To Hilda
From Pat and Fran

# JACKSON STREET AFTER HOURS

## THE ROOTS OF JAZZ IN SEATTLE

# *JACKSON STREET AFTER HOURS*

## THE ROOTS OF JAZZ IN SEATTLE

PAUL DE BARROS

WITH PHOTOGRAPHS BY
EDUARDO CALDERÓN

RESEARCH ASSISTANCE
Ted Dzielak

SASQUATCH BOOKS
SEATTLE

For Ernie Murdock



Printed in the United States of America.

Cover and text design: Art Chantry
Design and production assistance: Suzanne Brooker
Typesetting: Scribe Typography
Duotones: Trademark Color Separations
Front cover photograph: Oscar Holden. Courtesy of Grace Holden.

Library of Congress Cataloging in Publication Data
De Barros, Paul.
Jackson Street after hours : the roots of jazz in Seattle / by Paul de Barros ; with photographs by Eduardo Calderón ; research assistance by Ted Dzielak.
p. cm.
Discography: p.
Includes bibliographical references and index.
ISBN 0-912365-86-2 : $35:00. — ISBN 0-912365-92-7 (pbk.) : $22.95
1. Jazz — Washington — Seattle — History and criticism. 2. Jazz musicians — Interviews. I. Calderón, Eduardo. II. Title.
ML3508.8.S4D4 1993 93-24939
781.65'09797—dc20 CIP
MN

Sasquatch Books
1008 Western Avenue
Seattle, Washington 98104
(206) 467-4300

# contents

# preface

*Jackson Street After Hours* began as an oral history project through a grant from the King County Cultural Resources Division Heritage Program. Interviews began in August 1988 and continued through 1991. Subjects were interviewed if they had worked as jazz musicians in Washington State. Most of the long quotations used in the book are excerpted from these oral histories. Transcripts of the interviews were placed in the University of Washington's Suzzallo Library and the Seattle Public Library; relevant interviews were also placed in the Tacoma Public Library. The interviewees range historically from the late Floyd Turnham, who performed with his mother Edythe's band in Seattle in 1927, to Floyd Standifer and Chuck Metcalf, who still live and work in Seattle.

In choosing interview subjects, I leaned heavily toward the black community, since it was black musicians who had most often received the least recognition. (Musicians referred to in the text are black, unless otherwise identified.) I interviewed musicians born or raised in Washington who went on to national acclaim, such as Quincy Jones and Patti Bown, as well as some who spent only a short time in Washington but made a major impact on the local scene, such as white multi-instrumentalist Gus Mancuso. (Interviews were conducted following guidelines set out by Willa Baum in *Oral History for the Local Historical Society* and *Transcribing and Editing Oral History*.) Sessions also were taped with secondary sources, including nightclub owners, bartenders, and others who had some direct involvement with the scene. Of eighty-three interviews, I conducted over half; the others were done by volunteers, most of whom were associated with Seattle's Earshot Jazz Society, which initially sponsored the project by serving as the fiscal agent for fund-raising.

The project was originally intended as a more modest volume, a series of transcripts of selected oral histories tied together loosely with narrative material. As it progressed, however, I became increasingly disenchanted with oral history as an exclusive or primary research tool. It left too many holes. The period before 1927, for example, was impossible to document through interviews, since none of the original players was still alive. Some of the best bebop players — Gerald Brashear, Milt Garred, and Cecil Young — had also died. Few subjects were able to provide an overview of economic, social, or racial conditions, or specific dates when important events occurred.

In late 1988, making use of a generous grant from the King County Centennial Commission, I decided to expand the project to its present, more ambitious scope — a book documenting the roots of jazz in Seattle, using printed materials and secondary interviews as well as the oral histories. I employed a research assistant, Ted Dzielak, to comb through African-American newspapers in the University of Washington Library's Special Collections Department, and began to supplement the interviews with other resources, such as material from the *Seattle Times*, local histories, and general jazz histories and autobiographies. Among the most precious sources of material were private collections of scrapbook memorabilia and photographs shared by interview subjects.

The Centennial Commission grant also enabled me to enhance the project with contemporary photographs — twenty-six exquisite portraits of interview subjects by photographer Eduardo Calderón. Watching Eduardo work was a joy. Together, we traveled to New York, Los Angeles, and other cities to catch our subjects in the comfort of their own surroundings, asking them the most detailed of questions about their lives and careers. Invariably, Eduardo managed to pull something personal and true from these sessions. His photographs tell as much of the story as the words beside them do. By portraying musicians as people, not as performing icons, Calderón reminds us that their music is an extension of their humanity. He also reminds us that most of our subjects are still very much alive; they are people who are making contributions to our community or to others, and not just historical figures. Calderón also reproduced the vintage photographs that illustrate the rest of the text. These photos were generously loaned by interview subjects or culled from a variety of archives.

The result is an illustrated historical narrative that builds a documented, factual framework from which to hang the voices and images of Washington's jazz musicians. The candor of those voices and images — their presence, wit, and honesty — is what gives this book its special flavor, and made researching it a labor of love.

# introduction

For such an out-of-the-way place, Seattle has had a remarkable jazz history. The action began as early as 1918, when Lillian Smith's jazz band played at Washington Hall. It kept going strong all through Prohibition, as an authentic black jazz scene developed around the hub of Jackson Street and Twelfth Avenue. Even Jelly Roll Morton stopped off to play in the district, in 1920; he later wrote a rag, "Seattle Hunch," to commemorate his visit.

The scene peaked between 1937 and 1951, years in which Seattle came of age as a nerve center of the defense industry. A plentiful supply of soldiers and civilians, out looking for a good time, made Seattle a boomtown for musicians. In 1948, there were over two dozen nightclubs along Jackson Street, clubs where jazz and bootleg liquor flowed as freely as money from a soldier's pocket. Pianist Gerald Wiggins, stationed at Fort Lewis during the war, put it best: "They did everything but go home." This same lively scene nurtured the early careers of Quincy Jones, Ray Charles, and Ernestine Anderson.

Other musicians who played in the Jackson Street clubs went on to national jazz careers. Bassists Buddy Catlett and Wyatt Ruther worked with Count Basie. Pianists Wiggins and Jimmy Rowles went to Los Angeles, where they became exceptional accompanists and soloists. Patti Bown forged a career in New York. Still others, such as Floyd Standifer and Roscoe Weathers, never became well known outside the region, but when touring musicians came to town, they treated these Seattle players as peers. The "locals" may not have taken to the road, but they kept an authentic tradition alive at home.

Seattle has never been as musically isolated as most people imagine. In 1910, the town was the center of the largest vaudeville circuit in the country, a network of theaters owned by Alexander Pantages. Seattle audiences heard W. C. Handy and Freddie Keppard in Pantages theaters. And at every successive stage of jazz history, most major exponents of each new style found their way to the Northwest. The So Different Orchestra, one of the most important early jazz groups on the West Coast, played the Black and Tan in 1920. Duke Ellington played Seattle as early as 1934. Charlie Parker and Lester Young came through several times. Seattle may have been an outpost, but it certainly never lacked for jazz.

And yet, while Seattle has produced its share of great players, as a jazz town it has made no stylistic contributions to the development of the music. Why, then, one might reasonably ask, write the history of jazz here?

For those of us who live in Seattle, the answer is easy. To learn more about who we are, we look back at who we were, hoping to find clues to our identity. We know, for example, that Quincy Jones and Ray Charles rose from among our ranks. Does this tell us anything about who we are or who we might become? Is there something about the music these people have made that reflects us or our city?

For northwesterners there is also the issue of cultural hegemony. Western American history, and certainly West Coast jazz history, seems always to have been written by people for whom the West was at best exotic and at worst an inconsequential footnote. Even "West Coast jazz," acknowledged as a bona fide aesthetic movement, has been largely interpreted as a kind of aberration, a diluted form of the "real stuff" happening back East — even though Eric Dolphy and Charles Mingus were every bit as much West Coast figures as Gerry Mulligan, Shorty Rogers, or Chet Baker. This, then, provides an important rationale for writing a book about Seattle jazz: to know it and to name it accurately.

But what about people outside the Northwest? Why should they be interested in this sort of local chronicle? Jazz history typically has been written as the story of a main stem, growing through certain locales and styles — New Orleans, Chicago, Kansas City, and so on. Such a model is useful for getting a handle on the subject, but American culture — literature, visual art, music, or whatever — has always been a product of our whole land, not just a handful of urban areas. As important as New York is to the culture of jazz, the music's pulse has made itself felt all across the country. Jazz scholar Gunther Schuller treats this idea in his book *The Swing Era:*

> *It is fascinating to contemplate the role that geography and chance encounters have played in the history of jazz. Although often the impression is that "it all happens in New York" — even Basie and his Kansas City cohorts had to go there to really "make it" — it is useful to remind ourselves that . . . the crisscrossing of bands over the length and breadth of this nation over the decades, with the chance encounters between musicians, has been a factor of virtually incalculable importance in the development of jazz. The long hard tours, the endless one-nighters, though at times painful in actuality, have also played a crucial fertilizing role in the growth of this music.*

Lionel Hampton, for example, who is associated with Benny Goodman and who grew up in Chicago, clearly formed his musical aesthetic in Los Angeles and, for reasons that seem to be mostly coincidence, drew upon Seattle for an inordinate share of his sidemen. Andy Kirk's swinging, blues-inflected style is associated with the Midwest, yet his most illustrious soloist, Dick Wilson, learned to play jazz from Joe Darensbourg, a Creole clarinetist who worked in Seattle, and from a Seattle-bred saxophone teacher named Frank Waldron. In the complexities of such relationships between the national and the local, in the crisscrossings of lines all over the American map by the great and the mundane, the sung and the unsung, lie the secrets of the real history of jazz. The point here is not to make an exaggerated artistic claim for Seattle, per se, but to illustrate the cross-pollination and interplay that make up the fabric of jazz's rich history.

There is another, related and perhaps even more compelling, reason for chronicling this local history, and that is to honor the people who made the music. If, living in the West, one feels from time to time a sense of having been written out of history, it is as nothing compared with the invisibility that African Americans have experienced in general. Anyone who has done research of this kind is well acquainted with the scarcity of public documentation about black people, but I was frankly unprepared for the sweeping neglect I encountered. As I scoured old newspapers and magazines for information about black jazz musicians, it became increasingly clear that a whole era had gone by unnamed, unhailed, and unrecorded. Musicians famous and not so famous came and went, put down roots, influenced other musicians, started bands, ended them, had heydays and down days, but no one bothered to take notice or keep track. It's astonishing that brilliant musicians like Quincy Jones, Ray Charles, and Ernestine Anderson — the very ones who would go on to be claimed by Seattle as illustrious native sons and daughters — could have been "coming up" in the late 1940s on Seattle's Jackson Street without any consistent observer publicly documenting their progress. It is doubly ironic to sift through old newspapers and find review after review of mediocre chamber music concerts during the same period. This amounts to a systematic veiling, albeit unwitting, of one of the richest aspects of Seattle's cultural history.

Looking back, we can see that constructs of race and class permitted this veil to be hung. Jazz often thrived in Seattle, as elsewhere, in what were perceived as "dives," in a black ghetto where gambling, prostitution, and illegal drinking were as central to the action as the music itself. The notion that something of cultural importance might be brewing outside the law, on the outskirts of respectability, was virtually inconceivable to the white reporters, editors, and cultural pundits who might have documented what was going on. Even when such people did take friends down to, say, the Black and Tan at 12th and Jackson for a drink and some hot jazz, as often as not they saw only a "colorful" diversion from their routines, not the unfolding drama of an American music culture in the making.

There were exceptions. Thank goodness for black newspapers such as the *Northwest Enterprise,* with their listings of local black entertainers and occasional articles about them. Without this information there would be virtually no historical record of early Seattle jazz. Thanks, too, for Washington's black historian Esther Mumford, who began this difficult investigative work long ago, documenting the contributions of blacks in Washington in the 19th century. Breaking out of the mainstream press mold were Johnny Reddin, the intrepid *Seattle Post-Intelligencer* reporter who kept track of night people, and Doug Welch, another reporter who clearly loved jazz and advocated it in the *Seattle Times.* For the most part, though, Seattle's newspapers and magazines ignored the music and the musicians who created it. (About the only time the clubs ever got any notice was when they were raided; today, these sensational reports are often the only reliable source of club addresses.) One needn't look very far to find a parallel in today's media coverage of black neighborhoods: the same kinds of cultural constructs are still very much at work.

Jazz was not only ignored by local pundits; in many cases it was actively suppressed. Though Seattle briefly turned into a "city of sin" during and after the Yukon Gold Rush, the predominant Northwest mood has always been a sober, pragmatic, and anti-expressive one in which the business of life is business. Though jazz was tolerated, even during the notoriously liberated Jazz Age of the 1920s bluenoses consistently pushed the music underground. As if national Prohibition itself were not enough, the city passed additional ordinances against dancing, imposed taxes on cabarets, and tried to enforce irrational regulation of entertainment of all kinds. Confusing prudence with intolerance, vice with artistic expression, these measures slowed the cultural progress of the region. A residue of that intolerance still exists, in the control exercised by the State Liquor Board over nightclubs.

Curiously, the culture of official corruption that arose in response to this repression kept Seattle jazz alive during the first half of the century. The city's notorious "tolerance policy," under which policemen were paid under the table for winking at illegal practices such as gambling, prostitution, and bootlegging, ensured that bold entrepreneurs could continue to open nightclubs where jazz musicians thrived. When the tolerance policy finally collapsed in 1969, a curious disjunction occurred. Jazz, already on the downswing with the onslaught of rock, went into a decade of near-hibernation. By the time it reappeared with force locally, almost all the major players of the old era had died, moved away, or given up music. As a result, a generation of musicians and fans knew virtually nothing about Jackson Street's heyday. The few remaining older black musicians who had been part of the lively Jackson Street era felt passed over when the jazz scene revived, somehow robbed of their own legacy.

This book is an attempt to restore that legacy. For, in the face of these obstacles — being forced underground, harassed by the authorities, ignored by the press — Seattle jazz musicians have fared remarkably well. It is good for Seattleites to know that behind the bland veil of the official story there is also this rich and expressive history. This book is a tribute — in many cases a memorial — to the musicians who lived that history, the "locals" who have kept the jazz fire alive in the Northwest for eight decades.

Paul de Barros
Seattle, 1993

# prologue *A FANTASY*

Noon. Seattle, May 1, 1864. A lone black man walks along the muddy street that will become First Avenue. Over his shoulder is slung a military snare drum, the kind whose tattoo can still be heard east of here as armies collide in the brutal War Between the States. The man's hair is thick and curly and well-groomed — he is a barber, after all — and his face open and proud. He is pleased to be here, in this new Northwest, where a man seems able to get a fresh start, away from slavery, abolitionism, and the caste-bound traditions of the East Coast.

His drumbeat sprays out over the stumps, half-built clapboard houses, and offices that have sprouted along the steep hill that rises from the edge of Puget Sound. The water sparkles below. A half-dozen sailing ships idle in the wind. One, from San Francisco, is taking up a load of fresh-cut timber. Smoke rises from a brickyard and mill. The man looks up. The sun is high. Time for a break, says the beat of the drum. Time for the noonday meal . . .

Below, on First and Main at the new Plummer's Hall (which everyone has taken to calling Snoqualmie Hall), excited preparations are under way. Mr. Charles Plummer, proud procurer of the county's first liquor license (1854) and owner of Seattle's first saloon (complete with tinkling piano), has engaged the first traveling theatrical company ever to play the hopeful little pioneer town. Tonight, the Excelsior Minstrels, with the Taylor Brothers and whistling Tom LaFont, "The American Mocking Bird," will introduce Seattle to an entertainment craze that will sweep the nation when the war is over.

The performance is to be upstairs, in the meeting hall. The troupe raised its sets and rehearsed the show this morning, hanging a curtain to create a makeshift "backstage" area. All the accoutrements of the trade — cork, charcoal, tap shoes, makeup — are laid out on a table behind the sheet. Tom LaFont himself, a tall actor in a top hat who has seen much of the States and all of Europe, descends the steep stairs to the barroom, where he discovers Mr. Plummer.

"Everything is at the ready, sir," says LaFont. "I wonder where I might find a dining establishment?"

Before Plummer can answer, the noise of the snare drum comes within earshot.

"Sir, what on earth is that noise? Has the war come this far west without my knowledge?"

"Why no, my good friend, that's only Lopes, the heartbeat of Africa itself, my dear sir. Every day at midday, he strikes up that rhythm, to spread the news of his barbershop and the midday meal. Manuel Lopes, the barber. From Africa, he says, though I have it on good authority he comes from somewhere in the Caribbean Isles. I don't know how he knows when it's noon, since the sun never shines on this wretched bay."

"Why Mr. Plummer, I do not mean to be disagreeable, sir, but it appears the sun is out today."

They step outside.

"Why, so it is, so it is."

“An African, you say?” LaFont’s stomach is rumbling. “I once had some hot peppered stew in Antigua that nearly singed off my eyelashes.”

“You don’t say, don’t say. Damn fine barber. Trimmed my whiskers just last week. Brought that chair around the Horn, he did. Finest damn barber’s chair north of San Francisco.”

Lopes’ beat begins to fade. He has turned his march back toward the shop.

“I do believe I’ll stroll over and have a look. Seven sharp, then, is it?”

“Seven it is!”

Mr. Tom LaFont strikes out toward the drumbeat. It is a fine day. As he enters Lopes’ modest shop, a step down from the street, he finds the African hanging his snare drum on a hook. His topcoat, much the worse for wear, looks like British military, with tassels and pleats. Beside the drum hangs a large fragment of whalebone; on the floor, two glass floats that have followed the current from Japan. The place smells of cologne and gumbo. LaFont spies a bubbling pot on the sawdust-burning stove behind the elegant barber’s chair. Lopes’ back is to the actor. When he hears LaFont’s footfall, he suddenly turns on one heel in a smooth, almost mechanical motion, smiles, and gives a mock salute. The poise of it catches the actor’s eye. LaFont makes a mental note. He can use it.

“At your service, sir,” says Lopes, taking in the fine cut of the thespian’s frock and his friendly eyes, which promise sympathy. “And what may I do for you?”

“I have found the emerald isle, yet am I sore confused,” says LaFont, adopting a mock Shakespearean manner. “Shall I answer the call of my lowly stomach, and sup on spicy gumbo, or succumb to vanity and fatigue and have you shape my face and sprinkle sweet waters on my hair, while I lay in the embrace of that soft and sloping couch?”

Lopes laughs.

“Gumbo first, since you are a man of such good taste. Then we cut the sauce out of your beard!”

“Done!”

# 1

# "SEATTLE HUNCH" 1864·1920

One night in August 1920, the great Ferdinand "Jelly Roll" Morton, who claimed to have "invented" jazz, sat down at the piano at Seattle's Entertainers Club at 12th Avenue South and Main Street, put his big, Creole hands on the keys, and shook the house until the sun came up. Playing with Morton was Seattle clarinetist and pianist Oscar Holden, who had joined Jelly's band on a gig in Vancouver, British Columbia, and would later become the number one piano man in town.

Morton wasn't famous yet. He was just another "sport" in the district, with a diamond front tooth and a cool hand for pool, trying to raise a dime. The pianist had been kicking around the West Coast since leaving New Orleans in 1917, playing piano, hustling pool, shooting craps, and—when he could—running a string of girls. After a stint in San Francisco, he and his wife, Anita, had opened a "rooming house" at Ponder's Corner, outside Tacoma.

The Entertainers Club was advertised in the *Seattle Republican*, a black-owned newspaper, its coy language reflecting that Prohibition was in full force:

1000 1000
Thousands of Barrels
of
Refreshing, Exhilerating, Intoxicating Music
Poured Out Nightly at the
Entertainer's Cabaret
1238 Main Street
By the Best
SYNCOPATED ORCHESTRA
on the Coast
DON'T MISS IT
ENTERTAINER'S CABARET
GILLIE RICHARDSON
RUSSELL WALTON

The club was in the heart of a thriving nightclub district, where music rang out day and night, crap games sometimes ran for a week, and a man on the prowl could find any kind of pleasure he was seeking, as long as he had the cash to pay for it. The hub of the district was the corner of 12th and Jackson Street. This is where Seattle jazz was born and where it flowered, from the late teens until the 1960s.

At first glance, early Seattle doesn't seem the sort of place where Jelly Roll Morton—or jazz of any kind—would be found. A sleepy, remote village in the Northwest corner of the country, it was settled largely by Scandinavian immigrants who worked in the primary industries of fishing and logging and by earnest businessmen intent on building a modest, bourgeois life. Yet several peculiarities made Seattle a fertile spot for jazz. Early on, the town had developed a culture of legalized corruption that tolerated vice in exchange for official payoffs, which in turn supported venues for music. In the 1890s, a honky-tonk atmosphere evolved in Maynard Town (today's Pioneer Square), where a logger or sailor could liven up his weekend. Jazz was also encouraged by the city's passion for theater, which continually exposed the populace to new forms of entertainment. Some of the earliest jazz acts to leave New Orleans—as well as minstrel shows, which preceded jazz and made important contributions to its development—toured the Northwest on a theater circuit that was well established by the 1890s. A migration of African Americans that began before the turn of the century made Seattle a likely spot for jazz, as well.

From the late nineteenth century, the district south of Yesler Way—"across the deadline," as they said in the early days—had been a tenderloin full of whores and touts, gamblers and pimps, where brass bands and saloon pianists competed nightly for customers' attention and loot. Originally, the district lay in a rectangle

Top: "Noodles" Smith.
Bottom: "Blackie" Williams.

bounded by Fifth Avenue, Yesler, the waterfront, and King Street. This was Skid Road, the raw neighborhood where Seattle pioneer Henry Yesler "skidded" logs down the hill to his mill. After World War I, as the city became more settled, the action moved up the hill, through the International District (also known as Chinatown, between Fifth and Eighth avenues) and on up to 15th, where it merged with the increasingly black Central District. In the teens and twenties, this was Seattle's version of New Orleans' fabled Storyville, where "sports" and hustlers provided entertainment and rooming houses for casual laborers, drifters, and railroad porters. Yesler Hill, where the Yesler Terrace housing project now stands, became an area of concentrated prostitution; the junction of 12th and Jackson served the gamblers, bootleggers, railroad men, and sailors. Above 15th, the neighborhood became essentially like the rest of the city—quiet and residential. But from First Avenue to Fifteenth, Seattle rocked with wine, women, whoopee—and jazz.

Seattle's founders encouraged this underworld of vice while maintaining an image of respectability. This contradiction in the city's psychology, a kind of dual personality that flip-flopped between sobriety and naughtiness, would endure for many decades. Running a "wide open" town was a profitable tradition that involved everyone from the cop on the beat to the mayor and chief of police. By the early part of the century, corruption was so deeply imbedded in local politics that candidates often ran for office on the "wide open" platform, arguing that Seattle's vice industry generated income and a healthy economy for its more prudent citizenry. Figures such as Police Chief Charles Wappenstein and Mayor Hiram Gill reaped fortunes from the payoffs they received from whorehouses, opium dens, casinos, and later—when liquor was outlawed, too—speakeasies. Seattle's flamboyant, Wild West attitudes attracted the attention of a national magazine, *McClure's*, which recorded breathlessly, "No American city has ever seen anything comparable with it. The most hardened sports would telegraph to their pals to come to Seattle and inspect it, if only as a curiosity. . . . The city seems to have been transformed almost magically into one great gambling hell."

Into this colorful fray of organized sin, where a man could run any kind of operation as long as he paid off the right fellow, came new arrivals from America's black population. As chance would have it, the first black citizen of Seattle was a sometime musician, an African sailor and barber named Manuel Lopes who in 1852 signaled mealtimes in the little village by marching down the main street beating a snare drum. More African Americans trickled into the Northwest once the transcontinental railroads were opened, in 1889. The Northern Pacific Railroad imported groups of black workers from the Midwest to break a strike (unbeknownst to the recruits) at its coal mine in Roslyn, east of the Cascades. In 1889, black domestic help was brought from Chicago to staff Seattle's new Rainier Grand Hotel, and two years later, the Oregon Improvement Company recruited 600 black strikebreakers to the mines at Franklin and Newcastle, on the western side of the mountains. In Yakima, William Jackson, a barber and violinist, put together one of Washington's first black bands in 1910. His daughter, LeEtta Sanders King, was sixteen at the time; she would later become an important piano teacher in Seattle. In the early twentieth century, hundreds of thousands of blacks left the rural South for the industrialized North, forming the great ghettos of Harlem and Chicago's South Side. By 1910, 6,000 blacks lived in the state of Washington, 800 in Seattle.

One of the earliest and most colorful black entrepreneurs to reach Jackson Street was E. Russell "Noodles" Smith, in some sense the father—or perhaps the midwife—of Seattle jazz. Smith was a gambler and a businessman who was nicknamed "Noodles" because no matter how much he risked in a crap game, he always set aside enough cash to buy a bowl of noodles before he went to bed. Smith came from Denver to Seattle during the Alaska Yukon Pacific (AYP) Exposition in 1909 with $17,000 in his wallet, a stake he claimed to have won gambling for two days and three nights in Tonopah, Nevada. Others say he earned it pimping in a mining camp. Smith was a hard-nosed, miserly man who amassed a fortune from nightclubs, bootlegging, gambling, and real estate. Musicians recalled Smith as a perennially exhausted boss who

was "so busy making money" that if he asked you a question, he would fall asleep before you could answer.

In 1917, Smith and Burr "Blackie" Williams —who had the letter "B" studded in diamonds on his belt buckle—opened the Dumas Club, at 1040 Jackson. This was primarily a social club for blacks. Three years later, Noodles and a partner named Jimmy Woodland opened the Entertainers Club at 12th and Jackson. (The original site of the Entertainers Club, where Jelly Roll had played in August, was at 12th and Main.) In 1922, in the club's basement, Smith and Blackie Williams christened the Alhambra, which by 1932 was known as Seattle's most esteemed and longest-lived nightclub, the Black and Tan. (A "black and tan" was a generic name for a nightclub that admitted both blacks and whites.)

Every kid who grew up in Seattle in the fifties and sixties knew the Black and Tan as the hub of Seattle soul music. What they probably didn't know was that in July 1920 one of the most important early jazz bands in the West, Reb Spikes' So Different Orchestra, played there. In 1934, ragtime pianist Eubie Blake played the Black and Tan, too; in later years, so did the entire Duke Ellington Orchestra, Lucky Millinder, and Louis Jordan.

Across the street from the Black and Tan, on the northeast corner, Noodles opened the Hill Top Tavern. Nearby, other operators started the Monarch Pool Hall and a gambling joint called the Main Event. Up the street, Bill Bowman owned a place called, simply, "Bowman's Joint." Noodles also opened the Golden West and Coast hotels in the International District. Touring celebrities such as Louis Armstrong, Duke Ellington, and Erskine Hawkins would come to know the little rooms of the Coast and Golden West well.

"Twelfth and Jackson *belonged* to Noodles Smith," recalls Marshal Royal, the great Count Basie alto saxophonist, who married Noodles' sister-in-law.

> *He was the ward boss. He was the biggest dude in that part of town. You see, in those days you couldn't open up a nightclub unless you passed by Noodles Smith. The man downtown would call him up and say, "Such and such a guy wants to open up a club over at such and such a place." And he'd ask Noodles if it was all right for him to open up or not. If you didn't pass his observations, you just didn't exist.*

The heavy action on the corner attracted big-time gamblers, including Lena Horne's father, George Horne, who lived in Seattle for a while and gambled with "Big George" Stevens. Bruce Rowell, a sometime-saxophonist who was Noodles' right-hand man, remembers Stevens well. "He'd go way back up here into his suit

**The Black and Tan nightclub, corner of 12th Avenue South and Jackson Street, 1937.**

**The marquee, washed out in the photo, says "Black and Tan." Originally called the Alhambra and founded in 1922 by Noodles Smith, the Black and Tan operated well into the 1960s. Note Japanese businesses flourishing in the area; these disappeared after Japanese internment during WWII.**

**Courtesy of the Washington State Archives**

coat—he had a pocket between his shoulder blades—and he'd pull out a thousand dollars. That's right! Right there in the Main Event, on Jackson Street. Then he said, 'Okay, let's keep gambling. Let the good times roll.'"

In the 1920s, Noodles and Blackie lived the lives of flamboyant gangsters, driving fancy cars and showering food and drink on their friends and relatives. The late Emma Gayton, wife of drummer Leonard Gayton, was a child when Blackie took a room in her mother's house.

> *He used to drive me to school sometimes. I'd feel so important. He bought me earrings for my birthday. He always drank a brandy when he got up in the morning. All the policemen used to come to wish him a happy Christmas! We had great big bowls of eggnog, great big turkeys on the table. We entertained all the celebrities in Seattle. I was just a little thing sitting on people's laps. They'd send me to bed when the party got good.*

Smith often staked other operators, taking a cut off the top. If the fellows he staked couldn't make a go of it, he'd collect their property. According to Rowell, Noodles kept a safe in the basement of a house he owned on 12th, just north of Jackson. The safe housed brown bags full of cash.

> *It was laying right there waiting for an opportunity. There's open-up money, for a joint. Under that open-up money, there is the poker game money. Here is the crap-table money. Here is the Chuck-a-Luck [a dice game] money. Here is working money. All in bags. Cash. These four or five bags are together. Here's another four or five. He would open a joint, right tonight. Just grab one of those bags. . . . It never went to the bank.*

Smith, who was married to Elbee Williamson, also kept a flamboyant mistress, a nightclub singer named Zelma Winslow. Noodles and Zelma carried on so brazenly that Elbee eventually filed for divorce, receiving as part of the settlement the Coast Hotel, where she became a popular host. Smith himself retired from the nightclub business in 1940. In his later years, he became a beneficent community elder who helped rehabilitate ex-convicts, paid the jail fines of losers and underdogs at Christmas, and bankrolled amateur sports teams. However, he remained a miser. When a relative told him, "You can't take it with you," he answered, "I don't intend to leave it to no one else." When he died in 1952 he left no will, and no one ever found his fabled sacks of cash.

Though jazz historians traditionally have focused on colorful, "sporting" districts such as Noodles Smith's Jackson Street empire, middle-class neighborhoods also have exercised a tremendous, if usually unheralded, influence on the music's development. Far from the raucous nightlife of the Black and Tan was Seattle's respectable East Madison neighborhood, where black pioneer George Grose had sold off a tract of land in parcels to churchgoing, middle-class families. Life there was pleasant, secure, and hopeful, especially compared with the horrors that beset blacks in other American cities. LeEtta Sanders King, born in 1894, painted a pastoral picture of the period during and just after World War I:

> *There weren't too many colored people in Seattle then. There was all kinds of things we did, though, just as if there were a lot of people here. We had activities, dinner parties, and outings. Oh, we had a great time. . . .Before the war there was just lots of pleasure: boat rides, dances, and just a great deal of pleasant, happy life. . . . Dances were given at the Renton Hill Club House, which was at 18th and Madison. We wore pretty party dresses and the men wore tux. . . .There was no segregation in the theaters as I recall it. We sat where we wanted to sit. So in a sense, Seattle was quite an open city. We went to the parks and we'd go to any of them and enjoy them. Sunday-afternoon band concerts were greatly enjoyed in those days.*

Church picnics provided the occasion for some of Seattle's early black music-making. In 1891, the Seattle Comet Band performed at the African Methodist Episcopal church's first picnic. These affairs continued well into the twentieth century. One of bassist Buddy Catlett's earliest musical memories is of hearing the great Creole clarinetist Joe Darensbourg at a picnic near Enumclaw, a small town outside Seattle, in the 1930s.

Residents of East Madison were not always sanguine about their less inhibited brethren on Jackson Street. Horace Cayton, son of a black

Seattle newspaper editor of the same name, vividly captured the division between the two neighborhoods—the one staid, quiet, and religious and the other noisy, illegal, and profane—in his autobiography, *Long Old Road*. "There were parts of the city, the sporting area," writes Cayton, who was raised in a Capitol Hill mansion, "where we were not even allowed to ride through in our carriage, for those people were morally corrupt and of great discredit to the race."

In spite of such class tensions, the two neighborhoods enjoyed a symbiotic relationship. For while young black musicians may have learned to jam all night in "hot" swing bands on Jackson Street, it was within the secure and hopeful boundaries of East Madison, with its church socials and concert band picnics, that many of them acquired the technical skills—not to say aspirations—that it took to become quality players. No individual better demonstrates the importance of this stable environment than alto saxophonist and music teacher Frank Waldron, one of the most important figures in early Washington jazz and a man whose influence would be felt on the scene for half a century.

It was probably during the First World War that Frank Dordan Waldron, born in 1890, came to Tacoma, where he played in a dance pavilion frequented by soldiers from Camp Lewis (now Fort Lewis). He most likely learned to play his instrument in the Army. When the war ended, Waldron came to Seattle and set up shop as a teacher on Jackson Street, first in Bessie Young's theatrical boardinghouse, then in his own studio, which he opened in 1919.

In the early twenties, the saxophone enjoyed a faddish popularity akin to the guitar craze of the sixties. Though the saxophone had been invented by a Belgian, for use in military parade bands, it was popularized in America by African-American jazz musicians. Saxophone studios, how-to books, and saxophone quartets sprang up all over the country. Seattle even had a saxophone orchestra.

By all accounts, Waldron was a master of the instrument. He had a classic tone, perfect articulation, and masterful phrasing. In 1924, he published a saxophone method book, *Syncopated Classic*, in which he used nine of his compositions, including "Climb Them Walls," "Pretty Doll," and "With Pep," to demonstrate the new jazz techniques of slap-tonguing and flutter-tonguing. The tunes are difficult, requiring complex fingering and advanced ability.

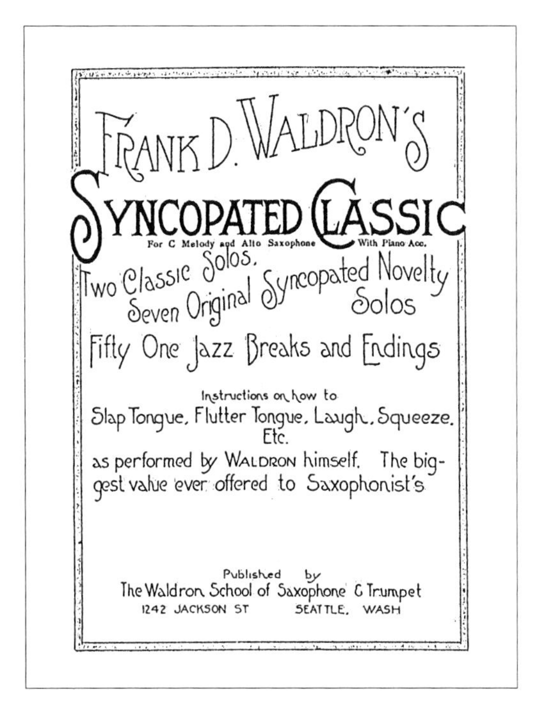


Waldron was more than a teacher. Throughout the 1920s, he performed with a five-piece group called the Odean Jazz Orchestra at the Nanking Cafe, a high-class Chinese restaurant with a dance floor, on Fourth Avenue between Pine and Olive streets. Waldron must have been very highly respected, since, as a rule, black groups were not allowed to play downtown, and integrated jazz groups were virtually unknown throughout the United States.

"Frank used to sit up there with his sun visor on and play alto," remembers white drummer and trumpeter Chet Ramage, whose Musical Knights later played in the same establishment. "He was a hell of a musician."

"Frank was bald-headed, big, and loved to drink whiskey," says pianist Palmer Johnson, who came to Seattle from Los Angeles in 1928, met Waldron not long afterward, and later roomed with him. "He played both [trumpet and saxophone], but he lost his 'lip' for trumpet. He was a hell of a good teacher."

Buddy Catlett, who started studying reeds with Waldron in the forties before switching to bass, remembers him as a superb technician who scolded his students fiercely if they didn't practice:

*If you came to your lesson and you hadn't been doing anything but playing football*

**Infantry Band, 1926. Left to right: Powell Newington Barnett (son of Powell Samuel Barnett), unknown, Albert Buford (father of Vernon "Pops" Buford), Floyd Turnham, Jr., unknown, Powell Samuel Barnett (tuba). Directly below Barnett, Charles Adams (cornet); third from right, Tim Waldron; second from right, Young; extreme right, Tom Jones.**

**Military bands were musical precursors of jazz bands, offering black musicians an opportunity to learn to play. This group often performed at Leschi Park.**

**Courtesy of Emma Gayton**

*all week, you'd be sitting there sweating bullets. He'd say, "You'll never play with Duke Ellington if you keep going this way." You'd play your lesson, and he'd light up a cigarette—he smoked so much he had safety matches laid out on his Victrola so he could light up one after the other—and he'd pour himself a glass of gin, and he'd stand up over you and say, "Now, boy, that's the worst batch of shit I ever heard!" Oh, and another thing. He'd say, "Listen here, I want to tell you something. I want you to leave them bitches alone. And leave that booze alone. And leave those cigarettes alone!" Him with a cigarette in one hand and a glass of gin in the other. Then you'd hear this voice from the back room: [falsetto] "Fra-a-nk? Are you through in there yet?"*

Waldron taught the same basics that white classical teachers did—sight-reading, tonguing, embouchure, phrasing—but to his more advanced students he also taught theory and ear training, using jazz improvisers as models. White clarinetist Ron Pierce, who also took lessons from Waldron in the forties, recalls:

*With my [white] teachers, it was all "Play time, play section, play in tune." [Waldron would] say, "Play me a seventh chord." Now the thing was, I had never experienced this kind of thing before. He was a memorizer guy. Then he'd lean over and play a record on the Victrola and show you how Louis Armstrong did it. This guy really turned on my ear.*

The list of Northwest musicians who reflected Waldron's legacy is long and deep: Not only Catlett and Pierce, but Quincy Jones, Dick Wilson, and Jabo Ward also came for weekly lessons. Waldron died in 1955, leaving no relations in the area.

Another early black immigrant who had a profound impact on Seattle's musical history was Powell Samuel "Shorty" Barnett, whose family had come from Indiana to Roslyn in 1906 to work in the mines. The son of a former slave, Barnett stood a few inches over 5 feet, had biceps as thick as tree trunks, and boasted that his hands were so rough he could scrape an inch of skin off before it hurt. Barnett started out on tuba in a brass band formed by Roslyn's black miners, then performed in Seattle concert and military bands at the gingerbread pavilions at the foot of Madison Street and at Leschi Park. Barnett also played for a time with the early Washington jazz band Edythe Turnham and Her Knights of Syncopation, as did one of his Seattle brass-band mates, trumpeter Charles Adams.

In 1909, when Seattle's city fathers were gearing up for the AYP Exposition, Barnett approached the fair organizers to ask if they wanted to hire his brass band. His request started a controversy that led to the foundation of a separate musicians' union for blacks. At that time, Seattle musicians were organized under the American Federation of Musicians (AFM), Local No. 76. There were no black members.

"I went to the man in charge of music for the Fair Association," recalled Barnett.

> *He told me that if I got the Negro band in the union they could play all year at the fair. But the Negro musicians wouldn't do anything about it. . . . I encouraged them to join the union, but they were determined to create their own. So I decided that half a loaf would be better than none. If they organized their own union, perhaps they could join the other musicians' union later.*

Later, indeed—it would be forty-seven years before blacks would get another invitation to join Local 76. The Negro Musicians' Union, Local No. 493, was formed in 1913. Barnett joined both the white and the black unions.

Seattle's segregated musicians' unions were not an anomaly. Rather than admit blacks to white unions, where they could compete for high-paying jobs, white locals across the country encouraged blacks to form their own unions. Territories were marked off. In Seattle, the dividing line between black and white was Yesler Way, which separated downtown from the honky-tonk neighborhood where Seattle had first sprung up from the mud. Though segregation was morally abhorrent, it had a bright side. Local 493, with its black membership, quite naturally became the focal point for Seattle's thriving jazz scene. Every major player, from Frank Waldron in the twenties to Quincy Jones in the forties, would at some point become a member of the black local, jamming on 493 sessions, studying with 493 teachers, and forming groups with 493 musicians. The Local 493 "clubhouse," the Blue Note, on 13th Avenue and Jefferson, hosted the hippest jam sessions throughout the late 1930s and 1940s.

Powell Barnett, who later became one of Seattle's most important civic leaders and had a city park named after him, spent much of his life trying to convince blacks and whites alike that segregation in any institution was a bad idea. He mounted several attempts to amalgamate the unions, but did not succeed until 1956. That he met with resistance from the black community as well as the white is not surprising in light of the black experience in early Washington. At the time, most unions didn't admit blacks at all. When they did allow them to work, anti-black violence often occurred. The fact that Barnett held a brief for unions in the early part of the century made him the exception in the black community, not the rule. As it turned out, an all-black band did play at the AYP Exposition, but it was not from Seattle. Lacy's Dixieland Band, a forty-five-piece group from the South, represented southern culture at the fair.

Had Powell Barnett and his brass band played at the AYP Exposition, however, they would have encountered the sophisticated scrutiny of a Seattle public already exposed to much of the best that show business had to offer. Pioneer boomtowns traditionally have erected opera houses as a badge of culture, but Seattle had a mania for theater that surpassed by many degrees even the most ambitious settlement. In 1859, eight years after the city was

**The Edythe Turnham family minstrel show, Spokane, c. 1910.**
**Bandleader Edythe Turnham, third from left; her sister, Maggie, second from left.**

**Early jazz musicians such as Spokane bandleader Edythe Turnham, who moved to Seattle in 1926, found plentiful work in minstrel shows.**

**Courtesy of Georgia Turnham**

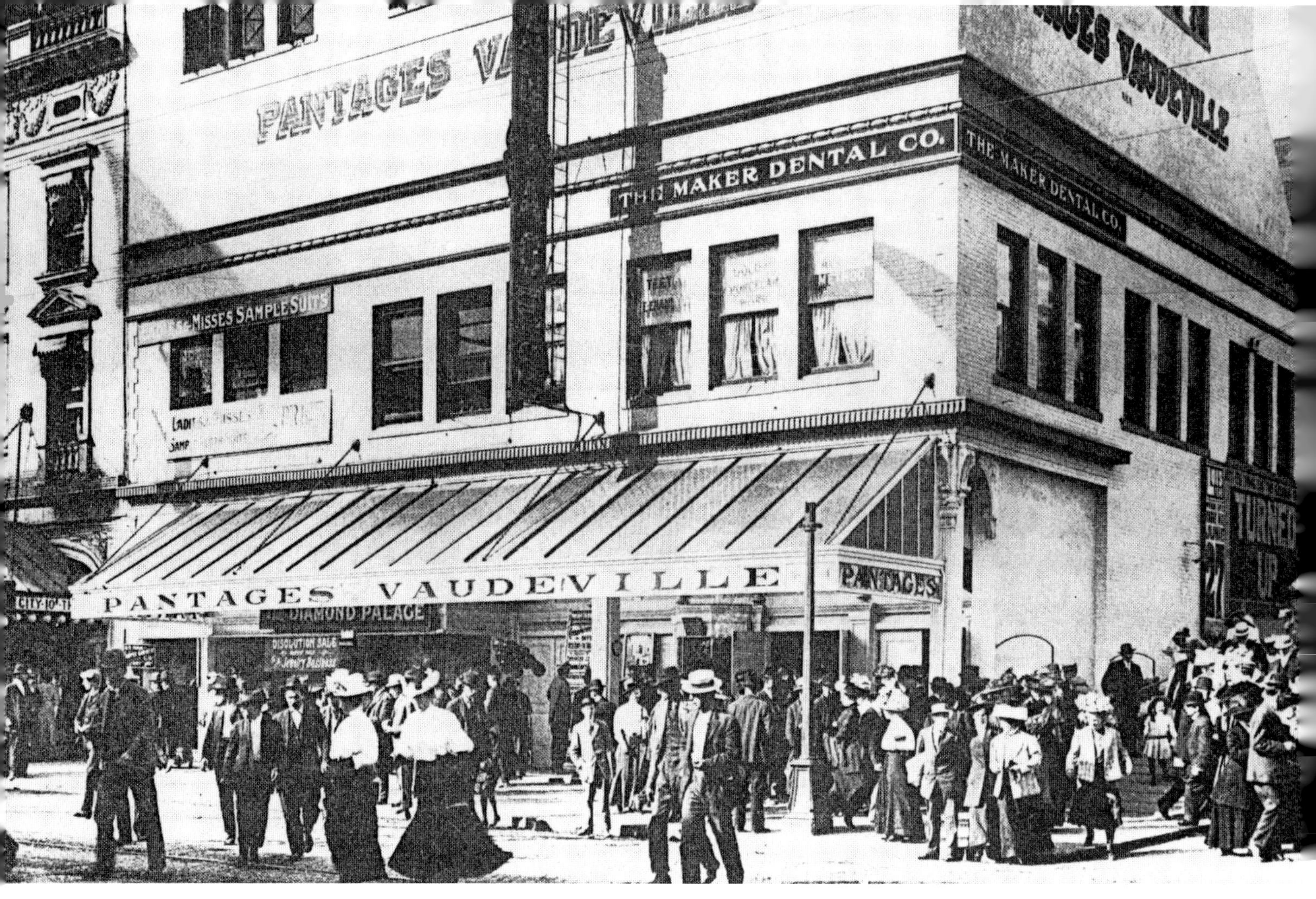


The Pantages Theater, on the corner of Second and Seneca, was the first theater to bear that name. It was the original house of what became one of the largest popular-priced vaudeville circuits in the United States. Built in 1904 with the profits Alexander Pantages earned in his Crystal Theater farther south on Second Street, it was remodeled in 1907 and continued in use until 1914 when a new Pantages Theater was opened at Third and University. Courtesy of the University of Washington Special Collections

founded, Plummer's Hall, one of the town's first buildings, was being used as a theater. (Pioneer Charles Plummer also obtained the county's first liquor license and operated Seattle's first saloon, thus establishing two precedents—boozing and theater—that would have a huge impact on local jazz.)

From Plummer's Hall forward, Seattle built one theater after another. The Great Fire of 1889 burned everything except a building called Turnverein Hall, at Fourth and Jefferson, but by the 1890s a golden era had dawned, helped by hard cash from the Yukon Gold Rush of 1898. An impresario named John Cort, who had broken into show business in New York as a blackface song-and-dance man, refurbished Turnverein Hall, renaming it the Seattle Opera House. Cort also opened the Standard Theater, at Occidental Avenue South and Washington Street, followed by the Moore Theatre, in 1907.

Across the street from the Seattle Opera House, John Considine operated the People's Theatre. Considine is credited with putting in place the world's first popular-priced vaudeville chain, eventually hooking up with a New York booking agent and building the $100,000 Grand Theater in Tacoma. Considine also monopolized a curious early Seattle institution called the "box house," a basement saloon with a theater attached, where rowdy entertainment was presented. Considine was soon eclipsed by Alexander Pantages, who would create the largest network of theaters outside New York City—the Pantages Circuit—with the entire business centered in Seattle. In 1904, Pantages built an eponymous theater on Second Avenue, relocating it to Third Avenue and University Street in 1915. This theater, later known as the Rex and the Palomar, hosted big jazz shows from the thirties to the fifties.

Seattle's wealth of theaters attracted a flood of vaudeville and minstrel shows, including the city's first visiting theater company—Tom LaFont's Excelsior Minstrels. Between 1864 and 1912, no fewer than 156 touring minstrel troupes passed through Seattle. In minstrel shows, actors—both black and white—smeared their faces with burnt cork and did outrageous parodies of black behavior (antics that were originally a parody of the pretentious behavior of white plantation owners). In spite of the genre's racially demeaning content, one of the ways early black jazz musicians such as Jelly Roll Morton, Eubie Blake, and Fats Waller made a living was by performing in minstrel shows. (Some of San Francisco's early black jazz musicians came from the Georgia Minstrels.) Vaudeville provided opportunities, too, sometimes with serendipitous consequences. In 1911, a black vaudeville troupe broke up in Seattle, stranding Nora and Ross Hendrix. Their grandson, Jimi, would change the face of popular music.

Ironically, as black entertainers such as Ross Hendrix trickled into town and began to establish the roots of a jazz tradition, the white population was more likely to attend a blackface show like Tom LaFont's than a jazz performance by blacks. This pattern—of white performers reaping rewards for imitating black artists while black artists went unrecognized—was rooted in minstrelsy and would permeate the history of jazz. Unreported in the newspapers and masked by socioeconomic custom, Seattle jazz developed with few whites ever knowing it existed.

W. C. Handy was one black musical figure whites probably were aware of in the early part of the century. Handy, who wrote "St. Louis Blues," among other hit songs, was musical director for W. H. Mahara's Minstrels, which played three times at the Seattle Theatre, at Third and Cherry Street, where the Arctic Building now stands. For his 1898 performance, Mahara brought twenty-six performers and offered a daily parade to drum up business before the show. It must have worked. There were no vacant seats at the opening.

A review from the *Seattle Times* of March 21, 1898, reflects the combination of exuberant approval and blatant racism the white press reserved for black entertainers:

> *In such a performance as that last night the attention of the musical ear is fascinated by the negro melodies, arranged for solos, quartettes or choruses, as the case may be, but all rendered in that vibrant, sympathetic passionate tone quality characteristic of the negro race. In all the range of musical art there is nothing quite like a negro melody rendered by a son or daughter of the African race. . . . An air quite foreign to the plantation tunes usually associated with colored minstrels, rendered by a quartette of well-trained negro singers, assumes a quality quite its own. Take the popular melody, "All Coons Look Alike to Me."*

**Nora and Ross Hendrix, Seattle, 1911.**

**Jimi Hendrix's grandparents were vaudeville performers who settled in Seattle after being stranded there.**

**Courtesy of Al Hendrix**

Early jazz acts followed minstrel shows in Northwest theaters. In 1914, the Pantages played host to the first jazz band ever to tour outside New Orleans—Freddie Keppard's Creole Orchestra. Keppard, an important early stylist on the New Orleans scene, was much admired by Louis Armstrong—and even by Jelly Roll Morton, who usually had nothing good to

The Original Creole Orchestra, 1912. Front row, left to right: Dink Johnson, James Palao, Leon Williams. Back row: Eddie Vinson, Freddie Keppard, George Baquet, Bill Johnson.

This early New Orleans jazz band played Seattle's Pantages Theater in 1914.

Courtesy of the Hogan Jazz Archive, Tulane University

say about any other musician. Keppard appeared in Seattle and Tacoma after spending six years in Los Angeles. His music was one of the hottest, most modern things going at the time, and Seattleites and Tacomans were hearing it—three years before the first jazz record was released. This, along with the visits of W. C. Handy, dispels somewhat the myth that audiences in the Northwest were isolated from national trends.

The presence of touring jazz artists in the Northwest in 1914 also is a good reminder that the well-known theory of the dissemination of jazz from the South, "up the river from New Orleans," has largely been discredited. Though jazz probably originated in New Orleans around the turn of the century, the past two decades of jazz scholarship have shown fairly conclusively that musicians were playing various styles of pre-jazz or jazzlike music in black communities in Texas, New York, Los Angeles, and San Francisco before jazz musicians found their way from New Orleans to Chicago in the 1910s. Tom Stoddard, in his ground-breaking book *Jazz on the Barbary Coast*, has shown that black musicians in San Francisco were improvising as early as 1907 and that early jazz-associated dances such as the Texas Tommy, the turkey trot, and the bunny hug originated before World War I in San Francisco—not in the South. The earliest known use of the word "jazz" in print is in a 1913 edition of the San Francisco *Bulletin*. Several of the musicians mentioned in Stoddard's book, including Buck Campbell and Gerald Wells, also spent significant portions of their careers in the Northwest. (Campbell was from Spokane.) Since small numbers of blacks began to trickle into Washington in the 1880s, it is quite possible that a young generation of African Americans in Seattle, Tacoma, and even Spokane was playing syncopated, pre-jazz music before 1920, though little evidence remains to support this theory.

One bit of evidence that does exist suggests that jazz may have traveled to the Northwest via the armed forces. The November 25, 1917, issue of the service newspaper *Trench and Camp* features this intriguing notice:

> *Originator of "Jazz" in 347th Orchestra*
>
> *Bobby Hayes—drummer and slide whistle player from San Francisco—is now stationed at Camp Lewis. He is famous in San Francisco and all of California. Hayes plays at Camp Lewis dances. He has, moreover, so many different kinds of technic that there seems to be no limits to the things he can do with the weird outfit which comprises that stock of a trap man.*

Though he sounds as if he was an authentic jazz man, research has turned up nothing about Hayes.

The first documented jazz performance by a local band in Washington took place on June 10, 1918, at Seattle's Washington Hall, which still stands at 14th Avenue and Fir Street. The performers were Miss Lillian Smith's Jazz Band, personnel unknown. The show was billed as a "Grand Benefit Ball" to raise money for the NAACP. On July 14, 1919, Smith was out playing again on a "Moonlight Excursion" sponsored by the Efficiency Club, and the following month she had engagements at the Renton Hill Club House at 18th Avenue and Madison and at the Odd Fellows' fifteenth annual picnic at Wildwood Park. In November, she was back at Washington Hall, leading the Grand Ball for the Elks Club. "Plenty of Jazz Music by the Best Jazz Band in Town," said the ad.

It's likely that Smith played syncopated dance music with a ragtime-to-jazz feeling, though it's hard to say just how "hot" Miss Lillian's band really was. Donald Gatewood, whose mother directed the choir at Mount Zion Baptist Church, remembers black society bands such as Smith's playing mostly ballroom dance music, with hot jazz numbers with solos thrown in for spice. Whatever her jazz quotient, Smith was the first in a long and honorable line of Seattle jazz bandleaders to come.

Just before leaving Seattle, Jelly Roll Morton lost almost everything in a high-stakes game. He commemorated this misfortune in a new rag, "Seattle Hunch." It is a cheerful, lilting composition laced with stop-time sections and quick little glissandos that zip up to melody notes. Did Morton have a hunch that Seattle was becoming a West Coast hub of jazz? If he had, he could have doubled his money. With the Jackson Street scene heating up and a stable black middle class in the East Madison district, forces were starting to line up that would create a fertile environment for jazz. The theater and vaudeville scene was in place, ready to bring in national acts. The port and military bases were bringing in individuals of curiosity and abandon who would patronize the clubs. And a corrupt political infrastructure was firmly in place to support the vices that supported the music. The style of Frank Waldron and Lillian Smith may have been somewhat old-fashioned, with the watch-fob and frock-coat trappings of the turn of the century, but the next generation would have all the flamboyance of the Jazz Age to come.

**Jelly Roll Morton, right, in Los Angeles, in 1917.**

**Morton was just another hustler on the make when this photo was taken, doing a "vaudeville single" up and down the West Coast, from Mexico to Alaska. He would not become famous until his 1923 recordings.**

**Photo by Duncan Schiedt Courtesy of the Hogan Jazz Archive, Tulane University**

# 2
# THE JAZZ AGE
# 1920-1933

*The orchestra was clashing out a "red hot" melody, flashily dressed women and escorts were laughing in the spacious dance hall and supper room—and upstairs, the agents declared, half a dozen couples were standing at the bar, drinking real bonded liquor while numerous others were shooting craps. . . . After more than a year of untrammeled operation Seattle's liveliest "night club" was closed and the rattle of its dice, the tinkle of its highball glasses, and the clashing cymbals of its jazz band were silent.*

Seattle Times, *March 23, 1931*

In the Roaring Twenties, Seattle, like the rest of the country, went wild. There were speakeasies, roadhouses, raccoon coats, bobbed hair, the Charleston, bootleggers, and federal agents. There was also jazz—not a lot of it, but certainly enough to qualify the town as more than a whistle-stop on the Jazz Age express. Because of a strong, rurally based anti-saloon movement east of the mountains, Prohibition started in Washington in 1916, three years earlier than in the rest of the nation. As a result, the hermetic arts of bathtub gin, "Joe sent me" speakeasies, and Canadian rum-running, which rose in reaction against Prohibition, got a head start in the Northwest.

In some ways, Prohibition fit right in with the Northwest ethos. Seattle and Tacoma already had an institutionalized underground firmly in place to deal with the distribution of vice. Bootleg liquor became simply another profit center—albeit a broader-based one—for the mayor and police chief to add to the casinos, whorehouses, and opium dens they already tolerated. On the other hand, the reaction against Prohibition broadened the clientele for such illegal activities, stimulating the nightclub business enormously. Whereas only single men—sailors, loggers, miners, and the like—had patronized Skid Road, everyone wanted a drink. And everyone, it would appear, had one.

Clarinetist Joe Darensbourg, who had seen a lot of action before arriving in Seattle from Los Angeles in 1928, found Seattle's speakeasy scene one of the wildest in the country. "There's never been a town like Seattle, to my idea," wrote Darensbourg in his hilarious as-told-to autobiography, *Jazz Odyssey*. "Seattle and New Orleans is the two distinct towns in the U.S.A., so different from any others."

Bootleg liquor was to be found practically anywhere. "The illegal stuff was ferried in by ship, dinghies, dories, speedboats, and even by canoe," according to the *Seattle Times*. "Booze arrived in Washington in the gas tanks of cars, by horse and wagon and airplanes."

Roadhouses, freestanding nightclubs on the outskirts of town, provided a popular form of entertainment during Prohibition. Beyond the reach of local police jurisdiction, and protected from the feds by lookouts, they were made possible by the sudden accessibility of the automobile. Because of Seattle's proximity to Canada, where liquor was still legal, roadhouses flourished along the highways going north to British Columbia. Dining and dancing clubs sprang up along the Everett and Bothell highways (now Highway 99 and Bothell Way, respectively), including the China Castle, Parker's Highway Pavilion, Marino's, Willard's, the Jungle Temple, and the Ranch. The Green Mill was named after the famous Al Capone hangout in Chicago. In February 1927, the Sid Saunders band was playing there. Johnny Maxon's Orchestra played for college students at the Coon Chicken Inn. (Part of a chain of southern-fried-chicken establishments that closed in the 1950s, the Coon Chicken Inn was a grotesque monument to racism whose front entrance was the mouth of a grinning redcap.)

Willard's, a roadhouse on Bothell Way that featured a fan dancer, was a good restaurant with a large dance floor that brought in "name" white musicians from San Francisco, such as Art Hickman and Paul Ash, as well as Johnny Robinson's Varsity Vagabonds, from Portland, considered by some observers to be the hottest jazz band in the Northwest. To the south, down Marginal Way, there was the China Pheasant. Near Enumclaw, the Snake Ranch, also known as Red Neck Kelly's, flourished. Even Police Chief Forbes acknowledged with dismay in a 1931 interview that "everybody, nearly, carries a bottle on his hip when he goes to a roadhouse."

Along Jackson Street, from First Avenue to Fourteenth, with detours through the International District, a thirsty, fun-seeking citizen could find not only bonded Scotch, but jazz, dancing, and just about any other kind of entertainment, including opium dens, brothels for men and for women, elaborate casinos with roulette wheels and dice felts, and a daily Chinese lottery that sometimes paid big bucks. One establishment featured female mud wrestlers. Downtown, huge beer parlors, such as Lyon's Music Hall, on First Avenue, and the Virginian, on Stewart, featured music, dancing, terrible sandwiches, and all the beer you could drink, courtesy of beat cops who were paid off in an orderly fashion. Johnny Reddin, a columnist who remembered putting phony labels on bathtub gin as a kid to sell out the back door of a Queen Anne drugstore, liked to put it this way:

"A Seattle visitor asks a policeman where he can get a drink—'See that building on the corner?' says the man in blue. 'That's the Methodist church. It's probably one of the few places in town that you *can't* get a drink.'"

Not that the feds didn't try to squelch all this. As soon as Prohibition was enacted nationally, agents began making war on the clubs. In 1923 alone, 1,306 persons were arrested in Seattle for liquor-law violations. As fast as the feds busted them, the proprietors of the speakeasies devised new ways of evading the law. One clever bartender, known as "Doorbelly" because of the size of his gut, stored vats of liquor in the loft of his house and installed pipes down to the bar faucets, through which the gin ran like water.

The local cops, many of whom were on the take, were almost as frustrating to the feds as the operators. The night the Chinese Gardens speakeasy was busted in 1931, Seattle's sergeant of detectives was found working in the hatcheck room. The most celebrated tale of police corruption during Washington's Prohibition era involved police lieutenant Roy Olmsted, who was caught red-handed unloading Canadian liquor from a motorboat north of Edmonds. Convicted and expelled from the force, Olmsted was later caught again in his Mount Baker home, with a house full of liquor. When federal officers burst in, they found his wife broadcasting messages to smugglers over the radio, disguised as "Aunt Vivian's" bedtime stories for youngsters. Olmsted served four years at the McNeil Island federal penitentiary.

The most important musician to walk into this wide-open scene was Oscar Holden, the patriarch of early Seattle jazz. Born in 1887 in Nashville, Holden had played on Fate Marable's famous Mississippi riverboat excursions, where Louis Armstrong and other young New Orleans musicians had also honed their craft. According to Joe Darensbourg, Holden also worked with "Keppard and those guys" in the early days of New Orleans jazz. Anxious to get away from the South, Holden had settled in Chicago, where he taught and performed. In his autobiography, Jelly Roll Morton says he brought Holden to Seattle from Vancouver, British Columbia, where Holden played clarinet in Morton's band. Holden's daughter, Grace, says the year was 1919.

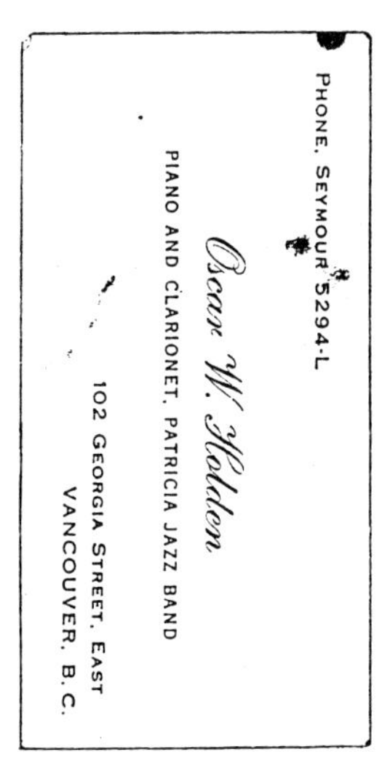


"He played piano, saxophone, clarinet, trumpet, and bass," says Grace, herself a pianist.

> *Our mother, Leala, played piano. The two met while playing different gigs in the North End of Seattle. Oscar was playing at the Jungle Temple, in 1928. A little further up the road was another night spot I don't remember the name of. One of them had a flat tire and my mother was asked if she wouldn't mind bringing Oscar back to town.*

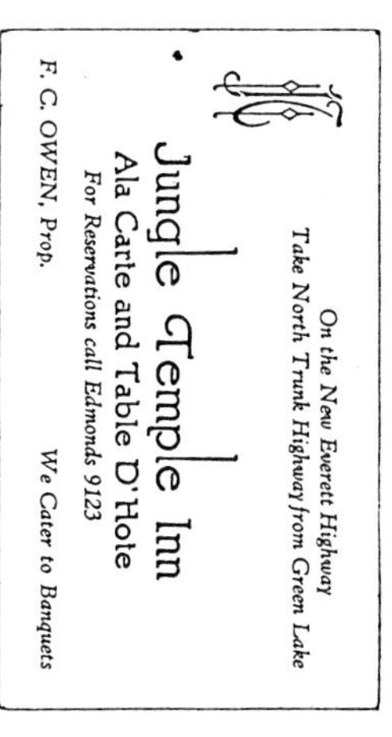


Holden was a powerhouse player with a deep classical background and a stride style similar to Fats Waller's. He could transpose tunes into all twelve keys, accompany singers sensitively, and work with a band or play solo all night long and keep it interesting. Recalls Palmer Johnson:

Oscar Holden, the patriarch of Seattle jazz.
Courtesy of Grace Holden

*Oscar was my idol, man, because he could read so good! Anything you set before him, he's gone! He had a wonderful musical education. He was one of the first ones up here. Oscar was real black and had a soft voice. He was a great, great performer. I always asked him to play some Chopin, and he did. [And] he'd play "Rhapsody in Blue" right off from the beginning to end.*

Holden had seven children, five of whom pursued musical careers. Probably the best-known is Ron, a vocalist whose calypso-tinged rock 'n' roll hit "Love You So" hit the *Billboard* charts. Seattle rhythm-and-blues fans know Jimmy Holden as the soulful electric keyboardist of the archetypal bar band the Reputations, while fans of an earlier generation know Grace as the original keyboardist and vocalist with the Charlie Taylor band, where Quincy Jones got his start, and Oscar, Jr., as that group's original alto saxophonist. Dave Holden worked in Seattle in an organ trio for years before moving to Los Angeles, where he started playing solo.

Like many musicians in the area at the time, Oscar Holden also held a day job, working as a pipe fitter at Todd Shipyards. Grace vividly recalls her father racing off to catch the ferry after work to play a graduation in Kirkland, or switching from his pipe-fitter's clothes to his tux for a job at the Clover Club downtown.

"He'd come home from swing shift," she recounts, "then go right straight upstairs, take his bath, change his clothes, and be right back out the door at twelve-thirty so he could be on the job at one o'clock. He'd play from one until four-thirty or five o'clock in the morning."

Holden had tremendous stamina. As a regular constitutional, he swam two miles across Lake Washington. His family would drive around the lake—there was no bridge—and pick him up on the other side. Holden also fixed old pianos in his spare time.

Ron Holden recounts:

*One of the fondest memories was Friday and Saturday nights. . . . I can remember lying in bed with butterflies in my stomach because I knew any minute my mom would come in and kiss me good night. She would come in all dressed up for the gig and Dad would be in his tux. I would go to sleep with that in my mind. Two glamorous people kissing me good night.*

According to Ron, "Every Sunday, the family would get together and play the same music that they played for the dances." "There was a piano in the basement, and a parlor grand upstairs," adds Grace. "We ate music, we lived music."

Unfortunately for posterity, Holden so despised life in the South that he never talked to his family about his past with New Orleans musicians. He did not mention, for example, that he had been cited in Jelly Roll Morton's autobiography. (This may have been out of pride. Jelly Roll wrote, "[Holden] was no hot man, but he played plenty straight clarinet.") He often told his children he purposely did not marry until he had fled Dixie, so his children would not have to be born there. "He hated that music," remembers Grace. "He associated that with the South and the bad old days. He could play that type of jazz, with the banjo in there doing its thing, but the Al Jolson kind of thing was against his nature. That was what he left behind."

Oscar Holden performed until 1966, when he had a stroke. He died three years later. The musical traditions Holden carried to Seattle from the South and the Midwest have lived on through his children, but only rarely has his contribution been acknowledged. Jimmy Holden fondly remembers an exception.

"I was playing at the Scarlet Tree one night, and this guy, a local saxophonist, passed me a note that said, 'Your father was one of the greatest piano players in Seattle.' That did a lot for me, to know that somebody remembered him the way we do."

One of the places Oscar Holden played as a regular was Doc Hamilton's Barbecue Pit, on 12th Avenue, across from where Seattle University stands today. Of all the illustrious Prohibition hangouts, none was more famous—nor its owner more widely heralded—than Doc Hamilton's; it was Seattle's Prohibition equivalent of Harlem's Cotton Club. John H. "Doc" Hamilton was a tall, dapper man with a devastatingly deferential, gold-toothed smile that masked an angry pride. A man of sophisticated airs, he held a lifelong passion for dice and barbecued meats. (According to Darensbourg, Hamilton registered a patent for his "secret" barbecue sauce.) Born in West Point, Mississippi, Hamilton was twenty-three when he came to Seattle in 1914. He left to serve in France in World War I in the Ninety-second Infantry Division (the black "Buffalo" division). When he returned, he opened his first speakeasy in his home at 1017½ East Union Street. (When the cops axed their way into the place in July 1924, hacking through three barred doors, they found a cozy nightclub with four pianos, silver cocktail shakers, and high-class glassware.)

Hamilton later owned or operated several other illegal clubs, including a roadhouse just north of the King-Snohomish county line, on Highway 99, called the Ranch. "When the running boats would dock," recalls saxophonist Bruce Rowell, Noodles Smith's old right-hand man, "they would come right up on the beach where the Ranch was, on 99."

Doc's most famous establishment, however, was the Pit. Doc Hamilton's Barbecue Pit was elegant. Limousines lined the curb out front, while Seattle's social elect, including the mayor, ducked in and out of the club. At the door, Jim Baker, a short fellow in an admiral's uniform, variously called "Buttons" or "Napoleon," welcomed the guests. Inside was the restaurant and bar, where "liquor was to be had with no more effort than asking for a glass of water." Here, Doc worked at his huge barbecue pit, turning the spit and slicing southern-cured ham. Downstairs was the "action"—roulette and an all-night dice game. Should there be a raid, the Barbecue Pit was prepared. A complete alarm system, with a complicated system of bells, bars, and pulleys, snaked through the building. A button convenient to the foot of the cashier at the lunch counter was wired to a buzzer at the triple-barred doors of the cabaret in the basement.

Usually, Doc had singers working in his place. Oscar Holden accompanied them or played solo (sometimes falling asleep at the keyboard, according to one account). The place was a hangout for the best musicians. Says Joe Darensbourg:

*Doc's was a good job. We made good money and tips, got all our food. . . . I met*

*Jimmie Lunceford for the first time at [Doc's] place. We went to breakfast. The next night, after the band got through playing, Willie Smith and Trummy Young came in and sat in with us. Willie brought his saxophone and his clarinet down there.*

Like the rest of the speaks, Hamilton's club was protected by payoffs. Nevertheless, it was raided so often one begins to suspect someone downtown had a grudge against this elegant black man who was raking in the dough. Terry Pettus, an old Seattle radical, went to his grave convinced that Hamilton had offended public sensibilities by building a house in Mount Baker, at the time an all-white neighborhood. Whatever the reason, Hamilton eventually was hounded out of town by the police, who raided the club again and again. What had started as a joking cat-and-mouse game, played out in the press between the cagey Hamilton and Sheriff Harry Lewis, eventually turned ugly.

"If some dice accidentally fell out of someone's pocket," Doc told a reporter after one of his periodic busts, "I was too busy roasting chickens to notice."

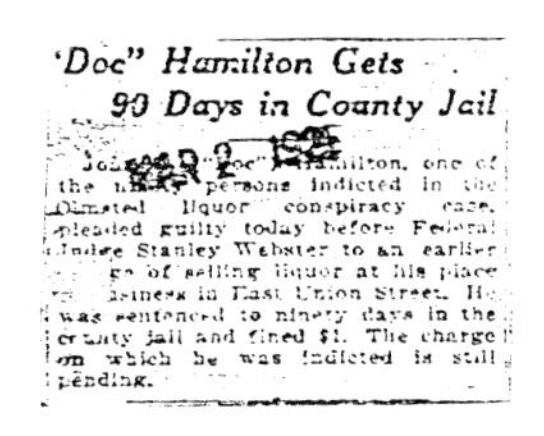
'Doc" Hamilton Gets 90 Days in County Jail

[illegible] "Doc" Hamilton, one of the [illegible] persons indicted in the Olmsted liquor conspiracy case, pleaded guilty today before Federal Judge Stanley Webster to an earlier [illegible] of selling liquor at his place [illegible] business in East Union Street. He was sentenced to ninety days in the county jail and fined $1. The charge on which he was indicted is still pending.

Doc Hamilton, Freed In Olmsted Liquor Case, Asks Divorce

THE matrimonial firm of Hamilton & Hamilton—consisting of "Doc" and Queenie—is on the rocks, according to a divorce action begun in Superior Court yesterday by John H. Hamilton, better known as "Doc."

Hamilton, [illegible] barbecue pit has been [illegible] into the public eye by its [illegible] and by the Olmsted conspiracy trial in which "Doc" appeared as [illegible] defendant and was exonerated [illegible]

When Doc Hamilton was hauled off to jail after an undercover raid by Lewis on May 25, 1931—"This place is pinched!" Lewis had shouted—he was smiling. "I guess the sheriff wanted some extra good cooking in his jail kitchen," he quipped. But when the judge padlocked the club and sentenced Hamilton to federal prison instead of the usual overnight stay in jail and light fine, Hamilton angrily appealed the case.

"I ask you," Doc pleaded, "is this right? Can they do this to a man? Can Prohibition agents come into a man's restaurant with liquor, mix their drinks behind his back, and then padlock his place because drinking has been done in it?"

When he lost the appeal, Doc was devastated. The judge sentenced him to five years. Hamilton gave an eloquent courtroom farewell, charging Judge Howard Findley with racism. After all, Doc argued, no white speakeasy operators were going to prison.

*Your Honor, sir, you know that the laws are unjust, and that because I am a colored man I can shine shoes or scrub floors or cook for somebody, but that if I try to rise above that position, the public is against me. If I go to the penitentiary, sir, there will be twenty-five people who will starve to death. They are my father, mother, my children, and my employees. If you send me to the penitentiary, sir, God Himself will curse you for it.*

Hamilton was pardoned two days before Christmas, 1933, after serving ten months. Despite his early release, he was a broken man. He had lost his Seattle house. He farmed for a while in Auburn and made several unsuccessful attempts to reopen his club. He died in 1942, alone in a Chinatown hotel.

When running his famous Barbecue Pit, Hamilton had catered to whites, as the Cotton Club in New York did. The white population caught on quickly to the mania for jazz through the media and phonograph records, despite the fact that most early jazz stars did not visit Seattle during the twenties.

Though "jazz" was discussed in the black newspaper *Cayton's Weekly* as early as 1917, whites probably first saw the word in print on January 4, 1920, in an ad for a vaudeville show at the Palace Hip, at Second Avenue and Spring Street. The ad touted an act called Tom Brown's County Officials, featuring a routine dubbed the "Rube Jay Jazzers." For the rest of the year, "jazz" was the buzzword for vaudeville shows coming to town. The following month, Ole and Abie's Jazz Band played the Orpheum. In June, Fanchon and Marco, a popular West Coast vaudeville team and production company, produced "A Jazz Opera," featuring "a jazz orchestra and 30 of the most beautiful girls in the world." Modeled on the Ziegfield Follies, the show had an all–West Coast cast and made a successful East Coast tour.

The following year, San Francisco cornetist Paul Ash, who would later become famous in Chicago as a conductor, was billed as "Mr. Jazz Himself," performing in a "Jazz Revue" in which the band's drummer juggled drumsticks and ran up and down the aisle beating time. It's hard to gauge just how much "jazz" content there was in these early shows. The use of the word in advertising suggests that the acts probably were capitalizing on a fad word.

Fad or not, by 1925 jazz shows had begun to appear in major Seattle theaters with some regularity. The first group to be touted as a "big name" jazz act from out of town was the Sid Hall Orchestra, a hotel band from New York, which played the Palace Hip on May 12, 1925. The USS *Nevada* Jazz Band had already played the Pantages in January of the same year, and the twelve-member Colorado Jazz Band played there as well, on May 3, 1925. In March, a group with the intriguing name the Chinese Stringed Band, billed as "six syncopated players of modern jazz," played the Columbia Theatre "on their way East." This may have been an early jazz band on its way to Yokohama, Manila, or Shanghai. According to Bruce Rowell and Emma Gayton—whose mother's rooming house Blackie Williams had lived in—the great blues singers Bessie Smith and Mamie Smith also performed in Seattle, though no record of their shows can be found. It's possible, since Seattle was on a main touring circuit, drawing major celebrities in other fields. In 1925 alone, Anna Pavlova, Sergei Rachmaninoff, the Hungarian musician/composer Ernö Dohnányi, American tenor Roland Hayes, violinist/composer Fritz Kreisler, and the Russian basso Feodor Chaliapin all performed on Seattle stages. By 1928, jazz had taken over the popular music scene to the extent that theater orchestra leader Jules Buffano would warn the musicians' union that "legitimate players who refuse to deviate into the jazz realm are finding it increasingly difficult to find and hold good jobs."

Buffano's use of the verb "deviate" is revealing. Like rock 'n' roll in the 1950s, jazz was greeted by many as a cacophonous symptom of a society run amuck. When local newspapers and magazine editors wrote about it, they were often less interested in the music than in the social behavior that accompanied it. "Jazz is a return to the primitive, to the savage who used music as a physical stimulant," wrote the comically dubbed "Jazz Investigator" for the *Seattle Times* in June 1921. "Jazz is a cross rhythm that carried far enough could so irritate the nervous system as to derange it entirely. . . . Jazz is one of the greatest contributing factors to the recklessness of young people today."

The Musical Arts Society agreed with the *Times*. The same year, it passed a resolution denouncing jazz as something that "tears down the moral fiber." Four years later, a Spokane music professor went them one better, bringing a $4,000 suit against the leader of a local orchestra for syncopating the old masters.

One of the most intriguing responses to the new music came from *Cayton's Weekly*, which, though a black newspaper, was beside itself with bourgeois embarrassment over jazz. Owner Horace Cayton's daughter, Madge, wrote:

> *One must be careful that the alluring god of jazz, Mumbo Jumbo, does not lead us so far from the true god of music, Pan. . . . Is there not a chance of jazz becoming the key to open our souls to the passions our forefathers once spent generations in trying to overcome?*

All of this publicity for jazz was a great boon to local black entertainers, who could now command not only an audience of sailors looking for action at one of Noodles Smith's joints, but a more middle-class crowd in a speakeasy, as well. The pianist who became more popular in this vein than anyone else over the years was Palmer Johnson, whom Oscar Holden took under his wing after his arrival in Seattle from Los Angeles.

A big-framed, straight-backed man with enormous hands, childlike eyes, and the booming intonation of a country preacher, Johnson was born in Houston, in 1907, and grew up from the age of three in Los Angeles. His childhood along Central Avenue near 33rd Street, where his mother ran a soul-food restaurant, is rich with musical memories. Johnson was nurtured in an era when pianists Henry Prince and Harvey Brooks were at their peak, Paul Howard and his Serenaders had just hired Lionel Hampton to play drums, and Louis Armstrong had come out to play at Frank Sebastian's Cotton Club. Johnson remembers his mother and aunt talking about Jelly Roll Morton playing at Normandy Hall.

> *In those days they gave parties every Friday or Saturday night, or a stomp, as they called it. We weren't allowed to play jazz, or rags as they called it in them days, in the house, so all the neighbors from around who knew that we kids could play would say, "Come on over. Friday night, so and so's going to have a ball." You walk*

Alcohol Still Of 1,000 Gallons Is

STILL IS RAIDED

4 BLACK-TAN NIGHT CLUBS SHUT UP BY U.S. RAIDERS

Three White Men, Two Negroes Arrested in 'Doc' Hamilton's Pit, Yesler Way Cabaret JAN 25 1932

Federal prohibition authorities planned abatement proceedings against four "black-and-tan" night clubs today as a result of liquor raids staged Saturday night by six deputy sheriffs and an out-of-town federal prohibition agent.

Five men, three of them white, were arrested in hip pocket searches, and several hundred merrymakers were momentarily alarmed when the officers made whirlwind entrances.

At Doc (J. H.) Hamilton's Barbecue Pit, 908 12th Ave., the officers, led by Deputy Claude Latimer, arrested three white guests, A. A. Houghian, 31 years old, 6012 14th Ave. N. W.; A. L. Coleman, 206 Harvard Ave. N., and Paul D. Clyde, 40, 138 Galer St. Houghian posted $250 bond. The others were released to friends.

New Yesler Club Raided

At a new and elaborate Negro night club at 926 Yesler Way, the officers entered while twenty couples were dancing, just after a floor entertainment. They found the bar "dry" but arrested Archie Jackson, 32-year-old Negro musician, for a small quantity of liquor. He had just dropped in, he said, after playing at another club.

Leon Green, 29, Negro laborer, was arrested for having liquor, in a Negro pool room and men's club at 1205 Jackson St., the former Alhambra Cafe. When searched, he was carrying $6.81 in Canadian money, three knives, two watches and a ring.

"Suckers" in Formal Dress

[illegible] Miller, 32, Negro, was arrested [illegible] a small amount of liquor *down the street, you could hear the player pianos, playing "Down at the Savannah lives a fellow named Hosanna. . . ." "Bluein' the Blues," that was called, on a pump piano. Hear that all over town, man.*

*In 1923, my cousin took me to Doctor Gordon's Hummingbird, on Twelfth and Central, where Harvey Brooks was playing piano. . . . Harvey Brooks, Leon Hereford played alto, and Paul Howard, tenor. Jazz player, but he played in church, too, on Sunday. I used to follow them around getting pointers how to play. . . . Every time I had an opportunity to see Henry Prince play, who lived in Pasadena, I'd stand outside the Parish Hall. I didn't want to go inside, just stand outside and listen to Henry.*

Johnson started on violin, at age seven, but soon turned to piano. His first professional job was in 1924, playing Friday and Saturday nights at the Chicken Inn, across the street from Frank Sebastian's Cotton Club, with an entertainer named Gutfoot. A year or two later, Johnson and a friend hitchhiked to the San Francisco Bay area, where they heard one of the region's early black jazz piano men, Wesley "Fess" Fields.

In 1927 Johnson returned to San Francisco and began working at a lesbian bar, where he remembers playing "Two Cigarettes in the Dark" and "Valencia," new tunes at the time. The following year, he traveled by boat from Los Angeles to Seattle to play a gig at the Maryland Tavern with guitarist Freddy Vaughn. Vaughn had been working one night a week in Los Angeles with Curtis Mosby's Blue Blowers when he heard of steadier work in Seattle. He invited Johnson, saxophonist Elmer Fain, drummer Ellis Walsh, and (male) vocalist Sally Harper to come with him. Remembers Johnson:

*We caught a boat. We landed here in about November 1928, and we were scheduled to go to the Maryland Tavern, which is out Old Bothell Highway. It was almost to Everett. It was the farthest one, and just before you got to it, there was another one called Rubenac's Tavern and then across the street was the Ranch, where they used to do a lot of gambling. Didn't do any gambling at the Maryland Tavern. It's a roadhouse. We had an old Victrola, with one of those horns on it, and we fixed it to a box and [you could] throw silver dollars in it. That was the kitty. All silver dollars in those days. The songs we played were "My Blue Heaven" and "When Evening Is Nigh." The music at the Maryland Tavern was loud. The louder you played, the better. Because there was so much noise going on, the music had to drown out that noise. There wasn't no microphones then —we took a megaphone and sang. Until we got to the sweet stuff, like "My Blue Heaven."*

*The Charleston was still in vogue, but we were tired of the Charleston. It's monotonous. And here's some guy just learning it. And we said, "Oh nuts. We saw that stuff down in Los Angeles." Every person that you looked at could do the Charleston. . . . We had to educate them.*

Johnson was considerably advanced as a player when he got to town, a master of stride, boogie-woogie, chromatic modulations, and a deftly sliding left-hand chordal style that used tenth intervals. He also had picked up the flowery, classically influenced pianisms of the Los Angeles players.

"Palmer Johnson used to always laugh to himself as he played—'Ha-ha-ha-ha-ha!'—looking at the keys," recalls Julian Henson, a Portland pianist who moved to Seattle in 1932. "He'd be playing and laughing. He was just marvelous!"

"Palmer was very good," says Joe Darensbourg. "Played with the class of Billy Kyle and could work with anybody's band."

Johnson was good, but still counted Oscar Holden his superior. "In those days, Oscar was very, very much better than I was. He was kind and considerate and he wanted to see me learn. I loved him. He helped me so much. He helped me on my reading. He gave me inspiration."

The band Johnson came to Seattle with had some intriguing players. Sally Harper has been described by trumpeter Buck Clayton, who knew him in Los Angeles, as a "beautiful lyric tenor singer." Harper popularized an old gambling tune from the Klondike, "Ace in the Hole," and made it a permanent part of the Seattle repertoire, much to the chagrin of singers who were still fielding requests for it thirty years later. Elmer Fain, who could not read music but was a good improviser, later returned to Los Angeles, where he worked with Clayton at the Paradise Club and became the business agent for the black Los Angeles Musicians' Union, Local No. 767. Drummer Ellis Walsh went on to a career that included playing on the Louis Jordan record "Is You Is, or Is You Ain't."

When the Maryland Tavern was shut down by federal agents—hacked to pieces with double-bitted axes—the band broke up. Johnson moved on to Marino's, another "joint" on Bothell Highway, known for its excellent food. He played there with trumpeter Charles Adams, then worked briefly at the Main Event, a small gambling joint near 12th and Jackson. He next found himself working with clarinetist Darensbourg and alto saxophonist Gerald Wells, at the China Castle, a spectacular-looking Prohibition-era roadhouse with "lookout towers," prostitution "cribs" in the basement, and, some say, an underground escape tunnel to the college hangout across the street, the Coon Chicken Inn. The China Castle, near NE 87th Street on what is now Lake City Way, was closer to town than the Ranch or the Maryland Tavern, but still very much "in the woods" in those days. It opened in 1929, shut down for a while in the early 1930s, then reopened in 1934 as the Jolly Roger, with a pirate flag flying from the turret, to capitalize on its purple Prohibition past. For many years, it was a roadside restaurant; in the 1980s it reopened as a blues nightclub; it burned down in October 1989. Palmer Johnson describes it as a rip-roaring place, where college kids and others with a few bucks in their wallet would drive out in their new automobiles to kick up their heels.

*Sometimes, there was nobody in the joint. We'd be sitting around the table playing a game called mellow, something on the order of whist. We'd see some lights from a car coming and the band would jump on the stand and play like mad, like there was something going on, you understand! And pretty soon, they'd come in. It was a funny thing how that happened. As soon as that bunch came in, here was another bunch that came in. Pretty soon, the joint would be rolling. Jumping, man. And we playing all their requests. . . .*

*The madams would close down their whorehouses about, say, two o'clock, and go out nightclubbing. They bring the whores down there. The gals, gee whiz, man, when you had those girls come in, they'd be coming out to spend some money. Probably a thousand dollars, which was nothing to them then. All five or six of her girls, and they had a chance to dress up in their new rhinestone slippers and their new dresses and their new capes or whatever they got. Some of them had mink, or imitation mink, and they came out to show it off.*

The gig at the China Castle ended in a couple of months, and in 1929 Palmer went to work at Herman Myers' Taxi Dance Hall, on the corner of First and Yesler, this time with Darensbourg, Freddy Vaughn, Seattle trumpeter Lee Philips, a drummer whose name no one remembers, and Gerald Wells. The job lasted two years.

The taxi dance was a curious institution in which girls were paid by a hall to dance with customers. Myers' establishment catered to soldiers and sailors. Explains Johnson:

*It was ten cents a dance. The band just played continually, never stopped. Just round and round and round. A guy buys tickets and all these girls are sitting around and he chooses his partner, and he dances and dances and gives her so many tickets. Then when he runs out of tickets, he goes to the counter and gets some more. A man would hold up his finger. Like, [if] he wanted a waltz and then he wanted a two-step or a fox-trot, he held it up, or if he wanted a real fast one he held up his fingers and the band knew how to answer him with these numbers. That was a good job. I think we made thirty-five dollars a week then.*

Joe Darensbourg says that he and Johnson worked at a roadhouse on Everett Highway called the Jungle Temple, with a group named the Jungle Temple Syncopators, "around the back end of 1929." The Jungle Temple had two incarnations, numbered accordingly, but it's

The Freda Shaw band aboard the SS *H.F. Alexander*, 1928. Shaw, center; Joe Darensbourg, far right.

Jazz musicians like Darensbourg often played on cruise ships to Los Angeles, Hawaii, and the Far East in the 1920s.

Courtesy of Emma Gayton

often unclear which one musicians are referring to. Johnson doesn't remember the band.

Darensbourg's recollections of his time in Seattle are anything but reliable—even he admits he was drunk most of the time—but they are undeniably colorful and entertaining. An olive-skinned Creole clarinetist from Louisiana who would later play a major role in the New Orleans revival, Joseph Wilmer Darensbourg was an immensely likable, openhearted man who loved to spin tall tales, cook jambalaya, drink tremendous quantities of alcohol, and play practical jokes on his bandmates. Born in Baton Rouge, Louisiana, Darensbourg was a student of the great Alphonse Picou (noted for his clarinet solo on "High Society") and toured as a young man with minstrel and medicine shows. In 1925, he played briefly in St. Louis with Jelly Roll Morton and, like Oscar Holden, on Fate Marable's riverboat excursions, before being recruited into Hill and Vesthon's Original Dixieland Jazz Band. The band broke up in California and Darensbourg settled in Los Angeles, where he continued to work as a musician and an instrument repairman. Darensbourg got his first glimpse of Seattle in 1928, while traveling up and down the West Coast with the Freda Shaw band aboard the SS *H. F. Alexander*. In 1929, attracted by the easy money and wild lifestyle, he decided to move there.

> *When I was in Los Angeles a lot of musicians would come back from Seattle and tell you how great it was, how much money you could make. When I was offered the job on the boat I had that in mind. . . . We'd get in, just for two nights, and meet some broads, and when we got through we'd go down to 12th and Jackson. [Seattle] was a money town. You went to work in a joint there and you always had forty-five dollars a week guaranteed. They had legitimate red-light districts, which consisted of Jackson Street, King Street, and Yesler Way. At these after-hours clubs we had a lot of the sporting class of people used to come in, like pimps and prostitutes. They'd come to show off . . . and see who could outspend each other putting money in the kitty. The house usually had a kitty cast out of plaster of paris and painted; it would have a big mouth and they put a light in it. You had a lot of silver dollars in those days, and people would throw a dollar into the kitty and hit a little lever inside and its eyes would light up. People got a kick out of that, seeing the goddamn cat blink his eyes. . . . In a place like the Black and Tan we'd have several entertainers that would go to the tables and sing songs. We would wind up sometimes making 200 or 300 dollars apiece.*

Darensbourg had worked briefly with Palmer Johnson in Los Angeles, so it was only natural that his first Seattle engagement would be with the big pianist. In addition to their gigs at the Jungle Temple and Herman Myers' Taxi Dance Hall, they worked at the Blue Rose, a "pretty elaborate after-hours joint" on 14th and Yesler, later called the Rocking Chair, where Darensbourg stayed for about six or eight months. The band included "Banjoski" Adams (on banjo, of course, plus vocals) and drummer Bill Hoy.

Darensbourg also worked with Oscar Holden often, first at the Jungle Temple, then later at the Blue Rose and the Black and Tan. In 1932, he formed a quartet with white pianist Vic Sewell. Sewell and his brother, Monty (a trumpet player), were the sons of Slim Sewell, a trombonist who played at the Pantages Theater for thirty years and also played with the Seattle Symphony. Because Vic lived on Genessee Street, Darensbourg, who had a name for everything, dubbed the band the Genessee Street Shufflers.

The Shufflers was a popular band and featured, in addition to Darensbourg and Sewell, drummer Jack Foy and bassist/guitarist Bill Rinaldi, both white. Darensbourg, an unremitting practical joker, played one of his best tricks on Foy while performing with the Shufflers. Remembers Foy:

> *I kept smelling this terrible smell around my drums every night, you know? I figured a cat died under the riser or something. Finally, I kept smelling it on my hands. Joe had put Limburger cheese under all of the cymbals. I'd touch them with my hand and I'd get it on me. As the days went by, it got riper and riper, of course. Oh, my God, it smelled!*

Bill Rinaldi, one of Seattle's most enduring sidemen, whose career bridges the "hot jazz" period and the swing era, was a roughneck, a husky ex–prize fighter remembered as much for his solid sense of time as for his continual scraps.

"Bill was a jealous guy," according to Darensbourg. "If he'd see Lorna [a chorus girl he married] getting too close to a guy or the guy holding her too close, he would jump off the bandstand and hit the guy in the mouth. He'd start a big fight like that. It was a lot of fun."

Jack Foy agrees:

> *He was the toughest guy I ever met in my life. Joe called Bill Rinaldi "Tiger." If he went down the street and somebody beat him to a parking place, he'd jump out and beat the hell out of the guy, just for kicks. Loved to fight. If there was a fight in the joint where we worked, he'd go and throw the guy out, like a bouncer. He was the unofficial bouncer of every place we'd work.*

Darensbourg and Palmer Johnson both worked at various times with another important early Seattle musician, Gerald Wells. Though Wells was a better reader than improviser, he is an extremely important figure in the story of early West Coast jazz, and his influence ranged from Los Angeles to Honolulu. Wells' birthplace has been given variously as Saint Vincent, Port of Spain, and Jamaica; locals identify his accent as "Jamaican." As early as 1914 he was playing flute in Sid LeProtti's jazz band in San Francisco. Wells first came to Seattle in 1913, but spent most of the late teens traveling with one of the most influential groups in the West, Reb Spikes' So Different Orchestra. In 1917, the So Different Orchestra shipped out to Honolulu for a six-month engagement at the Alexander Young Hotel. When the United States entered World War I, the whole band was absorbed into the service, becoming the first jazz band to play in Army uniform. When an offer to tour the East Coast developed, Wells wanted to go and the others did not, so he left the band and returned to Seattle. It's not clear whether Wells rejoined the So Different Orchestra when it subsequently came north to play the Alhambra in July 1920, but it makes sense that he would have, even if he had already left the band. Remembers Darensbourg:

> *[Gerald] played saxophone and piccolo. Gerald was a prominent bandleader in Seattle and always had a pretty good little band. It was a mixed band: We had about seven pieces and some good arrangements, and we considered ourselves the top band in Seattle. . . . Originally he had been in San Diego working at Jack Johnson's club.*
>
> *. . . Gerald was a fine musician, a good legitimate man, but he wasn't a jazzman by any stretch of the imagination. . . . Most of our stuff was for dances and we had singing entertainers in there with us, like Lillian Goode. We'd play for the vocalists and sometimes for shows, where you had to do a lot of reading.*

Evelyn Bundy with her son, Charles Taylor, c. 1935. The Bundy-Taylor household was a focal point for the jazz community for two generations. Evelyn Bundy led one of Seattle's only swing bands in the 1920s; her son, Charles, started the band in the 1940s that gave Quincy Jones his start.

Wells later became president of Local 493, playing a prominent role as host of the Blue Note, the informal 493 union hall, on Jefferson and 14th. Wells, Holden, Johnson, and Darensbourg were the most influential immigrants to Seattle in the 1920s. They brought with them sophisticated new styles and a higher technical standard than had existed in town before. Without recordings from the period, however, it is difficult to know what they sounded like. From talking to them and other sources, and listening to their more recent recordings and to other music from the period, it is clear that they were not playing traditional New Orleans jazz, or "Dixieland," as it is sometimes called. Oscar Holden's children make a point of saying that the pianist had "left all that southern music" behind him. "We didn't play no Dixieland," says Darensbourg. "In the first place, Gerald [Wells] never knew anybody in that style or anything about the music. Our group was a jazz band; we didn't call it Dixieland."

Johnson is even more emphatic:

*We never used any Dixieland. Only on a few, certain numbers. We played "Tiger Rag" on request, but we weren't crazy about "Tiger Rag." Even in those days that was what we called old-time stuff. We were all the time getting something new. For instance, when we heard Duke Ellington's record, we'd study that record. And you never heard no tuba in it. These guys tried to make their playing sound as near to the Duke [Ellington] as they could. Not only the Duke had a good band, at those times McKinney's Cotton Pickers was a hell of a band.*

*We played pops. What I call pops is, when you can get a tune and fix it up the way that we wanted to fix it. We learned how to take one of them tunes apart, man, and put it back together again. We learned it by ear, then we'd tear it to pieces. No Dixieland and no two-beat. The drummer made four beats. One-two-three-four. Four beats. No two-beat stuff. That's old-time stuff. It was jazz, man.*

What Johnson and Darensbourg seem to be saying is that their little combos were playing classic jazz, danceable rearrangements in four-four time of popular tunes, played in small ensembles, with some improvised solos and a looser, less "ricky-ticky" feeling than the ragtime bands of an earlier era. Swing, or simply jazz, is a more accurate description of what they were playing than Dixieland.

Another distinction between Seattle jazz and Dixieland is that many early New Orleans musicians played by ear. Johnson, on the other hand, came from a generation of Los Angeles musicians who put a premium on the ability to read sheet music and play European classics. This was the milieu that produced Lionel Hampton, Curtis Mosby, Les Hite, and Charlie Echols. The fact that Gerald Wells had been playing on the West Coast since the early teens, but, according to Darensbourg, knew nothing of the New Orleans style, goes a long way toward making a case for the existence of an independent West Coast jazz style that had developed very early in the music's history, in which Seattle participated at the outer edge, picking up influences as musicians moved in and out of town. Like West Coast jazz of the 1950s, this music emphasized melody, intricate arrangements, an accommodation of popular taste, a somewhat pretentious intimation of "classical" overtones, and a light-footed sense of swing.

Seattle jazz was also, at least at this early stage, not very bluesy. Johnson even expresses a distaste for this basic building block of jazz, preferring technically complex music to the simple folk lines of blues: "I never did like blues anyway, from having it for breakfast, dinner, and supper when I was a little kid coming up. That's all you could hear around the neighborhood is blues, blues, blues. I wanted to hear something fantastic. I used to like to go and hear Yehudi Menuhin." Not until the 1940s, when a wave of African Americans came to Seattle from Louisiana, Texas, Arkansas, and other points south, would the blues, gospel, and the gutsier side of black music arrive in the Northwest.

When Johnson and Darensbourg got to town, there were two organized bands working on a regular basis. One was led by pianist Evelyn Bundy and drummer Leonard Gayton and the other by Edythe and Floyd Turnham. Bundy and Gayton's band was called the Garfield Ramblers. Formed in 1926 and named after Garfield High School, the Ramblers played for high school and tennis-club dances and various black society affairs. In addition to Bundy and Gayton, the band included Wayne Adams on saxophones, Jimmy Adams on trumpet, and Creon Thomas on piano, drums, violin, and banjo. When Evelyn Bundy graduated from high school, the Garfield Ramblers became the Evelyn Bundy band.

Bundy, who played piano, banjo, drums, and saxophone, and sometimes sang, was born in Seattle. Her father, who had sung in a local quartet that sometimes performed at the Rainier Club, encouraged her to study classical piano. She studied with Frank Waldron and began performing professionally at thirteen. Emma Gayton, Leonard's widow, remembered Bundy's mother traveling with the band to "make sure Evelyn was in good company. She would dress her out of this world."

According to Emma, Leonard "would walk from table to table, singing through a megaphone, with high hat and brushes in tow. Money was collected in a kitty." This is the earliest known reference to "table singing" in Seattle, a custom that became even more popular during the 1940s. Singers would roam the floor of a club or dance hall, sometimes accompanied by a horn player (but not usually a drummer), and collect tips from customers for playing their favorite tunes. This not only pleased the customers, it provided the musicians a living wage. In the early days of jazz, salaries were low; the only way to really make money on a gig was through tips.

In 1929, Bundy married Charles Taylor, a plasterer who promoted the band on the side. The Garfield Ramblers was usually a four- or five-piece group, with alto man Kenny Pernell sometimes replacing Wayne Adams. "They used to go to their gigs in a hearse," recalls Bundy and Taylor's son, Charles, Jr. "That's right, one of the guys that was playing worked at the undertaker's. And so that was a joke of theirs." Horn chores in the Bundy band were covered by the Adams brothers, two of the strongest sidemen in town. Both were students of Waldron and played music well into the 1930s. Jimmy Adams led his own band in 1931 at Faurot's Hall, worked with Joe Darensbourg at the Jungle Temple, and was billed as the "trumpet king" at a 1932 summer ball at Washington Hall. He later committed suicide. Wayne Adams left Seattle with Palmer Johnson in Earl Whaley's band in 1934.

Multi-instrumentalist Creon Thomas had perfect pitch. "A streetcar would go by and he'd say, 'A-flat!'" recalls Julian Henson. "Guys used to play a note on the piano and take bets if he could guess what it was. Creon was always going along humming or playing drums. Music was in his mind twenty-four hours a day." Thomas later moved to San Diego, where he played music through the forties and fifties.

When Leonard Gayton graduated from Garfield in 1927, he, too, struck out on his own, playing the 908 Club (formerly Doc Hamilton's), the Plantation, and the New Harlem. In 1930, he was the inaugural act at a club that would have a venerable local history, the Chinese Gardens, at Seventh and King; he also performed on pleasure cruises that ran to Alaska and California.

In the thirties, the Bundy-Taylor household became a hub of the Seattle jazz world. When touring musicians came to town, they would congregate in the basement music room and bar of the Bundy-Taylor home, adorned to this day with jazz photos and memorabilia, to socialize and jam after the gig. Charles, Jr., who

Edythe Turnham and Her Knights of Syncopation, 1926. Left to right: Floyd Turnham, Sr., Sam Barnett, Dave Hendricks, Charles Adams, Floyd Turnham, Jr., Edythe Turnham, Babe Hackley.

This photo was printed on a business card.

Courtesy of Emma Gayton

later formed an important band of his own, remembers, "In those days, black people didn't have any place to stay or to go. There was a lot of singing. Everybody would play. Everybody would take turns singing songs and telling stories and laughing. Lionel Hampton, Erskine Hawkins—they all came to our house."

Taylor remembers his mother as a sophisticated, two-handed pianist, rather than a strictly stride, "boom-chunk"–type player. Her band, he says, played with the dignified blend of Duke Ellington's orchestra. Bundy stopped performing regularly in 1937.

On April 30, 1926, Seattle's Northwest Enterprise quaintly noted, "Mr. and Mrs. Floyd Turnham, 'popular musicians,' bought a house at 707 22nd and will be moving in shortly." The Edythe Turnham Orchestra (also called the Knights of Syncopation) was already a going concern when it arrived from Spokane and became the other important jazz group in Seattle in the mid-1920s. Turnham was born Edythe Pane, in Topeka, Kansas, around 1890, and started playing piano when she was three years old. She came to Spokane in 1900; about eight years later she married Floyd Turnham, a carpenter from Texas. With her sister, Maggie, she put together a vaudeville act featuring two blackface comedians, and toured throughout eastern Washington and Idaho. Edythe also worked solo in Spokane. Sometime in the early twenties, she formed a five-piece family band, the Knights of Syncopation. Edythe played piano; Floyd was on drums; Floyd, Jr., played saxophone; Maggie was a dancer and entertainer.

Floyd, Jr., recalls his mother taking him to 12th and Jackson in Seattle as early as 1922, where as a twelve-year-old he sang "The End of a Perfect Day" for tips. He also remembers playing in a five-piece band at the Black and Tan for Noodles Smith. Once the Turnhams were in Seattle, they played at the Copper Kettle, the Alhambra, the Tennis Club, the Coon Chicken Inn, Willard's, the black Elks Club, and the Bungalow Dance Hall. The Copper Kettle, owned by "Six Fingers" Taylor, was on Madison Street, near 21st Avenue; the Elks Club, down the street at 18th. The Bungalow was located on Third, just north of the Bon Marché department store. Gigs downtown were normally reserved for whites, but, according to Bruce Rowell, who briefly played saxophone with the band, engagements for fashion shows at the Bon Marché and Frederick & Nelson got Turnham past the color bar. When the Bungalow moved to Eighth Avenue, however, Local 76 protested, says Rowell, and Turnham's orchestra was not permitted to play.

Edythe Turnham's style of music was "right on the edge between Dixieland and ragtime we classify as jazz," explains saxophonist Marshal Royal, who heard her later in Los Angeles. "The only one that survived out of that into the new era was the son, Floyd. He turned out to be a good saxophone player."

Floyd, Jr., remembers that the band played tunes in sets of three—"waltz, fox-trot, and standard little jump tunes. We'd always start a slow one, medium one, and a little fast one . . . three tunes. When we played [Fats Waller's] 'What Did I Do to Be So Black and Blue?' the whole audience stopped."

Floyd, Jr., and his sister, Frances, attended Garfield High School, where they came to know Wayne and Jimmy Adams and Creon Thomas, then playing in the Garfield Ramblers, bass and tuba player Joe Bailey, and the rest of the Garfield jazz crowd. Floyd says he remembers Oscar Bradley, a drummer with whom he later worked in Los Angeles, peeking through the window of the Tennis Club to listen to Edythe's band. Edythe's band played the Garfield Funfest using all the kids in the family; Floyd, Jr., became the leader of the pep band. He also studied saxophone with Frank Waldron and pursued his goal of being a complete entertainer—singing, dancing, and performing on violin, saxophone, and piano. Edythe, for her part, played rehearsal piano for a dance school and occasionally took bands out on Alaska cruises, while Floyd, Sr., worked part-time as a tailor and drove the band around in a huge Hudson. According to Floyd, Jr., his father "had a hell of a rhythm on the bass drum, and snares and socks in them and stuff. He was solid. Never missed a beat. Right on the beam. He was a card." Al Hilbert, Floyd Turnham, Sr.'s nephew, recalled hauling the band to a gig in the back of a truck, in 1928, with the piano strapped down and the band playing as he drove for fifteen or twenty blocks.

In 1928, the Knights of Syncopation got their big break—an audition for the Orpheum Theater circuit. The band was booked in theaters from Winnipeg to Long Beach. A few months later, however, they found themselves stranded in Los Angeles. The Turnhams eventually flourished in southern California, where the band became known as the Dixie Aces, featuring, in addition to the three Turnhams, many of Los Angeles' finest sidemen, including Frank Pasley and Teddy Buckner. In 1934, Duke Ellington heard Edythe at the Jazzland Cafe. "Girl," Duke reportedly said, "you sure can play. You sure are heavy." Floyd, Sr., died in 1936, but Edythe continued to work until 1945, at one point playing at Los Angeles' Cotton Club with a band led by Charlie Echols that included Bumps Myers, Paul Howard, and Lee Young. Floyd, Jr., meanwhile, became a prominent fixture on the Los Angeles scene.

A lanky fellow given to naughty winks and stories, Turnham was an amiable, slow-talking man, proud of the way he played yet completely unpretentious. After leaving the Dixie Aces, in 1933, Floyd, Jr., worked in both jazz and rhythm-and-blues groups, as a regular for Les Hite, Gerald Wilson, Joe Liggins, and Bardu Ali, and subbing or working short stints with Count Basie, Benny Carter, Teddy Wilson, and others. From 1938 to 1941, he led his own orchestra, which had a moment of glory in Los Angeles when he won a much celebrated "cutting contest" in 1939 against tenor saxophonist Vido Musso. In late 1939 or early 1940, Les Hite took over Floyd's men, adding some of his own, including Oscar Bradley and the great trombonist Britt Woodman. (Hite, one of the best early bandleaders in Los Angeles, used several sidemen with Seattle connections over the years, including Joe Bailey and pianists Phil Moore and Gerald Wiggins.) In 1942, when Dizzy Gillespie came into the Hite organization and made the first recording of a bebop solo (on "Jersey Bounce"), Turnham, Bradley, and Wiggins were all in the group. Turnham and Woodman continued to be close associates after their tour with Hite. When Johnny Hodges and Lawrence Brown made their famous defection from Duke Ellington's band to form a group of their own, Turnham and Woodman were recruited as replacements. Floyd played dates in Los Angeles with Ellington but never left town with the band. Curiously, he never seemed to regret this, despite the fame and wealth the Ellington chair might have yielded. He turned down Coleman Hawkins once, too. "I guess I was just so in love with my wife," says Turnham, "that I wanted to stay home."

Duke and Hawk were no doubt attracted to Turnham's firm, elegant, solidly projected alto sound—in the old-fashioned tradition of Hodges, Benny Carter, and Willie Smith—a perfect fit with Duke's conception, which, like Turnham's, was formed in the 1920s. Count Basie also admired that sound. He dubbed Turnham "Iron Jaw" because he played so loud. Albert McCarthy, in his book *Big Band Jazz*, mentions being impressed by "several of [Hite's] soloists, notably an alto player who was almost certainly Floyd Turnham."

In the late 1950s, Turnham started playing rhythm-and-blues tenor saxophone with Joe Liggins and His Honeydrippers. His shift from jazz to R & B was not surprising, since Los Angeles was a hotbed of the new dance music after World War II, and one of the Turnhams' first important contacts in Los Angeles had been the father of Jack McVea, whose song "Open the Door, Richard" was one of the first big R & B hits. Turnham was a featured soloist with Liggins on "Red Top" and "Flyin' Home." He retired in 1974, but an offer in 1979 to tour internationally with a revivalist show called "1000 Years of Jazz," led by British jazz aficionado and drummer Barry Martyn, rekindled his career. Turnham toured all over the world in the 1980s with Martyn's group—an unusual one in revivalist circles, since the band featured older black musicians. Revivalist, or Dixieland, groups are usually white.

Turnham is represented well on several recordings. He has a good alto solo on Les Hite's "The Lick" and also plays on "T-Bone Blues," recorded when T-Bone Walker was with the Hite band, "T.B. Blues", and "Board Meeting Time," with Joe Wilder and Dizzy Gillespie. In 1946, Turnham waxed Melba Liston's tune "Mores," with Los Angeles bandleader Gerald Wilson. Turnham died in Los Angeles in 1992 in comfortable circumstances, cared for by his wife, Georgia, a jazz fan who loved nothing better than to hear him play.

The twenties in Seattle were represented by vocalists as well as top instrumentalists. Easily the most important was Mildred Bailey, who, like Edythe Turnham, came west from Spokane. Bailey was the first white jazz singer of any significance. Born Mildred Rinker, she grew up in the small farming community of Tekoa, sixty miles southeast of Spokane, then moved to Spokane in 1912. Her mother, Josie, was one-quarter Coeur d'Alene Indian and taught Mildred Native American songs, which she later performed. When Mildred's father married a second time, following Josie's death, Mildred was sent to Seattle to live with an aunt. She had a rough time of it. Before the age of eighteen, she had been married twice and developed a pattern of overeating that would plague her the rest of her life.

As a teenager in Seattle, Bailey played piano in silent-movie houses, plugged songs in downtown department stores, and demonstrated sheet music, first at Woolworth's, then at Bush and Lane's music store. Her first, and very brief, marriage was to a man named Bailey, from whom she adopted her stage name. Probably around 1925, she moved to Los Angeles, where she married her second husband, a bootlegger named Benny Stafford.

Bailey's brother, Al Rinker, had a duo with another famous Spokaneite—Bing Crosby. Al [and Bing] followed Mildred to Los Angeles the following year, stopping off in Seattle long enough to sing at the Butler Hotel for two weeks with bandleader Jackie Souders. In Los Angeles, Mildred helped Al and Bing get an audition with the "king of jazz" himself, Paul Whiteman. Three years later, when Crosby and Rinker were gaining fame as the Rhythm Boys, Rinker convinced Whiteman to hire his sister. Bailey sang her way to fame on a recording led by the innovative Whiteman sideman guitarist Eddie Lang, on Hoagy Carmichael's "Rockin' Chair." It became her signature song.

"Rockin' Chair" marked the first recording by a "girl singer" with a big band, an innovation that would set the pattern for the swing era. Bailey's successors could scarcely have had a better model. She sang impeccably in tune, in a hauntingly pure, tiny voice that seemed to float in thin air. Her phrasing incorporated the blue notes, sudden swoops, dives, and surprise leaps of the great black blues singers, but she never sounded like a white singer mimicking black vocal effects.

Bailey was popular with improvisers, a jazz-singer's singer. Her small-group sides over the years with Johnny Hodges, Benny Goodman, Teddy Wilson, and others hold up well against similar, better-known recordings by Billie Holiday. After working with her third husband—bandleader Red Norvo—through much of the thirties, Bailey went into decline. In 1944, she made a comeback at Manhattan's Cafe Society and secured a national radio program, "The Mildred Bailey Radio Show." (The producer was ex–Seattle pianist Phil Moore.)

*Time* magazine described her in a feature article as "just about the greatest popular songbird in the U.S.," and the jazz journal *down beat* put her picture on the cover. Her comeback didn't last long. She died in 1951, broke, alone, and unhappy.

While Mildred Bailey was in Seattle learning the ropes and listening to records by Bessie Smith, there were black vocalists in her own backyard whom she likely never heard. One of the best was Evelyn Williamson, who was raised by Noodles Smith. (Noodles had married Evelyn's older sister, Elbee.) The wealthy entrepreneur made sure that Evelyn wanted for nothing. Born in 1910, she graduated from Garfield, where she and Frances Turnham had won first place for their cabaret act at the Garfield Funfest. Afterwards she went to finishing school in Washington, D.C., where she studied voice and piano. Williamson lived in Los Angeles with her husband of over fifty years, saxophonist Marshal Royal.

> *In those days, to be a cabaret singer meant you were classified with a lower element. But I always wanted to be a singer. I went to Doc Hamilton, who had a little after-hour club. Just select people could go down there. I went there as a waitress, then in between customers I would go downstairs and sing. That's where I met Oscar Holden.*

Williamson was soon making her living as an entertainer, singing mostly with piano accompanists in small clubs, and occasionally at dances. *Cayton's Weekly* lists her at Washington, Finnish, and Greyerbiehl halls, and working with Palmer Johnson at the Chinese Gardens, in 1931. She did some "rhythm tunes" but admits she "wasn't too good" on blues. Her real specialty was ballads. Johnson recalls her as having a "sweet" voice and doing "more than justice" to "Rockin' Chair." She must have been a good sport, too. At Doc's, a rich lumberman who always brought his own Champagne perennially asked her to sing "Street of Dreams"—all night long. "He would stay there for hours. And that's a very short song! I'd sing it and he'd say, 'Sing it again.' When I first met him was at Doc Hamilton's. He would give me twenty to thirty dollars every chorus. I'd never seen so much money in my life."

Though Williamson and pianist Evelyn Bundy were Garfield schoolmates and the best of friends, Williamson preferred working with Oscar Holden, by far the better musician. Oscar was always tied up at Doc's, though, so she usually worked with Marion Fulmighter or with "Princess" Belle, who had come to Seattle from New Zealand. For a while, Williamson worked at the Jungle Temple No. 1, on Everett Highway, with the great Seattle-bred tenor saxophonist Dick Wilson, who later played with Andy Kirk.

In 1935, an amusing mishap befell the demure, polished Williamson when she and Fulmighter got their first break to sing on Seattle radio. "I was going to sing 'Smoke Gets in Your Eyes.' I don't know whether Marion was drunk or nervous, but she started in the wrong key. I had a pretty good range, but that

**Mildred Bailey, on the cover of *down beat* magazine, 1944.**

**Originally from Tekoa, Washington, near Spokane, Mildred Bailey honed her skills as a jazz singer in Seattle before moving to Los Angeles in 1925.**

**Courtesy of John McDonough**

The Edythe Turnham Orchestra, 1927–28.

Left to right: H. A. Jones, Charles Adams, Floyd Turnham, Sr., Boone, Edythe Turnham, Fats Wilson, Floyd Turnham, Jr., Bruce Rowell.

This larger version of Edythe Turnham's group had different personnel than her Knights of Syncopation.

Courtesy of Georgia Turnham

was just a little too high. I had never sung on radio and the first lick I took, I said, 'Shit! That's too high!' That was our first opportunity and our last."

Evelyn and her friends were quite naive about the rough-and-tumble life going on around them in the clubs. Once, when they were rehearsing with Darensbourg, he got drunk and became unruly with a policeman. They tried to bail him out by going down to the jailhouse and "entertaining" the officers. "We were lucky to get to our rehearsal," laughs Williamson.

In 1936, Evelyn Williamson married Los Angeles tenor saxophonist Bumps Myers, who had worked with Joe Darensbourg at the Jungle Temple and come back to town with Les Hite. Her destined love, however, was another sax player in the Hite band, Marshal Royal, whom she married two years later. This took her away to Los Angeles for good, where she pursued a career as a big-band singer with Hite and Lionel Hampton. She would later return to Seattle for a triumphant visit with Hamp at the Trianon, riding high with her popular number "I Nearly Lost My Mind," which she would later record with the band. After the war, she sang in exclusive supper clubs in Hollywood and retired in the early 1950s.

Williamson sang in Seattle for ten years, from 1928 to 1938, working six or seven nights a week, usually until the late hours of the next morning. There was lots of work, and a pleasant spirit of cooperation, she says, between her and other singers.

"There was never any jealousy or competitiveness. If I was working and somebody called me for a job and I couldn't take it, I would immediately call up one of the others and tell them it was open."

Some of the jobs Williamson referred her friends to were likely at various small resorts, outside of town. Seattle is surrounded by little lakes. Before the days of suburban sprawl, nearly every one of these puddles had a "resort," sometimes just a little dance hall. The Grove, at Angle Lake, the present site of Sea-Tac International Airport, was one. Another was the Bungalow Inn, at Silver Lake, east of today's Interstate 5 and north of Lynnwood (not to be confused with the Bungalow in Seattle, where Edythe Turnham's group played). The Bungalow Inn burned down in 1929.

Another venue for work-hungry musicians was the steamship lines that ran pleasure cruises to Alaska, California, and the Far East. Joe Darensbourg, Leonard Gayton, Palmer Johnson, Oscar Holden, and Edythe Turnham all played on the President Line steamship cruises, making good wages and often bringing back "booty" from Asia to sell stateside at inflated prices.

Lillian Goode, who had been an entertainer at Frank Sebastian's Cotton Club, in Los Angeles, may have come north to Seattle on just such a steamship. "Goody," as she was known to her friends, influenced Evelyn Williamson with her interpretations of ballads and impressed Palmer Johnson a lot. "She had a voice like a canary," he recalls, "way up high.

She could sing stuff like 'Indian Love Call,' which was very prominent at that time."

Not a great deal is known about Goode. She sang for a while with Gerald Wells and the Hi-Hatters and performed at a benefit dance with Williamson and Zelma Winslow (Noodles Smith's mistress) at Broadway Hall. Leon Vaughn, a trumpet player who came to town somewhat later and remembers her singing at the Black and Tan, says, "She could really sell a teary-type ballad."

Zelma Winslow was the other fine singer on the scene at the time, though she was so hot-tempered and had so much trouble with Noodles that she didn't have a lot of time to concentrate on her career. Once during an early Sunday morning raid on the Black and Tan by the county constables, she got so mad at a cop who swore at her that she socked him in the jaw. It was quite a melee. At her trial, the officer dared her to hit him again, which she did. Zelma did a little time for that.

Winslow worked at the Jungle Temple with Oscar Holden and later at a private room upstairs at the Chinese Gardens. Noodles Smith kept Winslow highly visible but strictly off-limits. She "could sing like nobody's business," according to one habitué of the clubs at that time. "She had dimples you could put your whole finger in," remembers pianist Julian Henson. "She was so beautiful! She did torch songs and blues."

The zaniest entertainer in this period by far was a fellow from Los Angeles named Eddie Rucker, who had performed there with the early jazz group the Black and Tan Orchestra. (The term "entertainer," as used by Darensbourg and Johnson, refers to a table singer with an "act," not necessarily a dancer or comedian, as it might today.) Says Darensbourg:

> *People came from all over the Pacific Northwest to hear Eddie. He used to do a lot of X-rated, off-color tunes. He made so much money. The Jungle Temple had little individual booths with a drawn curtain so you could have private entertainment. You had to pay Eddie a lot of money to come in and sing for you. He might keep the curtain open a little, push in a little roll-away piano which had four octaves, and we'd stand around outside and play. We would average seventy-five or a hundred dollars a night in that kitty!*

Souvenir photo card from the Black and Tan Club.

Rucker worked most of the time at the Entertainers Club, an intimate speakeasy, like a little apartment where a few customers would go up for a drink, laugh, and make requests.

"It was the upstairs of a four-plex," recalls Bruce Rowell. "On one side of the upstairs, there was a front room that wasn't used, then there was a room where the poker game was. Then there was the barroom. And then you go across the hall and the next two rooms was the dance floor and the musicians."

"Eddie liked that room all for himself," says Williamson. "He didn't like when I worked with him up there. Whenever my brother-in-law [Noodles] would get mad at me, he'd send me up there."

Rucker was a jive artist. He often told customers he could sing in French, which he would promptly do, making up a lot of nonsense, to their delight. One night, however, he got caught. As Joe Darensbourg remembers it:

> *One night at the Black and Tan, Harold Weeks, the Seattle composer who wrote the swing hit "Hindustan," came into the club. Eddie prided himself he could sing any song you could name. For songs he didn't know, he would make up the words. So he said, "Why, sure I know that song." He started singing "Hindustan" and told the band to make an introduction, although we had never played it or heard it before. Then Eddie sang some funny words and Harold let him finish. Eddie asked Harold how did he like his version of the song and Harold said, "I like it fine, but it ain't the one I wrote!"*

Palmer Johnson worked several times with Rucker, in both Seattle and Portland.

"Great? He sure was!" Johnson says. "When he first walked into the joint and we were ready to play, he'd tap that cane on the floor, singing, 'She's my weakness now!' The only thing, Eddie had to get full of his cocaine. He used to booze it down with whiskey. He liked them straight shots of Scotch. I sure remember that."

Working with Rucker at the Jungle Temple or on society dances at Finnish Hall was drummer "Baby" Borders, called "Baby" because of his high voice. Little is known about Borders, but since Johnson describes him as being from the South, Borders may have been the Samuel Borders who played drums in the Black Birds of Paradise, a Montgomery, Alabama, band formed in 1925. In any case, Baby Borders came to Seattle via Los Angeles and in 1931 was playing a dance every Monday night for the Elite Social Club; in 1933, he worked with the ten-piece Harlem Knights at the Black and Tan. Borders was in town until at least 1938; he later moved to Detroit. He lived with Marion Fulmighter, Evelyn Williamson's accompanist, who, according to Julian Henson, had a "cute" style and later left town in a show with Mae West.

Williamson, Fulmighter, and Zelma Winslow were all arrested one night in a police sweep of the Chinese Gardens, but this club was tame compared to the one across the street. At 511½ Seventh South was the Hong Kong Chinese Society Club, known colloquially as the "Bucket of Blood," a ghoulish nickname it picked up because of a notorious murder that occurred out front one night after a raid. It was rowdy, but musicians liked to go there because it was a good place to jam. Recalls Darensbourg's drummer Jack Foy, "You could play anything you wanted there. They'd have an organized band, about four pieces, and they'd always have at least eight or ten on the stand, jamming." Three blocks away, at No. 710, was the Golden West Club, on the fourth floor of the hotel of the same name. (The faded red lettering can still be made out on the side of the building.) After finishing up at Herman Myers' Taxi Dance Hall, Palmer Johnson often worked at the Golden West after hours, as a single.

Thanks to the action in Seattle, many musicians drifted in from Los Angeles or elsewhere, and stayed awhile before moving on. One outstanding immigrant was Los Angeles–born banjoist and guitarist Ceele (pronounced "C. L.," short for Cecil Louis) Burke. Burke and Palmer Johnson had been schoolmates in Los Angeles, and they worked together in Portland in 1931. After leaving the Northwest, Burke picked up Hawaiian steel guitar and moved to Honolulu. His Hawaiian bent earned him a small niche in jazz history: it is his wonderfully slinky steel-guitar introduction on Louis Armstrong's classic version of "I'm Confessing."

A better-known music business figure who spent a short time on the Seattle scene as a youngster was pianist Phil Moore. Moore was born in Portland and studied briefly at Cornish College of the Arts in Seattle. Evelyn Williamson recalls Moore coming into the Black and Tan for his first job, when he was fifteen. Moore became one of the first blacks to break into the Hollywood studios, eventually working as a staff arranger and conductor for Metro-Goldwyn-Mayer, scoring the films *Broadway Melody* and *A Song Is Born*. He also worked as an accompanist and vocal coach for Lena Horne, wrote the popular wartime hit "Shoo Shoo Baby," and led a popular bebop quartet on New York's 52nd Street, the Phil Moore Four.

One player Johnson much admired was Beverly Harrison, an alto saxophonist who led a band Johnson worked with around 1931. Harrison made a smart arrangement of Duke Ellington's "It Don't Mean a Thing If It Ain't Got That Swing" that was quite popular locally. The Hoy family had the respect of Seattle musicians as well. Bill Hoy worked with Oscar Holden at the Jungle Temple and his sister-in-law, Sue Hoy, was a well-known entertainer on the Los Angeles scene whom Buck Clayton describes as "one great singer." Joe Darensbourg, for his part, admired guitarists Rudy Goldberg and Bill Page.

*I remember one time we was playing some place with Page and a guy came in with the score of "Rhapsody in Blue" in a special arrangement. On the part which old [Mike] Pingatore did on banjo with Paul Whiteman, he had it written out for guitar. Now, Bill had fooled us all that he could read, he had such a good ear. But when he got to the guitar solo he didn't know what to do. Finally, Gerald Wells says, "That's a guitar solo. I thought you could read. Why don't you play it?" Bill admitted he couldn't read at all, but he says, "One of you guys play that thing and let me listen to it once!" Old Gerald took his piccolo and played it for Bill. After that Bill just played it like nothing happened, the whole thing.*

Johnson credits Ivan Ditmar, a white staff pianist at one of the radio stations, with being one of swingingest players on the scene. Wilbert Barranco was another pianist who commanded both Johnson's and Darensbourg's respect. Darensbourg had known Barranco in Baton Rouge; Barranco later had his own group in Oakland in 1933–1934 and played with Los Angeles bandleader Curtis Mosby's group, fronting the traveling show "Change Your Luck," which came to Seattle in 1933.

Other names from the late 1920s and early 1930s that crop up again and again, but about whom there is little information, include Jack Brackman (saxophone, also mentioned by Buck Clayton), Slim Taft (trombone), Bill Trent (vocals), Glover Compton (piano), P. G. Lowery, Oscar Low, Jack Henshaw, Frank Bufaro, Arnie Sewell, Eddie Swanson, "Big Foot" Smitty, "Shelby," Moses Johnson, Tommy Thomas, Lee Caldwell, and Jim Juicy.

Since it was illegal, the roadhouse and after-hours scene where most of these musicians played was largely an underground affair, where only the more bold pleasure-seekers ventured. It was also where one was likely to find the hottest music, since that was where the progressive black musicians played. As jazz became more popular locally, however, the music caught on with white musicians, as well, and scores of more visible but usually less authentic bands cropped up.

Throughout the 1920s, white bands with pasted-down hair, wire-rim glasses, and starched collars, holding saxophones, banjos, and violins and often calling themselves "syncopators" or "serenaders," were continually described as "jazz" groups on the entertainment pages of the *Seattle Times*. Jackie Souders, who would become one of Seattle's leading sweet bandleaders, was billing himself in 1921 at the Pantages as "Offering Jazz Music in the College Style." The white orchestra conductor Jules Buffano, playing at the Seattle Theatre (which later became the Paramount), described himself as the "Crown Jewel of Jazz." The Del Monte Blue Dogs, the J & V Syncopators, the Highway Pavilion Dance Orchestra, the Goodrich Silvertown Cord Orchestra, Warren Anderson's Symphonic Dance Orchestra, the Rainier Serenaders, the Charmed Land Serenaders, the Stevens Dance Orchestra, the Honeymoon Serenaders, Gene Paul and his Seattle Sax Band, and Shorty Clough's Melody Boys are some of the other bands that gave themselves "jazz" billing.

How much jazz these bands played is open to question. Hot, improvised jazz, says white drummer Chet Ramage, was mainly confined to the speakeasies where blacks performed, in the clubs along Jackson Street and the roadhouses. "Local 493 had most of the jazz players," he says.

There has been perennial controversy among jazz enthusiasts over the authenticity of this or that band. In the 1920s and early 1930s, the terms of the argument were expressed as the opposition between "sweet" bands and "hot" bands, though such a distinction was often more a matter of taste than musical detail. Among early jazz fans, a "sweet" band was one that played satiny, lilting rhythms for ballroom dancing, with an eye to variety. A "hot" band, on the other hand, would play a good portion of jump rhythms, with lots of surprising solos and blues feeling.

The new rhythms of jazz and ragtime were originally incorporated into popular dances for the masses by Irene and Vernon Castle, just before World War I. The Castles took the hot rhythms of the "animal dances"—the Texas Tommy, turkey trot, and fox-trot—and domesticated them for the middle class. In the teens, ballroom and taxi-dance establishments sprang up all over the United States and Europe to accommodate this new "social dancing" craze. By the twenties, however, the excitement of these rhythms had worn off or been watered down. That's why when bandleaders like Fletcher Henderson came along in the 1920s with a harder-hitting, hotter style, jazz fanatics turned up their noses at the "ricky-ticky" two-step feeling of the hotel bands.

Some of the "syncopating" hotel groups, however, probably played pretty hot jazz. Of all of them, the Del Monte Blue Dogs had the most success as a touring item. The members were from Seattle, except pianist John Murphy. The other players were John Ashton, violin, banjo, sax, and leader; Frosty Hedden, trumpet; Joe Adams, saxophone; and Mike Mallia, drums. In 1928, the Dogs hit the road on the Keith Orpheum circuit; an Ohio reviewer described them as "red hot." The year 1929 found the Blue Dogs playing in New York and Chicago. The next year, under the name the Ashton-Hedden Blue Dogs, they were home, minus Murphy but with pianist Wally Anderson and bassist Clyde Willison. Anderson later led a "tenor band" (a sweet band with three tenor saxophones) at the Olympic Hotel and worked at the Magic Inn behind the Will Mastin Trio, with Sammy Davis, Jr.

The song list for the Goodrich Silvertown Cord Orchestra suggests that this band, like the Blue Dogs, was genuinely inspired by the jazz hits of the day. Listed under "Jazz" on the *Seattle Times*' weekly "radio page," they played "There'll Be Some Changes Made," and "Popular Street Blues." The J & V Syncopators listed "Copenhagen" and "Arkansas Blues" in their repertory and advertised, "You'll love these Harmony Hounds." Groups who promoted themselves as "dogs" or "hounds" and played blues generally had some connection to jazz.

Chet Ramage, who played with white drummer Shorty Clough, says Clough's Melody Boys were jazz-oriented and that Clough was a "very fine drummer" who taught at Hopper Kelly's music store. In 1929, Shorty and his boys played Seattle's Bungalow, with "Tia Juana Slim" Pratt, Jim Murphy, and Perry Ridder. *Musicland*, the official newsletter of the white musicians' union, referred nostalgically to the Bungalow as a place where "the boys played their hearts out." This language, as well as the self-consciously jazzy nicknames of Shorty's outfit, suggests that Shorty's group played some authentic jazz.

A couple of other white sidemen have been singled out by observers as having jazz chops. One was trumpeter Paul Clifford, who played at the State Theatre (later the Rivoli); another was guitarist Virgil Ireland, who came to Seattle from Kansas City to work on the pleasure cruises. Ireland was described by one musician as an advanced guitarist in the style of Eddie Lang, who played single-string solos and some "chord jazz."

One important white group that certainly played bona fide "hot" music in the Dixieland vein during the 1920s was Barney's Jazz Band, led by drummer Clarence Barney. Barney was born hunchbacked and grew up in the teens in Sedro Woolley, a rural town in the upper Skagit Valley, about fifty miles south of the Canadian border. In 1924, he brought an enthusiastic bunch of guys from the northern counties into Dick Parker's Highway Pavilion, on Bothell Way, just outside the Seattle city limits. (This was the original Parker's Pavilion, open at least as early as 1923, which later burned down; in 1928, Parker moved his operation to Aurora and 170th, where it stands as Parker's today.) Chet Ramage recalls Barney's Jazz Band as an extremely popular five-piece that commanded high prices.

Barney's sidemen included the hot Sedro Woolley clarinetist Clarence Thue; Lou Lillpop on piano; a trumpet man from Anacortes named Charlie; Clarence Smith, from Mt. Vernon, on banjo; Bellingham violinist Art Thal, later replaced by Dave Burnham, from Anacortes; and Bill Stendal, also from Sedro Woolley, on vocals. Clarinetist Doug Finch, who grew up with Barney and Stendal in Sedro Woolley and subbed in the band, played saxophone and clarinet with another jazz group, the Washington Ramblers, throughout the twenties.

Another white bandleader who had a great deal of influence on local acceptance and understanding of jazz was the stately Jules Buffano, the orchestra conductor at the Paramount Theater. Buffano was another musician who had worked with Fate Marable's Mississippi riverboat bands and was a successful leader in Chicago before moving to Seattle in 1928 to open the newly constructed Seattle Theatre at Ninth and Pine. On opening night, Buffano conducted a show called "The Mikado of Jazz," written by Paul Ash. According to Palmer Johnson, Buffano was not only an impressive conductor, but also a "fine jazz pianist" with a strong left hand. He spent the years 1937 to 1939 in Hollywood, then returned to Seattle, where he worked at the Town Ranch and the Senator Ballroom.

During Buffano's heyday, theater orchestras were a popular form of entertainment. They played everything from light classics to jazz, similar to the fare one might hear at an outdoor band shell. In that era, one had to go hear musicians playing live in order to hear music at all, but there were musicians playing everywhere. Jackie Souders was at the Olympic

The Vic Meyers Orchestra.

Courtesy of the Museum of History and Industry *Seattle Post-Intelligencer* Collection.

Hotel, Sam Wineland at the Coliseum, Hermie King at the Palace Hip, Otto Crowhurst at the Pantages, Leonard Hagen at the Blue Mouse, William Winder at the Egyptian, George Lipschultz at the Fifth Avenue, Francesco Longo or Liborious Hauptmann at the Columbia, Charles Burnett at the Orpheum, and Henri Damski at the Camlin. Many of the theaters employed organists. There were also bands playing at the burlesque theaters, roadhouses, and nightclubs, and in radio orchestras.

"We had 680 members and 610 of them were working steady," says Chet Ramage, who joined the white musicians' local in 1926 and served as president for many years. "We had theaters. We had music in the lobby of the Olympic Hotel. We had ballrooms. The guys could make a living." It was from this vast pool of musicians that the budding white jazz players on the underground scene arose.

Many of them worked for Vic Meyers at one time or another, the most famous of the pops bandleaders and one of the most eccentric figures in Washington history. Meyers and his notorious venue, the Rose Room of the Butler Hotel at Second and James Street, with its chandeliers and bootleg whiskey, would go down in the memories of white Seattleites as the very life of the Jazz Age. Technically, Vic was a drummer, but he was known primarily as a front man. His orchestra featured elaborate saxophone and brass sections, as well as tuba, banjo, violin, piano, and drums. Joe Darensbourg played with Meyers for a short time (on saxophone), as did Ramage.

Vic Meyers was a charismatic figure who was leading his own dance orchestras in the Seattle area by 1922. He recorded several sides for Columbia and Brunswick, and also had a hand in composing "Ada," with Seattle songwriters Harold Weeks and Danny Cann. In the early 1920s, the dapper bandleader toured his men down the West Coast to Monterey and San Diego, then crossed the country to New York's Arcadia Ballroom and several venues around Chicago. When he returned to Seattle, in 1926, he found himself a genuine celebrity. His band was regularly aired live on Seattle station KFOA, and, in 1932, his orchestra became the first in Seattle to be broadcast over national radio, on Walter Winchell's NBC show.

The Butler Hotel was a college hangout where couples danced and drank and, on the night of the Apple Cup (the University of Washington versus Washington State University football contest) occasionally shacked up in one of the dollar-a-night rooms upstairs. Meyers and the proprietor of the hotel, John

RUM NET SPREAD
BANNICK TAKES

RAIDERS SAY CHINATOWN DRINKING HAD BEEN IGNORED

—MAR-23-1931

Chief to Inquire Reasons Why Patrolmen Entered Chinese Gardens, Passed Up Bottles on Tables.

Summary shakeup of Chinatown beat patrolmen was forecast today when Chief Louis J. Forbes declared he was summoning several officers before him to answer charges by federal dry agents that policemen in uniform were going in and out of the Chinese Gardens, 516 Seventh Ave. S., during a government liquor and gambling raid there Saturday midnight. The Gardens, after more than a year of untrammelled operation as Seattle's liveliest "night club," was closed, and the rattle of its dice, the tinkle of its highball glasses and the clashing cymbals of its jazz band were silent as a result of the raid.

M. J. McNamee.

Charles (Cholly) Louie, one-time Federal Court interpreter, its dapper Chinese proprietor, who slipped away during the excitement as the raiders gathered in sixteen other prisoners, including a former police detective sergeant, had promised to surrender when he got around to it some time today. Several hundred merrymakers, caught in the raid, were driven into the streets after being "frisked" for flasks.

"I'm going to find out from my Chinatown beat men," Chief Forbes said this morning, "if it is true that they were going in and out of that place, and that there were bottles on the tables and open drinking going on.

"The federals have said they got a lot of bonded liquor in the raid. If that is true this bonded liquor must have come from some place, and it makes me wonder why the federals don't stop it at the border. But, be that as it may, open drinking in public won't be tolerated as long as I'm chief of police, though I'll admit it's almost impossible to stop it. Everybody, nearly, carries a bottle on his hip when he goes to a roadhouse."

The chief said he was first calling in Sergt. J. F. Harrington and Patrolman Tom Feek, who were on duty in the district at the time the Chinese Gardens were raided. He indicated others might be questioned later concerning conditions on the beat.

Climaxes Drive.

The federal action climaxed a week's drive against South End resorts in which Sheriff Claude G. Bannick played a leading role, going over the heads of the police to raid several reputed gambling joints.

The surprise of the Chinese Gardens raid was the arrest of Michael James McNamee, former sergeant of

Savage, flaunted the new flapper culture of the twenties in the face of Seattle's authorities. They did not go unnoticed.

One of the curious anomalies of Seattle's Roaring Twenties is that while the city was, on the one hand, excitedly embracing each new trend of the Jazz Age in a vast underground of nightclubs and hot spots, on the other it was continually passing laws and regulations that spoiled the party. With almost predictable regularity, one administration would encourage a "tolerance policy," under which nightclubs flourished, and the next would emphasize reform, passing increasingly convoluted laws against drinking, dancing, music, and cabarets. It was an ambivalence deeply rooted in the city's psyche and sometimes exemplified in a single person. The notorious opportunist Hiram Gill, for example, was first elected mayor on a "wide open" ticket, then re-elected as a reform candidate. During the 1920s, Bertha Landes, councilwoman and then mayor (1926–1928), waged a continuous war against not only alcohol but dancing, which she apparently found disgusting, much to the financial chagrin of ballroom and hotel operators. In Seattle, the celebrated Jazz Age of hedonism and permissiveness was a kind of post-pioneer hysteria that delighted in sophistication at the same time as it rejected it.

The first raid on the Butler Hotel was in 1918. Over the next eleven years, the Seattle Police Department and federal authorities waged war on the hotel, citing the establishment on average once every two months, for everything from illegal sales of alcohol to dancing on Sunday. Though other music venues were harassed during this period, the Butler's size and visibility made it a favorite target, particularly for the redoubtable Bertha Landes. In 1921, Landes began a campaign to give the city more control over the taxi-dance establishments, citing that such places attracted the "wrong kind of girl." Judge J. T. Ronald, who backed Landes, agreed. "There is a potential evil to society in all dance halls," he argued. The 1923 Landes Ordinance, as it came to be known, outlawed taxi dances and required regular dance halls to hire a police-department matron as a chaperone. It also specified a lengthy inspection process, a nightly closing time of twelve-thirty, and draconian control to the city in regard to licensing. (The effects of this ordinance would be felt as late the 1950s, when matrons were still legally required at certain kinds of dances.) In June 1922, the Alhambra, the Butler Hotel, the Bungalow (the one in town), and the Lodge all came under attack for not conforming to Landes' idea of what a dance hall should be. The following year, the Butler was hit again for allowing dancing on Sunday, about which there was yet another, older city ordinance. In 1929, Mayor Frank Edwards, following Landes' lead, closed the ten-cent dance halls in the South End, calling them a "moral menace."

But John Savage, operator of the Butler, was a survivor. He charmed the press into treating his various transgressions as harmless fun. Meyers, ever the prankster, fell into the scofflaw mood. When the feds filtered into the Butler to make arrests, the bandleader would strike up a jaunty version of "How Dry I Am."

The Butler was finally padlocked as a "nuisance" on May 7, 1929. Its demise, however, had no dramatic effect on the career of either Savage or Meyers. Savage moved over to the Trianon Ballroom, and Vic opened his own club (named after himself, of course) upstairs at 2221 Fourth Avenue. For a year, Club Victor kept alive the spirit of the Rose Room, which the newspapers described as the culture of "jazz and whoopee," until the feds closed it in late June of 1930. Undaunted, Meyers moved to a new location on Sixth Avenue. But by this time, other forces were at work in the bandleader's life.

In 1932, on a whim, Meyers ran for mayor of Seattle, poking fun at the political process in a way that has ever been appealing to northwesterners. When all the candidates were invited to speak at a luncheon, Vic arrived dressed as Mahatma Gandhi, leading a goat. He lost the mayoral race, but to the horror of his sponsors, he was shortly elected lieutenant governor. Meyers hung on to his post for four consecutive terms, retired from music, and became a noted authority on parliamentary procedure. He also fathered Sun Lakes State Park and, more relevant to the story of Washington jazz, led the fight in the 1937 Legislature against a bill that would have made interracial marriage illegal in Washington, as it was in Oregon. Ironically, in the 1960s, Meyers took a political dive in a scandal over an anti-gambling petition, just the sort of issue he had spent a lifetime laughing at. He died in 1992.

As a bandleader, Meyers was cut out of the mold of the famous Paul Whiteman. Both men understood that the white public liked jazz but perceived it as music from the gutter, so they cloaked its hot rhythms and raucous self-expression in phony orchestral sophistication. The public liked its jazz thus disguised, just as it had preferred minstrel shows by white actors in blackface. When Whiteman himself made a sensational appearance in Seattle in 1930, it was probably the closest the general public had ever come to hearing real jazz. They could have done worse. Though Whiteman may have been pompous and stilted, he hired some of the greatest jazz musicians who ever lived—Bix Beiderbecke, Joe Venuti, Jack Teagarden, and Jimmy Dorsey—and won over a white middle-class world which at that time would not have dreamed of setting foot in a speakeasy. He also commissioned George Gershwin to write *Rhapsody in Blue*.

Whiteman was a huge celebrity, one of the few jazz bandleaders to cross over to the "middle of the road." The Seattle papers gossiped over his impending arrival. The day before his six-day appearance at the Civic Auditorium (where the Opera House now stands), a dinner-dance was arranged at the Spanish Ballroom of the Olympic Hotel (now the Four Seasons). The governor, the mayor, and their wives attended, along with the rest of Puget Sound high society. Whiteman's every move was noted, as he drove through the winding, mountainous roads from Los Angeles behind the wheel of his V-16 Cadillac. The *Seattle Times* noted that the Rhythm Boys, with Spokaneites Bing Crosby and Al Rinker, were in the show. (Mildred Bailey was almost certainly in this performance as well, though she is not mentioned.) Three thousand people attended Whiteman's first show. Wrote the reviewer for Local 76's *Musicland*:

> *Jazz so presented that it tore down the prejudices of even the most cynical was offered Seattle. . . . Outstanding among the numbers was the interpretation of George Gershwin's "Rhapsody in Blue." This piece, which has been heralded as one of the most significant works of American composers, was presented with such masterly finesse and expert attention to coloring and cadence as would have been worthy of a symphonic ensemble. Swinging from the sublime to the ridicule were the antics of an amazing trick fiddler, Wilbur Hall. Cutting ludicrous capers, and deftly juggling his bow while playing, he indulged in clowning acrobatics and danced a measure or two without missing a note. . . . Clever stuff.*

The Meyers/Whiteman model of the jazzman belongs decidedly to the 1920s—carefree, showy, pleased with its own naughtiness, a little stiff, and still tied to the grandiosity of early-twentieth-century ringmasters. In the next jazz period, the swing era, the music would be looser, bluesier, immensely more popular, and quite a bit less concerned with concocting links to classical music. In Seattle, some of the foundations for the new era had already been laid. Musicians were moving in, the state was welcoming African Americans, and a jazz tradition had been established in after-hours joints and major theaters. In 1928, the city went on a building spree that would also be important to the future of local jazz. All in one year, the Civic Auditorium, the Trianon Ballroom, McElroy's Spanish Ballroom, and the Seattle Theatre rose on the skyline. These venues would become the focus of the swing craze, providing thousands of dancers with the strains of Gene Krupa, Tommy Dorsey, Harry James, Jimmie Lunceford, and the rest.

Even more significant than the construction boom, Prohibition was on its way out. On November 7, 1933, the liquor ban was finally repealed. Bashes were held all over town. At the Marine Club, the Mardi Gras (the new name for Doc Hamilton's), Ciro's, the New Yorker, the Little Silver Slipper, Bill Hengely's Argonaut, Don's Alaska Bar, and the Alhambra, crowds merrily lifted their glasses, hailing the end of the days of federal agents, bootleggers, and bathtub gin. In the same year, Washington passed the Steele Act, legalizing the sale of beer and wine—but not hard liquor—by the glass and creating the Washington State Liquor Control Board.

Still, the swing era would be slow to take root in Seattle. The Great Depression cut deeply into the number and scope of venues, and the state's Calvinist reluctance to legalize whiskey prolonged the speakeasy culture of the twenties. The 1930s would be a scuffling era for jazz musicians.

# 3
# COMBOS AND DIVES
## the depression years

The Great Depression hit Seattle with full force in 1933. For jazz musicians things were slow, if sweet. Most of the action was in small clubs, played by combos struggling to get by on tips. Marion Fulmighter and Baby Borders were the top act in town, working at the Black and Tan. The most intriguing musician on the scene was pianist Julian Henson, who would later have a tremendous influence on pianist Jimmy Rowles. An almost completely unknown player who transmitted a great deal of jazz tradition during his two decades in Seattle but never received any recognition for it, Henson is emblematic of the "unsung local" whose career thrived out of the limelight. A self-taught player who never learned to read music, Henson was born in Omaha, Nebraska, spent his early childhood in Minneapolis, and started to play piano by ear after moving to Portland when he was fourteen. In the thirties, he came under the spell of Art Tatum and began to copy the master's intricate, filigreed improvisations and complicated harmonic developments. Henson had perfect pitch, which helped him find on the keyboard the melodies he heard in his head.

When he was eighteen, Henson struck out for Seattle. He connected immediately with the city's early generation of black performers—Joe Darensbourg, Wayne and Jimmy Adams, Baby Borders, Marion Fulmighter, Creon Thomas, Frank Waldron, and others. Henson himself worked the Blue Rose, an intimate, two-room club in a house on Yesler Way, between 12th and 14th. The Blue Rose was owned by "Big Lewis" Richardson, who poured liquor in the kitchen and brought it out to his customers, who were seated on the club's three davenports. During Henson's break, Big Lewis cranked up the jukebox.

When he arrived in Seattle, Henson was probably the most advanced pianist in town. He played in a flowery, ornamental style that showcased intricate runs and arpeggios, modulations from key to key within one tune, and complicated chord extensions. Henson credits Archie Jackson, the St. Louis–born pianist who worked with Frank Waldron at the Nanking, as one of his early mentors.

> *Archie was a power piano player, a big guy with great big hands. He played those big tenths [an interval spanning ten white keys]. Anything I'd ask him, he'd show me. Because my hands were small, I learned to play tenths between this [ring] finger and my thumb. I used to push my hands against the piano keys until I got my hand stretched out.*
>
> *There were so many marvelous piano players and they were all very open and generous. There was a guy named Ralph Richardson. He was fantastic. He was from some small town in Washington—Yakima, I think. He was better than most.*

Henson also names Palmer Johnson, Oscar Holden, and Princess Belle as among the finest pianists in town. Princess, whom Evelyn Williamson and most other singers in the area counted as their favorite accompanist, was reputed to be a Maori, from New Zealand. She dressed "like a schoolteacher" and played exclusive places downtown—a "real elegant lady," in Henson's words. Joe Darensbourg, who remembers working at a roadhouse with her, says she was the girlfriend of Los Angeles bandleader Curtis Mosby. Drummer Duke Turner says he played in San Francisco with Princess Belle in a band led by Elmer Fain.

But for Henson, there was more to life on Jackson Street than piano players. The district was also home, providing a world of rich street life in a safe, relaxed, multiracial atmosphere that is hard to imagine today. The neighborhood was a great cultural stew of immigrant groups, dominated by Jewish and

Japanese populations. Blacks were the next-largest group, with Italians and Chinese close behind. Japanese businesses flourished (though they were later destroyed, when the Japanese were interned during World War II), including beer parlors, hardware stores, movie theaters, and restaurants. There were Asian dance bands, too. Filipino saxophonist Frank Osias played with the Moonlight Serenaders; the Manila Serenaders were active at the Manila Dance Hall; and the Rizal, a taxi-dance establishment, had its own orchestra in 1933. The Tokiwa Hotel, at the corner of Maynard Avenue and King Street, was home to many jazz musicians, some of whom were stragglers from vaudeville shows that had crashed in Seattle. Rooms at the Tokiwa were only a dollar or two a week, which made survival fairly easy for a young musician. Despite hard times, Henson remembers life along Jackson Street in those days as fairly idyllic:

> *Most of the musicians who lived at the Tokiwa owed them money, but they wouldn't put you out. You could go to these Japanese restaurants and get twenty-cent meals. You could have four or five different kinds of bread in there. Then down on Skid Road, they had some places where for ten cents you could get some great beef stew. Good meals. Most of the entertainers, they'd get off and they'd go down there. Then there was Bob and Freda's. They sold beans for ten cents a bowl up there on 12th Avenue, right off Jackson. Everybody went to Bob and Freda's to get some beans. They sure were good, too. Out on the street, there was a guy they called "Whistling Jim." He was always whistling and he sold hot tamales out of a cart. They'd cost ten cents apiece.*
>
> *My dad was a bartender at the 411 Club, so he had a lot of friends. I was on my own, but every once in a while, I'd go in there and he'd say, "Kid, you doin' all right?" And he'd hand me a ten. Hell, that'd pay my room rent for a month. It was a town-and-a-half, man. It had so much going for it. You could get drunk and lay down in the middle of the street all night long and nobody'd bother you! Nothing happening 'til after twelve o'clock, then it came alive! All night, people running from club to club. It was an after-hours circus.*

**The Tokiwa Hotel, Jackson near Maynard, 1937.**

**Musicians and stranded show people often stayed at the Tokiwa during the Great Depression.**

**Courtesy of the Washington State Archives**

Alto saxophone man Marshal Royal also fondly recalls the family atmosphere Seattle provided musicians in those days:

> *They were a different type of people up in Seattle. You had a lot of fun. They were nice, they were cordial. I'm not just speaking of black people. I'm talking about the Chinese guys that owned the cab companies and things. They were our buddies. Everybody was just in it for a family. Like the Mar boys, big-time tong [gang] people out of Fresno, we had a ball. After we finished our job, they would have a midnight picture at the Atlas Theatre, open all night long. You could go in there and tell the owner what picture you wanted and he'd have it for you two or three days later.*

But out on the road, making it as a jazz musician during the Depression was still a scuffle. Joe Darensbourg's peripatetic career during those years is fairly suggestive of the unpredictable and often dangerous enterprises a journeyman musician had to undertake to survive hard times. Darensbourg had a run of hard luck that reads like a Woody Guthrie talking blues. First, the clarinetist took a trio to Green River, Wyoming, in 1931, where he was stranded. In Billings, Montana, he was hit by a truck, which put him in a cast for almost a year with a broken back and punctured lung. When he developed tuberculosis, he spent the winter taking the cure in Phoenix. Feeling better, he played with dance bands, and with a Mexican band. In Prescott, Arizona, he pumped a player piano while playing clarinet. But the job dried up and he was stranded again.

In 1932, Darensbourg was back in Seattle,

Combo at the Shantytown, 1937, near Bellingham, Washington.

Left to right: Junie Bradford, "Banjoski" Adams, Lee(?) Philips, Buddy "Moose" Groves.

Courtesy of Vivian Ewing

first with the Genessee Street Shufflers, then with Oscar Holden at the Blue Rose, and later at the black Elks Club, on 18th and Madison, with Zelma Winslow, Bill Hoy on drums, Bill Page on guitar, and Bill Trent and Oscar Low on vocals. A multiplicity of jobs, both musical and non-musical, followed: he did a stint in a food distribution warehouse, cooked in the galley of a crab boat, taught kids through a WPA "make work" program, ran his own Italian restaurant in Seattle, and made several trips to the Far East and Portland on cruise ships. In Asia, Darensbourg confesses, the band bought cymbals and smuggled them back inside the bass drum, selling them back home for an exorbitant profit.

In 1935, things picked up for Joe. He landed a regular gig on Kitsap Lake (near Bremerton) at a place called Houghton's (later, the Shellback Inn), sometimes working with a barrelhouse pianist known to posterity only as "Big Foot Smitty." It was on the Bremerton ferry that Darensbourg first met his future employer, Louis Armstrong, who was delighted to discover "another home boy" way up in the Pacific Northwest:

> *He was going over there with his band to play a one-nighter. . . . It just happened all of us was on the ferry boat together. I ran into "Fireman" George—old "Pops" Foster—who was there drinking beer, so I says, "What the hell you doin' on this boat?" and he says, "Well I'm here with Pops, with Louis." He seemed surprised to see me. He said, "Would you like to meet Pops?" I hadn't seen Fireman George since '28 and the days with Papa Mutt. He took me over to where Louis was eating and, right off from there, Louis started calling me "another home boy."*

Back in Seattle, Darensbourg went to work at Doc Hamilton's, where he played with saxophonist and vocalist Tootie Boyd, another struggling musician, originally from Ellensburg, Washington, who settled in Seattle in 1935 and worked with Phil Moore and Herman Whaley in the early 1930s. Boyd modeled his tenor saxophone playing on the great Illinois Jacquet and worked with Palmer Johnson and the early Seattle swing-band leader Al Pierre. "Tootie sang beautifully," asserts Palmer Johnson. "He used to sing 'I'm going to move way out on the outskirts of town. . . .' What a voice he had!" Boyd often took groups east of the mountains for work, or into California, Oregon, or Vancouver, British Columbia. One of the steadiest gigs the saxophonist secured was at the Shantytown, a country roadhouse near Bellingham. He held a regular job there for over a year, working with drummer Junie Bradford, "Banjoski" Adams, and bassist Buddy Groves. But working conditions were less than ideal.

"They had pianos in there that you'd come home bloody from playing," remembers Julian Henson. "The keys'd be all jagged. I remember I was playing there one time, playing 'Willow Weep for Me,' and I used to do a gliss on that and I did like that right along the edge of the keys and I sliced my finger right to the bone. The only piano in town with red keys!"

Darensbourg left Seattle in 1936. After a brief reunion of the Genessee Street Shufflers in 1938, he took bassist-guitarist Bill Rinaldi, pianist Jack Henshaw, and guitarist Virgil Ireland out to Grand Coulee, where construction forces were completing the great dam on the Columbia River. They found work at a rough-and-ready saloon called the Silver Dollar and played after hours at another joint.

Far away from the Shantytown, in Kansas City and New York, jazz style was changing dramatically during the Great Depression. On the models of Fletcher Henderson and Bennie Moten, the big-band format developed, with brass and reed sections trading riffs in a dynamic "call-and-response" pattern. Rhythm took on a loping, lighter four-four feel. Written arrangements became more important, as bands got bigger and each searched for a signature style. Individual soloing styles became more complex. This new, big-band style of swing music didn't enter the public imagination at large until 1935, when on-location radio broadcasts by Benny Goodman lit a musical brushfire that wasn't put out until the middle of World War II. But "swing" had been taking shape in black communities since the late 1920s.

In Seattle, swing caught on, but for a variety of reasons it was played in small combos rather than big bands through most of the thirties. Earl Whaley, an alto saxophonist and bandleader from the Bay Area, led an early West Coast swing band, the Red Hot Syncopators, at Seattle's Broadway and Finnish halls in 1932, as well as working in a variety of combos with Palmer Johnson, Joe Darensbourg, and Evelyn Williamson. In 1934, Whaley took a bona fide swing band that included Palmer Johnson to Shanghai, China.

But the first real harbinger of modern swing to reach the Northwest was Gene Coy, an Amarillo, Texas, bandleader and drummer who played a series of engagements in Seattle beginning in 1933. Coy's hot, nine-piece unit came from the heart of the Kansas City/Houston belt, where the foundations for the loping, blues-drenched new music were being laid. Coy had been associated with some of the most illustrious names developing in swing. The great saxophonist Ben Webster had worked with him in Amarillo in 1929–1930. Bassist Walter Page (with Count Basie) remembered Gene Coy and his Happy Black Aces from this period as "really jumping"; John Lewis, the influential pianist who would later found the Modern Jazz Quartet, recalled being impressed by the band and the playing of Coy's wife, Marge, whose piano sounded like that of the great Mary Lou Williams as early as 1927, he said. The Coy band found its way to San Diego, Los Angeles, and Tijuana in 1932, and on January 5, 1933, the *Northwest Enterprise* announced breathlessly:

> *Coming to Seattle! Gene Coy and His Eleven Black Aces, famous broadcasting and recording band. . . . At Washington Hall. "You'll Rock. You'll Roar, You'll Holler For More. They're Hotter Than Fire!"*

Al Turay, a white guitarist and bass player born in Seattle, remembers Coy and the Black Aces as "the closest thing we had around here to jazz—along the lines of Jimmie Lunceford and Bennie Moten, Kansas City–style." Palmer Johnson concurs, singling out the Coy band as the one superior, up-to-date group in the area at a time when Seattle was decidedly behind the times stylistically. The Coy band, which changed its name to the "Nine Rhythm Racketeers" while in Seattle, booked a string of engagements at Finnish Hall and Broadway Hall in January through March 1933, then took its "entrancing, enthralling syncopating" music to Portland.

During this first Seattle period, Coy picked up his most important soloist—the great and almost completely forgotten tenor saxophonist Dick Wilson. Wilson, originally from Illinois, had lived in Seattle since he was five years old and had attended Broadway high school. He was a handsome young man with reddish curly hair, a light complexion, and a thin mustache—"a great lady-killer," according to Andy Kirk. He started out as a pianist and vocalist, but after finishing his high school years in Los Angeles he returned to Seattle, where he took lessons from Frank Waldron and Joe Darensbourg. Darensbourg tells the story like this:

> *Around this time I got to know a kid who would probably have been the greatest of all tenor men if he'd lived. This was Dick Wilson. His father died when he was real young and he was raised by his mother, a nice iron-willed woman. . . . When Dick was about seventeen years old his mother asked me if I would teach him saxophone. I didn't really want to be bothered with pupils, but I said if he came over to the house I'd give him some pointers, just as a favor. I started giving him lessons on alto sax. When he started playing he kinda copied my style a little, but he had an individual sound even then. He was just a natural. A year after I taught him he was a better saxophone player than me.*

Wilson played with Darensbourg's band briefly, then, with Dick's mother's permission, Joe sent the young sax man off to Portland to apprentice with pianist Don Anderson's big band, using Joe's tenor sax. Wilson returned to Seattle a mature player, rejoining Darensbourg at the Jungle Temple No. 1 in a combo with Jimmy Adams (trumpet), Babe Hackley

A combo at the Jungle Temple No. 2, c. 1931.

Left to right: Dick Wilson (playing clarinet), Baby Borders, Oscar Hurst, Freddy Vaughn, unknown.

Dick Wilson, one of the premier tenor saxophone stylists of the swing era, got his start in Seattle.

Courtesy of Emma Gayton

(piano), and Baby Borders (drums). The band reportedly played a style that later would be identified with John Kirby—understated, small-group combo swing—and broadcast on the radio twice a week. Sometime in early 1933, Wilson left town with the Gene Coy band. A year later, he joined Zack Whyte, followed by Andy Kirk's Clouds of Joy in 1936.

Andy Kirk had one of the best of the Kansas City bands. His biggest hit was a ballad that featured vocalist Pha Terrell on "Until the Real Thing Comes Along," but Kirk swung like mad on other recordings. It was during Wilson's tenure with Kirk that the saxophonist recorded the dozen or so solos on which his reputation rests. "Lotta Sax Appeal" (1936), "Christopher Columbus" (1936), "Moten Swing" (1936), "Wednesday Night Hop" (1936), "All the Jive Is Gone," "In the Groove" (1937), and "Little Miss" (1940), among others, show Wilson as a soloist with a light but substantial and highly personal sound, advanced harmonic concept, a genius for melody, and a faultless execution that put him in a class with Chu Berry, Don Byas, and Herschel Evans. Like his Kirk bandmate Byas, Wilson occupied that interesting transitional style between the gruff, vertical, diatonic approach of Coleman Hawkins and the more loping, chromatic, "modern" style of Lester Young. Darensbourg claims that Byas confessed in a conversation in Paris that he had been influenced by Dick Wilson. Albert McCarthy, the prominent swing-era historian, casts Wilson as "one of the five or six best tenor saxophone soloists of the swing era"; Dizzy Gillespie, in a 1989 interview, emphatically agreed:

> *Dick Wilson was a bitch. . . . Stylist, too, creator of a style of sax. You know, not very many musicians followed in his footsteps, or learned his style, but he was right up there with Lester Young and Herschel Evans. He was considered one of the best. The head guys then were Coleman Hawkins and then Chu Berry. Coleman Hawkins was the king, but Dick Wilson and Chu Berry, they were the crown princes.*

Wilson returned to Seattle at least once, in 1941, billed as "Seattle's own Dick Wilson," when the Kirk band performed at the Senator Ballroom. Photographer Al Smith caught Wilson standing up in the saxophone section, wearing sunglasses and playing one of his memorable solos. It would be one of Wilson's last choruses. A few months later he died at age 30, of a lingering disease which some report was tuberculosis; Joe Darensbourg says it was syphilis contracted from a prostitute in Canada. Wilson was the most important swing figure to come out of Washington State, and his early death was understandably a blow to his friends. Darensbourg described him as "one of the guys I sincerely liked in this business." Palmer Johnson remembered Wilson as "a soft and easygoing guy. . . . He was very nice, always happy and smiling."

Wilson was not the only member of Gene Coy's band with Seattle connections to achieve notoriety. Alvin "Junior" Raglin, who later joined the Duke Ellington Orchestra, also played with Coy's Eleven Black Aces. Raglin and trombonist Andy Duryea apparently left the band during one of its Seattle gigs, because both their names begin to appear on Seattle combo announcements in 1938. Marshal Royal says the Coy band was falling apart at this point: "They came to town raggedy as a nickel mop. They weren't making too much money, so they broke up and went all different kind of ways. Junior Raglin was the guitar player. After they got stranded, that's when Junior took up bass playing."

For a time, Raglin and Duryea both worked for Palmer Johnson at the Congo Club in a sextet with local tenor saxophonist Aaron Davis and drummer Gilbert "Punkin" Austin. Raglin, an exceptional talent, was born in 1917 in

Omaha, where he started on guitar. Twenty years later, he was working with Gene Coy at Seattle's Ubangi Club, one of the Jackson Street district's most successful and glamorous black-owned nightclubs. In the words of Palmer Johnson, who played with him in Coy's band for that engagement, "Junior could play guitar and walk the dog on a bass." Al Turay concurs: "Junior Raglin was a real great bass player. He was playing bass when I would come into the 411 Club with my guitar. He was also just one bitch of a guitar player. God, he was just an amazing guitar player. So he'd play guitar, a Gibson L5, which he loved to play, and I'd play bass. We'd switch off like that."

Raglin at this time was said to have been playing a two-necked guitar with bass strings on one neck and guitar strings on the other. Today, this is not such an unusual instrument, but it was a rarity in the 1930s, perhaps the first one ever made. Raglin worked in Seattle for a couple of years with Palmer Johnson's sextet, in a duo with Seattle guitarist Milt Green, and in at least one gala jazz concert at the Metropolitan Theatre. Sometime after 1940, he went to Los Angeles and joined the Duke Ellington Orchestra, replacing Jimmy Blanton. Duke was based in Los Angeles from 1939 to 1941, recording and writing film scores and producing an original musical. In these years Jimmy Blanton was rewriting the book on jazz bass, extending the range of the instrument from its undifferentiated "thump! thump! thump! thump!" into a precise, single-note style, the signature for which became his melodic bass introduction to "Jack the Bear"—an announcement to the world that the bass fiddle would no longer be just a rhythm instrument. But the young Blanton was cursed with tuberculosis. He was hospitalized in late 1941 and died the following June. Junior Raglin reportedly played beside Blanton in the band for a few nights before joining the band. Soon, he went into the recording studio with a close approximation of Blanton's sound. On December 2, 1942, Raglin recorded, with Duke, Billy Strayhorn's great new tunes "Raincheck" and "Chelsea Bridge," issued on Victor. Two weeks later he was back in Seattle playing with Ellington at the Palomar Theatre. The *Seattle Times* noticed

**The Andy Kirk Band, with tenor saxophonist Dick Wilson (wearing sunglasses), Senator Ballroom, February 17, 1941.**

**Photo by Al Smith**

the performance: "Seattle's Alvin Raglin won great applause with his work on the fiddle in 'Jack the Bear.'"

Raglin spent the next four years with Ellington, appearing on over thirty sides with the master. It is Raglin who plays on "Come Sunday," "The Blues," "Worksong," and other sections of Ellington's masterful suite *Black, Brown and Beige*, which debuted in Carnegie Hall. That's also Raglin on the 1945 recordings of "Black and Tan Fantasy" and "Caravan." During and after his stint with the Duke, Raglin went out with two of the small groups that spun off from the Ellington band—with Ray Nance in 1944, and Johnny Hodges in 1948. In 1945, Raglin left the Ellington organization, and enjoyed some success. His picture appeared in *Life* magazine in 1944; *Esquire* gave him the New Star award in its 1946 jazz poll, and *down beat* pictured him leading his own trio at the Three Deuces, on New York's 52nd Street, the same year. However, Raglin's career went downhill after this brief blast in the limelight. By the early fifties, he had moved to Boston and stopped performing. He died in 1956, reportedly from the effects of alcohol abuse.

Long after the departure of Dick Wilson and Junior Raglin from his band, Gene Coy remained a popular figure in Seattle, playing between 1938 and 1940 at Lyons' Music Hall, the Finnish Hall, the Ubangi, and other venues. Coy's prolonged tenure in Seattle is important not only for the sidemen who flowed in and out of the band, but because of the stylistic authenticity he offered young musicians. It is surprising, then, considering the availability of authentic stylists and the popularity of swing, that a black swing band along the lines of Coy's did not emerge from Seattle. But one didn't. Why?

It could be argued that Gerald Wells' ten-piece group, which played the Hi-Hatters club in 1931, took a step toward orchestrated, large-group jazz, but no one who heard this band is prepared to confirm that it played in a modern, swing-era style. And Earl Whaley's group, though it evolved closer to the swing model, never grew beyond combo ambitions.

The most obvious reason Seattle remained a combo town without big bands in the 1930s was the small number of blacks in the region. Four thousand, to be exact, in the entire state of Washington—population, three million. "You didn't have forty [black] musicians in Seattle," comments Marshal Royal dryly. "Probably

Veteran Seattle jazz musician and Local 493 president Gerald Wells, center, plays tenor saxophone in a swing band with Joe Gauff (alto saxophone) and Len Brooks (piano), 1940s.

Photo by Al Smith

didn't have twenty. It was a very, very small scene."

Add to the small population the fact that big-band leaders had to keep fifteen or twenty men on the payroll, week in and week out, and it becomes more clear why no large local band evolved. Besides, downtown venues were closed to black musicians. Even if an enterprising black bandleader had tried to start a big band, the lucrative jobs in the hotels and theaters would have been off-limits. Big bands would not develop until the 1940s, when the black population of Seattle grew by thousands.

In the meantime, Seattle's combo scene heated up, as the Depression passed into the more prosperous war years. From Fifth Avenue in the International District to Fourteenth Avenue in the Central Area, nightclubs and speakeasies such as the Ubangi, the 411 Club, Two Pals, the Green Dot, the Congo Club, the Black and Tan, and the black Elks Club had opened, reopened, or rebounded with the economic impetus of Roosevelt's war-readiness plan. Though America didn't join the war until 1941, the president's strategy to make the United States the "arsenal for Europe" had boosted the shipping industry and secondary jobs related to it around Puget Sound. Young single men had begun to arrive in Seattle and Tacoma, a migration that would continue through 1945. Many of these men were looking not only for work, but for a new home in the West. Some, like the black railroad porters and waiters who had made Noodles Smith's ventures a success, also were looking for a good time on the town and for the recreational music that was familiar to them—jazz and blues. They had money in their pockets.

Talented musicians came and went, dropping out of "name" bands, staying long enough to sow the seeds of new styles developing around the country, then packing up again. Local musicians, in turn, were picked up by well-known bands. This constant interchange between local and national scenes was the underground interstate highway system on which the jazz tradition traveled.

One of the brightest travelers was Jimmy Rowles, a young musician from Spokane who would later become famous as a band pianist with Benny Goodman and Woody Herman, as a superb accompanist for Ella Fitzgerald, and finally as a trio artist of the first order. Born in 1918, Rowles is a gruff, gravel-voiced customer whose exterior belies the extreme sensitivity and subtlety of his music. An unabashed disciple of Lester Young and Art Tatum with a love for reworking harmonies, Rowles can find more beauty and intricacy in one simple popular tune than most musicians can find in a night. As a teenager in Spokane, Rowles was taken on as a protégé by a Blackfoot Indian from Montana named Tom Brown who played tenor saxophone. Rowles remembers the day they met:

> *I was fiddling around with the piano in the gym one afternoon, and this guy came around. He was a genius, I found out later. He was arranging for the pep band. He said, "That's not it." Then he left. One day he came [and played me] a Benny Goodman Trio record. It was "Someday Sweetheart." He put that on the windup and said, "Listen to this." And I heard Teddy Wilson playing. He says, "That's the way you're supposed to play, and I can help you." That quick, my whole life changed. I had a purpose. I didn't know what I was going to be, but I knew I wasn't going to be a lawyer.*

For the rest of that year in Spokane, Rowles studied informally with Brown, listening to every note of Teddy Wilson, Art Tatum, and Fats Waller, and working with Brown in clubs. One night, when Les Hite's band came through town, Jimmy went backstage and played for Marshal Royal, who at that time was Hite's alto saxophonist. Royal counseled, "I think you could do well, but you've gotta get out of here. Go to Seattle first. You can learn in Seattle. Then come to L.A."

Rowles happily took Royal's advice, telling his stepfather he wanted to study pre-law at the University of Washington. That fall, with his portable record player in tow, Rowles found a room in a Seattle boardinghouse and enrolled at the university. He attended one lecture—"It was in anthropology, I remember"—and promptly cadged a ride from a roommate to Jackson Street. "It was like the beginning of a new, whole life," Rowles remembers. "In Spokane there was nothing like this. This was a city. And it was right at Seattle's almost peak period."

For a young pianist like Rowles, the Jackson Street combo scene actually was preferable to a big-band milieu, since in small groups he could learn to improvise and develop his own style. That first night in 1937, Rowles heard

Gene Coy at the Black and Tan—but he was much more interested in the solo style of a twenty-three-year-old Kansas City tenor saxophonist named Aaron Davis, who came on for a jam session after Coy had finished. Rowles describes their first meeting:

> *This guy sounded like Lester Young, like all the records I'd been listening to. I had memorized those solos. So I'm sitting over there itching for the keys and I finally went over and told Aaron I was from Spokane and told him I'd been listening to Lester Young, and asked him if I could play "Lady Be Good" with him. He laughed. So I sat down and whipped off Count Basie's first chorus on "Lady Be Good." He came in and played Lester's solo. I was laughing, and he was laughing.*

When the evening drew to a close, Davis told Rowles that if he wanted to find more action, he should go down to the 411 Club and introduce himself to Palmer Johnson. Johnson remembers the night Rowles walked in.

"Jimmy Rowles! He had kind of short, cropped hair, rosy cheeks, and he never had a nickel. Tall, skinny kid. Going to school. He used to come in and I'd want to get off for a little while. Let Jimmy up and play, while I took a little walk."

The club Palmer occasionally turned over to Rowles was one of Seattle's better—and newer—ones. The 411, on Maynard, was a long and lean establishment that extended all the way to the back alley. The bandstand stood about halfway down the room and was big enough to support a five-piece band. On weekends, students from the University of Washington jammed the place.

"If Louis [Armstrong] was in town, or Duke, they'd come down to the 411 Club and jam," remembers Johnson. "Ben Webster came down one night. This is where we met this kid Corky Corcoran. He was fifteen years old and we let him in the back door. I'll never forget that night. Little baby-faced kid, but he could play saxophone."

"The sun was up when I'd get on the streetcar to go back to the University District," recounts Rowles. "The streetcar guy never even used to charge me. He says, 'You! For Christ's sake, are you ever going to sleep?' 'I'm going to sleep today, I promise ya.' Next morning I'd see him again, he'd say, 'Jesus Christ, you're really after it, aren't ya?' 'Yup, I gotta learn.'"

Jam sessions at the 411 gave Rowles his first experience on the firing line, with eager musicians calling tunes he might or might not know, in keys he might or might not have rehearsed. It was priceless training and it was the time-honored method for learning to play jazz among musicians of the old school. But if Johnson gave Rowles the simple gift of turning over the piano bench to him, it was Julian Henson who initiated him into the mysteries of modern harmony.

"Julian Henson played crazy chords," Rowles recalls. "Palmer was sort of Fats Wallerish; he played nice, full piano, but he wasn't too modern. Julian Henson showed me things. I'd hear something and I'd ask, 'What the heck you doing there?' and he'd show me. He had some good stuff. I used to love the way he played."

Rowles continued to soak up as much as he could, subbing in sweet bands led by Center Case and Jimmy Crane and jamming at the Blue Rose—once, when Jimmie Lunceford's vocalist, Dan Grissom, was there. Gene Sargent, the Seattle arranger, composer, and accordionist who would later record with Woody Herman, hipped Rowles to Duke Ellington's harmonies, and Ike Young, a dapper alto saxophonist playing with Gene Coy, befriended and encouraged him.

Rowles grew weary of maintaining the ruse on his family, however, who still thought he was attending the University of Washington. He returned to Spokane, briefly attending Gonzaga University and working for his father. But Spokane was not where he belonged, either. Rowles declared to his parents that he was going to be a musician, not a lawyer, and, like Crosby, Rinker, and Bailey before him, he left Spokane for Los Angeles. It was the right move. By the fall of 1940, he was playing every night with his idol, Lester Young, and sitting at Art Tatum's feet after hours. A call from Benny Goodman in 1941 set fire to Rowles' career. Today Rowles, who is honored at jazz festivals around the world, is known as a distinctive, mature stylist who respects the tradition of the popular song (often rarely played ones) without descending into cocktail sentimentality.

It had been Marshal Royal who encouraged Jimmy Rowles to come to Seattle in the first place. No one was in a better position to know just how hot the Jackson Street scene was cooking in those days than Royal and his colleagues in the Les Hite band. In 1936, Hite had been the opening attraction at the Ubangi. This was Seattle's first floor-show nightclub, which opened as a response to the booming swing-band business from out of town.

The Ubangi was also the last hurrah of Noodles Smith. Located at 710 Seventh Avenue South, just off Jackson Street in what is now the International District, it was a large, beautiful upstairs cabaret with potted palms. Big-time entertainers such as Cab Calloway worked there, as well as up-and-coming black entertainers.

According to Bruce Rowell, who managed the Ubangi with Noodles Smith's nephew, Harold, the club catered mainly to a white clientele. To kick off the place, Bruce and Noodles took a trek to the Cotton Club in Los Angeles to find talent for the club's debut. They recruited Les Hite's band, plus a line of chorus girls. According to Rowell,

> *We had 'em for twelve weeks. We had the chorus line from Frank Sebastian's Cotton Club and got all of our costumes from Madame Ouida in Los Angeles. They'd change the show every two weeks. After Hite left, we got an offer from a guy by the name of Basie, out of Kansas City. Noodles said, "I never heard of this Basie guy." So we booked some band from the East Coast that wasn't any good, got rid of them after two weeks, and then brought in Wyatt Howard.*

Howard was a major local white bandleader who later led the house band at the Town and Country Club, downtown on Sixth Avenue. Local musicians who followed Howard into the Ubangi included Palmer Johnson, who remembers working as a single on the "mezzanine level" of the club ("Gee, how the people used to flock to that joint!"), Marion Fulmighter (billed as Marion Fullove), and Noodles' consort, Zelma Winslow.

The Ubangi was occasionally nabbed by the state liquor board, and Rowell had a unique way of dealing with raids that hearkened back to Prohibition:

> *There were secret doors and slides and you could get down below the street. 'Til this day, there's still old gambling setups, places to one side where there's cribs to smoke opium. You could go down there and come up in the alley by the Wah Mee Club [the Blue Heaven in those days, the site of a notorious mass murder in 1986.] That's how I got away from the Washington State liquor board, three times. Heh-heh-heh-heh! When they came in, I'd go to the office, see, and say, "Let me get my overcoat." Then I'd zip down that little deal, you know, near the floor, and* shee-oop! *I'm downstairs in the basement. Next thing I know, I'm coming out, go down to the Mar Hotel, get a room, take a bath, and go to bed! They're all up there lookin' for me and I'm in the shower!*

Usually, the "fix was in," however, and a designated man was sent down to the Courthouse to be arrested. He would be back to work in half an hour. At one time, says Rowell, Noodles had as many as seventy "cases" pending against him.

The Ubangi only lasted a couple of years. When the building was sold in February 1938, the *Northwest Enterprise* bid the club a sad farewell, touting it proudly as the "largest race-owned enterprise . . . north of Los Angeles." For a while, Rowell and Harold ran a place on Maynard Street, the 416, next to the Atlas Theatre. Noodles also bankrolled Louis Todd for another club, the Big Apple, located on King between Fifth and Sixth. Neither lasted very long.

In about 1940, a lavish place owned by Sherman Spates on the north side of Jackson, between Maynard and Sixth, took up the slack. The Congo Club was the classic Prohibition-style "blind," a circular bar and ballroom hidden behind a swinging door at the back of a spacious, well-lit restaurant called the Congo Grill. Johnny Reddin, a *Seattle Times* columnist who liked to hang out in after-hours clubs, wrote that the Congo was his favorite place to eat in the district.

In 1940, Johnson took a band into the Congo with Herman Grimes, one of the best musicians ever to linger in Seattle. Grimes grew up in Birmingham, Alabama, in a family band that included his older brother Johnny, a well-known swing trumpet player in New York. In 1923, Herman led Roger's Sunshine Minstrels (out of Florence, Alabama), and during the Depression worked with several Kansas City bands, including Tommy Douglas'. "He was one of your top trumpet players, one of your real

Herman Grimes, trumpet, gives the boys in the Gay Jones Orchestra a few pointers, c. 1940.

Left to right: Grimes, Carle Rising, Floyd Tebbelman, Sven Sandstrom, Ernie Sears, Freddie Thompson, Dick Krafft, Glenn Martin, Aaron Shearer.

Courtesy of Gaylord Jones

powerhouse men," recalls Darensbourg, who heard Grimes in Alabama before meeting him again in Seattle. According to Marshal Royal, who later played with Grimes in a Bay Area Navy band during World War II, Noodles Smith "sent for" Grimes from Kansas City. "He thought Herman Grimes was just the greatest," says Royal. "He thought he was better than Louis Armstrong."

Palmer Johnson was a fan, as well: "I call Grimes the greatest trumpet player out of this Northwest. He could play as much trumpet as anybody in the country. And he could sing and he was a comic. Watching him walk up and down that floor, with his trumpet under his arm and singing. And his big eyes! Oooh! Those high notes, when we'd play 'Chinatown.' He went way up, to the trumpet's high F, man! He had a lip of iron!"

"Every band that came to Seattle—the Dorsey brothers, any band—they came down to try to steal Herman Grimes," according to Bruce Rowell. "But Herman Grimes would not go on the road! 'I want to stay right here in Seattle,' he'd say. 'I got a lady I'm living with, she's doing all my laundry, cooking all my meals. We split the kitty every morning. When I was nine years old, I was third trumpet on the Barnum & Bailey's Circus, riding on the band-wagon and the parades. I've *been* on the road.'"

During the day, Grimes wrote horse-race tickets at the Green Dot, a barbershop also owned by Sherman Spates across the street from the Congo Club, which sometimes featured piano players in back. Later on, Johnson worked with Grimes at the Green Dot and at Coe's Tavern, on Roosevelt, and Grimes himself led a trio at the Dutchman Tavern with Beulah Bradford (Junie Bradford's sister) on piano and Art Bradford (no relation) on drums.

In 1947, after his stint in the Navy, Herman Grimes briefly replaced Shorty Baker in the trumpet section of the Duke Ellington Orchestra. In November 1947, he recorded "Do Nothin' Till You Hear from Me" with Duke. Royal says Grimes subsequently joined the merchant marine and died aboard one of the boats sometime in the 1950s. He does not appear to have come back to Seattle.

The Congo Club, the Ubangi, the Blue Rose, and the 411 were bootlegging establishments devoted to entertainment, alcohol, and, sometimes, gambling. But the International District also sported legitimate Chinese restaurants friendly to jazz. One of the most venerable was the Chinese Gardens, on Seventh, near King. The Chinese Gardens, it will be remembered, had been inaugurated by Leonard Gayton back in 1930 and shut down by the feds in a spectacular raid the following year. The restaurant was owned by Charlie Louie, who was well-liked by musicians, even though they joked about his habit of requesting his alma mater tune, "The Stein Song," from the University of Maine. The Chinese Gardens was more formal than the clubs. Women wore evening gowns and men wore ties. It survived until after World War II, hosting a variety of bands and jam sessions.

Outside of town, one of the most illustrious Chinese-run establishments was the China Pheasant, a roadhouse casino between Boeing Field and the Duwamish River operated by Harry Lew. Seattle also had a few downtown venues for jazz-oriented white musicians during this period. The State Theater (where Al Jolson had once played), just up the hill from First on Madison, hired players for burlesque shows. The Virginian, a large, plain beer garden at Virginia Street and Fourth Avenue, used three dance bands, alternating sets from one o'clock in the morning until dawn. On First, near Union Street, was Lyons' Music Hall, owned by Al Lyons, who would later build the Showbox Theater, where many of the greatest swing era bands performed; and at 11th Avenue and Pine was the Cocoanut Grove, a vast basement establishment that seated a thousand.

But the music downtown was mostly commercial. If musicians wanted to play jazz, they

had to go to Jackson Street. Jack Foy, the drummer who played with Darensbourg's Genessee Street Shufflers, would go down to jam at the Hong Kong Chinese Society:

*A bass player named Ben Johnson showed me more things. He knew enough about the drums that he could show me how to play with a bass, or with a rhythm section, you know? [He] really taught me how to play with a band, which was most important. How to play behind a guy taking a solo. Be a little different between clarinet and saxophone and trumpet, trombone, piano.*

Foy also recalls an unusual place named the Jailhouse, where one night he met Lionel Hampton, Marshal Royal, Walter Page, and Les Hite.

*It was quite a joint. The tables were all cells, with bars. The keeper—the "jailer"—would show you to your cell like a maitre d', you know, like a guard, and put you in the table and lock you up. Then the waiter'd come and unlock the cell and take your order. Kind of a crazy place. The band was dressed in convict uniforms.*

Palmer Johnson did his share of scuffling during the Depression, too. Though he managed to snag a steady Seattle gig with Herman Grimes at the Dutchman Tavern, on Spokane Street and First, he spent two years of the Depression in Portland (1931–1932) working in speakeasies and whorehouses. In 1934, he took the most exotic flyer of all—a three-year trip to the elegant ballrooms of Shanghai.

During the 1930s, a wealthy international elite lived in Shanghai, enjoying greyhound racing, jai alai, gambling, and jazz. Scores of elegant bands—both black and white—were ferried over to play in the ballrooms owned by wealthy Chinese promoters, including groups led by trumpeters Buck Clayton and Tommy Foy (Jack's brother).

By all accounts, Shanghai was a good deal for the musicians, particularly blacks, who say they were treated with respect for the first time in their lives. Players were given excellent

**The Earl Whaley Band at St. Anna's Dance Hall, Shanghai, China, 1934. Left to right: Fate Williams, Oscar Hurst, Punkin Austin, Earl West, Wayne Adams, Earl Whaley, Palmer Johnson.**

**Courtesy of Palmer Johnson**

quarters in the international settlement, with maids and personal tailors who made them uniforms on request. There were American cooks to provide familiar meals. The pay ranged from $100 to $200 a week, and the city was full of exotic attractions, including rickshaw rides and a newly popularized drink from Russia called vodka. Everything about the place, from the palm-lined streets to the elegantly turned ballrooms—the Canidrome, St. Anna's Dance Hall, the Casa Nova—was like a Hollywood movie, complete with international spies and exotic women dropping handkerchiefs on the ballroom floor.

Palmer Johnson went to Shanghai reluctantly. The pianist was making good money in Portland speakeasies, but bandleader Earl Whaley finally convinced him to go. Whaley's original band had three horns and three men on rhythm: Wayne Adams (saxophones), Oscar Hurst (trumpet), "Fate" Williams (trombone), Earl West (guitar), Johnson (piano), and "Punkin" Austin (drums). Later, Whaley picked up bassist Reginald Jones from Buck Clayton's band. Jones, known as "Jonesy," was another Gene Coy veteran who had moved to the Northwest. (His brother, Reunald, played trumpet for Count Basie.) The band was given its quarters and immediately went to work at St. Anna's Ballroom. As Johnson remembers:

> *It was the most beautiful ballroom you ever looked upon. They had revolving chandeliers, man, that go around and around this way. Three of them. It was a vast place. And all these Chinese girls and some Russian girls, sitting around there, and prospective customers came along and choose a girl to dance with. Music never stopped. Just one after the other. The Chinese were crazy about "This Evening About a Quarter to Nine." Fred Astaire and Ginger Rogers had made this movie,* Flying Down to Rio, *so we played "Carioca" and "Cheek to Cheek," "Accent on Youth" and "Stay as Sweet as You Are." Buck's band played afternoon tea dances. Ours never started 'til around seven o'clock, so sometimes I went over and heard his band. After he left, they brought up another band from Los Angeles.*

Before long, bad weather blew over Johnson's Asian retreat. The way he tells it, he had befriended a tap dancer, Buster Dunston, who was gay.

> *We were working in the open-air pavilion one night, at the outskirts of the city. This was in 1935. It was raining cats and dogs. Buster and I had just gone out to eat one of the delicacies over there, frogs' legs. They were delicious, man. Tastes better than chicken. About two o'clock, in walks Buster, and he had two fellows with him. And Earl Whaley says, "Here comes Palmer's boy."*
>
> *I just waited. Just waited until after the band played the last number. And I says, "I didn't like that crack you made about Buster when Buster walked in here." And he said, "What you going to do about it?" and I let this left go, and it hit the piano and broke this finger and busted his nose. So they bandaged my finger up and I quit.*

After leaving Whaley, Johnson took a job with a Filipino band in Penang, in what is now Malaysia, led by a trombone player, then worked six weeks at Singapore's famous Raffles Hotel.

In January 1937, after an apology and a raise, Johnson rejoined Whaley in a Hong Kong dance hall. The following month, the band was back in Shanghai's Ambassador Ballroom, across the street from the racecourse. But the atmosphere in the colorful cosmopolitan city had gone sour. Japanese soldiers were doing maneuvers in the streets, a foreshadowing of the invasion and occupation to come. Musicians began to think seriously about getting back to America. Some ballrooms had deducted a small amount from each player's paycheck for the passage, but many musicians were stranded. Being that far away from home with no way to get back was frightening, according to Johnson:

> *I had been watching these Japs, riding around up the main road in these little tanks. They were gathering troops to go to war. I says, I don't want none of this. I started going to the jai alai games to try to win my fare back. I want to get the hell out of there. So I read this paper, it said, "'President Grant' [the ship] arriving." Beautiful Shanghai day. I put on my whites and I go down to the Wussong River and hire a water taxi and go out in*

*the middle of the stream and get on board the* President Grant. *It just so happened that one of the waiters had took a dose of clap in Manila and they had him quarantined on the ship. I played piano and waited tables all the way back, man. When I got back, they used to call me "China Seas."*

Not all the musicians in Shanghai were as lucky as China Seas. Weeks after Johnson left, the Japanese shelled the city from the river. Several musicians were interned. Earl West died before he could return to the States. Whaley was imprisoned, and, according to one account, his hands were broken when he became defiant with his captors. He worked as an interpreter for American troops in prison, then came home and worked for the Post Office. He was alive until at least 1964, when he lived in Los Angeles. Jones is thought to have been imprisoned, but he did make it back. He later turned up in Los Angeles, where he worked for Local No. 47 of the AFM. Wayne Adams was interned, but two years after his return to America he died of complications from a disease he had reportedly contracted overseas. Punkin Austin returned to Seattle.

Palmer Johnson's return in 1937, the year the young Jimmy Rowles came to town and subbed for him, marked the high point of the senior pianist's career. His engagements at the 411, the 908 Club, and the Congo Club set the pace for the district and for Seattle jazz. But in 1942, wanderlust seized the chuckling pianist again, and he made for Alaska, where fortunes were to be won entertaining servicemen and the rough pioneers who were guiding the snow-blown territory toward statehood. Johnson would not return to Seattle until 1977.

Johnson's contribution to the Seattle scene, spanning fourteen years and three decades, is enormous. Along with Elmer Fain, Bumps Myers, Frank Pasley, and others, he brought to the Northwest the new, sophisticated sense of jazz that had developed in Los Angeles, as well as a high level of reading, transposing, and improvising that would become the standard for all jazz players who followed him. He was generous to younger musicians and accessible to audiences, and conveyed a sense of joy in what he was doing that was contagious. If any one jazz musician can be so chosen, Johnson is the prime symbol of the "living tradition" of jazz in Seattle.

Johnson's departure also marked the end of an era. His colorful style of solo piano and combo swing belonged to the early phases of jazz that had been forged in the teens and twenties, a style that was fast being replaced by the new style of big-band swing. But the combo scene during the Depression, with its colorful characters and speakeasy flair, had been a great school for young players such as Dick Wilson, Junior Raglin, and Jimmy Rowles. Rowles, in particular, would not forget his debt to the town.

"To have been able to participate in that experience in Seattle," he says, "and learn at the same time from all these musicians—not be standing around watching, like it is today—I was very lucky."

Meanwhile, though it had been a long time coming, Seattle's next generation of jazzers was developing a top-notch swing culture of its own. Ironically, the first big band to become well-known in Seattle wouldn't come out of the black community, but from two white college kids. Their energy would bring Seattle into the big-band era, and leave the scuffling Depression behind.

**The Palmer Johnson Quartet at the 908 Club, 1940.**

**Left to right: Punkin Austin, Milt Green, Tootie Boyd, Palmer Johnson.**

**Courtesy of Palmer Johnson**

# 4
# SWINGMANIA
## the big bands roll in

Swing was a youth craze, much like Beatlemania in the 1960s, and very popular on campus. Part of the reason for this popularity was that the music was more danceable than early jazz, even at fast tempos, and therefore fit nicely into the adolescent ritual of growing up and falling in love. This was the era of the jitterbug and dance marathons, when the lindy hop replaced the fox-trot and the Charleston.

Swing was also big business. Bands led by Benny Goodman, the Dorseys, Duke Ellington, Jimmie Lunceford, and Woody Herman made enormous sums of money touring the country, playing one-nighters in ballrooms. Bandleaders became stars both on radio and in the movies. When Artie Shaw married Betty Grable, it was front-page stuff. When Gene Krupa was busted for smoking pot, the roof came off. Local copy bands sprang up in every city, imitating the name bands. Even the underground slang of jazzmen seeped into the mainstream. Swing fanatics called themselves "jitterbugs" and "alligators" and picked up expressions like "groovy" and "cool" from black musicians. Cab Calloway published a tongue-in-cheek *Dictionary of Jive* that became a cult favorite. A cult of enthusiasm and experience, which would have its apogee in the bebop 1940s, spread through America's teen culture, which had been created by the automobile and affluence. White drummer Don Manning, who later became an important jazz collector and historian, recounts:

> *In 1941, I remember going down to interview Duke Ellington in his dressing room for the school newspaper. They did five shows a day, which a kid could get into, and they had a special matinee, down at the Showbox on First Avenue. When I met Duke, I talked to him in "jive." Duke was so tickled, he brought the band out. "Say that again to these guys!" he said.*

Though black swing bands such as Ellington's started coming to Seattle in the mid-thirties and black swing combos such as Palmer Johnson's had been playing in the clubs for years, the first local swing big band was formed and popularized by white college students. Norm Bobrow, who was raised in New York's Westchester County, had been to more Broadway shows by the time he was a teenager than most Seattleites would see in a lifetime. More important, he had been taken up to Harlem, where he'd fallen in love with black music and style at the Apollo Theater. When the Bobrows moved to Seattle in 1936, the town seemed strictly from squaresville to the young New York– bred university freshman. The most popular orchestra on the University of Washington campus was an "ickie band" (swing slang for a corny group) led by Jimmy Crane, who was also a yell leader. While the rest of the country was stomping at the Savoy, Seattleites had yet to hear Lunceford live.

"One morning," explains Bobrow, a still-boyish older man who exudes a disarming Broadway enthusiasm, "I decided that with all these bands around here, there must be one that is playing good Benny Goodman, good Artie Shaw, good Duke Ellington, good Jimmie Lunceford. I called Gay Jones off a blind list in *The Daily*. When he answered the phone I said, 'I'd like to present a good, listenable band that has a jazz flavor.' Gay said, 'We're having a rehearsal right now, come on over!'"

Gaylord Jones and his young wife, Marilyn, had been living hand-to-mouth ever since graduating from West Seattle High in 1936. Gay was a student at the University of Washington, but he spent most of his time rehearsing the band, listening to hot new records, and writing his own arrangements—that is, when he and the guys weren't down at the Black and Tan or the Dutchman Tavern. Music was their life. Gay's best friend since childhood, Tiny Martin, lived down the street and played bass. Their new takeoff on the Bob Crosby hit "Big Noise From Winnetka" had become one of the highlights of their act. Sven Sandstrom, the band's jazz trumpet player, lived in Gay and Marilyn's basement; he had the annoying habit of getting up early and practicing Bunny Berigan's solo on "I Can't Get Started."

Gay had grown up with music. His father had played solo jazz piano at Lundeen's. In their early teens, Gay and Tiny had started a "kid band," the Cosmopolitans, which played dances, assemblies, and sock hops. Some of the players from the Cosmopolitans—Floyd Tebbleman (sax), Dick Kraft (sax), and Carle Rising (trumpet)—were now with the Gaylord Jones Orchestra. Marilyn, who used the stage name Mars Mercer, was a fan of the Boswell Sisters, the hip harmonizers with the Benny Goodman band. She had a vocal trio that sang at the Spanish Castle, in Tacoma. When they all graduated, they expanded the band to five saxes, four trumpets, three trombones, and four rhythm players, and started looking for jobs. They had no idea that the happy-go-lucky student who came around that morning to give them a listen was going to help them so much.

"When I got there," recalls Bobrow, "they were doing 'One O'Clock Jump,' 'Begin the Beguine,' and 'Back Bay Shuffle,' and all the Artie Shaw and Benny Goodman charts. Man, I just flipped out! I never expected to hear a band which was so organized and tight. Gay was a goddamned perfectionist."

This was the beginning of Bobrow's fifty-year career as Seattle's most important jazz impresario and the much-belated starting gun for the city's swing era. On March 2, 1939, in a sensational style that would become his trademark, Bobrow announced a concert by Gaylord Jones and the formation of the Husky Hot Club, a new campus organization dedicated to swing. The show attracted a turn-away crowd of 250 to Clark Hall, not to mention the unwanted attention of the university president, who told Bobrow he objected to having a campus organization with the word "hot" in its name.

There it was, the puritanical face of Bertha Landes looming over Seattle again. "I believe that some people believe that 'hot' has licentious connotations," said the president.

Bobrow played it cool.

"I reminded him," Bobrow remembers, "that there was a very famous, legendary Hot Club of France, which had nothing whatsoever licentious about it at all." The president thought for a moment. "Well—could you at least change the name?"

Overnight, Bobrow had discovered the causes he would ride for the next five decades—the cultural superiority of jazz, the rights of black people, and local neglect of local talent. He moved the show off-campus to the basement of the nearby Meany Hotel. The mob scene there soon rippled through town, and the Gay Jones Orchestra became the most popular swing band in Washington. Bobrow got the band booked into the Trianon Ballroom. Because of the

Top: Glenn Martin, Norm Bobrow, and Gaylord Jones (left to right) discuss a new arrangement, c. 1940.

Courtesy of Gaylord Jones

VICTOR
For best results use Victor Needles
27316-B
I NEARLY LOST MY MIND—Fox Trot
(Casi Me Vuelvo Loco)
(Lionel Hampton-Gay Jones)
Lionel Hampton and his Sextette
Vocal refrain by Evelyn Meyers

Victor record label, "I Nearly Lost my Mind" (Lionel Hampton-Gay Jones).

*A Message from the*

**Husky Hot Club**

*to the University Students:*

We're off the campus now, but not really. Our objective remains the same—to help make Washington students happy. That's what makes the Hot Club happy.

So we're putting on the first

**"Husky Hop"**

especially for you at the "U"

The Place?—BOTHELL WAY PAVILION, 6.9 miles north of Coon Chicken Inn.
The Time?—FRI., TOMORROW, 9:30 to 12:30.
The Band?—

**GAY JONES!**

*'Nuf said we think—only Hep! Hep!*

Left: Advertisement for the Husky Hot Club.

Jitterbugs. Photo by Al Smith

publicity generated from the Hot Club incident, people lined up around the corner. The jitterbuggers turned out in full force.

"Some of them were really spectacular," describes Jones, "throwing the gal around and under their leg and up in the air. There were some of those tunes we'd play where the whole doggone place would—I'd be worried about the floor giving way. Everybody was really jumping."

TRIANON
FRIDAY NIGHT ONLY
Dance the Gay Way with "The Sweet Swing Sensation of the West"
GAY JONES
AND HIS ORCHESTRA

TRIANON
FRIDAY NIGHT ONLY
Dance the GAY Way
GAY JONES
AND HIS ORCHESTRA
AND ENTERTAINERS
"The Sweet Swing Sensation of the West"

From 1939 to 1942, the Gay Jones Orchestra was the house band at the Trianon. The ballroom, which was becoming the nerve center of Seattle's swing era, was already a venerable institution when he started playing there. Built for $175,000 in 1927 by John Savage—the notorious crony of Vic Meyers at the Butler Hotel —and bankrolled by bandleader Herb Wiedoeft, the Trianon covered half a block at Third Avenue and Wall Street. It was the biggest ballroom in the Northwest. The dance floor, made of springy white maple, spanned 30 by 135 feet, accommodated over 5,000 dancers, and was fitted all around with ducts that sucked away stale air. Around the dance floor were 150 three-person settees; upstairs, the loges seated 300 to 400 people, and there were 16 arched, open-air balconies where lovers could retreat. In later years, Ted Harris, who managed the ballroom for Savage from 1930 until it closed in 1956, would say, "More people met their future wives and husbands at the Trianon than anywhere else in Seattle." The ceiling was draped with cloth and had a huge glitter ball, and the walls were decorated with tropical scenes. At the far end of the room was the prize of the establishment: a silver clamshell hood over the bandstand that projected sound beautifully out over the dancers. Out front, or backstage managing the autograph hounds, was a six-foot, four-inch deputy sheriff named Elmo Hudgins who loved swing enough to have requested the ballroom for his beat.

Herb Wiedoeft's Orchestra, a syncopated jazz regular on KFOA radio broadcasts, opened the Trianon in May 1927. According to local legend, the bandleader subsequently lost the venue to John Savage in a card game. At first, Savage booked sweet dance bands from the West Coast, such as those led by Vic Meyers, Owen Sweeten, and Anson Weeks. But in 1933, Savage started experimenting with national acts, bringing in Ted Fio Rito (who came in with an unknown sixteen-year-old singer named Betty Grable). Popular sweet-band leaders Guy Lombardo and Ted Lewis followed.

At about the same time, black revues featuring swing bands started to come to town, as well. Los Angeles bandleader Curtis Mosby brought his Dixieland Blue Blowers to the Rex Theatre in August 1933, in an "all-Negro revue" titled "Change Your Luck." The next year, blues queen Ida Cox visited with the show "Darktown Scandals." In 1935, three similar acts followed: "Harlem Follies," with dancer "Jazzlips" Richardson; "Harlem on Parade," with the Lennox Avenue Boys and dancer Tommy Harris (in blackface); and "Brown Skin Models," featuring what it advertised. Today, the ads for these shows featuring half-naked "brownskin beauties" and parodies of African features strike us as racist, but they were also the sincere legacy of the Harlem Renaissance, which, in great black musicals of the 1920s such as *Shuffle Along*, had affirmed Africanness in African-American culture.

In 1934, Les Hite brought his twelve-piece unit to the Paramount. That same year, Duke Ellington played the Music Hall Theater. Major Pigford, a budding trombone player who would later work with Quincy Jones, was eight years old when he attended the concert:

> *When the band came on, as each instrument played, there was a spotlight on him and it went through this blue gauze which sparkled. I thought it was pure magic. I vividly remember [clarinetist] Barney Bigard was playing a solo, and then a trumpet, and then Tricky Sam [Nanton] on the*

*trombone. He was making some of the most unbelievable sounds I'd ever heard in my life. Then this magnificent figure came out in this white tuxedo. And that was Duke Ellington. I was completely awestruck.*

Ellington's visit to Seattle was followed by Lionel Hampton's first band, on its inaugural road trip from Los Angeles. The group played the Rex Theatre, but dissolved when work dried up. "Most of the musicians decided to sign on with a ship that was taking a pleasure cruise somewhere," according to Hampton. (Hamp wasn't the only bandleader to have trouble making ends meet in the Northwest. Even Guy Lombardo lost money at the Trianon.)

In 1936, Duke returned, playing five shows a day at the Palomar (the old Rex), and Glen Gray, the great white bandleader whose Casa Loma Orchestra was one of the seminal big bands, played the Trianon. Fletcher Henderson hit the bandstand the following year. By the early 1940s, nearly every jazz name of note, black and white, had passed through Tacoma and Seattle, and sometimes Spokane: Earl Hines, Andy Kirk, Gene Krupa, Ella Fitzgerald, Benny Goodman, Eli Rice, Harry James, Charlie Barnet, Sammy Kaye, Kay Kyser, Phil Harris, the International Sweethearts of Rhythm, Roy Eldridge, Bob Crosby, Jack Teagarden, Lawrence Welk, Teddy Hill, Cab Calloway, Count Basie, Artie Shaw, Jimmie Lunceford, Woody Herman . . . they all came through. Oddly, Glenn Miller was the exception; he never got any closer than Jantzen Beach, outside Portland.

As swing caught on, more ballrooms sprouted up, including McElroy's, Parker's, the Senator, the Showbox, Faurot's, the Everstate, and the Palladium. In Fife, outside Tacoma, there was the Century Ballroom; outside Olympia was the Evergreen, a roadhouse/ballroom; in Tacoma were the Spanish Castle, on the Seattle-Tacoma Highway at Midway, plus the Cinderella, the Crescent, and the Aragon. The crowds outside the ballrooms became news items in themselves. Particularly after the war had started, witnesses report that lines of thousands streamed along Third Avenue, by the Trianon. Swing-shift dances lasted until five in the morning. A Tommy Dorsey show was moved from the Trianon to the larger Civic Auditorium, where it drew a crowd of 6,500. There

**Posters from the 1940s for concerts by Duke Ellington and Jimmie Lunceford at the Trianon Ballroom.**

**Courtesy of Don Lanphere**

**Left top:** Flyer for Norm Bobrow concert at the Metropolitan Theatre, with photographs of Palmer Johnson (left) and Gaylord Jones (right).

Courtesy of Gaylord Jones

**Right top:** Seattle's first swing concert, Metropolitan Theatre, February 4, 1940. Top row of photos, left to right: 1) Palmer Johnson, Norm Bobrow, Gordy Challstedt; 2) Andy Duryea (trombone), Herman Grimes (trumpet); 3) Mars Mercer; 4) Gordy Challstedt. Second row, left to right: 1) Joe Darensbourg, Aaron Davis, tenor saxophones; 2) Palmer Johnson, piano; 3) Frank Spencer and Irv Ashby play guitar as band watches. Third row, left to right: 1) boy and girl, unknown; 2) Andy Duryea, Herman Grimes; 3) Herman Grimes, at microphone facing left; 4) Norm Bobrow, at microphone facing right. Bottom row: 1) unknown; 2) Gay Jones Orchestra saxophone section; 3) Gordy Challstedt; 4) Gay Jones Orchestra, with Illinois Jacquet, tenor saxophone, at right end of sax section.

Courtesy of Gaylord Jones

**Right:** Corky Corcoran, Los Angeles.

were lines five blocks long in both directions.

Though Seattle teenagers no doubt would have discovered swing music on their own through recordings, they were assisted immeasurably by the promotional zeal of Norm Bobrow. The enthusiastic presenter, described by the *Seattle Post-Intelligencer* as "a young visionary who believes that swing is fraught with significance," came to jazz with a liberal, civilizing mission as well as a genuine love for the music. One way of expressing this sense of mission was to present jazz in a concert hall, with the notion of "dignifying" the art for a mass audience, an idea that had gained currency with the legendary 1938 "Spirituals to Swing" concert at Carnegie Hall. Like Bobrow, many fans felt that American racism kept jazz buried in the underworld of nightclubs. Putting the music in a concert hall would take a much-needed swipe at Jim Crow.

On February 4, 1940, Bobrow produced the first bona fide jazz concert on the West Coast, at Seattle's Metropolitan Theatre, pre-dating by four years the Norman Granz shows in Los Angeles normally credited with that accomplishment. (In part, Seattle was fertile ground for such a show precisely because the town had erected so many theaters earlier in the century.) The bill included Gay Jones and the Palmer Johnson Sextet, with Aaron Davis, Andy Duryea, Punkin Austin, Herman Grimes, and guitarist Milt Green. Bobrow was quite aware of the historical importance of what he was doing.

"I would like to see swing music attain in Seattle the same respect with which it is regarded throughout most of the country," he wrote in what amounted to a manifesto in the *Seattle Star*. "After all, swing is an American music and Seattle an American city. Why shouldn't we accept the music of our own country—or at least try to understand it?"

The concert was a resounding success, with a full house of "alligators" attending the three-hour bash. Emboldened, Bobrow planned an even more ambitious night later in the year. Lionel Hampton, at the height of his popularity after leaving Benny Goodman, was debuting a new band at the Trianon. Bobrow rented the nearby Moore Theatre and booked Johnson, Grimes, Jones, and an all-star Hampton combo, with guitarist Irv Ashby and the great tenor saxophonist Illinois Jacquet. The house went bananas.

Seven months later, Bobrow got a call from Gerald Wells, who had become president of Local 493. The members wanted to book Fats Waller for a dance at the Senator Ballroom, but they didn't think they could raise the money. Could Bobrow possibly book a concert around the same time? Fats was in the twilight of his career, but was still hot on the charts. "Jitterbug Waltz" had just come out, a novelty Fats played on the Hammond organ. The two dates would probably make it worth his while to come out. The night Fats played the Moore Theatre—July 13, 1941—Ozzie Nelson's big band was at the Trianon Ballroom and *Citizen Kane* had just opened at the Metropolitan. The show was a critical, musical, and financial success, and would remain a calling card for Bobrow for years to come as he booked dozens of national acts, including Charlie Parker and Dave Brubeck.

Meanwhile, in Los Angeles, Norman Granz was advancing the cause of jazz in the concert

hall, as well, with shows that featured a Northwest swing musician—Corky Corcoran. Tenor saxophonist Corcoran was the region's most important contributor to the swing era. Born Gene Patrick Corcoran in 1924 in Tacoma, at 15 this sawed-off Irish kid was catching rides to Seattle to sit in at the 411 Club. Guitarist Al Turay was there the night Corky came in and blew the famed tenor saxophonist Ben Webster off the stand. "Webster was mad," recalls Turay, "because he'd been drinking. He slammed his horn down." The following year, Jimmie Lunceford heard Corcoran in Tacoma and invited him to join the band. "I'll have to ask my mother," had been his reply. Corcoran played briefly with Lunceford, then joined the Sonny Dunham orchestra in 1940 and Harry James in 1941. James and Betty Grable legally adopted the underage saxophonist so he could tour with the band. James, an avid baseball fan who habitually organized intra–big-band games, is rumored to have asked Corky if he could play second base before hiring him. It was the right question. Corcoran had Babe Ruth's jersey number—3—etched on his saxophone. Corcoran became a star while he was with James. In 1944, *down beat* readers voted him No. 8 in the Best Tenor Saxophonist category. His name was featured in ads for the band, and he played on all of James' Columbia recordings.

Corky played with a swaggering, virile tone on swing tunes and—like his idol, Ben Webster—with full-bodied tenderness on ballads. He had a natural melodic imagination. His normal tone was woody and piping, with a burry edge and broad vibrato, but he wasn't afraid to

The Men About Town, c. 1942. Left to right: Dick Woodhouse, Alf Lauritsen, George Hartwell, Stan Ball, Bob Bateman, Pete Barrington; drummer (hidden), Dave Stetler.

Courtesy of Dave Stetler

abruptly alter his timbre with salty exclamations, honks, and wails. Corcoran performs on one of the most famous jazz albums of all time, *Just Jazz*, a live recording produced by Los Angeles promoter Gene Norman of a 1947 concert at the Los Angeles Civic Auditorium, with Lionel Hampton's All Stars. Corcoran's solo on "Stardust" is a tour de force in which he spits out jawbusting explosions, chuffing descending figures, and dazzling harmonic substitutions.

As is the case with so many prodigies, Corcoran's story did not turn out well. Belligerent, spoiled, and eventually alcoholic, the young tenor saxophonist habitually got into fights. He was married and divorced several times. One drunken night in Tacoma, a bus pulled up and he jumped on, thinking he was still on a road trip. Corcoran quit drinking in 1955 and eventually regained his musical stature, if not his marquee value. He appeared at the Newport Jazz Festival in New York in 1974 and presented his own group at the New York Jazz Museum. "He was such a sensitive player," recalls Fred Radke, a Seattle trumpet player who later led the Harry James ghost band. "All he ever wanted to talk about was baseball and golf, but when he put his horn into his mouth, he was so deep." He died in 1979, and Fred Radke established a scholarship in Corcoran's name at North Seattle Community College.

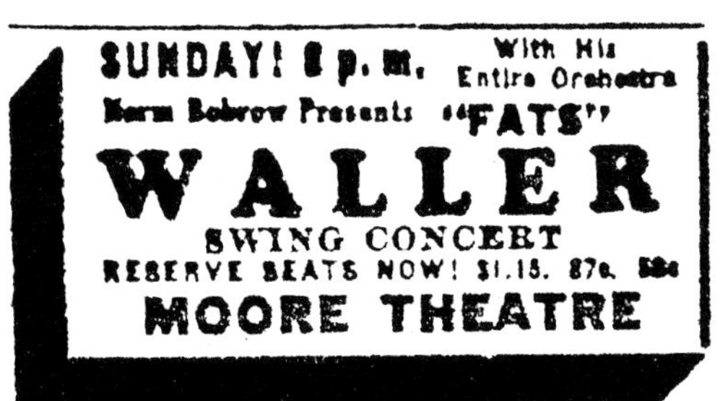


Along with Dick Wilson and Junior Raglin, Corky Corcoran was one of the few Northwest musicians who achieved notoriety during the swing era. None of the big bands that came out of Seattle became well-known. In a way, this is not surprising. Because the economic machinery of the music business—agents, advance men, critics—was far away from the Northwest in the thirties and forties, even when local bands were good, they had trouble moving into the limelight. However, quality music was being made in the region. Many musicians feel some groups deserved to be better known. Says Gay Jones' trumpeter Pete Barrington:

> *You know, I traveled a great deal after that—L.A. especially—I went to a lot of jazz concerts and I didn't hear anything, especially at the local level, that was a hell of a lot better, and a lot of it was definitely inferior to what I used to hear around Seattle. I always felt that if Tommy Dorsey or Jimmie Lunceford had heard the Gay Jones band of '38, '39, '40, he might have said, "Wait a minute here, let's get some financing, put this thing together, and get some records and some air dates." Because it was a good band. I always kind of resented that.*

Of the dozens of local musicians who had the talent to make the "big time," Jones is at the top of the list. When his band broke up in 1942, as the draft claimed its members, the bandleader struck out for Los Angeles. He got on as staff arranger for Freddie Slack, the ex–Dorsey pianist who started the boogie-woogie craze. (Bassist Tiny Martin went on to a career with the Boston Symphony.) Jones had sold several charts to Lionel Hampton, including his own theme, "I Nearly Lost My Mind," "Standing Room Only," and a riff called "Boogie Woogie." The whiz from West Seattle High also penned Slack a winner, "Riffette," which shot up to the Top Ten on the Harlem Hit Parade, and did some arranging for Dave Hargrave. Several months later, Jones was drafted. He returned home to Seattle to play club dates downtown and in Chinatown until the early 1950s.

Occasionally, he toured with Curt Sykes, who succeeded him as house bandleader at the Trianon. As the swing craze died, Jones and his wife, Mars, were drawn more and more to their second love, sport fishing. Today, still married, Gay and Mars run a successful charter fishing boat out of Port Angeles. Jones plays in a local trio, for fun. He has no regrets. "I never had the push," confesses the mild-mannered pianist, adding that if it hadn't been for Norm Bobrow, the band never would have gotten as far as it did.

Of course, as Woody Herman has pointed out, "Few of the swing-era bands . . . ever played jazz," a distinction that swing nostalgists often fail to make. What made Gay Jones stand out from other, less jazz-oriented white dance-band leaders, such as Putt Anderson, Wyatt Howard, and Archie Loveland, was his unmitigated commitment to swing—in particular, to the hot, two-beat feeling of the Lunceford band and a "fat" jazz arranging style with extra notes added to the chords for color, a style Stan Kenton and Woody Herman would make famous.

There were a few other white bandleaders who played jazz, as well. Chuck Reisdorf's organization featured drummer and vocalist Charlie Blackwell, who sang the nonsense bebop lyrics of the Glenn Miller hit "Wham!" in a Cab Calloway style. Blackwell left Seattle in 1942 and later worked with Benny Carter, Stan Kenton, Count Basie, Art Tatum, Nat "King" Cole, and Dave Brubeck. Vern Mallory, who came to Seattle during the Depression, led a hot dance band that was highly influenced by Jimmie Lunceford and Erskine Hawkins. Mallory's band was so hip that it was booked to play for black audiences at the Savoy Ballroom, on Madison. Trianon bandleader Curt Sykes toured the Northwest and provided steady work for many jazz musicians, including Gay Jones, Pete Barrington, Dave Stetler, Fred Greenwell, Red Kelly, Don Manning, and the incredible drummer Buzz Bridgeford, Seattle's version of Dave Tough, Woody Herman's rhythm ace. In 1948, Sykes' band placed No. 34 in the *down beat* poll's Best Swing Band category, largely on the strength of Bridgeford's reputation.

Sykes, Mallory, and Jones often drew sidemen straight out of high school, particularly once the war had siphoned off most of the professional talent. These high schoolers usually were already playing in kid bands, which were a breeding ground for a generation of new players.

"You could buy arrangements for seventy-five cents," recalls Manning. "We could buy those Count Basie charts, Duke Ellington charts. Glenn Miller. We had a kid band first and then bands in high school. The Men About Town were the best. And then came the Chevaliers."

The Chevaliers was a college-age dance band led by Stanton Patty. (Patty later became a reviewer and travel editor for the *Seattle Times.*) Playing saxophone in the band was a zany 14-year-old named Ronnie Pierce, whose entrepreneurial exploits later became a part of local music legend. Pierce joined the Noteworthies at Seattle's Roosevelt High School, a kid band that included pianist Kenny Kimball, trombonist Bob McDermid, and drummer Keith Purvis, all of whom would play significant roles in jazz after the war. The Men About Town was started before the Noteworthies, by fourteen-year-old trumpet prodigy Pete Barrington, who, like Gay Jones, was a big Lunceford fan. Barrington remembers:

> *Art Doll, a saxophone player from Tacoma who didn't play in the band, would sit down and laboriously transcribe these Lunceford arrangements for us, those double-timing saxophone things. Lunceford came out to an assembly at Roosevelt and we played that stuff for him. Well, he went nuts. He had us down to the Trianon that night, as his guests, and offered us any charts we wanted.*

Many of the youngsters in the Men About Town became professional musicians, including bassists Red Kelly and Hal "Champ" Champeness, who later worked with comedian/ musician Stan Boreson, and drummer Dave Stetler.

When Dave Stetler came home after a Men About Town gig and told his mother he had decided to become a professional musician, she was horrified. "I thought she was going to cut my throat," says Stetler, who has lived and worked in Seattle all his life, playing with both jazz and commercial groups. He became a professional musician right out of high school, in the International District, where he paid some dues:

> *[Combos] generally didn't have a bass because the Chinese figured if you had a piano and a drummer you had two rhythm.*

*They'd hire another horn, but they wouldn't hire a bass, which is pretty grim, from a drummer's point of view, when the bass drum is your bass note. . . .*

*At the Club Maynard, [there were] no civilians except on the bandstand. They had a little two-by-four around the bandstand. [One night], two great big girls got into a big, screaming fight right next to me, over a sailor, and one of them caught the other one by the throat and leaned her over the two-by-four and bam! her head is right on my snare drum, and she's gouging her eyes. About a half-hour later, some sailors and soldiers got into it. And now, it's like a John Wayne movie, smashing tables and bodies are flying around the floor and the guys are clubbing each other. The SPs and MPs come in and the whistles are blowing and the clubs flying and they're knocking guys on the head. They dragged out about twelve guys. Down the stairs they go. And we're playing through all of this.*

After failing an audition with the Bob Chester band because of sight-reading problems, Stetler took lessons from Shorty Clough, whose syncopated salad days with the Melody Boys had given way to teaching in a drum studio downtown. Stetler worked with Bob Harvey's band at the China Pheasant, the Marginal Way roadhouse operated by Harry Lew. Bass player Tiny Martin and trumpeter Carle Rising from the old Gay Jones Orchestra also were in the band. In 1945, Stetler took a brief look at the 52nd Street scene in New York. He was dazzled by the music but decided to come home, where he joined Wyatt Howard at the Town and Country Club.

As a young white musician, Stetler had the option of taking a steady commercial job at a place like the Town and Country when hot jazz work was scarce. Because of segregation, however, his counterparts in the black community did not.

Stetler remembers his ingenuous horror at coming up against Seattle's segregated musicians' unions as a young man: "At the time I joined the union, I wasn't even aware that there was a black union. I'd been playing at dances with [black] kids like Sonny Booker and Billy Tolles. . . . Then I got in the union and it was suddenly, 'Wait a minute, you can't have any black guys in your band.' The rules were very strict."

Though black name bands often played under the Trianon Ballroom band shell, local black bands rarely did, and black audiences were forbidden to attend, except under special circumstances. (The Trianon did not admit Filipinos or Hawaiians, either.) As a consequence, the memories of black swing-era musicians in Seattle, though nostalgic to be sure, have a somewhat more complex flavor.

Blacks were not allowed in the Trianon because owner John Savage did not want them there. He felt that it was "bad for business." During the 1920s, when he ran the Butler Hotel, he hadn't allowed blacks, and he wasn't about to change his ways for swing. On the contrary, as the black population of Washington mushroomed during the war years, many whites, like Savage, dug in their heels even more resolutely against blacks.

This dogged racial resistance was emblematic of a social upheaval taking place all over the West, where an unprepared white population, with little experience of African Americans, particularly from the South, suddenly found itself dealing with a large group of people whose accents were different, whose food seemed peculiar, and whose manners struck them as rustic.

Things came to a head at the Trianon in 1940, when Lionel Hampton's new band was booked. Hampton was well-known in both white and black communities, and, because he and Teddy Wilson had been the first blacks to play regularly with Benny Goodman, he was also something of a hero. Naturally, blacks wanted to see the band, as did the white swing alligators, who had kept their ears pressed to their radios listening to live broadcasts of the band since 1935. There were local Hampton connections, too. Hamp's new vocalist was Evelyn Williamson, who had been raised in Seattle by Noodles Smith. Her first husband, tenor saxophonist Bumps Myers, was also in the band. Evelyn's featured number was the Gay Jones tune "I Nearly Lost My Mind." Hamp's drummer, Oscar Bradley, and his alto saxophonist Floyd Turnham had also spent time playing in Seattle. The black community swung into action. They approached the Trianon's manager, Ted Harris, and pressured him to open the ballroom to blacks.

Harris responded by asking the *Northwest*

*Enterprise* to sponsor a special "Jim Crow" night, for blacks only. The editors were appalled. Why should they agree to Jim Crow in the ballroom when they were fighting it everywhere else? They refused. Gerald Wells, however, already inured to segregation as president of Local 493, agreed to the sponsorship, no doubt hoping for more cooperation down the line. The result, as with Powell Barnett's hopeful acquiescence in the original formation of Local 493 three decades earlier, was less happy. After the Hamp dance, the Trianon instituted a regular policy of hosting "Colored Folks" Monday-night dances (known pejoratively in the black community as "spook nights"), while continuing to bar blacks during the rest of the week, thereby tightening racism's hold over the Seattle music business.

Ted Harris and John Savage justified this segregation policy by disingenuously citing a Seattle city ordinance against "mixed dancing" that prevented them from admitting blacks, even if they had wanted to. For over five decades, this schoolboy's tale of a segregationist city ordinance has been repeated in dozens of newspapers and journals, but in fact it was nothing more than a cynical ruse on the part of ballroom operators to keep blacks out. No such law ever existed. That locals actually believed there was a law in Seattle against blacks and whites dancing together—and could accept its existence—says as much about Seattleites' ignorance of their own special history as it does about the general American acceptance of racism as a fact of life. For despite frequent de facto segregation, in most areas Seattle had always rejected segregation as retrograde. The state of Washington has a remarkably progressive civil-rights record, in comparison not only to the South, but to other western states.

The reason most blacks gave for moving to Washington in the early 1900s, for example, was that "Black Laws" in Oregon prohibited African Americans from owning land or marrying whites. Washington adopted civil-rights legislation before many other states did. As early as 1890, the year the state constitution was adopted, the Legislature approved a Public Accommodations Act, which provided for "equal enjoyment" of inns, public conveyances, restaurants, theaters, and other public places. Writes Esther Mumford:

> *Some of the most prominent black members of the Seattle community came here in quest of "free air." Almost without exception, they came to Seattle with expectations of a better life. They found few legal*

**Evelyn Williamson sings with the Lionel Hampton Orchestra at the Trianon Ballroom, December, 1940.**

**Photo by Al Smith**

*barriers erected against them, although race prejudice was often as effective as proscriptive laws. . . . Despite numerous obstacles to the realization of their full capacities as useful human beings here, Seattle and Washington State offered considerable improvements over the places most blacks had left.*

This is not to say that racism and segregation did not exist. Pianist Patti Bown remembers that well into the fifties, a black entertainer as famous as Marian Anderson would stay with her parents rather than undergo the humiliation of staying in one of the hotels in the International District reserved for blacks—the Coast, the Tokiwa, the Golden West, and the Mar. Restrictive real-estate covenants against blacks, Jews, and Asians—so-called red-lining—were also common, and created the segregated residential patterns that exist today in Seattle, Tacoma, and Spokane. But such policies were milder and less predictable in Washington than elsewhere—and illegal. Theater facilities, for example, were sometimes segregated and sometimes integrated. The balcony of the Palomar Theater, known as "Peanut Heaven," was reserved for blacks. At the Liberty Theater, seating was open.

During the 1940s, the Seattle tradition of tolerance between the races was put to the test. Prior to the war, fewer blacks than Japanese Americans lived in Seattle. Between 1940 and 1950, Seattle's African-American population grew from 3,789 to 15,667. It was the promise of war work—in the aluminum plants, shipyards, and airplane and electrical power industries, plus the armed services—that drew these new immigrants. What they found, unfortunately, wasn't always as hospitable as the "free air" they had hoped for. Boeing, for example, had a whites-only hiring policy, which it blamed on the charter of the Aero-Mechanics Union. As we have seen, the musicians' union was also segregated.

White migrants from the South attempted to impose their "separate but equal" customs on the Northwest; some northwesterners, panicking at the sudden multiculturalization of their home turf, found themselves chiming in. The black press bristled with angry stories. Signs saying "We cater to whites only" sprang up in all but three restaurants in the city of Bremerton. The town's Housing Authority built separate facilities for blacks and whites. (The Navy base spent hundreds of thousands of dollars constructing duplicate facilities for black families; Quincy Jones grew up in one of them, called Sinclair Heights.) The commander at the Bremerton Navy Yard recommended blacks be rerouted "somewhere else." An advertisement for Christmas help placed by the Frederick & Nelson department store in the November 12, 1941, *Seattle Post-Intelligencer* requested white applicants only. Five black soldiers were told by the owner of Tacoma's Grill Cafe, "I won't feed you in here—you'll have to go back to the Chicken Coop." The Admiral Theater, in Madison Park, attempted to eject a black family for sitting "on the wrong side of the house," and a downtown roller rink refused admission to a group of black children on a birthday outing. The Pacific Foundry Company in Renton segregated its bathrooms; the black workers struck. A race riot broke out at Fort Lawton, in Seattle, and a white soldier was lynched.

When episodes of violence threatened to erupt into full-scale riots, such as the one that occurred in Detroit, black leaders, in concert with the NAACP, appealed to the mayor, City Council, governor, and the courts. The membership of the Seattle chapter of the NAACP increased from 85 to 1,550. A Committee for the Defense of Negro Labor's Right to Work at Boeing Airplane Company was formed. Eventually, jobs began to open up. By the summer of 1944, Boeing had 1,600 black workers.

It was against such a background of racial struggle that the swing era unfolded for black musicians and fans.

For whites, the Trianon Ballroom was a gala, glittering dreamland, one that would provide nostalgic memories for decades. For blacks, it was an off-limits place where one could attend dances only on "spook night." For whites, after-hours clubs were an optional, "colorful" recreation. For blacks, they were the only places where a musician could make real money and where black fans were allowed to enjoy the music. For whites, the swing era was a great job at the Boeing Company or Kaiser Aluminum, with plenty of money to spend to see Tommy Dorsey. For blacks, it was joining the NAACP to see if the Renton Foundry would stop trying to shove them into a "colored" bathroom.

For black musicians, the main issue was finding a place to work. Though apparently there was no written policy at Local 76 prohibiting blacks from working in downtown venues, they didn't, and every musician, white or black, who played during this era speaks with certainty of "turf," "jurisdictions," and "color lines." Downtown—the area north of Yesler and west of Eighth Avenue, which included all the theaters—was for whites only; "cross-town," from the First Avenue dives up through Chinatown and the hub of 12th and Jackson, was for blacks, as were the all-night roadhouses outside of town. Exceptions were few.

Ken Boas, a young white player who worked mainly with black musicians, became so furious at the segregation policy that he resigned from Local 76 and joined Local 493. Other white musicians, including Bill Rinaldi and Traff Hubert, followed suit. The black union, for its part, was pretty loosely run. Gerald Wells ran the union out of his house, though much of its business was conducted from the Blue Note "clubhouse" at 14th and Jefferson, where musicians congregated to jam after their gigs and take advantage of the twenty-five-cent drinks. At its peak, the black union probably had no more than 150 members. Emmett Lewis took over the presidency in 1954, tightened it up, and eventually presided over its merger with Local 76.

From the white point of view, the benefit of maintaining two unions was that it reserved the best-paying, "legit" gigs—in the pit for touring theatrical shows, and in ballrooms and downtown hotels—for whites. The after-hours "dives" were left to black musicians. Musicians in the white union sometimes defended this exclusionary practice by charging that black musicians had crude musical skills, couldn't read music as well as whites, played out of tune, and were not dependable. This was a racist and self-reinforcing argument for perpetuating segregation and obviously not accurate as a generalization. But there was enough truth to it, especially from a white point of view, to keep the stereotype alive.

Part of the conflict was cultural. Jazz has a different set of standards than European music. To play it effectively, a musician must develop an inner metronomic time sense, the ability to improvise, a personal sound with varying timbres, and a rhythmic attitude usually called "swing." The white European tradition, on the other hand, stresses rigid intonation, strong sight-reading, section playing, and conformity.

An early band of Al Pierre's in Portland, 1930.

Left to right: Russell Jones, Jimmy Adams, Charles Wilson, Al Pierre, unknown, unknown.

Courtesy of Al Smith

As long as the unions were segregated, white musicians had the advantage of being able to freely mine the skills of black musicians in after-hours clubs—sitting in, collecting ideas, and honing their improvising jazz skills—while blacks did not have the reciprocal privilege. How could a black musician learn to sight-read effectively or play in section with standard European intonation when he was denied the right to play in the very situations where he might learn to do so? This one-way street guaranteed that while white musicians could learn to play jazz, black musicians would continue to be barred from the "legit" jobs. When whites in turn went on to make a great deal of money playing and recording jazz, black musicians were understandably bitter.

Leaving the "dive" jobs to black musicians did have an ironic effect, however. Many of the gigs in the black clubs paid five-fold in tips what the downtown jobs could yield. "All those others, you go down there and make a little piddling salary, maybe twenty-five dollars a week," recalls trumpet man Bob Russell. "And we were doing better than that. At least a hundred to a hundred and a half, anywhere in there. So that's one reason why we stayed with those after-hours clubs."

The band that epitomized this situation—and, indeed, the black swing era in Seattle—was led by a man who had been in the area since 1932 and had paid his dues on the Depression scene up and down the coast. Though Al Pierre did not start a bona fide swing band in Seattle until 1944, his Portland group, the Royal Knights, must count as the first indigenous black swing band in the Northwest. Pierre, who learned to play piano from his mother, grew up in Midland, a rural suburb of

Tacoma, in a big house, formerly a hunting lodge, with a stone fireplace and a winding staircase. In the fall, the boys would hunt pheasant with their father in the nearby woods. Musicians often came out for rehearsals and fried-chicken feasts.

Pierre left Tacoma early in his career. He worked in Los Angeles with Charlie Echols in 1926 and Joe Darensbourg in 1927. Duke Turner, the Oakland drummer, remembered playing with Pierre in Palo Alto, California, perhaps even earlier: "Al was a very good pianist. . . . You put a piece of sheet music in front of [him] and [he] could play. [He] played in a dance style and improvised quite a bit."

In 1932, Pierre based himself in Portland, where he again played with Darensbourg; in February of that year, Al Pierre's Royal Knights played Seattle's Washington Hall; in August, they hit Tacoma's Valhalla Hall. At this time, vocalist Russell Jones and drummer Chester Wells were working with Al. Leonard Gayton left Seattle for Portland to do the same.

Pierre was well-liked, an amiable, professional leader who could easily get the best from his musicians. As a player, he was a competent stride man who knew his scales in all twelve keys, but his style seems to have been somewhat ornamental. "Al was a 'butterfly' piano player," says trumpeter Leon Vaughn, who worked for him. "*Phur-ur-ur-ur*—you know. He wasn't the real jazzy piano player with a steady beat, like Mary Lou Williams." Joe Darensbourg's main recollection of the pianist was that he owned a tuxedo, which other musicians habitually borrowed: "We used it so much the knees was stretched out of shape; look like they had a couple of footballs in there. It was all frayed to hell. Anybody would see us, they'd say, 'I see you got Al's tuxedo!'"

Pierre seems to have settled in Seattle around 1934. For a while, he owned his own club at 12th and Yesler, Al's Lucky Hour. In 1943, his band had a steady gig every Tuesday at the Savoy Community Center, on 21st Avenue and Madison. In the same era, he put together his own book of arrangements for a little big band and started working after hours at the Union Club (also called the Marine Club) at First and Cherry. The Union Club was a large speakeasy with a long bar, a dance floor, and a casino where you could often find prizefighter Eddie Cotton's manager rolling dice. The waitresses wore drape trousers and gabardine shirts.

Pierre used mostly stock arrangements of commercial and jump tunes, and relied on table singers—usually Palmer Johnson's old cohort, Russell Jones, and torch singer Dee Dee Hackett—to please the crowd. The band was impeccably rehearsed. A 1944 acetate recording of the tune "Jammin'" reveals the Pierre band as fiery and vivid, with nattily executed lines crisscrossing each other in an excited, Lunceford-like manner. The lineup included Pierre on piano, Bill Rinaldi on bass, Vernon Brown on drums, William Joseph on alto saxophone (later replaced by Terry Cruise), Jabo Ward on tenor saxophone, Bob Russell or Leon Vaughn on trumpet, and Major Pigford on trombone. "It was primarily a dance band," remembers Al Turay, who sometimes sat in after his own gig. "But it was a black dance band, and their type of dance music was jazz."

**Top:**
**The Little Harlem Rondivoo, in Tacoma, 1935. Pianist is unknown.**

**Courtesy of the Tacoma Public Library**

**Bottom:**
**The Al Pierre Band at the Yukon Club, 1944–48. Left to right: Vernon Brown, Al Pierre, Bob Russell, Terry Cruise, Jabo Ward.**

**Courtesy of Wanda Brown**

According to saxophonist Jabo Ward, who worked with Pierre from 1943 to 1949:

*The band played tunes by Ellington, Basie, and blues things. We played at the Union Club from 1 a.m. 'til 5 a.m. Sometimes Harry Fox sang bawdy songs. He'd get to singing [at one table] and everybody would want to know, "What is he singing over there?" So they'd be wanting to go over there and listen, too. We'd tell 'em, "I'll be over to your table in a few minutes."*

*The place used to be packed. They had two bands. We were the late band. People were ready to hear music by the time we got there. They were ready to dance and drink. After a while, it'd be just like a little floor show. The band would play a number, then we'd have the singer come on and do two or three numbers, then the band would play, then they'd feature one instrument, then we'd go back to the dancing. In other words, one musician would be in the spotlight. Floor show, table singing, band.*

Pierre himself played in the flowery, California manner, but his band was steeped in modern, Kansas City swing. Vernon Brown, Bob Russell, Leon Vaughn, Jabo Ward, and William Joseph all came to Seattle from the Midwest. The importation of these five players marks a stylistic turning point in Seattle music, the birth of a blend between California and midwestern influences.

Vernon Brown may have been Al Pierre's greatest gift to Seattle. Brown grew up around the great nascent swing bands in Kansas City and performed intermittently with several minor ones, including those of Grant Moore and Eli Rice. In 1943, through a mutual friend, Pierre got word to Brown that he would pay him $100 a week if Vernon would come to the Northwest. "Vernon Brown was the Jo Jones–

**The Vernon Brown band at the Marine Club (aka the Union Club), 1945.**

**Left to right: Bob Russell, Roscoe Weathers, Vernon Brown, Jabo Ward, Bill Rinaldi, Lucky Cook.**

**Courtesy of Bob Russell**

LOOK! LOOK! LOOK!

# DANCE

*Brotherhood of Sleeping Car Porters*
*and Ladies' Auxiliary*

---

**Tuesday, July 31, 1945**

**9:00 p. m. to 1:00 a. m.**

*Presenting*

## AL PIERRE'S ORCHESTRA

*Featuring That Mad Drummer*

**VERNON BROWN**

*and the Three Rhythm Jesters*

---

**W. O. W. HALL**
528 S.W. 11th AVENUE

**ADMISSION**
**$1.50 Inc. Tax**

type drummer—Kansas City–style," remembers Leon Vaughn. "He would catch up real quick on your riffs and back you with the drums. Vernon accentuated what you were doing. He was one of the best big-band drummers that I played with."

Brown became one of the city's legends, a steady timekeeper who sat behind his cymbals and played all night, sipping from a bottle of Thunderbird. Bob Russell remembers that, unlike many other musicians, who were led to ruin by liquor, Brown seemed to thrive on it:

> *Vern would drink just as much as you'd pass him and it never bothered him. He'd sit there with his big self, just sittin' there, never strain. He got so that he would get tired of straining and he'd get comfortable. When he'd get tired, he'd work on the sock cymbal. When he'd get to working on that there wasn't no need to bother him, 'cause he was going to do nothing but keep a steady rhythm all night. I don't think I know of anybody around here that was any stronger than he was.*

"They'd say that once that he set a time, you could not shake him from it," remembers his wife, Wanda, a white vocalist whose career paralleled Vernon's. "He would never go away from that. He was steady. He wasn't a flamboyant-type drummer. He didn't throw his sticks up in the air and all that sort of stuff. He just kept good time."

Bob Russell, trumpet "screamer" supreme, brought a K.C. resume to the Pierre wind section paralleled by no one else in Seattle. An opinionated but gentle fellow whose health was failing badly when he was interviewed in 1989, Russell was born in Zion, Wyoming, and raised in Kansas City and Denver. Russell says that despite the legends about Bennie Moten, Harlan Leonard, Count Basie, and others who were reshaping jazz in the 1920s, there wasn't a lot of steady work in Kansas City.

"Moten organized a band and talked to me about joining, but I decided, no, I'd stay right where I was at, playing in theaters and nightclubs. Right across the street [from the club where he was working] was the Lincoln Theater. We'd finish there around 11:05 or 11:10 at night and I'd go right across the street, go upstairs and play until four or five o'clock in the morning." Russell worked for Harry Dillard in a small pit band. Everyone in the band could read: "There wasn't no goofin' there. Wasn't no sliding over and saying 'Let's play this.' You played what was on that sheet." At intermission, the band played jazz.

Sometime around 1928, Russell went out with Bennie Moten's chief rival in Kansas City, George E. Lee, who billed himself as the "Cab Calloway of the West" and later hired the young Charlie Parker. One of Lee's calling cards was his gold-plated instruments. Even his tuba was gold. Russell didn't care for Lee's ostentatiousness ("All that gold just didn't look right to me"), but indirectly, the shiny array of instruments led to a chance meeting that jazz fans are still grateful for.

One day, when the Lee band was playing Parsons, Kansas, a young man named Wilbur Clayton happened to come to the dance. Recalls Clayton:

> *We all went to the dance and as soon as I entered the hall I saw all of those beautiful instruments standing on the bandstand and I flipped. . . . I stood in front of this band and watched them as they began to tune up. I became rooted right to the spot. During the dance, I talked with*

*one of the trumpet players in the band, Bob Russell. He was one cool cat and so sharp. He had four or five different kinds of horns in front of him. He took me under his wing a little bit and told me how much money they made, what nice times they had, and how he enjoyed playing. He had just joined George's band and was a well-known trumpeter among the "territory bands," as they were called. . . . After talking to Bob I said to myself, "This is it! I'm going to get a trumpet."*

Of course, Wilbur was none other than "Buck" Clayton, who became not only a seminal stylist in the Basie band, but a leader in his own right.

While Bob Russell was in Texas with the Lee band, Grant Moore and His Original New Orleans Black Devils sent for him. With Moore, Russell toured a circuit of ballrooms in Iowa, Nebraska, Oklahoma, the Dakotas, and Minnesota. Russell soloed on two sides Moore recorded, the driving "Original Dixieland One-Step" and "Mama Don't Allow," a novelty number.

Russell left Grant's band and joined Tommy Fox, a nightclub bandleader in Milwaukee, then played with Burt Bailey, in whose band he worked with Vernon Brown. Brown referred Russell to Al Pierre.

"He was experimenting with mouthpieces," recalls Major Pigford, a trombone player familiar with such practices. "He would take a mouthpiece and shave it down crossways so with that very little cup he would play high notes." Leon Vaughn remembers Russell as "one of those guys who could stand up and take ten choruses above high C." Russell worked with Al Pierre until the band broke up in 1951, then worked in a big band with saxophonist Terry Cruise throughout the fifties and sixties while holding down a day job at Seattle City Light.

Leon Vaughn was the other trumpet player who worked a lot with Pierre. Like Bob Russell, Vaughn, who was born in Topeka, Kansas, had a deep background in Kansas City music, though jazz took a back seat to college before he came to Seattle. Vaughn's story reads like a textbook illustration of the way racism forced many African Americans into the music business.

Leon Vaughn is a compact, straight-talking fellow with a head for statistics, a knack for telling a good yarn, and a great impatience with anything he calls "bull." Retired after 25 years as a site engineer for Boeing, Vaughn is an avid gardener (he grows herbs for a local restaurant), an ex–elk hunter, and a proud grandfather. The walls of his spacious home above Madison Park are covered with plaques

**The Terry Cruise Orchestra at Dick Parker's Ballroom, c. 1957.**

**Left to right: Johnny Moton, Terry Cruise, Bob Moffat, Kenny Pernell, Junie Bradford, Carlos Ward, Dick Thorlakson, Bob Russell, Ish Dotson, Don Glenn, Leon Vaughn, William Joseph.**

**After playing for many years with Al Pierre, Terry Cruise led his own orchestras throughout the 1950s. Note alto saxophonist Carlos Ward, who later led the saxophone section for Abdullah Ibrahim.**

**Courtesy of Don Glenn**

and certificates marking his many ventures into community service.

Born in Topeka, Kansas, in 1915, Vaughn graduated from Washburn University with the intention of becoming a civil attorney. When he finished college, he won a statewide legal contest, the Corpus Juris.

*The winner was supposed to join one of the big white firms, in Topeka. When I went in there I had an appointment with the top partner. He looked up and saw me and said, "We don't need the janitor up here at this time." I knew then that it was a dead issue. At that time the only thing a black lawyer could do was criminal law and I didn't want to do that.*

The idea of becoming a musician grew on him slowly. When he was four, his mother started him on piano; at seven, he started trumpet, playing in the school concert band and marching band.

*When I was twelve years old, Jo Jones came to town. He was playing what they call "Ten Cents a Dance" at the Kansas State Fair. His trumpet player got appendicitis and had to be operated on, and they wanted somebody that could read music, so they recommended me. I can remember the first tune I ever played as a jazz musician was "When Kansas City Kitty Smiles at Me."*

*Jo Jones took me down to Kansas City, but before he took me away my mother made me promise I would play music in the summer, but in the fall I had to come back and finish school. So I faithfully went back and finished all of my school. Jo Jones paid us twenty-eight dollars a week. When I brought that home, my dad went through the ceiling. He was making seventeen dollars with four kids. From then on, I found out I could put my brother and sister through school with my money from playing music.*

Vaughn formed a small band. He played around Kansas City clubs and on jaunts outside of town, sometimes working with luminaries such as Mary Lou Williams, Ben Thigpen, or bassist Adolphus Alsbrook, who also later moved to Seattle. Vaughn greedily drank in the new sounds, hanging out at the Sunset Club and the Reno Club, listening to Jay McShann, Big Joe Turner, George E. Lee, Bennie Moten, Count Basie, and the rest. "We would grab up anybody we could—Wynton Graham, Ben Webster, Cliff McTier, Jay McShann. Take off on a little gig in the surrounding towns. None of the bands had steady employment. It was all one-night stands."

After a couple of brief stints in Omaha with Cluss Webb and his Spiders, and the Nat Towles band, Vaughn worked in Minneapolis for a while, then got a telegram from Colorado, where Alsbrook was playing with Eli Rice. A Midwest tour with the Rice band landed him in North Carolina, where he remembers finding the Pettiford family band stranded (including the great bassist Oscar Pettiford), and helping to take up a collection to send them back to Minneapolis, where Vaughn returned, as well.

As the nation moved toward war, musicians were subject to conscription unless they took on vital work in factories or in the transportation industry, so in 1940, following his friend Alsbrook's lead, Vaughn got a job with the railroad.

*I gave away all my old band uniforms—I must have had eight or ten of them—but I kept my Bach trumpet. We were running on the* Great Northern Empire Builder *from Chicago to Tacoma. We'd catch the train in Minneapolis, go to Chicago, then come back and "walk across the country." We were waiters. We would stop in Seattle for the day. Then the next morning we had to put new groceries in the train for the ride back across the country. We came out here a couple of times in December. The grass was green, the roses were blooming.*

**The Vern Mallory Orchestra, USO Club, Second Avenue, Seattle, 1943–1944.**

**Left to right: Don Lindley, Bob Mullay, Jabo Ward, Marv Thomas, Chet Pietruszewski.**

**Courtesy of Don Glenn**

Clarence Williams sings with the Leon Vaughn band at Basin Street, 1948.

Left to right: Ralph Stephens, Leon Vaughn, Aaron Davis, Clarence Williams, Milton Walton.

Photo by Al Smith

*It had been thirty-six degrees below zero for thirty-six days in Minneapolis. So I decided I had enough of that!*

One night in Seattle in 1942, at the Porters and Waiters Club (a.k.a. the Black and Tan), Leon met a white bandleader named Bud Storm who needed a singer/entertainer to spice up his group. Vaughn, who had done some ballad singing with the Rice band, agreed to play the part. His railroading days were over. With Storm, Vaughn played trumpet and sang, doing the popular Bunny Berigan feature "I Can't Get Started." Vaughn stayed with Bud Storm for ten months before joining the Al Pierre band in 1943 or 1944.

Leon remembers Pierre's group as having a raw and bluesy Jay McShann sound and featuring novelty songs favored by gamblers, such as "Ace in the Hole" and "Big Fat Butterfly"—the latter a silly blues takeoff on "Poor Butterfly" that crowds went crazy for.

*I had never heard this song. But it got so famous around here. They had a lot of songs that people in this section, especially from Alaska, the gamblers, liked. I can remember one night when one of the landladies from Alaska who ran one of the big whorehouses up there came in. She started off giving us twenty dollars for a song. Well, there's a guy in there that's a gold miner and a fisherman. He says, "Don't play that bitch's song, play mine! Here's a hundred dollars." So they started a little bidding war. We ended up making something like eight thousand dollars in that one night. We stayed 'til about ten o'clock in the morning. It was real wild, something that I'd never seen before.*

When he left the Pierre ensemble, Vaughn formed his own band at a basement club on Maynard, the Basin Street club, using Adolphus Alsbrook and ex–Pierre alto man William Joseph, among others. Vaughn also occasionally used Clarence Williams, a blues singer/guitarist who was still working in Seattle in the 1990s, as well. Even after Vaughn went to work

Eastside Hall, early 1950s; originally the Gala Theatre, later called the Savoy Ballroom, then Birdland, at 2203 Madison Street.

Billy Tolles and the Savoy Boys played here in 1941. Ray Charles, T-Bone Walker, Larry Coryell, Jimi Hendrix, and others played here in the 1950s and '60s.

Photo by Al Smith

for Boeing in 1948, he continued to play music with Pierre, Terry Cruise, and Joe Gauff, and in his own big band composed of other Boeing employees during the 1950s.

Terry Cruise, the lead saxopohone player for Al Pierre—and, later, the emcee and front man for the band—was originally from Los Angeles. "He had a tone big as a house," according to Bob Russell, who contributed arrangements to Cruise's band in the 1950s. "He wasn't too fast as far as getting it down the horn. But he had such a beautiful tone. And he could swing it for you. And when he would swing it, he still kept it beautiful."

Cruise, who also played excellent clarinet, later became a board member of Local 493 and managed the Blue Note. He also worked with saxophonist Jabo Ward at the New Chinatown, an after-hours place on Sixth and Main, and he played for many of Norm Bobrow's shows. In the fifties, Cruise went to work for the state liquor board, days, and led a big band that included many of the sidemen who had worked with Al Pierre. He died in 1988.

The other reed man in the Pierre organization was Ulysses "Jabo" Ward, a remarkable musician who turned a late start into an asset, studying music so intensely he pushed past his swing-era counterparts into the world of bebop. Ward, like Vernon Brown, was from the Midwest. While Ward did not play music as a teenager, he was nevertheless exposed to the best of the swinging Southwest sounds.

A tall, thin man who speaks in nervous fragments that are a bit like the bebop phrases he plays, Ward was born in Kansas City in 1918. He sang in the school glee club and in a quartet. He remembers his father playing blues piano in the living room and his mother singing in the church choir. He heard Kansas City locals Count Basie and Thaymon Hayes, and "Harlan Leonard and the Kansas City Rockets was a local group that we used to go and hear all the time and dance to," he recalls.

Jabo's father was a Pullman porter. In 1937, he gave Jabo a ticket to Seattle to visit a couple of schoolmates and look for a job. Jabo wound up staying for three years, working in a lumber mill near Onalaska before joining the merchant marine. He returned to Kansas City briefly in 1940. Once back in Seattle, he boarded out.

Ward had started teaching himself the trumpet, but on one of his trips to Alaska he decided he really wanted to play the saxophone. "As soon we docked in Seattle, I went right downtown and bought a Buescher sax. I went to a teacher, Frank Waldron, and paid for lessons in advance. I'd take a couple of lessons ashore and then be on a ship for eleven days. Because we were moving troops to Alaska, and not cargo, the ship would be empty on the return trip. I'd go up into my stateroom and play and play. That's how I learned."

From Waldron, Jabo learned the "countermelodic" method of improvising:

> *You learn the melody and then you play your own melody behind that note. [Waldron] was technical, very technical. He liked finger independence. He loved execution. He loved tone quality and, above all, he wanted you to practice. He didn't have any time for students that didn't practice. And he could tell when you practiced. I've heard him tell his students, "Have your*

*parents come over with you next time, that's right. Because you're wasting your parents' money."*

Other models of technique and style for Ward at the time included saxophonist Aaron Davis and trumpet man Frank Walton. "These were my idols," he says. Ward was studying both tenor and alto saxophone—he would later take up flute, as well—but for Al Pierre, he generally played the baritone sax. Ward played at first with a white band led by Vern Mallory, then joined Al Pierre, with whom he stayed for six years, from 1943 to 1950, playing six nights a week at the Union Club. During this period, he also played in nearly every other after-hours venue.

*When we got off from work, we'd usually tend to look for the jazz places. So there's where 14th and Jefferson [the Blue Note] came in. That's the place to unwind. Or we'd go to the Basin Street, where we could have sessions and everything. There's where we let our hair down and played the things that we wanted to play. "How High the Moon," "All the Things You Are," "Indiana"—you could take those tunes and increase the tempo and make them jazz.*

Ward tells of one late-night jam when Vido Musso, Kai Winding, and Ray Wetzel, in town with the Stan Kenton band, came down. It was those after-hours sessions, oddly enough, that led Ward into an obsession with golf: the top of the piano in his Central District home is covered with golf trophies.

*The guys who played at the Union Club would go out in the mornings after playing all night and play a round of golf. I thought it was pretty stupid, 'til one day they got me out there as a kind of joke, and I got hooked. When you play golf you have to relax and concentrate at the same time; you have to overcome obstacles like sandtraps; you have to challenge yourself to get better every day. It's just like music.*

Swinging instrumentalists such as Ward and Vernon Brown were the musical backbone of Pierre's band, but what kept the customers coming back night after night were the vocalists, Russell Jones and Dee Dee Hackett. The vocalists were also the key to making tips. A good night could net several hundred dollars in requests in the kitty—a lard can, in the case of the Union Club.

Saxophonist Billy Tolles remembers watching the Al Pierre band work the tables:

*They had two singers, a man and a woman. They always had a saxophone between the band and the singer to play a little phrase to let the band know what the singer wanted to sing, what key it was in. Maybe this big pimp would have ten girls here and he'd be supporting the party, and this girl would want "How Deep Is the Ocean" and this one would want "Poor Butterfly," or "Stardust," or "Body and Soul." They'd be there at that table twenty or thirty minutes, just singing for them and getting three-, four-, and five-dollar tips. They could never go to their pocket, they had to keep it in between their fingers. When they'd get their fingers all full of money, they'd come back and drop it in the big, galvanized tub, sitting right here by the side of the piano player. And boy, in the middle of the night, man, Al Pierre would be taking his foot, stuffing that money down in that tub. They'd take home eighty, ninety, one hundred dollars a night [apiece].*

Dee Dee Hackett, who came to Seattle from Oakland, was by some recollections not only a crowd-pleaser, but a stylist of national caliber. In Palmer Johnson's words:

*When Ella first came out with "A Tisket . . ." Dee Dee was around here singing up a storm, and the band was way up in tempo and she was out there scatting. She had a sense of timing, man. Dee Dee was the best I ever seen. Absotively! She learned her singing as a child in church, like spirituals and stuff. She was a singer, man.* A SINGER. *She loved to swing with the band. You could see her bouncing, and never, you could never lose her, no matter what riffs you made.*

Hackett often worked with Palmer Johnson at the Two Pals, on Jackson Street, but most of her work throughout the 1940s was at the Union Club. One of her specialties was blues with truly "blue" lyrics, no doubt a favorite with gold miners and Yukon types. "She could sing all them nasty songs," remembers Russell.

"Good, bad, nasty. When we had Dee Dee singing with us, why, it was just buy, buy, buy, buy, buy, man. Give her five, ten . . . and guys think nothing of it."

Russell Jones kept the rounders happy, too, with songs that celebrated the gambling and hustling life, including the perennial "Ace in the Hole," plus "True Blue Lou" and "Carry the Torch." Born a year before Palmer Johnson, Jones had grown up in the same Los Angeles neighborhood, serving his apprenticeship in the Charlie Echols band in 1931, along with Bumps Myers and Kid Ory. The following year, Jones was in Seattle playing the African-American Mid-Summer Ball, but appears to have returned to Los Angeles during the 1930s. Jones worked with Palmer Johnson as well as Al Pierre. In 1943, a *Seattle Times* review of a Paramount Theater show with Johnson noted Jones' "rich baritone voice" and his "ability to use [it] well, as he demonstrated in his second number, often sung by Paul Robeson, 'Without a Song.'" With Jones' voice and Johnson's boogie-woogie piano, the hour-long act brought the house down every night. They took it to the Cave, in Vancouver, British Columbia, and to Portland's Cloud Room, then returned the following year to the Palomar Theater in Seattle. When Palmer left town for Alaska, Jones continued to sing with Al Pierre, at the Union Club, Charlie Beale's Rizal Club, and the Basin Street; in February 1946, the singer performed with a ten-piece group called the Basin Street Band for a big dance at Finnish Hall.

In 1949, Al Pierre's little swing band moved from the Union Club to the Showbox Theater, on First Avenue. But the swing era was over; business started to wane. When the band's bookings were cut from five to four to three nights a week, Al Pierre, like Johnson, began to look north to Alaska. He found the band a regular job in Fairbanks, at the Green Lantern, but his musicians didn't care for the cold climate and remoteness of the Far North. The band gradually fell apart.

"We went up there with six pieces," remembers Russell. "Dee Dee was with us. Everything but the bass player—Vern, Al, Jabo, Terry, myself, and Dee Dee. Dee Dee came back first, then Jabo. Then I come down in 1950. And that's when the band was split up."

Al Pierre became ill in Alaska; he died the next year.

Stylistically, Al Pierre's group represented the pinnacle of black swing in Seattle—danceable music with hot solos, table singing, and, due to the small market it catered to, some accommodation to the popular taste for romantic and novelty songs. Though Pierre and his arrangers did not generate an original style, the group afforded an authentic opportunity for young players to learn what real jazz music was. The band also had a genuinely local flavor, with its emphasis on the Alaskan rounder tunes.

Al Pierre spent most of his working life in Seattle along First Avenue, in the white honky-tonk area dominated by sailors and transients. There was a reason for this. The Central District boasted dozens of small after-hours clubs, but there was no major ballroom or social center for African Americans, comparable to the Trianon Ballroom, in their own neighborhood. This glaring lack of recreational facilities was a major civic issue for blacks.

"There wasn't too much for us to do, as a group, unless you were a musician, or some sort of hustler," recalls Buster Clayborn, an African American whose father had been a friend of Noodles Smith's and who worked with a citizens' committee to integrate Seattle's Jefferson Park golf course in the 1940s. "That's the thing that bothered me more than anything else when I come out here. There wasn't nothin' for us to do."

As early as the 1920s, black leaders had approached the City of Seattle to complain about statutes and encumbrances that barred the way of black entrepreneurs attempting to

**Top: Billy Tolles as a teenager, when he started with the Savoy Boys.**

**Courtesy of Billy Tolles**

**Bottom right: Betty Marshall was a pianist and Billy Tolles a tenor saxophonist, but here they are shown competing as a jitterbug team.**

**Photo by Al Smith**

create social venues in African-American neighborhoods. One city ordinance prohibited dance halls east of Eighth Avenue or south of Dearborn Street. In 1920, Powell Barnett, who had railed against segregated unions a decade before, chaired the Committee to Establish the East Madison YMCA, arguing that the Central District needed a neighborhood place to keep black youth from getting into mischief. (Ironically, his opponents argued this was a "Jim Crow" idea, because the new "Y" would be all black!) Barnett's success on the YMCA issue would later mean that kids like Quincy Jones and Gerald Brashear had a neighborhood place to try out some of their first music. (In the mid-1930s, "Doc" Hamilton had made the same argument, though admittedly from a rather different perspective.)

In 1939, members of the black community took a petition with 118 signatures to the City Council and hired an attorney, requesting a dance-hall license be given to Ira F. Norris, who owned a tavern at 21st and Madison. He was turned down.

Two years later, a neighborhood entrepreneur named Lemuel Honeysuckle succeeded where Norris had failed. Though the City Council didn't officially grant him a dance-hall license until February 1946 (by which time it was under new ownership), Honeysuckle went ahead and remodeled the Gala Theatre at 21st and Madison (originally a roundhouse for streetcars), named it the Savoy Ballroom, and started throwing Saturday-afternoon dances there. For the next two decades, in its numerous incarnations as the Savoy, the House of Joy, and Birdland, this establishment, along with the East Madison YMCA, would ring with the sounds of black swing, blues, jazz, and rock 'n' roll. The Trianon might have Curt Sykes and Gaylord Jones, but the Savoy would host Al Pierre, Billy Tolles, the Jive Bombers, Bumps and Charlie Blackwell, Vern Mallory, Al Hickey, Tootie Boyd, Banjoski Adams, Ernestine Anderson, and Dave Lewis, among others.

The first black swing band to debut at the Savoy Ballroom, in December 1941, consisted of a bunch of high school kids led by tenor saxophonist Billy Tolles. Called the Savoy Boys, it would be the spawning ground for a new generation of hot swing-to-bebop players who took the music to the next stop beyond Al Pierre.

Billy Tolles is one of the more colorful characters in Seattle jazz. Arrogant, natty, vain, and restless, Tolles combines a college education with a streetwise wit, a pairing that has led him into all kinds of social and musical situations. Tolles seems more like the kind of saxophone player you'd meet on the road with James Brown than with Duke Ellington, but he is a complete master of the instrument. Born in Waukegan, Illinois, in 1924, Tolles came to Seattle when he was five. (His father was a cousin of the midwestern territory bandleader Nat Towles, though their names were spelled differently.) Tolles grew up in the East Madison District, with all its attendant cultural aspirations. He remembers:

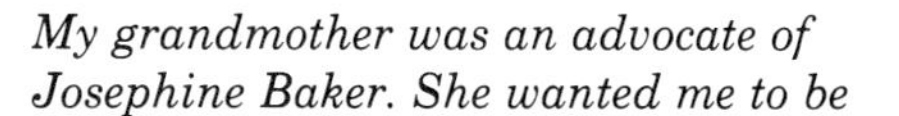

*My grandmother was an advocate of Josephine Baker. She wanted me to be*

Palmer Johnson and Russell Jones
To Be at Palomar Theater
Week Starting May 10

*artsy and have the "right kind of background" so that I could do something else besides wait tables or be a domestic, which is what most black people were doing in those days. I started on piano at about the age of nine or ten, then I studied dance with Syvilla Fort, a disciple of Katherine Dunham. But the real music came from Mount Zion Baptist Church, where I sang in the junior choir. That's where I got my foundation.*

Tolles learned to play trumpet from a friend of his mother's, and in high school played in the marching band. He also played in a swing quartet, the Four Sharps, formed by Charlie Blackwell, with classmates Gerald Brashear and Sonny Booker. A couple of years later, he lost his front teeth playing football, and switched to sousaphone. Tolles was a popular dancer. He and his jitterbug partner, pianist Betty Marshall, won prizes for their performances. But up to this point, Tolles had had no desire to be a professional musician, nor had he considered playing the saxophone. Then he saw Illinois Jacquet at a Norm Bobrow concert at the Moore Theatre.

*That Illinois Jacquet almost made me jump out of the balcony, man. I've never been so roused up in all my life. From that day on, I started listening to the saxophone. One afternoon, I was in Bill Washington's basement, lagging tax tokens to the wall, and I beat him out of some money. I accidentally kicked open this old saxophone case. We opened it up, and here's this moldy, C melody saxophone. I said, "I'm going to take this saxophone for security 'til you pay me." I took it home and rubbed it all up and put rubber bands on it and made all the notes work, and put some kind of reed on it and played "I Love You Truly," right off the bat. Bam! It scared me. That was the end of my piano career. I was thirteen years old.*

*I went over to Gerald's to show him what I was doing and, lo and behold, here's Gerald sitting on his back porch, playing a C melody saxophone that he had got from someplace. So we set out there and played duets. Gerald was probably about a year or so older than me. We decided that we should have a swing band. We all met down at Gerald and Buddy [Brashear]'s house.*

At first, the group copied Count Basie records. The saxophones would go into the kitchen and the rest of the band would stay in the living room. Then Tolles began to write simple arrangements of his own.

*I wrote out parts for Charlie Barnet's "Redskin Rumba" and Erskine Hawkins' "Uncle Bud," and I came back and taught each one how to play his part at a rehearsal. Boy, that neighborhood jumped! People came from miles around. The police came! That was the beginning of the Savoy Boys orchestra.*

This was in 1941. The personnel of the Savoy Boys was Billy Tolles, Gerald Brashear, Floyd Franklin, and George Francis (the son of vocalist Lillian Goode), saxophone; Don Alexander, Carl Valley, and Sonny Booker, trumpet; George Turner, Major Pigford, and Billy Anderson, trombone; Bobby Catlett (Buddy Catlett's brother), guitar; Delbert Brown, drums; and Kenny Boas, the only white member of the group, piano.

Don Manning, who was playing over at Roosevelt High in the white counterpart to the Savoy Boys, remembers the Savoy Boys playing Charlie Barnet's version of "Cherokee." "Boy, did they swing. They just swung like maniacs."

"It was a good band," according to Major Pigford. "We played a lot of things from written music, from orchestrations I guess that Billy bought. Then a lot of things we just put together by head. We featured Bobby Catlett on 'Floyd's Guitar Blues.' Sonny Booker could play the heck out of 'Stardust.' Buddy Brashear played 'After Hours.' We also did 'Tuxedo Junction,' 'Stompin' at the Savoy,' and 'Blues in the Night.'"

The Savoy Boys got their name, their first gig, and early guidance in the ways of the street from Lemuel Honeysuckle, who had owned a pool hall on Madison Street. "Honeysuckle and his brother owned a lot of property on Mercer Island," remembers Sonny Booker. "Honeysuckle always had a nightclub or a bootleg joint. He was like a pillar of the community. He'd put jobs up on the board if you wanted to work a certain place downtown. He had good connections with City Hall."

Sonny Booker, Savoy Boys trumpeter, became pretty well-connected himself. Booker is a slight, slow-talking man with delicate features, a sweet smile, and bedroom eyes. He is remembered by fans from the 1960s as the proprietor of the Checkmate nightclub, at 23rd Avenue and Union (at one time the informal clubhouse of the Black Panthers), and as the co-owner of the Silver Fox limousine company. A generation of Hollywood stars also knows him as a fencing coach, a sport at which he is still a master teacher. But in his youth, Booker was a star quarterback at Garfield High School who discovered that his charm and wit could win him as good a living on the street as his trumpet. His sense of the district, its characters and milieu, has a special, knowing quality.

Born in Canada in 1923, Booker was raised on a farm by one of the only black families on Mercer Island, just southeast of Seattle. He started music as a bugler for the Boy Scouts. At Garfield he was given a trumpet by guitarist Al Mitchell; lessons from Frank Waldron and a chair in the high school band followed. While at Garfield, Booker and Gerald Brashear took a quartet into the New Chinatown, a legitimate Chinese restaurant at Sixth and Main with a thriving bootleg business upstairs. Booker was astonished at how much money he could earn, and how much respect he suddenly commanded on the scene as a musician: "Musicians, they were the glamorous part of life, in those days. The peak of the jobs for the black community were like mailmen and porters and skycaps. So if you weren't a musician or a pimp, you were riding on the boats or a shoe shine or a skycap, or on the railroad."

Booker's comment illuminates the important point that before the civil rights movement, playing jazz was one of the few economic opportunities available to African Americans. Booker's easy parallel between playing music and selling sex—"if you weren't a musician or a pimp"—also highlights that the various "hustling" professions of gambling, pimping, and bootlegging, viewed as lowlife criminal activity by mainstream society, were entrepreneurial choices open to blacks. These were often the professions chosen by the most intelligent, ambitious, and magnanimous people in the community, who became highly respected regardless of their dealings. Booker continues:

*Prostitution was always a part of the black community, in a sense, because that's what we ended up doing to make money. But the black pimps that you had in those days were different than what you have today. They were like gentlemen. They dressed up. It was a way of life. A lot of the pimps were musicians—musician/pimps. Most of the pimps and hustlers were the pillars of the society, because they had the money to donate to the church. The pimps were respected and everybody knew they were pimps, and the whores, everybody knew they were whores. They were dressed up and they had money and everybody talked about them "going to work." It was just an understood deal, a way of life.*

**The Savoy Boys at the Savoy Ballroom, c. 1941.**

**Buddy Brashear, piano; Sonny Booker, trumpet; Billy Tolles, tenor saxophone; Gerald Brashear, alto saxophone.**

**Photo by Al Smith**

Booker freelanced throughout the late forties, playing with Al Pierre, Jabo Ward, and bandleader/promoter Bumps Blackwell, then left music in the early fifties, when he and fellow Savoy Boy George Francis became the first black bartenders to work in a downtown restaurant, the Barbecue Pit. In 1952, he moved to Pasadena, where he studied bass at the Westlake School of Music, played with Gerald Wilson's big band and saxophonist Teddy Edwards, and worked as a fencing coach for movie stars. In 1965, he returned to Seattle to open the Checkmate. In the early nineties, Booker was a silver-haired gentleman with a bit of Jackson Street mischief still in his eyes, who occasionally showed up at Lofurno's restaurant to blow a few tunes of sweetly crafted music.

Sitting behind Sonny Booker in the Savoy Boys was Major Pigford, a huge, imposing trombone player. Pigford's career was notable in that it extended through the three major 1940s black bands—the Savoy Boys, the Al Pierre Orchestra, and the Bumps Blackwell Junior Band. Born in 1925, Pigford started out on clarinet but switched to trombone at age eleven. He asked Frank Waldron to teach him, but Waldron didn't feel qualified to teach trombone. Through studying the standard method books and by playing in the Washington Middle School band, Pigford learned the instrument. At Garfield High School, music teacher Parker Cook was his mentor. According to Pigford, the Savoy Boys got together for the express purpose of playing the Garfield Funfest, which had a nightclub theme in 1941. Then the group started working at the Black and Tan.

There, Major and his mates discovered the same high-rolling world that had opened Sonny Booker's eyes. "Those clubs," he says, "some nights you'd sit around and make nothing but scale—eighty-four dollars a week. Other nights, here comes a big spender and every time he wants to hear a tune, he throws ten or twenty bucks in the kitty. Sometimes I'd go to school with five or six hundred dollars in my pocket!"

Like many others, Pigford learned to play his instrument through jam sessions, sometimes taking it on the chin, but always returning for more:

*You ran your scales at home, but the only place you could really learn to play was at a jam session. I mean sessions of the Jazz at the Philharmonic type, where you start a blues number, then anybody could come in and play two or three choruses. If you played halfway decently, they let you play. If you didn't, they'd tell you to get off the stand. You see, they'd make you feel so bad if you messed up, you had to go home and learn it if you wanted to keep on playing. Say, "Hey man, look past your foot so you can come in on time," or "Listen to yourself, you're playing flat," you know, whatever.*

*One night, an all-girl band called the Darlings of Rhythm were playing at the Black and Tan. Quincy [Jones] and us, we all went down to hear them. I was drinking a lot. I got to feeling real good, and somebody said, "Hey, man, go up there and blow against that trombone player!" I didn't want to have no woman playing no trombone, you know. I hauled out my little horn and went up on the bandstand. They were playing some blues. I played one chorus, then she'd do the same thing I blew. I looked at her and then I blew what I thought was something a little more difficult. And she played what I played and also played something even a little more difficult. Pretty soon . . . "The hell with this!" I put my horn up. Well, the trombone player was Melba Liston!*

Major Pigford went straight from the Savoy Boys to Al Pierre's band, later playing with a group Pierre put together for a locally mounted black revue, "Blackbirds." He then joined the Bumps Blackwell Junior Band, which nurtured the next generation of Garfield kids—Quincy Jones, Buddy Catlett, and others. When the Blackwell band broke up, Pigford shipped out to sea, playing in a band in Yokohama. In 1953, he gave up music and moved to Detroit, where he earned a degree in biology. He returned to Seattle in 1974 and began working as a bookkeeper for Pacific Northwest Theatre Associates and playing private parties and dances with an eight-piece band, The Mixed Bag.

The Savoy Boys stayed together until the fall of 1943, when Tolles left town to attend A & T (Agricultural and Technical) College, in Greensboro, North Carolina. Some of the other sidemen in Billy Tolles' extraordinary "kid band" who went on to pursue music careers include

Floyd Franklin, who played rhythm and blues gigs in Seattle in the early fifties; Gerald Brashear, who became, at least briefly, the most successful and certainly the best bebop saxophonist in the city; Ken Boas, also a top early bebopper and an intimate of Ray Charles; and, of course, Tolles himself.

The world of music these young men faced after returning from the war was much changed. Once the boys came home, the vogue shifted from swing to vocalists. Peggy Lee and Frank Sinatra replaced Tommy Dorsey and Benny Goodman as the public's idols. Soldiers came home, married, and stopped dancing. Ballrooms began to close. Money did not flow so freely. In addition to the new sweet vocals, three principal genres emerged to replace swing—bebop (or "progressive" jazz), lounge trios, and rock 'n' roll. Bebop quintets inherited and expanded upon the tradition of the featured swing combo, which had stepped out in front of the bandstand during the swing era to play a hot tune or two. Rock 'n' roll was a commercial distillation of the blues-charged shuffles and jumps played by the post-war "little big bands" of Louis Jordan, T-Bone Walker, and Jack McVea. While bebop and rock 'n' roll were worlds apart—the former became difficult "art music" that demanded attentive listening, while the latter was simple and direct music for dancing—they both shared the common root of the swing band, which had, for a while, combined the two functions of art and dance. The piano or guitar lounge trio, developed by Nat Cole, was an extension of the big-band rhythm section, combining a modern approach to the keyboard with the once-over-lightly style of the Kansas City Six. The development of these post-war styles was influenced, at least in part, by an economic pinch that forced bandleaders to cut down from large groups to small.

The new styles also expressed the freedoms won by the black community after the war. Bebop asserted the intention of African-American musicians to think of themselves as artists and intellectuals, not grinning entertainers. Rock 'n' roll signaled that blacks would express in public the raucous blues culture they had previously kept to themselves. Nat Cole's sophisticated piano and smooth crooning let the world know there was an upwardly mobile, black middle class as suave and cool as—or cooler than—the white elite.

The intimacy of the new musical styles reflected a change that crossed racial boundaries—namely, a shift in mood that occurred after the war. Gay Jones' trumpet player Pete Barrington captures it nicely:

> *You know, when the war ended, a great deal of sentimentality went out the door. There were songs during the war about the soldiers and their girlfriends and the loneliness. That kind of disappeared when the guys came back. And I've always thought this contributed to the demise of the big-band thing. Guys wanted to go to a small place, with an intimate little group, three or four guys. They weren't interested in competing at the ballroom level. They wanted to sit down and have a few drinks and talk to their lady.*

All of the post-war styles emerged along Jackson Street between 1946 and 1951—sometimes in the same band—even as swing bands themselves continued to hang on. A great, cacophonous swell came over the town as bebop, southern blues, swing, rhythm and blues, piano trios, and even Dixieland revivalist groups played all night up and down Jackson, from First to Fourteenth, and along the Madison Street hub between 21st and 23rd. Musicians moved to town from Florida, Texas, West Virginia, Louisiana, and Chicago, bringing new sounds and ideas with them.

When Billy Tolles came back to Seattle after the war and heard the Al Pierre band again, it sounded old-fashioned. "I said, 'Boy, that style is going out, man. That's that old-time "comp," playing the bass note and the chord [stride piano].' I had been in New York and heard piano players like I was trying to play. Quincy played piano like I wanted to play. And Ray Charles. People like that. I knew I wanted to be more modern than that."

The after-hours scene was headed for its zenith.

# 5
# ERNESTINE ANDERSON and the first beboppers

Imagine a time when Seattle, which now rolls up its streets at 10 o'clock, was full of people walking up and down the sidewalk after midnight. When you could buy a newspaper at the corner of 14th and Yesler from a man called Neversleep—at three in the morning. When limousines pulled up to the 908 Club all night, disgorging celebrities and wealthy women wearing diamonds and furs. When "Cabdaddy" stood in front of the Rocking Chair, ready to hail you a cab—that is, if he knew who you were.

Since the war had begun in earnest, the district had gone plain wild. Whatever a young sailor or soldier wanted—liquor, drugs, gambling, women—he could pretty much get on demand. There were clubs with full casinos upstairs—roulette wheels, blackjack, craps—and poker games that ran night and day. There wasn't a brand of liquor you couldn't buy. Women? There were gentlemen pimps behind and in front of the bar; sometimes they doubled on the bandstand, too. Even heroin and cocaine were for sale. According to pianist Gerald Wiggins, who was stationed at Fort Lewis during the war,

> *Seattle was a hot town then. Believe me. You could get anything you wanted. It didn't make any difference. They had a guy, he'd come by your home and take your order. You want Johnnie Walker or Seagram's? You tell him. Half-pint, fifth, quart. He'd bring it to you. The music was good and money was like dirt. It was everywhere. Talk about high rollers. You couldn't believe it. You know, boom time. Shipyards and all this. Guys didn't know what to do with their paychecks. They did everything but go home.*

Trumpet player Leon Vaughn says that in 1948, if he started walking up Jackson from First Avenue, by the time he reached Fourteenth, he had passed thirty-four nightclubs. Veteran establishments such as the 908, Two Pals, Congo Club, Showbox, Black and Tan, Yukon, and Union clubs were still going. In addition, new venues had opened, including the Washington Social Club, the black Elks Club (relocated from Madison Street to Jackson Street, near Sixth Avenue South), the Savoy Ballroom, Club Maynard, and the Basin Street, Rocking Chair, Blue Note, New Chinatown, Spinning Wheel, and Mardi Gras. There were bars where jazz came and went, as well, like the Forty and Eight Club, the Submarine Room, the Aeromarine Club, the Tuxedo, the Athens Club, and the Green Dot. The military bases, too—Fort Lawton, Fort Lewis, Sand Point Naval Air Station, and McChord Air Force Base—hired musicians for both enlisted men's clubs and NCO clubs.

Many of these spots were full-fledged cabarets, with a floor show, fancy décor, doormen, and waiters. Others were simply joints set up as an excuse to sell bootleg booze. As white bassist Chuck Metcalf remembers:

> *There was this tremendous pressure during the war to have liquor on Sunday and liquor after hours. So what you had then was a lot of little clubs. A lot of them were like a little hole in the wall . . .really a small place with just a bar in the corner of the room that would be set up as a bandstand with round, plastic-covered tables and some chairs and a space cleared away for a dance floor. It would be kind of crowded and there'd be a jukebox and there would be a band.*

Large or small, the clubs brought out the customers. "Along Jackson Street, it was almost like Mardi Gras," says Al Turay. "Musicians would be traipsing up and down the street with their instrument cases, going in one club, sitting in, and going from one place to another." According to Wanda Brown, then a "dice girl" and singer who later married drummer Vernon

Brown, "You could practically walk out of one door and walk right into another one."

"It was a very serious, New Orleans–kind of feeling," says white saxophonist Freddie Greenwell. "Just gala whoopee-time, all night long."

Since liquor was still an illegal business, to flourish it had to be subsidized by either organized crime or City Hall. In Seattle, there was no "mob." The boys in blue were on the take. The amusing colloquial name for this institutionalized graft was the "tolerance policy," which meant that in exchange for police "tolerance" of alcohol, gambling, and prostitution, operators would pay fixed prices on a regular basis.

Al Hilbert, a Spokane native and nephew of bandleader Edythe Turnham, started working as a card dealer at the Basin Street club when it opened in 1940. His boss, Dave Levy, paid a professional gambler to teach Hilbert how other gamblers cheated. Recalls Hilbert:

*He made me go to a man who showed me how to run up a hand in poker and deal seconds and to read the cards that were marked. Then he gave me the game. I got forty percent of all the take in this game for two years. Completely run for two years, twenty-four hours! I got ten percent of the other shifts, because I was the head of it. The game was mine. So I made a lot of money.*

While surreptitious gambling went on behind closed doors, anyone could play the "Chinese lottery" out in the open. A form of keno in which customers bet on daily numbers, the Chinatown lottery was a popular form of entertainment that yielded hefty jackpots. Lottery headquarters was on Maynard, across from the Basin Street. Sonny Booker remembers:

*The Chinese lottery was funny, because you could look right in the window. There was a storefront. They'd turn this thing up and the dice would fall down, and the numbers would come down. You could watch.* Bloom, bloom, bloom, *these little dice would fall down. They'd be marking the numbers all in Chinese.*

As a dealer, bartender, and, later, assistant club manager, Al Hilbert became a savvy fellow, familiar with all aspects of the tolerance policy and how its system of payoffs worked.

"Someone got six hundred [a month] for gambling and they got six hundred for the liquor," explained Hilbert. "The policemen on the beat were supposed to get twenty-five dollars a week."

Every once in a while, to keep up a good front for the public, the police staged a raid. It was all quite routine. They would call in advance, and an employee—usually the bartender—would be chosen as the designated arrestee for the evening. As a precaution, Hilbert had all of his bartenders fingerprinted in advance at the police station, so they wouldn't have to waste time downtown when they were arrested.

"When the bartenders got busted," says Al, "we'd give him an hour, so he could stop someplace and get him a hamburger on the way back to the club. The jail was not that far from Maynard and Jackson. And all you had to do when you went down there was sign your name."

"It's an old, old story for many of the prisoners," reported the *Seattle Times* in a 1940 exposé of the system.

*They stand around for a few minutes in the booking office until their regular bondsmen post necessary bail. Then they are freed. . . . Almost without exception—it is always the same group of men who are defendants. They trot in and out of the jail and in and out of Judge Knott's court with surprising regularity. . . . The addresses at which they operate are usually typed on the complaints.*

Though Seattle had no organized crime in the 1940s, the tolerance policy and many of the clubs were controlled by small-time hoods. The most notorious was a dapper but menacing fellow named "Russian John" Lasso, who specialized in the clip joints along First Avenue, including the Yukon Club, where Al Pierre played for a while. Lasso had come to Seattle from Russia by way of Alaska, and he spoke with an accent as thick as his cigars. He liked ladies with furs and large diamonds, sported a fifty-dollar hat and expensive suits, and always wore a gold four-leaf clover on his lapel. John made sure he was well-connected downtown. When a rival tried to compete for the peep-show business on the strip, he got the cops and a crooked judge to set up his rival on a drug rap. He was also rumored to have a homemade collection of "dum-dum" bullets.

"He owned a club I worked in called the Cabin, in Tacoma," recalls drummer Jack Foy. "He was married to a White Russian girl, a singer, the whitest blonde you ever saw in your life. She kind of took a liking to me, which he didn't like, so one of the guys in the band told me I better find another gig. I did."

Though fellows like Russian John were occasionally arrested, essentially they operated with impunity. Periodic public outcries against the speakeasies led to police crackdowns, but soon enough, everyone would be back in business. A month after a particularly gruesome triple murder at the 410-B Tavern (which had been "raided" twenty-two times), a Times columnist spent a whole evening in illegal establishments and even received directions to the clubs from policemen.

Despite what sounds like a dangerous underworld atmosphere, almost everyone who spent any time on Jackson Street in the 1940s reports that it was surprisingly safe. Wanda Brown describes the scene this way:

> *You could walk up and down Jackson Street and you didn't have any fear. . . . I used to carry my whole bankroll up Jackson Street, used to go in the alley away from Jackson over to Maynard to catch a cab to come home. By myself. Nobody ever bothered me. I'd just be swinging this bankroll in my hand. And everybody knew I was a dice girl. They knew I had money in there. I used to go up to the black Elks Club and I'd sit there with the bankroll and open it up, and pay for my drinks out of it.*

Jackson Street was not only safe, it was racially relaxed to a degree that would be startling to a contemporary observer.

"For people who came of age in the 1960s," says Chuck Metcalf, "it's really hard to imagine what race relations were like in those days. As someone who was totally naive, going into this club where practically everybody was black, I can't think of any time when I didn't feel totally safe."

Jim Gilles, a white pianist who played the black Elks Club in the early 1950s, echoes the sentiment: "In those days, it was actually easier to mix racially than it is now. Even though there was strict segregation, it was like the back-door thing that everybody understood and nobody paid any attention to. On that particular scene, it was very harmonious."

Seattle's racial tolerance was not lost on mixed couples, for whom Seattle became—and remains—a beacon. Drummer Leonard Gayton recalls friends coming to Seattle from Portland because interracial marriage was illegal in Oregon. On the Jackson Street scene, mixed couples were common: Wanda and Vernon Brown, Leon and Lorraine Vaughn, and Al and Dorothy Hilbert are three examples.

This easy give-and-take between the races in Seattle's nightlife district had a profound influence on music. Barriers between black and white traditions were never as clear-cut as they were in other western cities, such as Los Angeles, where a "cool" white school evolved in contradistinction to the "hard bop" played by blacks. In Seattle, the music of both blacks and whites tended to merge toward an agreeable middle, resulting in a melding of traditions that later was felt worldwide in the work of Jackson Street denizens such as Quincy Jones, Ray Charles, and Bumps Blackwell.

While Seattle's reputation as a harmonious place for racially mixed couples sizzled on the underground wire, few people outside the city knew it was also a hot spot for nightlife. This turned into a lucky break for fifteen-year-old vocalist Ernestine Anderson, whose father, ironically, was in part trying to get her away from the nightclub scene in Houston when he moved to Seattle in 1944.

Like thousands of Americans, Joseph Anderson was searching for a big paycheck in the shipping industry when he came to the Northwest; and like thousands of African Americans, he was seeking a better life—away from the South—for his wife, twin daughters, and two sons. Joseph was a fanatical blues fan who often spent his evenings listening to records by Bessie Smith and Lightnin' Hopkins. He sang bass in a male gospel quartet. Music was part of his life. But ever since Ernestine had won a talent contest at the Eldorado Ballroom, at the age of twelve, she had thought about nothing but singing and jazz. Her grades were slipping.

> *I got my first professional job when I was twelve. My godmother entered me in a talent contest. At the time, I only knew two pop songs. They were "Sunny Side of the Street" and "So Long," a song that was very popular at that time, written for servicemen going off to war. I won the contest and got to sing at this ballroom in Houston, one night a week—with a chaperon,*

*of course. I would go every Thursday night and do my two songs and they would give me all the pop I could drink. People would throw big silver dollars on the stage. I can remember trying to stay out of the way. . . . This Eldorado Ballroom where I won the contest used to have dances for the kids on Sunday. Big, big huge ballroom, upstairs. Russell Jacquet [Illinois' brother] had a seventeen-piece band there, and it was bad. I l-o-o-o-oved to dance. I used to go every Sunday and dance and dance and dance until I just dropped.*

Concerned that his daughter was slipping onto the wrong path, Joseph wrote a letter to his old quartet partner, Joe Denman, who had moved to Seattle, and asked what the situation was. A few weeks later, Denman wrote back. "Anderson—Come on up. There's plenty of work, the weather's mild and there's no nightclubs for a hundred miles around!" Denman was right on two counts, anyway, but he obviously hadn't taken a walk down Jackson Street lately. The action there would be the undoing of Joseph's plans, and the making of one of the great vocal careers in jazz.

Ernestine Anderson is a petite woman with a stunning, youthful complexion and a cheerleader grin that belies her age. She stares out from a firm presence with strength and candor, though one gets the feeling she would rather laugh, which she does often and fetchingly. Her conversation is punctuated with responsive "Yeah's" and evenly accented "You know's." Her voice is deep and soft. Sometimes her sentences trail down to a close, like dying phrases of music. Overall she gives a feeling of warmth, vulnerability, and a perhaps sorely won sense of self-preservation.

Seattle was a big shock to her, after Texas. Since Houston was segregated, Anderson had never been around white people. The local kids found her accent a curiosity. She soon made friends, however, and before long was teaching everyone in school the Texas Hop.

The word spread that Ernestine could sing. Two weeks after she'd arrived, the son of the very man who had assured Ernestine's father Seattle was a dead town took her to the YMCA on 23rd and Olive Way and introduced her to Sonny Booker and Gerald Brashear. When the two young hipsters saw this cute Texan gal wearing penny loafers and bobby socks, pleated skirt and sweater, they enthusiastically invited her to sing.

"I don't remember what I sang," says Ernestine today, "but they asked me to join the band. I told them my father would never allow me to sing on dance jobs. But somehow, they talked him into letting me do a few gigs, on a trial basis. My father said, 'You must keep your grades up. If your grades start to suffer, no more working.' "

Soon, Sonny and Gerald had Ernestine working weekends with their band, playing parties, weddings, and bar mitzvahs. Bumps Blackwell, the local promoter and bandleader, noticed her, and started placing Anderson with the bands he booked at the Washington Social Club, Finnish Hall, the 908, and, occasionally, the Trianon Ballroom, to open for a national act. Blackwell took Anderson under his wing, making sure she wasn't hassled at the clubs.

"I remember they had this security lady on the door at the Washington Social Club," says Ernestine. "When I'd come to work, she would turn her head and look the other way. This place got raided several times and we had routes that we would take to get out of the clubs. Many times, I would be outside the club, sitting in a car watching them load up the paddy wagon. I'd be the first one they got out of these places."

One night in 1946, without waiting for Blackwell's cue, Anderson ventured into the Basin Street, a huge speakeasy full of smoke with a floor show and a crowd full of rounders ("Adults went there," she says, with mock awe), and introduced herself to the bandleader, Ernie Lewis. Lewis was a pianist and union honcho from Oakland who was making waves on the West Coast with a nimble new sextet. The group included the remarkable alto saxophonist Pony Poindexter and tenor man Vernon "Pops" Buford, plus Walter Oakes (bass), Warren Thompson (drums), and Earl Boatley (guitar). Pianist Gerald Wiggins played when Lewis was away on business. (Boatley also played trumpet with Andy Kirk, under the name Earl Thompson.) Lewis was an excellent pianist with an ear for the new, once-over-lightly Kansas City Six style that had caught on with modern players. The band smoked. He was also a powerful, well-connected figure who would become involved in strengthening black locals and helping them amalgamate with the white unions. Hooking up with Lewis set the stage for Anderson to make the jump from sometime-kid singer to full-time professional.

"Bumps was trying to hold her," says bassist Wyatt Ruther, who had come to Seattle by way of Fort Lewis. "But he couldn't hold her very long after Ernie Lewis got up there. Ernie started exposing her to some of the other people that were coming to town. And then she took off."

Basin Street had opened in 1940, when Davey Lee, a local businessman, won a stake playing the Chinese lottery. The club was on Maynard, just off Jackson, in a basement that extended from the Bush Hotel to the area underneath what is now Hing Hay Park. Al Hilbert ran the card game at street level; below was the nightclub. Though it was an after-hours club, Basin Street was a tightly run ship with strictly enforced rules. As you entered down the stairs, the first person you saw was the bouncer, Gorilla Jones, an ex-middleweight champion and an old beau of Mae West's, who still sent him a fresh white carnation every day. On the wall behind Jones hung a sign: STAY WITH YOUR PARTY AND OUR SERVICE IS YOURS, a rule aimed at keeping people at their tables, to discourage quarrels.

The club held about 200 and, unlike the 908 Club, was open to people of all colors. At the height of its popularity, twenty waiters and five bartenders worked there full-time. The music began at noon with a single pianist, graduated to trios at three, and a four-piece band at nine, followed by the main attraction—the Ernie Lewis band—at 1 a.m. The after-hours set lasted all night, six nights a week. Every once in a while, out-of-town acts came in, including the Ink Spots, Dexter Gordon, the great tap dancer Teddy Hale, and Sammy Davis, Jr., who at that time was working with his uncle's vaudeville group, the Will Mastin Trio. Jabo Ward considered Basin Street one of the two or three places where, musically, players felt they could let their hair down. Floor shows with chorus girls and exotic dancing were a specialty, including a drag act in which one dancer flung another around by the hair. The club's habitués included an eccentric fellow named Harold Curry, who came in nightly with a pet turtle on a leash, and another guy who routinely brought a bucketful of silver dollars.

"He had two bodyguards bringing them in," according to Leon Vaughn. "When we'd play, he'd throw a whole handful at you. You had to tell him to 'Watch it! Don't hit me with that stuff!' "

The women who danced at Basin Street also had a colorful idiosyncrasy, as told vividly by Vaughn:

> *On the last number of the evening, everybody played a solo and then got off the bandstand. The last solo was taken by the drummer. I don't know why, but he seemed to instill in these chicks the idea to come out, pull up their dresses, and dance. That used to be one of the things that people came down there to look at. I used to say, "Show your linen, baby! Show your linen!" And they would!*

This was the after-hours atmosphere in which the seventeen-year-old Anderson was learning the art, and the business, of singing jazz. One of the biggest things she learned there was how to "work the room."

> *From the stage, I could see people coming down the stairs. In those days, there were lots of pimps and prostitutes, people from the sporting life. They would be out with their number one girl for a good time. What you would do was learn everybody's favorite song, so when these hustlers would come down the stairs, their song started playing. This made them feel good. That was a big tip for you. I learned a lot of songs that way.*

Even though Davey Lee paid the beat cop weekly to keep his poker game and bootleg business afloat, occasionally there were raids. The young singer found the atmosphere intriguing.

> *They had a light in the dressing room that would flash when there was a raid. One night, I was dressing with these two dancers and the light flashed. They grabbed me and shoved me under the table and pulled the drapes. I heard this running and romping and people trying to get away, but I couldn't see anything that was going on. It was exciting.*

Anderson made a strong first impression on anyone who heard her during this period, both for the purity of her voice and her surprising versatility.

"Ernestine sounded like honey at dusk,"

recalls Quincy Jones. "Yes, Lord. She could kill 'Lover Man' and 'Body and Soul.' And she didn't do too bad on 'Big Fat Butterfly,' either. 'All of Me.' She was a killer."

Anderson had been raised on home-fried Texas blues, but the melodies of popular songs such as "How Are Things in Glocca Morra?"—and a yen to improvise on the melody—came naturally to her.

> *My family was blues people. They loved the Bobby Blue Blands and B. B. Kings and Muddy Waters. They had stacks and stacks of old blues records. We had an old Victrola that you had to wind up. Whenever bands would come—Jimmie Lunceford, Andy Kirk, Cab Calloway, Basie—they would go. I would hear them talking about them the night before, about how crowded it was. When I was a little kid in Texas, they had this one record by Bessie Smith that my mom and dad said I used to sing all the time—"Bumblebee, bumblebee. . . ."*
>
> *When I went to audition at the Eldorado Ballroom, the piano player asked me what key did I do these two songs that I knew in. I automatically said C. It turned out to be the wrong key. So I improvised around the melody, because my grandmother had told me that if I wanted to be a professional singer, once you start singing, you don't stop. When I finished, one of the musicians told me I was a jazz singer.*

By 1946, Ernestine had become a thoroughly modern devotee of bebop and of the beboppers' favorite singer, Sarah Vaughan, whose polished technique, huge range, and improvising ability paralleled the advances in instrumental jazz.

Anderson is known currently for her raspy, dark sound, but in the 1940s her voice was lighter and clearer and her style more "ingenue" than "wise woman of song." Norm Bobrow still waxes eloquent over the teenage Ernestine, whom he preferred even to Vaughan.

"Ernestine had that vulnerability," he says. "I didn't hear that vulnerability in Sarah. The people that had heard the story of Ella [Fitzgerald]'s discovery, you know, when she was fifteen, sixteen at the Apollo, playing with Chick Webb, it's almost like this was what it was like. Ernestine was just a spellbinder."

NORM BOBROW PRESENTS

STARRING IN CONCERT

THE ERNIE LEWIS BAND ★ THE GAY JONES COMBO
THE WEIR TRIO

Gerald Wiggins - Pete Barrington - Ernestine Anderson - Dave Tuttle - Dave Stetler - Frank Pressnall - Pony Poindexter - Lee Howe - Freddie Greenwell - Earl Boatley - Vernon Buford - Juanita Cruz - Ruben Walker Johnny Warren - Warren Thompson - Rollie Morehouse - Walter Oakes J. D. Weir - Ernie Lewis - Gay Jones

METROPOLITAN THEATRE
SEATTLE

MONDAY, NOVEMBER 4, 1946

*The Next Concert in the Northwest Jazz Series Will Be Announced in the December Issue of Norm Bobrow's*
JAZZ LETTER
*Available at All Northwest Music Shops and Mailed by Request*

Bobrow did everything he could to promote Anderson, calling her the "new Ella," praise that at one point drew fire from a local critic. Reviving his concept of all-star, all-local jazz shows, in November 1946 Bobrow put Ernestine in front of the Ernie Lewis band at the Metropolitan Theater on a blockbuster show with Gerald Wiggins doing a solo piano set; the Gay Jones combo; a trio fronted by Ernestine's only serious rival, Juanita Cruse; and a virtual catalog of Seattle sidemen, among them Fred Greenwell, Rollie Morehouse, and Dave Tuttle. Ernestine sang "Rich Man's Blues" and "Can't Help Loving That Man." Over the next two years, she enjoyed star status on Bobrow's shows, singing the tunes each week from the "Lucky Strike Hit Parade."

After this taste of stardom at home, Anderson became smitten with ambition.

"I was determined to make it," she says. "I told my folks that when I was eighteen, I was going to go on the road with a band."

As it happened, she was right. In early 1947, Ernestine Anderson became the first of the

Garfield High School crowd to be picked up by a name band.

*Shortly after my eighteenth birthday, the big band of Johnny Otis came to town. Paul Quinichette heard me at a jam session and he asked me to come down to the theater where Johnny was working. When I got there, Johnny said, "They tell me you sound like Sarah Vaughan." I auditioned and got the job.*

*Johnny at that time had a seventeen-piece swing band. That was a really rocking band. Paul Quinichette. Preston Love. Some "bad" players. He was on tour with the Ink Spots, Honi Coles, and Cholly Atkins and Slappy White and his partner Lewis, I forget his last name. Comedy team. And a woman singer named June Richmond. I talked them into letting me come on the band earlier than I was supposed to, so that I could watch June Richmond, learn from her. This woman was one of my idols. She had a great voice and great control. She used to sing, "Figaro, Figaro, Figaro. . . ." She was something else. Every performance, she would have people just laughing. She could do to an audience whatever she wanted. She just had 'em. I watched her and tried to figure out how she did this. She was a big lady. I did my apprenticeship, ironing her gowns in the dressing room and wondering if I'm ever going to get around the whole length and breadth of this gown!*

After three months of ironing, Anderson finally got to sing. She toured with Otis for six months, winding up with an extended engagement at the Club Alabam in Los Angeles. When Otis disbanded there, Ernestine decided to try her luck in California. She had a rough time of it.

"When I left home, my folks bought me some alligator luggage. I'll never forget it, because I'd sit there [in Los Angeles] and think, 'Who needs luggage if you don't have no clothes?' I was just so poor. I was there for over a year. In all that time, I never got out of that area."

It wasn't such a bad place to be. Central Avenue in Los Angeles was popping, much like Jackson Street. After-hours clubs flourished. Dexter Gordon was coming on strong; so were Howard McGhee and Wardell Gray. There were jam sessions every Monday night, sponsored by Gene Norman. Cedric Henry, a mild-mannered junkie affectionately known as "Shifty Henry," kept an eye out for Ernestine.

*Shifty was like a big brother to me. He was always trying to help me. He was a great jazz bass player. Somehow, he always managed to work and he always managed to be on top of it, even though he was a junkie. I knew when he was high, but he always took care of business and he was always very protective of me. He got me my first recording. He had to find me. That's how bad things were. I was moving from place to place and nobody could keep a finger on me. A few jukeboxes had [my record] in L.A. I knew where each one was. I'd go there and put my nickel in!*

An unusual—some would say psychic—experience led to Anderson's return home from her first shot at the road. Her twin sister, Josephine, is developmentally disabled. All their lives, the two have been extremely close. When things hit bottom for Ernestine, her sister seemed, somehow, to be tuned in to her misfortune.

*I finally got a job working weekends at Jack's Basket Room on Central for meals and room and board. He had some houses in back of the club. Little rows of houses. Units. He let me stay back there. And fed me. Then I got sick. I had strep throat. I hadn't been to work in days, which turned into weeks. Nobody came back to see me or anything. I was just so sick, I couldn't eat, couldn't do anything.*

*My family was living out in the projects [in Seattle], above Sicks' Stadium. [They] were up this hill. My sister sat in a window, looking down the hill. She sat in the window for a week and they couldn't get her to eat. They couldn't get her to go to sleep. She just kept looking down the hill, calling my name. My mother finally thought, "Well, there must be something wrong with Ernestine, because she just keeps calling her name." So my dad got the Seattle police to get in touch with the L.A. police. When they found me, I was so sick I couldn't move. They got me to a doc-*

*tor who gave me penicillin. I don't remember how long it took me to recuperate, but I came home. Josephine saved my life.*

While she was on tour with Johnny Otis, Paul Quinichette had taken Ernestine aside and advised her to stop trying to sound like Sarah Vaughan and start sounding like herself. It was a revelation.

"That sort of sunk in," she recalls. "I started thinking about it. 'How do I change? Where do I start?' So I stopped listening to singers. And I started listening to Diz and Bird."

During the war, Dizzy Gillespie and Charlie "Bird" Parker were in the vanguard of the bebop movement. Coupling the harmonic evolutions of Art Tatum and Lester Young with fierce new rhythms and angular melodic lines, the beboppers created a fast and furious, sometimes shrill music that well reflected the anxiety of the post-war period. The music also reflected new attitudes on the part of young blacks, who, after fighting a war for the United States, were reluctant to remain disenfranchised or, worse, to be hoisted onstage as entertainer buffoons. Quincy Jones explains:

*Charlie Parker was saying that inside, we have some musical ideas that go just a little bit beyond entertainment. We do not feel like shakin' our heads and grinnin' and stuff when we play. That, to me, was a social comment—that we have minds, too. And that was much more important than being "natural rhythm machines." To me, it was a prelude to Martin Luther King, to that social awareness.*

The first bebop records had reached Seattle by 1946, before Ernestine left town with Johnny Otis. A tiny group of young musicians had begun to listen to, and try to play, the new music. Ernestine was one of the first:

*We used to go to each other's houses. In those days money was really tight, so whoever was fat enough to buy a record, or an EP, we'd gather at their house. Usually nobody had any furniture. They had pillows and we'd sit on the floor. That was the days of the red and blue lights. There had to be colored lights in the room. Mood lights. They'd put a red light on the ceiling and put the records on and everybody would sit around and groove on these records and we'd learn all the licks. . . .*

Janet Thurlow, 1951.
Courtesy of Janet Thurlow

*You had to be able to sing all of Bird's solos, and all of Dizzy's solos. And if you couldn't do that, then you weren't happening.*

As her style matured, Anderson continued to sing locally, on Bobrow's shows and elsewhere, but Seattle couldn't keep her. After a couple more false starts, she was swept into the maelstrom of the modern-jazz era, first with Lionel Hampton, then as a star in her own right.

While Ernestine and her friends were soaking up the new sounds of bop, another future Hamptonite and acolyte of Sarah Vaughan's was working behind the counter of a downtown Seattle record store, making plans of her own to make it big in bebop. White vocalist Janet Thurlow is a special figure in the Jackson Street story. Today, she probably would be called a "groupie" (though that is too crass a term for such a gentle soul), because she made a virtual profession of tracking the action in the district and of putting musicians in touch with one another. It's amazing how often her name comes up in interviews as the key that unlocked the scene for this or that player. But Thurlow was also a quality vocalist, the second Seattle musician (after Evelyn Williamson) to get in the Lionel Hampton group, and the first white singer to work with a black big band. Once she was "in," she encouraged Lionel to bring up the troops left behind in Seattle.

A Seattle native, Thurlow started her musical career on violin at age five, then studied classical voice. Her youth was marked by sadness. First her parents got divorced, then her mother died. At age twenty, Thurlow was left with four younger siblings. She recalls:

*After she died, it just didn't seem like there was anything left. She and I were very close and I didn't have anything, I didn't have anybody. So I started going around and listening to jazz. The black musicians, I grew very close to. They seemed to fill a kind of void that I was lacking. Prior to that, I hadn't heard any jazz. It was a growth period for me. I had never been out on my own at all. It was a little scary at times. I didn't have any idea what I was going to do or what was going to happen to me.*

When Jimmie Lunceford died in Seaside, Oregon (in 1947), Thurlow became friends with his band while they waited in Seattle for passage home. Soon thereafter, she moved into the Central District with her younger sister, Diane, just a few blocks from where Ray Charles had moved, in 1948. Living in the Central District was an extraordinary thing for two young white girls to do during this era:

*Ray Charles used to call me quite a few times to come down and fix his lunch for him, or his dinner. He'd play piano and I'd sing with him. I started going out to the after-hours places. I had a really good record collection—Sarah [Vaughan]'s old things on Musicraft— "Lover Man," "Black Coffee," "Summertime." I knew I liked jazz and I wanted to sing.*

Thurlow took a job—as well as voice lessons—at the Sherman and Clay music store, but soon moved over to Al Siedel's record shop on Third Avenue, which carried more jazz. Whenever musicians came in, she gave them a free listen to the latest sides: "When Floyd [Standifer] or Freddie Greenwell would come in, I'd tell them, 'Oh, man! I got this great record and you gotta come in and hear it. 'Course, a lot of the time they didn't buy anything. My boss didn't like it too much."

As Standifer remembers it: "We'd listen to things like [Dexter Gordon's] 'The Chase.' I wrote all this stuff down and took it off the record right there in the booth."

Thurlow, who sometimes sported a fashionable spit curl and a blue jacket with shiny buttons, worked in a combo with pianist Cecil Young, drummer Eddie Cole (Nat's brother), and Gerald Brashear at the Officers' Club at Fort Lewis. Once, Sammy Davis, Jr., working in town with his uncle's group, the Will Mastin Trio, came along. Thurlow recalls that "Sammy went with me for nothing—would you believe it? He used to come over to my house and I'd give him ice cream and Coca-Cola."

When Anna Mae Winburn came through town with the Sweethearts of Rhythm, Janet auditioned; she didn't get a call-back. When Ivory Joe Hunter passed through, the tables were turned: He liked her singing so much he not only asked her to join the band, he asked her to marry him. She declined both offers.

In 1950, Thurlow received her first public notice, for a performance at the Trianon, which described her as "the home-town girl who starts in where Mildred Bailey left off as a soulful interpreter of modern songs."

The comparison was apt. Like Bailey, Thurlow was a lonely girl who found solace in hip black music and the after-hours life. Though Thurlow was not in Bailey's league—jazz inflections never quite supplanted her operatic training—she got a pure, bell-like sound that was attractively innocent.

"A few years ago, when I first heard Diane Schuur, I used to think of Janet Thurlow," says Fred Greenwell. "She used to sing like a record copy of Sarah Vaughan. Clear, and in tune, and muscular."

In the fall of 1950, Thurlow got her big break, and, as it turned out, she met her future husband, Jimmy Cleveland, in the deal.

*I was staying [in Portland] on the "other side of the tracks" with a black family. It was a place where everybody came through town and jammed. Hamp was playing one night and he came over, and Jimmy came, too. When he took his horn out of the case and started playing, I said, "Man, I've never heard the trombone played like that. I gotta meet him." Right after he finished playing, I walked up to him and told him I thought that was just great. He asked me if he could take me to breakfast.*

*Then I heard that Hamp was going up to Seattle to the Palomar Theater for a week. I invited Jimmy to dinner [in Seattle]. Hamp asked me to do a show with him that day. I was all excited and I got in my best evening gown. I went down and I did "Tenderly." And it went over good! Then I did "I Can't Believe You're in Love with Me." That's the one I recorded with him. Five months later, they sent me a telegram and the money and a plane ticket to come and join them in Baltimore, at the Royal Theater.*

Hiring a white singer was a deliberate experiment on Hamp's part. Writes Lionel, in his autobiography:

*It was Walter White who suggested that I take an integrated band down South. He thought it would be a good thing to show whites—because I was doing a lot of concerts at white halls and clubs—that black and white can get along together. So I took a band down that was half white and half black. I even took a white girl singer with me, Janet Thurlow.*

Janet's anomalous position in the Hampton band led to incidents. Pony Poindexter, also in the group at the time, relates that outside Lubbock, Texas, everyone was busted by a racist sheriff:

*It turned out that since Janet Thurlow, our girl singer, was white, we were breaking Texas law by her working with us and by her riding on the bus with us. It took all day to get this straightened out. . . . Janet was taken to the airport and put aboard a plane for Chicago. Then the band was released.*

Though Lionel's intentions were good, some of the material he gave Thurlow to sing made her less than comfortable, particularly an "Aunt Jemima"–type song, "Hominy Hoedown." But Hampton came from a generation of black entertainers weaned on the grinning "Shuffle Along" school of black entertainment, and he wasn't about to abandon it. As part of the same shtick, he picked up tap dancer Danny Alexander, an ace hoofer based in Seattle during the forties who had worked many a crowd at the Black and Tan. One of his specialties was picking up a table with his teeth.

Shtick or not, Thurlow was on the road with a name band, and on January 15, 1951, she came home to Seattle to prove it. Billed as the "white girl's singer of sultry songs," she sang her version of "Tenderly" at the Trianon. She was thrilled: "I said, 'Here I am, Seattle! I finally made it!' I felt real good that night. They compared me with Billie Holiday, Ella Fitzgerald." The following week, *down beat* praised her for her "amazing range and impressive styling."

Thurlow was in good company. She was appearing with one of the legendary Hampton groups, featuring, among others, Benny Bailey, Ed "Moon" Mullins, Jimmy Cleveland, Al Grey, Benny Powell, Bobby Plater, Jerome Richardson, Milt Buckner, and Don Lamond.

"That was the Lionel Hampton band that everybody talks about," remembers Jim Gilles, a Seattle pianist who worked at the black Elks and by coincidence once crossed paths with the Hampton group in Texas.

Quincy Jones also came into the Hampton orchestra, thanks to Janet's prodding.

"Janet Thurlow was sweet," Jones remembers. "She used to write me, 'Come on down to New York—Hamp wants to see you.' She kept bugging him about 'Don't forget about Quincy.' "

Thurlow and Jones crisscrossed the country with Hamp. On August 31 and September 1, 1951, the two young musicians had the pleasure of seeing both their names on the marquee of the Trianon Ballroom. Even the newspaper ad took notice of a couple of homies making good:

LIONEL HAMPTON
*Featuring two Seattleites*
*Quincy Jones & Janet Thurlow.*

While they were on the road with Hamp, Thurlow and Jimmy Cleveland decided to wed, an interracial marriage that would later inspire Charles Mingus to record Thurlow singing his brilliant ballad about such marriages, "Eclipse."

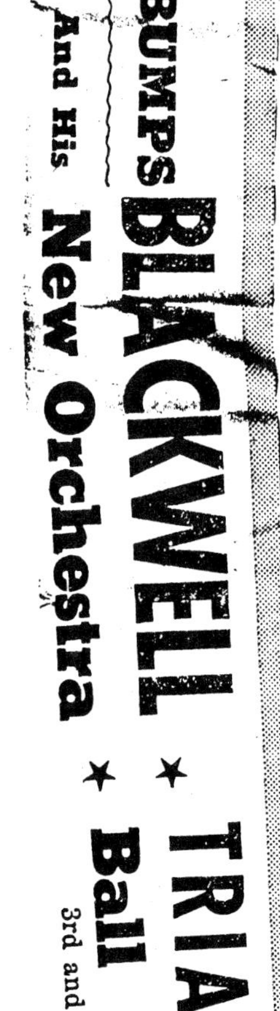

However, Lionel had a rule against married couples, so he dismissed the young singer from the band. She stayed in New York for a while, working with the Loumell Morgan Trio at Snooky's. It was at this point she became a Jehovah's Witness, a faith that has carried many other jazz musicians through hard times as well, including Andy Kirk, Benny Golson, Anna Mae Winburn, and Cozy Cole.

"When I worked at the Baby Grand in New York City with Nipsy Russell," says Thurlow, "he called me 'the Bible Lady,' because after I left the stand I'd go in my dressing room and read my *Watchtower*!"

Thurlow dropped out of public performance for a long time, but got back into singing in 1974, after moving to Los Angeles. In 1983, she and Jimmy started working in a wonderful, eight-piece "little big band" that has played at the Lighthouse, Marla's Memory Lane, and other Los Angeles venues. She performed a concert with Joe Williams in 1985. Sitting in the living room of her comfortable home with Jimmy Cleveland in Los Angeles, looking back on her Seattle days, Thurlow could still be the shy, modest, unassuming girl with the small, bell-like voice who got up and sang "Tenderly" for Hamp. In her view, there was nothing particularly glamorous about her Jackson Street days, though she remembers them fondly: "It was just ordinary people trying to make it, that's all. Our hearts were in music, we were young and we were out there, gung ho, singing with this band, singing with that band, jamming—anything for exposure."

Janet Thurlow advanced Seattle bebop by introducing musicians to one another and by alerting them to hot new records. Another vital source of the new sounds was Norman Granz's Jazz at the Philharmonic (JATP) series. Granz was the Los Angeles promoter whom Norm Bobrow had scooped by four years with his 1940 swing concert. In the JATP shows, Granz attempted to re-create the fervent atmosphere of a nightclub jam session in a concert hall. The JATP shows got underway in the fall of 1944 at Philharmonic Hall, and the name stuck when Granz took the concept on tour. Jazz at the Philharmonic reached Seattle on April 29, 1946, with an "All-Star Jazz Concert" featuring Coleman Hawkins, Lester Young, Meade Lux Lewis, Helen Humes, Ken Kersey, Charley Drayton, Buck Clayton, and Shadow Wilson. A similar lineup, with Bobrow attending to on-site promotional duties, returned the following October, with the addition of Roy Eldridge. By November 1948, Charlie Parker had made it to town, along with a couple of beboppers on the Los Angeles scene—trumpeter Howard McGhee and altoist Sonny Criss—as well as vocalist Kenny "Pancho" Hagood, Flip Phillips, J. C. Heard, Tommy Turk, and Coleman Hawkins.

"That was like the Beatles, man," recalls Quincy Jones. "People screaming, just happening. It was killer. There was so much heat. People just dying to see that."

The JATP shows brought modern stars in for a night, then they were gone. But before long, emissaries of the new music began to wander into town and stay a while, too. Roscoe Weathers, Pony Poindexter, and Gerald Wiggins were among the first to arrive. Weathers was a somewhat mysterious character. A likable fellow with a weeping mustache and sad eyes, he was originally from Memphis and worked with Jay McShann and Horace Henderson before coming west. Most sources say he jumped off the Jay McShann band in Seattle. McShann played Seattle's Civic Auditorium in 1945; Roscoe's name first appears in a Seattle newspaper that same year, when he was featured with Vern Mallory at the Savoy Ballroom.

Weathers played alto saxophone with a raw, biting tone and an oddly off-kilter sense of pacing that sounds almost avant-garde today, the way it veers haltingly between angular bebop lines and stretches of sweet caresses. He blew away the locals. Wyatt Ruther refers to him as "the Charlie Parker of the Northwest." Leon Vaughn remembers:

> *He was the first inkling that we had of how far bop had gone. He could put such unusual combinations together. He really knew his horn. He had the trio that came on from six o'clock 'til nine o'clock at the Basin Street for four months or so. He'd come in and jam a whole lot at the Basin Street and also at the Sessions Playhouse and the Blue Note. He was a hell of a sax player. Nobody could compete or compare with him. He could play all night long on "How High the Moon" and every chorus would be different.*

Weathers was messianic about spreading the gospel of bebop. Ken Boas, who worked with him for several weeks in Portland, remembers standing in the Basin Street with

Weathers, listening to the jukebox as it played Bird's "Scrapple from the Apple."

"I never will forget, Roscoe turned around to me and he had tears coming down his eyes. I said, 'What's the matter?' and he said, 'Oh, you don't understand. Those guys, it's just like they were praying.' "

Weathers was a generous teacher and didn't have a big ego. "There were a lot of tunes where they take the standard tune and put a different melody to it," Boas recounts. "He'd say, 'Here's what you do.' He'd know it just like nothing. He'd say, 'He goes up like this, and he goes down in chromatics and when he gets there, he stops, and he goes up,' you know? He'd show me on the piano, real slow."

In the fall of 1949, Weathers and Kenny Boas rented adjacent rooms in the Woodson Apartments (where many musicians lived), around the corner from the Washington Social Club. Their "pad" became a place for beboppers to congregate and socialize. Says Boas:

> *That was one of the happiest winters I ever spent, the fall of '49. We would listen to music, and play gigs. Roscoe liked to cook. He'd get a pot, and everybody would bring something and he'd boil a bunch of stuff. Guys would come by to see him, like Sonny Criss and Gus Johnson. And Paul Quinichette, you know? They were all friends, from playing together. You could tell by the way they [acted] that they respected him.*

Weathers played in a variety of pick-up bands in Seattle. Bassist Buddy Catlett tells of walking into Birdland one night and seeing the alto saxophonist smoking in a bebop group with Floyd Standifer (trumpet), Ray Charles (piano), Milt Garred (bass), and Jimmie Rodgers (drums). Despite his prowess and first-call status, Weathers' eccentricity and intensity made it difficult for him to adapt to making a living in music. "He'd come to work wearing these dark glasses with white rims with no glass in them," recalls Red Kelly. "In between tunes, he'd reach in and scratch his eye. I'd think—'Is he doing that on purpose?' "

"He had a mind of his own about things," remembers guitarist Garcia McKee. "If it wasn't right, he'd walk off." Major Pigford remembers one night in particular:

> *We were at the 102 Cherry and this drunk guy comes up and he's got this big old brown paper bag. He says he wants to hear Roy Acuff's "Blood on the Highway." [Pigford is referring to the 1942 country-and-western song "Wreck on the Highway."] Well, it just so happens that I happened to know the words to "Blood on the Highway." So Roscoe says, "Hey, man, don't you want to hear something by Charlie Parker?" And the guy says, "I don't know nothin' about that. I don't know no Charlie Parker." He wants to hear "Blood on the Highway." So I go up to Al [Pierre] and I say, "Look, Al, I know the words to one or two choruses of that thing. We can fake it." So we faked it and this guy took this whole paper bag and threw it in the kitty. It had eighteen hundred dollars in it. So I told Roscoe, "You wanted to play Charlie Parker. Hey, man, Roy Acuff gets you the money." You know, we split that together.*

Pigford's anecdote is a paradigm for the dilemma beboppers were beginning to face: as their art became more and more complex, it became less and less accessible to the average fan. The beboppers also took a humorless, almost adversarial, attitude onstage, which sometimes translated as contempt for the audience's taste. As a result, many of the early bebop musicians who remained true to their art couldn't find work, and ended up leaving music in despair. Weathers was among them. Though he had been a cup-bearer to Seattle and remained there through the early 1950s, ultimately he dropped out of music as a career. He toured Europe with bandleader Archie Savage, played Bop City in San Francisco, and in the sixties recorded an (uneven) album, *Roscoe Weathers and His Sterling Flute*. When Ernestine Anderson ran into him in the mid-1970s in Los Angeles, he had taken up jewelry-making and photography, though he continued to play on the side with former Seattle musicians Len Brooks and Garcia McKee. Weathers died in the 1980s.

Among the early westward bearers of the bop message must also be listed ex–Savoy Boy saxophonist Billy Tolles, who, by leaving town to go to A & T College in North Carolina, expanded his horizons to include both bebop and rhythm and blues. In the Southeast, Tolles played with young firebrands such as Lou

**Roscoe Weathers steps outside to have his picture taken in front of the Sessions Club, at 12th Avenue South and Main Street, c. 1948.**

**Courtesy of Wanda Brown**

Donaldson, James Moody, Dave Burns, and Joe Gales, who were stationed at a nearby Army post. Tolles made the transition to bebop easily. "We were playing 'Ornithology' and 'Billie's Bounce' and practicing every day," he recalls. "It didn't take us minutes to make the transition."

Tolles took a summer off from school in Seattle in 1945, gigging locally, but spent an even more important summer off in Newport News, Virginia, in 1947, working with the classic organ trio of Jack MacDuff, as well as with Redd Foxx, Ruth Brown, and Jimmy Scott.

In the East, Tolles not only picked up the new styles, he acquired an aggressive, professional punch that would set him far above most players in Seattle. Around Greensboro, he subbed with some of the best outfits on tour, including Louis Jordan, "Hot Lips" Page, Lucky Millinder, Benny Carter, Buddy Johnson, and King Kolax. In Boston, he worked with Sabby Lewis, then briefly picked up the tenor saxophone chair in Billy Eckstine's band, playing gigs on the Atlantic Coast all the way to the Apollo Theater, in New York. When he returned to Seattle in 1948 for a longer stay, Tolles scared people to death.

*When I came back, I came racehorsing and bebopping like a sonofagun. Sonny and Gerald and all the guys, they'd say, "Why you wanna play so fast, man?" "Cause I can." I'd been out in the world and I'd made it, man, and I'd played with everybody and I had an attitude. I'd been to New York City. I'd become twenty-one in New York, and I was really cocky, man, more than I should have been.*

Billy played a couple of times at the Washington Social Club with the Bumps Blackwell band, then started working with bassist Bob Marshall. Tolles went back into the Army briefly, at Fort Lewis, where he played with some of the other heavies stationed there (such as Earl DeWitt, Walter Benton, and Sir Roland Hanna) and also promoted jazz concerts at the theater on the post, including one or two shows with Ernestine Anderson. When he got out of the service in 1952, he went to Los Angeles and played for two weeks with Billie Holiday at the Tippin' In before returning to Seattle. That year, his band won the Combo Clash at the Eagles Auditorium, using Pony Poindexter and the magnificent trumpet player Kenny Dorham. (Dorham spent six months in Seattle, although he kept a low profile.) Billy Tolles moved away from bebop and into rock 'n' roll, as the fifties progressed, and became a Northwest rock pioneer.

Meanwhile, Tolles' Combo Clash band included another extremely important jazz messenger who had been making his mark on Seattle jazz since 1946. Norwood "Pony" Poindexter was a troubling figure, a versatile entertainer with a distinctively original style whose life was first plagued by drugs and crime, then consumed by anger and bitterness. A de-

*Norm Bobrow's Northwest*

# JAZZ LETTER

VOL. I — NOVEMBER, 1946 — NO. I

gree of the notoriety he craved came his way eventually, when he worked with Lambert, Hendricks and Bavan, but to Pony, it always seemed as if life gave him the short end of the stick.

Poindexter, who was born in New Orleans, grew up sitting in with Sidney Desvignes' combo on Bourbon Street and moved to Oakland, California, when he was fifteen. One of his first jobs in the Bay Area was with Vernon "Pops" Buford, the tenor saxophonist. Poindexter spent the war years playing hide-and-seek with the draft, squeezing in stints on New York's 52nd Street and playing a spell with Tiny Bradshaw, but he ultimately served in the Army as a musician in Naples, Italy. Poindexter then enrolled at the Candell Conservatory of Music, in Oakland, on the GI Bill. When he approached Ernie Lewis on the stand in 1946, Pony struck the older bandleader as not only feisty, but remarkably advanced. The great saxophonist and flutist Jerome Richardson was playing with Lewis at the time. When an offer to go to Seattle came up, Richardson didn't want to go, so Lewis offered the gig to Poindexter. It was Pony's first tour. The gutsy Louisiana fire in his tone fit right into the mix of styles evolving in Northwest clubs.

"He just took Seattle by storm," recalls Ernestine Anderson. "He was on everybody's list. Pony, little Pony. Pony Poindexter. He was called the 'ditty man,' because his solos were made up of a lot of different songs."

For the next ten years, Poindexter divided his time between Seattle and the Bay Area, exerting an enormous influence on technical standards and expectations in the Northwest. He married a Seattle woman in the early 1950s and spent a good deal of his time in the Northwest until 1958.

One of Pony's most prominent forums in Seattle was the weekly series of all-star concerts produced by Norm Bobrow, Jazz at the Metropolitan. Starting in May of 1946, nearly every Sunday for two years Bobrow presented jazz nights at the Repertory Playhouse, in the University District, and at the Metropolitan Theater.

As he had for Gay Jones, Bobrow went all out for publicity, promoting his shows as a deejay on two radio programs, courting the local press, and cranking out a mimeographed, 8½-by-14-inch promotional sheet titled "Norm Bobrow's Northwest Jazz Letter." The first (and only discoverable) issue—datelined New York City, November 1946—conveys Bobrow's sweet sense of regional advocacy in a breathless air of fandom and 'hep' talk: "The Northwest JAZZ LETTER is this moment being born on Editor Eddie Ronan's typewriter at the offices of down beat—That's the musicians' newspaper, father. This sort of makes DB's editors Michael Levin, Bill Gottlieb and Ronan godfathers to the Letter, and that kind of company is jazzy enough for us. Critic Leonard Feather, young man with apologetic manner, asking with keen interest about Northwest Jazz when we were introduced . . . Our Northwest jazz rates with the best in the country—I say that straight from 52nd Street. Norm Bobrow." Bobrow often participated in his own shows, singing tongue-in-cheek "jive."

Bobrow promoted anyone he thought was a good musician (and his critical taste was quite sharp), but he had his favorites. One of them was pianist Gerald Wiggins, another progressive voice who migrated to the area—if getting drafted counts as "migration." Wiggins spent four years in Seattle, 1944–1948, two of them at Fort Lewis and two of them in town, though his stretch at the camp was so light he was able to keep a Seattle apartment—with a grand piano.

Wiggins' only obligation in the 29th Special Service Band at Fort Lewis—which included Wyatt Ruther on trombone, Louis Jones (from Tiny Hill's band) on trumpet, and Junior Raglin on bass—was to play at the USO every Saturday night. "I don't think I spent over two or three days [in a row] in camp," says Wiggins.

The pianist started playing dates in town and became notorious in the jazz community

Unidentified saxophone player entertains soldiers out for a night on the town.
Photo by Al Smith

for playing sizzling-fast solos at concerts—while reading a book. "The Norm Bobrow shows were fun," recalls saxophonist Fred Greenwell, another Bobrow favorite, "because they were just [Gerald] and I and a rhythm section. A lot of the fellas around here could only go so far. Wiggins was in full control of whatever the spread was." Part of Gerald's book-reading act was sheer bravado. Though he was only twenty-two, Wiggins was a hip New Yorker who had already been on the road with Benny Carter and had appeared on the historic 1942 Les Hite recording of "Jersey Bounce" that featured the pioneering bebop solo by Dizzy Gillespie. Wiggins had been around the block, and he didn't mind letting the locals know. He also was just plain perturbed about being in the Army, which he had evaded until the MPs snatched him off the road in handcuffs. "I kept thinking about Benny Carter and all the cats having a ball on the strip," he reflects. "It took me a while to get over that." An Art Tatum disciple who could run harmonic circles around most any piano player anywhere, Wiggins quickly became known as the best keyboard man in town. "Nobody could catch up with Wig," remembers Lewis.

A short, puckish man with a scrunched-up face and a cagey sense of humor much like his oblique piano phrasing, Gerald Wiggins now lives in a large, comfortable house in Los Angeles. In his studio, there is a photograph of Marilyn Monroe, whom he coached for the singing parts in her 1950s movies, and another of Cybill Shepherd, whom he also coaches. "Wig," as he is affectionately known, seemed surprised and pleased that anyone was interested in his Seattle days, and also somewhat amused to look back on his crazy youth.

He blushes to admit that he probably came on like a New York know-it-all when he first got to town, but says there was one musician who humbled him—Julian Henson.

*Usually in a city like Seattle, there's one good musician that everybody talks about. The rest of the guys kind of look up to him. I thought at the time I was there that Julian Henson was the best piano player in town. Because he was doing things that I just couldn't figure out. That automatically made me say, "He's got something going." He was ahead of his time. He didn't know it was hard. He didn't read or anything. But he was really doing it. He was heavy. And he was fast. Oh, he was fast. I'd listen to him quite a bit.*

Wiggins worked five months with Al Hickey and the Jive Bombers at the Washington Social Club. He lived just two blocks away, at Madison and 23rd, but still he managed to come in late to the gig almost every night. The guys would tease him, but he had other things on his mind. One of them was the beautiful Seattleite I'Lee, whom he later married. The other was fishing.

"About seven or eight blocks up Madison, up the hill, there was a little pond that had catfish in it," he says. "Little baby catfish. We used to go over there at three or four o'clock in the morning and catch them. I'd go catch some catfish and bring them home and put them in the sink. My wife would find them there in the morning and I'd hear a shriek."

For a while, Gerald worked weekend gigs with his fishing buddy, saxophonist Tootie Boyd, in Portland.

> *He sure was a fast driver. He had an old Buick and it would do a hundred and twenty. And he'd get every bit of it every time. We used to go from Seattle to Portland in almost less than an hour. I was always afraid of riding with him. And you know he never got a ticket. People'd say, "You're crazy for riding with him. He's a maniac." And he was. But I was young and crazy and full of that juice. I didn't give a damn. "Can't you go any faster?"*

While Wiggins was in Seattle, he recorded a bristling 12-inch 78 with Fred Greenwell and Wyatt Ruther that attests to the heat and quality of music-making going on in town at the time. An extended bebop line over the changes of "Just You, Just Me," taken at a fast clip, it showcases Wiggins as a fleet, linear player in the style of Bud Powell who also throws in tumbling, whole-tone scales in the manner of Art Tatum. He swings like mad, and so does Freddie, whose easy phrasing and blowsy tone—dry, like Lester Young's, but broader—still sound immediate today.

After Wiggins was discharged in 1946, he went back to New York briefly, then returned to Seattle. He worked at the Rocking Chair with Wyatt Ruther, soloed in the AeroMarine Club (at the top of the Smith Tower), played duets with Julian Henson, and made an album with local vocalist Juanita Cruse. By 1948, he was ready to move on. Bassist Charlie Oden, who had played with Wiggins in the Army band, found a trio gig for them in the Bay Area. When Oden—along with guitarist/trumpeter Earl Boatley, from the Ernie Lewis band—was killed in a car crash, Wiggins struck out on his own, starting an illustrious career backing all the top vocalists, including Lena Horne, Dinah Washington, Helen Forrest, Eartha Kitt, Joe Williams, and Helen Humes.

In the fifties, he found a niche as a Hollywood vocal coach. After many years of sitting just outside the limelight, in the eighties Wig decided to "play for myself for a while." The result, a series of trio and solo albums for Concord and an expanded roster of dates that takes him to all the major festivals, has been highly rewarding. A somewhat ornamental player, Wiggins has a harmonic conception and feel for a romantic tune very much in line with another pianist who spent time on the Seattle scene studying the licks of Julian Henson—Jimmy Rowles.

The Wiggins/Rowles/Henson connection is an interesting one. All three pianists, with their flowery ornaments and sympathy for sentimental popular songs, were disciples in one way or another of Art Tatum (though Wiggins, the youngest, played in a more modern style), and their paths first crossed in Seattle. The stylistic trail is circuitous: Henson and Wiggins hear Tatum on record; Rowles learns firsthand from Henson in Seattle, then goes to Los Angeles and sits at the feet of Tatum himself. Wiggins and Henson duet in Seattle, then Wiggins also moves to Los Angeles, after Tatum dies, and carries on the tradition. Rowles and Wiggins, with their sensitive voicings and swing-era sensibilities, go on to become two of the greatest accompanists for jazz singers. Most interesting for the Northwest is that some of the qualities that made Rowles a great accompanist had begun to be transmitted to him by a bar pianist like Henson, on an obscure local scene like Seattle's, as early as 1937. This is part of the subterranean, unwritten history of jazz, the history that happens after hours and rarely gets acknowledged.

Though Ernestine Anderson was the most popular local singer during the forties, Gerald Wiggins thought enough of one of her competitors, Juanita Cruse, to cut a record with her in Los Angeles after they'd both left Seattle. It's not clear exactly how long Cruse was in the Northwest, but she was working with Elmer Gill at the Rocking Chair in 1946 and seems to have left sometime after 1948 with Jack McVea's band. Originally from St. Louis, Cruse played trumpet in high school before coming to Seattle, where she began to sing professionally. She was exceptional. Fred Greenwell says without hesitation that his two favorite jazz singers in town were Ernestine and Juanita. Wyatt Ruther says Ernestine caught your attention faster, but Juanita was more mature: "Juanita Cruse worked all over that place. She was one of the most popular singers around Seattle at that time. Juanita was a cross between Dinah Washington and Billie Holiday. She was very

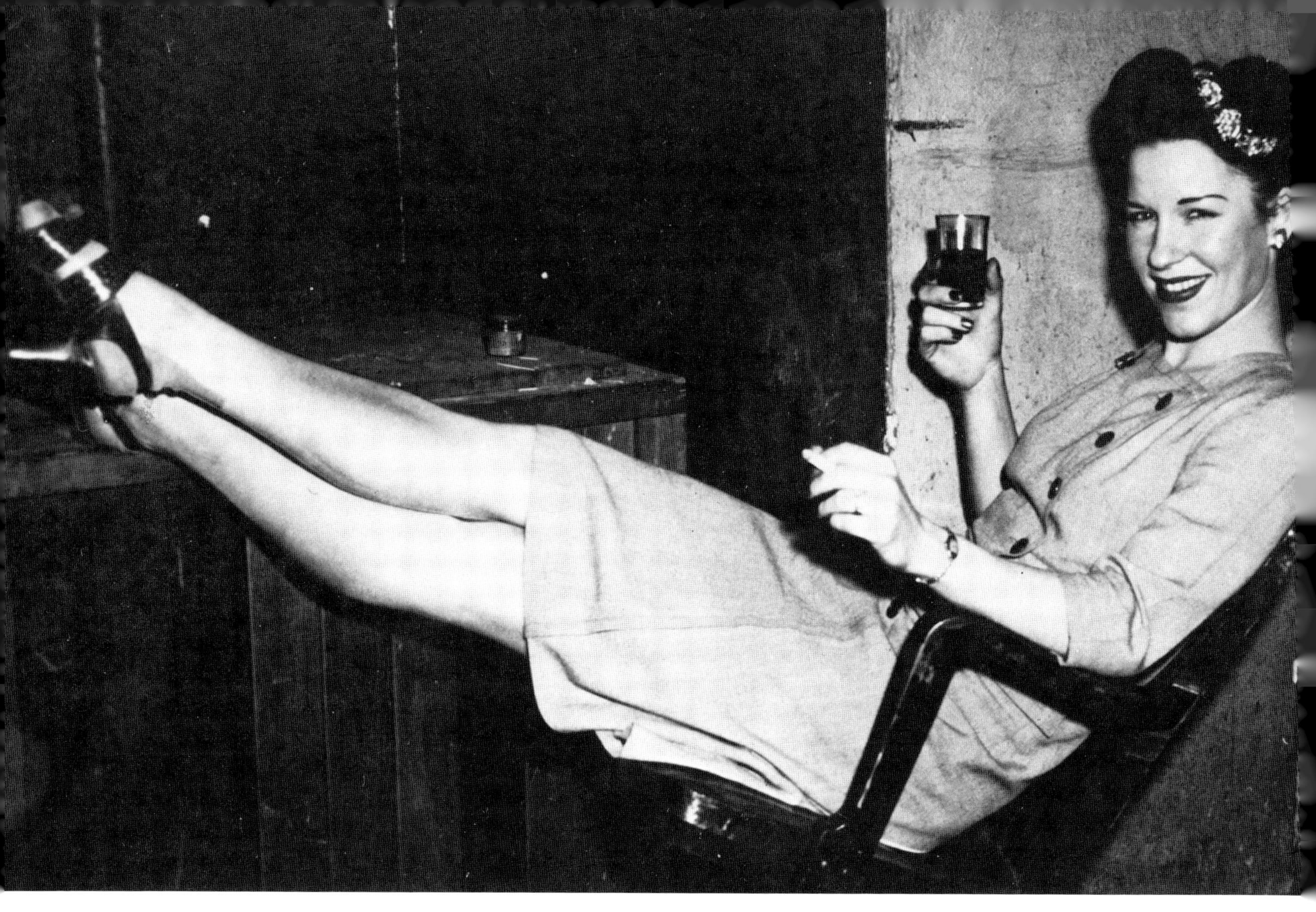

Wanda Brown.
Courtesy of Wanda Brown

good. She had her own style. She was one of those people that wouldn't sing a song exactly like somebody else sang it."

The album she made in Los Angeles with Wiggins, *Juanita!*, shows Cruse to be every bit as fine a singer as Greenwell and Ruther make her out to be, though not as expressive or individualistic as one might have expected. Critics ranked Juanita and Ernestine pretty closely. *down beat* awarded Cruse three stars (out of five) for her album in the same 1961 issue that Ernestine Anderson received three-and-a-half for *Moanin' Moanin' Moanin'*. She has a fine instrument, with true highs and a rich, raspy middle, and her conception of a song and execution are pristine. Cruse worked with Jeep Smith's band for eight years after she left McVea, then sang in Hollywood supper clubs.

Another modern singer on the scene was Wanda Brown, who had followed her drummer husband, Vernon, to Seattle in 1944. A good-natured, gravel-voiced gal who could often be found with a highball in one hand and a cigarette in the other, Wanda is a much-loved figure with a slow southern drawl who was still singing in the early nineties. In her heyday, locals compared her favorably to Billie Holiday, whose melismatic, emotionally direct style Brown seems to have picked up independent of Lady Day. Though she does not scat, Wanda is an improvising jazz singer who winds her way through the melody according to how she feels, like a horn player. She can belt out a jazz tune with blues feeling as well as anyone in town.

Brown was born Wanda Robertson in Oklahoma City in 1919. Her mother was a pianist with whom Jack Teagarden occasionally played; her father played fiddle and her brother, bass. Wanda sang in the glee club at school and remembers joining the young Charlie Christian in Oklahoma City jam sessions. Her Holiday-like style, she says, came to her by chance, much as improvising did to Ernestine:

*I used to sit in front of the nickelodeon and I'd listen to Ella Fitzgerald, whom I always admired, and still do. But she never, never sang in my key. I put nickel after nickel in, trying to learn the tune that she was singing. As a consequence of not being in my key, and me not knowing what key to sing it in, I sort of started singing around the melody. A lot of people I've talked with seem to think that is probably what makes me sound more like Billie Holiday. I admired Billie but my favorite was Ella Fitzgerald.*

When Brown was fourteen, she walked into a burlesque house in Oklahoma and boldly announced she'd like to be in the show. She soon found herself posing in "scanty clothes" singing in the chorus line (but not, she says emphatically, working as a stripper). Two years later, she left home, bound for Minneapolis, where the scene was hot. In 1939, she met Vernon Brown working in a club in Milwaukee and they got married in 1941. They moved to Detroit, where Vernon was called out to Seattle by Al Pierre in 1943. Wanda came out a few weeks later. She remembers having trouble at first adapting to the local custom of "table singing," which required vocalists to really belt out a song over the crowd noise, without a microphone. The protocol for Seattle's police raids was new to the singer, as well. One night she and Vernon were working the Sessions Club when the place was busted. "We heard the raid coming. Everybody stood up while I ducked out the exit door. Then Vernon ducked out. I wound up over here on 14th and Yesler, walking around on the street, waiting to see if Vernon was going to come and pick me up. I didn't know whether he got put in jail or not."

Toward the end of the war, Brown left Seattle with an all-girl band called Clarence Love's Darlings of Rhythm, but she only lasted about two months on the road.

*We had this sleeper bus, and the gal who played saxophone had the berth right above mine. She was alcoholic and her whiskey bottle kept falling down and hitting me on the head when I was sleeping. Several of the girls were definitely gay in the group and they were hitting on me all the time. I said, "This is not for me." In Klamath Falls, I said to heck with this noise. I sent Vernon a telegram to be prepared to send money, that I was coming home. When D-Day came, I said, "Goodbye, this is my D-Day also," and I came on home.*

After the war, Brown worked at the Washington Social Club with Wyatt Ruther, then with Billy Tolles in a fabulous but short-lived venue called the New Orleans Club, near the old Longacres racetrack. The club had a barbecue pit and a New Orleans chef; the band was as hot as the food. Billy's sextet had Neil Friel on trumpet, a trombonist from Los Angeles named Bones Robinson who could play like J. J. Johnson, Al Larkins on bass, and Gerald Frank on drums. There was a complete floor

**A CONCERT IN JAZZ**

**AMERICA'S FAVORITE MUSIC**

1. Theme Song .......... Band
2. Wood Sheddin with Woodie .......... Band
3. St. Louis Blues .......... Clarence Williams
4. Hindustan .......... Band
5. I Don't Care .......... Wanda Lester
6. Dark Eyes .......... Jab Ward
7. Stuffy .......... Band
8. Yesterday .......... Stanley Payne
9. My Buddy .......... Band
10. Ba Ba le Ba .......... Clarence Williams
11. The Classical Touch .......... Len Brooks

INTERMISSION

12. Boogie Woogie .......... Band
13. Out of Nowhere .......... Wanda Lester
14. Sweet Georgia Brown .......... Band
15. Little Fiddlin .......... Adolphus Alsbrook
16. Annie Laurie .......... Band
17. Buzz Buzz Buzz .......... Clarence Williams
18. Lover .......... Buster Coates
19. Basin Street .......... Bob Russel
20. Moon Nocturne .......... Roscoe Weathers
21. Fade Out .......... Band
22. A Study in Ivory .......... Len Brooks
23. I Got Rythm .......... Vernon Brown and Band

Produced by

**BOBBY RAWLS - VERNON BAKER**

**Directed by BOB RUSSEL**

Staff Arrangers

**ADOLPHUS ALSBROOK - LEN BROOKS**

Drums .......... International Star—Vernon Brown
Trumpet .......... He's Great—Bob Russell
Piano .......... NBC Star—Len Brooks
Alto .......... of Fletcher Henderson fame—Roscoe Weathers
Tenor .......... formerly Earl Hines—Stanley Payne
Tenor .......... Solid (You'll love him)—Jab Ward
Guitar .......... formerly Nat Towels Orchestra—Great Buster Coates
Bass .......... A Great Guy! A Great Musician—
Adolphus Alsbrook, Jr., formerly Duke Ellington Star

Featuring: CLARENCE WILLIAMS, Hollywood Singing Star
and
WANDA LESLER, International Sweetheart of Song

**The Al Pierre rehearsal band at the Union Club, c. 1948.**

**Left to right: Adolphus Alsbrook, Ish Dotson, Vernon Brown, unkonwn (trombone), Joe Gauff (alto saxophone), Skeeter Evans (trumpet), unknown (trombone), unknown (trumpet), Terry Cruise, Bob Russell, Wyatt Ruther, Jonas Weir, Hobson.**

**Courtesy of Wanda Brown**

show and, for a while, big-time traveling acts, like the one-legged tap dancer "Crip" Heard, performed there. One night in March 1949, when Ernestine Anderson was working the same show as Wanda, Billie Holiday dropped by the New Orleans. After hearing Wanda sing, she told Ernestine she thought Wanda must be black, "because she couldn't sing like that if she wasn't."

Brown herself, who has lived with black musicians most of her life and believes in minimizing racial differences, scoffs at the notion that there are "black singers" and "white singers." But Holiday's comment speaks volumes about the expressive and flexible style Brown uses on such tunes as "All of Me," "The Man I Love," "Ballin' the Jack" and "Body and Soul." Brown worked in the Seattle area throughout the 1950s, occasionally as a chorus girl at the Rivoli Burlesque, but usually as a jazz single. In the early 1960s, she picked up a day job as a secretary for King County Animal Control, and she retired from professional singing in 1964. After Vernon died in 1966, she lived with Gerald Brashear for about three years. Today, she occasionally appears at Patti Summers' club.

Wanda Brown's sometime–bass player, the big-framed, slow-talking Wyatt "Bull" Ruther, was another first-class musician (and future Basie-ite) who did his apprenticeship on Jackson Street. Ruther was playing trombone in the Special Forces band at Fort Lewis when, like Wiggins, he decided to stick around the area. His first local job was with a fondly remembered seventeen-piece rehearsal band Al Pierre had put together. Ruther made some of his first arrangements for this band. When Wanda Brown asked him to play bass, rather than trombone, at the Washington Social Club he decided to give it a shot. Ruther had started his conversion to bass at Fort Lewis when Charlie Oden left the Army band so the transition was not difficult. Besides, his general musical skills were already high. He had attended the Pittsburgh Musical Institute and learned to read both bass and treble clef, playing piano, xylophone, and trombone. When bass virtuoso and ex–Ellington sideman Adolphus Alsbrook came to town, he made Ruther his special project. "Adolphus Alsbrook taught me just about everything I know about bass violin," recalls Ruther. "In fact, when he died, he left me one of his fiddles. We were very close. He taught me how the instrument was supposed to be played."

Alsbrook's tutoring paid off for Ruther, who joined Ernie Lewis at the Black and Tan and later accompanied him back to the Bay Area in 1948. Work followed with Dave Brubeck, Lena Horne, Erroll Garner, George Shearing, and Count Basie. In 1955, Ruther moved to Canada, where he spent much of his professional career. He made a milestone album there with Canadian swing revivalist Fraser MacPherson, *Fraser Live at the Planetarium*. Around 1969, Ruther made a rather lackluster album with Gerald Brashear, *Easy Living with the Wyatt Ruther IV*. The bassist moved back to the Bay Area in 1984 and continued to work in the nineties as a first-call sideman, traveling to festivals in Europe and throughout the United States. He regards his time in Seattle as a significant ingredient in his success, saying, "I think it was very important to my musical career that I was there at that time. I was learning my instrument on the street. That's what a lot of us did. We learned how to play. If you walked in with an instrument, they'd call you up on the bandstand. If you could play, you stayed. If you couldn't play, you went back and you went to practicing again and came back when you could play. But you always had the opportunity."

Ruther's mentor, Adolphus Alsbrook, was a curious fellow. Originally from Kansas City, he had studied classical bass and harp and, according to Leon Vaughn, worked with Lester Young in Minneapolis and with Eli Rice on a Midwest tour in the thirties. Julian Henson remembers working with Alsbrook at the Rhumboogie Club in Minneapolis in the 1940s, where he says the bassist also taught judo in the police department.

Gene Ramey, the renowned Count Basie bassist, reports that Alsbrook was one of the only musicians ever to quit Duke Ellington's band:

> *The bass player who preceded Jimmy Blanton with Duke for a short time was from Kansas City. His name was Adolphus Allbrooks [sic], and I used to see him walking across the viaduct from Kansas City, Kansas, to Kansas City, Missouri, with his bass on his back. He was a great bass player, but he complained that Duke was using all the wrong chords. He was a great arranger, too, but he didn't want to consider that Duke was creating a new sound in music. He became a professor up at the University of Minnesota.*

Alsbrook came to Seattle at about the same time as Leon Vaughn, and worked with Vaughn as a waiter on the *Great Northern Empire Builder*, which ran from Chicago to Tacoma. He subsequently played with Vaughn's band at the Basin Street, and with Ernestine Anderson, Kenny Boas, and a variety of other players in town, including a brief commercial gig downtown with Wyatt Howard. Alsbrook had tremendous "legit" technique, with and without a bow.

Alsbrook suffered from narcolepsy, a disease that seizes its victims with sudden, brief bouts of sleep. He was notorious for dozing off while playing. Gerald Wiggins remembers Adolphus falling asleep as he walked up a flight of stairs. Despite the limitations caused by his affliction, musicians admired Alsbrook for his technical ability and his unusual intellect.

"He was a very mysterious person," says Ernestine Anderson. "He was very sophisticated. He stayed at a hotel down in Chinatown. In his room, he had an upright piano and walls of books. Everybody was, like, in awe of him. He introduced me to pearl tea—hot water with cream and sugar. We worked together for years. He was very protective of me. We talked and talked." Years later, Anderson discovered she was Adolphus' cousin (her grandmother's brother was Alsbrook's father). When she excitedly told him this one afternoon in Los Angeles, Alsbrook withdrew and never spoke to her again.

It's not clear when Alsbrook left Seattle. He was not around in the fifties, and he was working in Los Angeles in the sixties. His wife was a dancer, and Adolphus wrote music for Hollywood, including tunes for Herb Alpert's Tijuana Brass. He later moved to Vancouver, British Columbia, and died in the late 1980s.

Part of what made Jackson Street swing in the 1940s was its democratic embrace of gutbucket blues as well as jazz. There was little room for jazz snobs.

"If you couldn't play the blues," says Wyatt Ruther, "you couldn't play in Seattle. That was during the time when the smaller bands would be patterning themselves after Louis Jordan's band. There was Jack McVea and his 'Open the Door, Richard.' Everybody did that one. You had to entertain."

A venue that well reflected this eclectic and tolerant coexistence of dance music and art was the Washington Social Club, where all of Seattle's prominent musicians held forth at one time or another. Ernestine Anderson, Ray Charles, blues man Clarence Williams, Quincy Jones, and Bumps Blackwell all performed there, as well as national blues and jazz groups, such as B. B. King, Arthur Prysock, Red Allen, and Wardell Gray. The club was owned by "the Good Reverend" Sirless "Sy" Groves of Montana, who gave it an air of legitimacy that distinguished it from other after-hours joints. Incorporated in 1944, the club was large and out in the open, for one thing—many after-hours clubs were hidden in back alleys—and it was also in the heart of the staid Madison district, just a block or two from Mount Zion Church. The building still stands at the corner of 23rd Avenue and Madison Street. Pianist Patti Bown remembers climbing up the stairs many nights as a teen. "I always remembered the eighteenth and nineteenth stairs creaked," she says. "I used to go from seventeen to twenty for good luck." Though its full name—the Washington Educational and Social Club—sounds comically inflated, there were reasons to give it such a label. Though hard liquor was illegal, the state liquor board allowed private "clubs" to sell drinks to their members under special club licenses. Sy Groves actually had such a license, which made his place quasi-legitimate. To get in, you had to have a membership card.

The membership-card system was essentially a scam, part of the look-the-other-way tolerance policy upheld by the police. ("Most of my generation carried wallets fat with cards, each naming the bearer as a bona fide member of the 'Sahara,' 'Cavalcade,' or 'Blue Button' club, or numerous others," according to *Seattle Times* columnist Johnny Reddin.) But the Washington Social Club did, in fact, serve community purposes other than pouring drinks. "It was sort of organized like the center of the black community," asserts Sonny Booker. "Groves tried to do it right. They wanted to make it a social club. There'd be some women's meetings. They formed a young marching group for the parade."

Legitimate purposes notwithstanding, Groves still had to pay off the police, since he stayed open past the legal closing time, among other violations. Occasionally, of course, there were raids, some for show and some for real. It was an elaborate place. At the top of the stairs, a long bar lined the entryway, separated by a wall from the main dance hall. Across the floor was the bandstand, with a little railing around it. The room was half-filled with long tables—there were also some booths along the sides—where some of the best fried chicken and barbecue in town was served. The waiters offered "set-ups"—ice and soda—and customers brought their own bottles of whiskey, which they kept under the table. For an exorbitant fee, you could also buy a bottle from the house. The hall held about 250 customers. Like the Basin Street, the Washington Social Club had a floor show. Shake dancers with names like "The Flame" or "Zenobia" traded sets with the musicians and the tap-dancing emcee Teddy Felton, who did comedy routines.

Two of the most familiar faces on the Washington Social Club bandstand during the late forties were both blues-oriented tenor saxophonists—Vernon "Pops" Buford and Al Hickey. Buford was a contemporary of Pony Poindexter in Oakland and was the only musician from the Ernie Lewis band to actually settle in Seattle. In a wheelchair since 1977, when he had a stroke due to diabetes, which also required amputating both his legs, Pops speaks with a severe disability that makes him difficult to understand. His wife, Lillian, interprets for him as best she can, a process that often leads both of them into hysterical laughter. A cheerful, upbeat man who still loves music and life, Pops wears a massive gold ring on one hand and laughs loud and long at life's vagaries.

Buford was the son of a flutist who played in the same World War I military band as Seattle pioneer Powell Barnett. Both of his parents had died by the time he was eleven, so he was sent to Oakland to be raised by an aunt. A student of Jerome Richardson, by the time he was fourteen, Vernon was playing jazz up and down the state. Pops was a hard-swinging, blues-to-bop player in the style of Gene Ammons and Sonny Stitt, inspired as a youngster by the big bands of Erskine Hawkins and Jimmie Lunceford and by the solo styles of Charlie Parker, Lester Young, and Sarah Vaughan. He met Lillian in the Bay Area and they moved to Seattle in 1946 when the Ernie Lewis band came north. When Lewis returned to the Bay Area, Vernon and Lillian decided to stay in Seattle and raise a family. For a while, Buford made his living exclusively from music, working with Bumps Blackwell at the Washington Social Club and with Quincy Jones at the YMCA at 23rd and Olive. He also worked in Bremerton one night with Billie Holiday and in a hot quartet at the black Elks Club.

In the 1950s, when work died down, Pops took a day job at a car dealership and later was an orderly at University Hospital. He continued to make music, playing with guitarist Mike DeFillipis, drummer Gerald Frank, and, for several years, pianist Winfield King at a downtown club called the Textile. Vernon was good friends with guitarist Al Turay, who got him work in many white clubs in the North End that he might otherwise not have had access to. In 1957, Buford christened Seattle's first real jazz club, Pete's Poop Deck; in the 1960s he became the premier R & B tenor-saxophone honker in town, working in the burgeoning Fort Lewis rock 'n' roll scene.

Another exemplar of Seattle's heady mixture of blues and bebop was tenor saxophonist Al Hickey, who co-led a dynamic, Louis Jordan–inspired combo called the Jive Bombers from 1946 on. Though it suffered from continual personnel changes, the Jive Bombers was an extremely popular dance band in the black community. Hickey came to his Seattle success by a circuitous route. Born in Virginia in 1921, he grew up in New York, where he heard Count Basie, Chick Webb, and other hot big bands at the Apollo Theater. But it was Louis Jordan, whom he heard while outside the door of a little Harlem club on 133rd Street, who made him want to play music. Hickey's description of how he taught himself to play is a dramatic illustration of how jazz is often handed down as an oral tradition.

*I went to a pawnshop and started out with a clarinet. It cost about two dollars. I got a fingering chart. It took me about two months, practicing the fingering on a broomstick while I paid the pawnshop fifty cents a week to buy the clarinet. Then I did the same thing with a saxophone. Then I went around asking musicians*

**The Ernie Lewis Band, Oakland, 1944. Left to right: Vernon "Pops" Buford, Walter Oakes, Pony Poindexter, Warren Thompson, Earl Boatley (aka Earl Thompson), Ernie Lewis.**

**Courtesy of Vernon Buford**

*how you learn to play your horn. One person told me, "Learn your scales," so I went home and ran all the scales. Then another person told me, "Learn your chords." Well then—one, four, five, seven—I started learning the chords. Then one person told me, "What you need to do is not only play chords, but learn how to transition from one chord to the other." Pretty soon, if you were to sit down and call the chords, I would play. I didn't have to know the song.*

Hickey joined a trio and played his first professional gigs in upstate New York, then got an athletic scholarship to Fisk University, in Nashville. Jimmie Lunceford was also at Fisk, playing in a twelve-piece swing band called the Fisk Collegians. Hickey made the band, and in it, met his future Jive Bombers co-leader, a trumpeter from Ohio named "Doc" Wheeler. Hickey and Wheeler wrote arrangements for the Fisk Collegians and gigged in swing bands around Nashville. When war broke out in 1941, the two mates were sent to the Navy's holding tank for musicians at Great Lakes Naval Base, just west of Chicago. There they met William Funderburg, a territory bandleader and reed player from Birmingham, Alabama, who had enjoyed success leading a swing band during the Depression. (Funderburg is honored with a display in the Birmingham Jazz Hall of Fame.)

"All the musicians in the Navy started there," explains Hickey, who later retired to Portland following a successful, thirty-year musical career. "They'd get organized and then they'd go off to where they're posted for. Talk about jam sessions! Ernie Royal, Marshal Royal, Willie Smith, Clark Terry—everybody was there. Every noon, there was a jam session. There was also a seventeen-piece military band, which I wrote arrangements for."

Dave Bradford belting a "big note."

While Hickey was stationed at Great Lakes, he and some other sailors worked occasionally in Chicago in a small group they also called the Jive Bombers. When Hickey, Funderburg, and Wheeler were ordered to Sand Point Naval Air Station, in Seattle, in 1942, they kept the name alive for a Navy swing unit. Seattle bassist Bob Marshall, who was also stationed at Sand Point, joined them in the swing band and in a twenty-three-piece military band that played USO shows with traveling stars, including Jack Benny.

While the band was still a Navy group, the Bombers occasionally played local nightclubs, sometimes in uniform. In 1945, when Wheeler and Hickey were discharged, things had been going so well at the Washington Social Club they decided to form a civilian Jive Bombers, with different personnel.

"We had about seven arrangers in the Navy band," explains Hickey. "When the band broke up we exchanged arrangements, so we had a book from everybody. Anybody that was planning on being a leader when they got out of the service had a book. I was writing. Doc Wheeler was writing. And Bobby Braxton was writing. We had a hefty book going."

The core of the Jive Bombers was three horns and three rhythm, with Wheeler doing most of the arranging: Al Hickey, tenor saxophone; Doc Wheeler, trumpet; Bob Braxton, alto saxophone; Kenny Boas, piano; Al Larkins (later replaced by Wyatt Ruther), bass; and Duke Moore, drums. Wheeler left town in 1948 and became a high school principal in Oklahoma City. He was replaced by Dave Bradford; Gerald Wiggins played piano occasionally, and Johnny Moton replaced Boas on piano in 1951; John Willis inherited the alto chair from Braxton. Both Adolphus Alsbrook and Wyatt Ruther played bass with the Jive Bombers for a while, as well. In the fifties, Ralph Davis took over drum duties from Moore.

The Bombers were versatile entertainers. They did jive vocals in unison and jump tunes in the manner of Louis Jordan, and they got the crowd up dancing. Their version of "Flyin'

Home," which sometimes went on for half an hour, included Hickey or Braxton—or both—"walking the floor" for dollar tips, which customers stuffed into their horns as they passed by. Braxton also sang ballads, in the Eckstine manner, and Hickey did some jive singing. Dave Bradford, a song-and-dance guy from New Orleans who also did comedy, was the front man. The band did popular Nat Cole arrangements, such as "Straighten Up and Fly Right."

One night the Bombers got into a "battle of the bands" with Lester Young, the "Pres" himself, who worked at the Washington Social with a quintet for six weeks in 1948. (The group included Shorts McConnell on trumpet, Roy Haynes on drums, and possibly Argonne Thornton on piano. No one seems to remember who the bass player was, but he was from out of town.) Lester was in a far-out mood. Ron Pierce recalls:

> *Lester had long, long fingernails and he had this zoot suit on. He stood up at the microphone and said, "Now we're going to play 'Tea for Two,' and he bowed his head and played one note—*whoooooaaa!*—then he fingered 'Tea for Two,' and you could hear 'Tea for Two' but he would just be blowing air through the horn. On breaks between sets, he would stand very silently next to people sitting at a table. He would just wander up and he wouldn't say a word.*

The "battle" between the Bombers and Pres' band took place on February 5 at the Civic Auditorium. Hickey added some ringers for the occasion—Gerald Wiggins on piano, Roscoe Weathers on alto, and Bobby Braxton on vocals—and renamed the group the "Atomic Bombers." The Bombers reportedly gave Lester a run for his money.

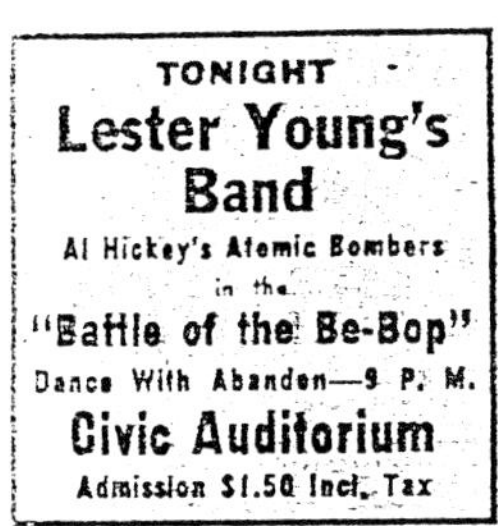
TONIGHT
Lester Young's
Band
Al Hickey's Atomic Bombers
in the
"Battle of the Be-Bop"
Dance With Abandon—9 P. M.
Civic Auditorium
Admission $1.50 Incl. Tax

By the 1950s, the Jive Bombers had dwindled to a quartet. Finding that jobs were less plentiful in Seattle, Hickey took a trio to Anchorage, Alaska—as did many Seattle musicians at this juncture—with drummer Duke Moore and pianist Elmer Gill. When he returned, he took a day job at Boeing and played in a rehearsal band there led by Leon Vaughn, then took a group into Bremerton to play. In 1953, Hickey moved to Portland.

Like many musicians of his era, Al Hickey looks back upon his Seattle years affectionately as a great learning experience. "When they had those jam sessions," he says, "if you weren't up to it, you were going to look like a fool. And if you've got any kind of competitive spark in you, you're trying not to let that happen. There were high-quality players. Anyone coming out of that era can handle any job they go on."

Hickey remembers one jam session in particular when he learned a lot, the night the great Los Angeles tenor saxophonist Wardell Gray came in. "Every tenor player in town came in and tried to blow out Wardell Gray," says Hickey. "Fools! They'd come in one by one, and disappear. About three hours later I said, 'Let's complete our discussion we had going, now that we've got rid of all them tenor players!' We sat up there on the bandstand, Wardell and I, talking all night long."

Before the decade was out, a new generation of Seattle beboppers would walk up the long flight of stairs at the Washington Social Club to continue the "discussion" begun by Hickey, Buford, Poindexter, and their cohorts. Quincy Jones, Patti Bown, Buddy Catlett, and Ray Charles—among others—would refine the Seattle mix of jazz and blues, shaping a music whose influence eventually would fan out to the rest of the world.

*When Paul de Barros contacted me in 1988 to ask if I would be interested in collaborating with him on the portraits for* Jackson Street After Hours, *I knew immediately how I wanted the photographs to be. I purchased a 1950s Rolleiflex and proceeded to photograph the musicians during the daytime and, with few exceptions, in their homes. No dimly lit nightclub locations for this project. I wanted intimacy. The friendliness I encountered with all the musicians helped make each session unforgettable. Each time I left, I had the confidence—rare in photography—that I had captured something special.*

**—Eduardo Calderón**

# A PORTFOLIO OF JAZZ ARTISTS

photography
by Eduardo Calderón

*"We caught a boat. We landed here in about November 1928,*
*and we were scheduled to go to the Maryland Tavern, which is out*
*Old Bothell Highway. It was almost to Everett. It's a roadhouse.*
*We had an old Victrola, with one of those horns on it,*
*and we fixed it to a box and you could throw silver dollars in it.*
*That was the kitty. All silver dollars in those days.*
*Sometimes, there was nobody in the joint. We'd be sitting around*
*the table playing a game called mellow, something on the order of whist.*
*We'd see some lights from a car coming and the band would jump*
*on the stand and play like mad, like there was something*
*going on, you understand! As soon as that bunch came in, here*
*was another bunch that came in.*
*Pretty soon, the joint would be rolling. Jumping, man."*

**— Palmer Johnson**

1989

Palmer Johnson

*"The first night we played at the Trianon Ballroom,*
*we had a huge night. They had the people lined up around the corner,*
*way down the block waiting to get in.*
*There were sailors and kids jitterbugging in the corners,*
*a group on each side, just going through all the gyrations.*
*Some of them were really spectacular, throwing the gal around and*
*under their leg and up in the air. There were some of those tunes we'd*
*play where the whole doggone place—I'd be worried*
*about the floor giving way."*

**— Gaylord Jones**

*1989*

*Jay Jones & Mars Mercer*

*"We would go to this table, play two or three numbers.*
*Somebody with a horn would be right next to the singer. Then the first*
*thing, they want somebody to play something else.*
*Then they're going to give him ten, twelve dollars. He'd get that lard can*
*about this big around—that used to be our kitty.*
*Every month or so we would change the can, just for luck. And that thing*
*used to be full. I've seen times we'd pull out a hundred*
*and four or five dollars a man.*
*That's the reason we stayed with those after-hours clubs.*
*That was the only way to make money."*

**— Bob Russell**

1989

Bob Russell

1989

Leon Vaughn

*"The Basin Street was under the Bush Hotel. You'd come down the stairs and you're met at the door by one of the most beautiful women in Seattle—Mike, black hair and real patrician-looking. Then you're escorted to your table by Gorilla Jones. He was a middleweight champion. Mae West gave him a lion for his birthday. There was another guy who would come into the club with a turtle on a leash, Harold Curry. And another guy would come in with a whole bucket full of silver dollars. When we'd play, he'd throw a whole handful at you. You had to tell him to 'Watch it! Don't hit me with that stuff!' Basin Street was known for its big floor shows. On the last number of the evening, we had a special number where everybody played a solo and then got off the bandstand. The last solo was taken by the drummer. I don't know why, but he seemed to instill in these chicks the idea to come out, pull up their dresses, and dance. That used to be one of the things that people came down there to look at. Yeah! I used to say, 'Show your linen, baby! Show your linen!' And they would!"*

**— Leon Vaughn**

*"What you do through your horn is project your own feelings.*
*Whether it's slow, fast, or medium I'm still projecting feelings, see.*
*And soul is one of the greatest things to have in music.*
*SOUL . . . SOUL. Project your inner self*
*through the bell of that instrument*
*. . . that's it!"*

**— Jabo Ward**

1988

Jabo Ward

*"When I came back from college, I came racehorsing*
*and bebopping like a sonofagun. Sonny and Gerald and all the guys,*
*they'd say, 'Why you wanna play so fast, man?'*
*'Cause I can.' I'd been out in the world and I'd made it, man,*
*and I'd played with everybody and I had an attitude.*
*I'd been to New York City. I'd become twenty-one*
*in New York, and I was really cocky, man,*
*more than I should have been."*

**— Billy Tolles**

1992

Billy Tolles

1988

Sonny Booker

*"Musicians, they were the glamorous part of life, in those days. The peak of the jobs for the black community were like mailmen and porters and skycaps. So if you weren't a musician or a pimp, you were riding on the boats or a shoe shine or a skycap, or on the railroad."*

**— Sonny Booker**

1988

Ernestine Anderson

*"When I went to audition at the Eldorado Ballroom,*
*the piano player asked me what key did I do these two songs*
*that I knew in. I automatically said C.*
*It turned out to be the wrong key. So I improvised around the melody,*
*because my grandmother had told me*
*that if I wanted to be a professional singer, once you start*
*singing, you don't stop. When I finished, one of the musicians*
*told me I was a jazz singer."*

**— Ernestine Anderson**

*"When he was young, he was the boss of everything, telling them whether everything was right or wrong, so he got the nickname 'Pops.' When Vernon played, everybody's feet would be flying."*

**— Lillian Buford**
**(speaking for her husband, Vernon, who suffered a stroke in 1977)**

1992

Pops Buford

*"You could walk up and down Jackson Street and you didn't have any fear. I used to carry my whole bankroll over to Maynard to catch a cab to come home. By myself. Nobody ever bothered me. I'd just be swinging this bankroll in my hand. And everybody knew I was a dice girl. They knew I had money in there. I used to go up to the black Elks Club and I'd sit there with the bankroll and open it up, and pay for my drinks out of it."*

**— Wanda Brown**

1989

Wanda Brown

1989

Gerald Wiggins

*"Seattle was a hot town then. Believe me, you could get anything you wanted. It didn't make any difference. They had a guy, he'd come by your home and take your order. You want Johnnie Walker or Seagram's? You tell him. Half-pint, fifth, quart. He'd bring it to you. The music was good and money was like dirt. It was everywhere. Talk about high rollers. You couldn't believe it. You know, boom time—shipyards and all this. Guys didn't know what to do with their paychecks. They did everything but go home."*

**— Gerald Wiggins**

*"I must have been fourteen years old and I wanted to write so badly. I used to listen to Billy Eckstine's band, 'Blowing the Blues Away.' I couldn't figure out how eight horns—four trumpets and four trombones—could play together at the same time and not play the same note. So Ray [Charles] hit a B-flat-seventh in root position and a C-seventh, which is a real Dizzy Gillespie kind of sound. They always had that eight notes or seven notes [in the chord]. And bang! He just hit that thing. When I saw that, it was like that whole world just opened up. Everything from then on made sense. Just that one chord started to let me know."*

**— Quincy Jones**

1989

Quincy Jones

1989

Patti Bown

*"When I walked home from school, I passed the pool parlor and the Mardi Gras and they always had jazz playing. My mother was saying 'No!' but the music was sensuous and it said 'Yes.'"*

**— Patti Bown**

1988

Buddy Catlett

*"The Army, the war, the shipyards, Fort Lewis brought the culture up here. That's why you had so many musicians that could play. We're fortunate. A lot of people resent the harshness of the blues, an intrusion on the values they already got set up. But it's the people in the fields that bring this culture value, that bring the spices to the stew. That made jazz what it was."*

**— Buddy Catlett**

*"What do they call this—bar mitzvah?—where you come out as a man? I think Seattle was kind of like that for me. The reason I put it to you that way is because in Seattle, at that point, all of a sudden I had to become a man."*

**— Ray Charles**

1991

Ray Charles

*"In those days, man, we just played for the playing. There wasn't any categories like they're having now. People played from their soul."*

**— Elmer Gill**

*1988*

*Elmer Gill*

1989

Fred Greenwell

*"We'd pile into two or three cars at one-thirty or two o'clock in the morning and we'd go out to the Straits, way out in the fields—no homes, out in the forest, the great green, wet Northwest—and we'd have our instruments, and in the middle of fields we'd play. Far out, boy. We had some wild times."*

**— Fred Greenwell**

1989

Chuck Metcalf

*"I was dap. I had my Mr. B collar and my peg pants, a flannel suit with wide rolled lapels and my wide knit tie with a Windsor knot. I was cool. I meant business. I had a pad at 3809 Brooklyn which was actually one of the scenes in the fifties. It was a building dated from Victorian times, probably from the Alaska-Yukon Exposition. I put foreign newspapers all over the walls and ceiling and I had apple boxes as a divider. I moved a piano in. We used to have sessions. I had the whole Stan Kenton band over to my pad in 1951 or '52."*

**— Chuck Metcalf**

*"That [Charlie] Barnet band was where the expression*
*'We saw the big man tonight' came from. Which meant that you go*
*into that thing where it was so powerful that you don't even know what*
*your name is or what the tune is.*
*It's just one big instrument, it's not a bunch of guys there.*
*'We saw the big man tonight.' Now once you do that, you spend*
*the rest of your life trying to do it again. And you do, maybe once*
*or twice a year. If there's a religion, that's mine."*

**— Red Kelly**

*1989* *Red Kelly*

1989

Jon Lanphere

*"During the summer that I had just turned sixteen
and was going to my senior year of high school, I came over from
Wenatchee. I had a room to myself at, I think it was called the Spring
Hotel. I worked with Wally Anderson at the Olympic [Hotel] Marine
Room seven to nine and then the other room there later at night.
The part of the gig my parents didn't know about was that I took
the bus to Maynard Street and played the Club Maynard until five
in the morning. It was the summer of 1944. The war was still going on,
so the Club Maynard was servicemen all night long.
I got introduced to life there."*

**— Don Lanphere**

1989

Troff Hubert

*"I was a 'jitterbug' originally. I was obsessed with jazz. I had about three thousand 78s. When Dizzy Gillespie and Charlie Parker first came out, I almost went crazy. I thought that was the greatest thing I had ever heard."*

**— Traff Hubert**

*"The first thing I learned, don't ever stand next to anybody in a raid. Keep your hands in your pockets. Don't take them out until you're told to. And when you do, make sure nobody's next to you, because you never know what'll end up in your pocket. Those were the days when I started carrying my horn either in a shopping bag or something light, because you could always keep it under your arm when you were running. There was a camaraderie, a fraternalism, that doesn't seem to be here anymore."*

**— Floyd Standifer**

1988

Floyd Standifer

1989 Bill Ramsay

*"There was a lot going on around Tacoma in those days.
Good Seattle musicians would come for sessions after their gigs.
I first heard Freddie Greenwell and Buzzy Bridgeford on Pacific
Avenue. There was quite a bit of Mafia control in those days.
Many times I remember playing at the New Yorker and
it was like some B movie, where the place would be full of people
and a couple of Vito's boys would come in and clear the place out.
Then they'd lay a long table right in front of the band. Then Vito and
his family'd come in and we'd end up
playing 'Come Back to Sorrento' all night long."*

**— Bill Ramsay**

1990

Larry Coryell

*"The black people were cool. They had a unified culture.
The white people had nothing. I mean, what did we have? Eisenhower?
Totie Fields? Pat O'Day? There was so much more emphasis
from our teachers here who happened
to be black on feeling, and very fundamental respect
for rhythmic principles."*

**— Larry Coryell**

# 6
# THE NEXT GENERATION
## Quincy Jones and company

On February 16, 1949, the Dizzy Gillespie Afro-Cuban big band, with Cuban drummer Chino Pozo, played Seattle's Senator Ballroom. This was a Bebop Event of the first order. Gary Steele, a white saxophone player from South Bend—a remote town in the southwest corner of the state—still remembers convincing his parents to drive him up to Seattle—130 miles—to hear the band. Steele, a high school student who was familiar with Gillespie's quintet records, thought he was going to hear a small group.

> *Here I came from this fishing village straight into the best thing that was happening musically in the world. . . . The thing that struck me most was the offhand and casual way that these guys looked when they were playing this music. Slumped in their chairs just like it was nothing, throwing it away. The whole band was kind of framed around this carnival-style conga player. He played with a strap over his shoulder. He was kind of the focal point of the whole thing. He was just unbelievable. What he was doing with the band. You could hardly take your eyes off him. He was a charismatic creature. And this band was just this living, breathing monster thing. I remember every little thing that happened. I remember Lester Bass was playing and he was up on a riser and he dropped his hat down through the risers and it kind of clattered down through there. He never did get it again. He just shrugged his shoulders and the band kept on roaring and nobody cared.*
>
> *Diz sat in front of the band in kind of a straight-back chair and he had another straight-back chair in his hand this way. He was trying to make a top out of it. He was trying to make it spin. Like he was totally preoccupied, you know, like he didn't give a shit. They were playing "Manteca," and all these great tunes they are still playing today.*

The night Dizzy's big band played the Senator (later called the Eagles Auditorium), the Bumps Blackwell Junior Band had a gig. No one in the group was too happy about missing Dizzy, least of all a young trumpet player named Quincy Jones. All through the job that night, he was thinking about going up to the Washington Social Club, where he knew some of the guys from the Gillespie band would probably fall by afterward. As luck would have it, a couple of them did. Recalls Jones:

> *I never will forget, they had those big, furry coat collars and those hip, New York pimp hats, you know? Ray Brown came up. These guys were bringing the sounds. That's the only contact we had. I couldn't believe it. It was like New York. Heaven. See, there was no way to communicate [in those days]. There was no MTV or anything. And* down beat *was the only way you could get any word out in a big city, outside of word of mouth, talking to the guys in the band—"Man, what's Bird doing?" "Bird put some Benzedrine in Rubberlegs Williams' coffee, man." All these stories would come out of there.*

Quincy Jones belonged to the young generation of modernists who would shape the next phase of Seattle music. Just sixteen when Dizzy came through town, Quincy was playing with a group of Garfield High kids originally led by tenor saxophonist Charlie Taylor before being taken under the wing of promoter Bumps Blackwell.

The Bumps Blackwell Junior Band is a legend in Seattle's black community. Not only did the band nurture the young Jones, it also served as the staging ground for the careers of

Buddy Catlett, Billy Johnson, and Tommy Adams. Because Bumps himself was a flamboyant character who also used Ernestine Anderson and, occasionally, Ray Charles, the band is a focal point in people's memories of the Jackson Street scene.

The Bumps Blackwell Junior Band was started by Charlie Taylor in the fall of 1947. Taylor is an intellectual whose influence on Jones as well as the scene at large has been unjustly overshadowed by the self-promoting Blackwell. Taylor was the son of Evelyn Bundy, the pianist who led the Garfield Ramblers in the 1920s. When he was growing up, famous touring musicians came to his parents' home to socialize or jam in the basement.

"We used to have their pictures all pasted around on the walls," recalls Taylor, who now holds a degree in anthropology and runs a computer business. "They'd eat there and sign the pictures and we'd put them on the wall. Lionel Hampton bought me a set of drums."

Taylor didn't start playing music until he was seventeen. His description of how he came to music says a lot about the role of jazz in the black community when he was growing up:

> *All the black kids I knew had a favorite instrument that they liked to listen to and could "pose" to. I liked to pose to a tenor saxophone, so that's what instrument I got. Everybody knew how to pose. We didn't really know how to play, but we just kept on doing it, so it went from posing to playing. We were listening to Jazz at the Philharmonic, Illinois Jacquet, Gene Ammons, Lester Young, and Coleman Hawkins. I could make sounds like all those different ones. The first thing was, you pose, then you can make some sounds. The first sounds you make are being able to sound like Lester Young or being able to sound like Coleman Hawkins or whatever.*
>
> *I got a saxophone for Christmas. I took lessons from Frank Waldron. For six months, I practiced about six hours a day. And when I couldn't play with a mouthpiece, when it got late, then I would just play with my fingers, fingering. Then the rest of the time I would just imagine it. At the end of six months of lessons—running chord changes and reading—I quit lessons and started a band.*

**Quincy Jones' high school yearbook photograph.**

When Taylor began to recruit musicians for his project, he turned first to his best friend, a kid who had just moved over from Bremerton, Quincy Jones. Jones was a handsome youngster whose spirit seems to have attracted good people and good projects from the start.

At sixty, Jones is still as unpretentious and enthusiastic as he must have been that night sitting at the feet of his musical idols at the Washington Social Club. His great celebrity and wealth have not prevented him from being one of the most genuine and disarming personalities in the music business. Today, Jones lives in a wood-sheathed hillside house in Bel Air, California, decorated in earth tones and warm surfaces more in keeping with jazz than with the glitz of the Los Angeles techno-pop he currently produces. His voice is sensitive and urbane, with a high, caressing edge. He touches when he talks.

Born in Chicago in 1933, Jones moved west with his family when he was ten, to the Navy town of Bremerton, about forty-five minutes by ferry from Seattle. His father had been offered a good wartime job as a carpenter in the naval shipyards. The family was placed in Sinclair Heights, a segregated housing project built for African Americans whom the Navy needed—temporarily.

"They made sure it was way away from town," recalls Jones. "You had to walk three miles up this hill to get into town. They also didn't put phones in the homes. You had to go to a telephone booth. They didn't want the black people to get so comfortable there after the war. They wanted them to get out. I didn't even realize this until someone told me that later."

Jones attended school in Bremerton, where he received hit-and-miss musical instruction.

His first instrument was French horn, an interesting concidence in light of Jones' colorful use of that instrument as an arranger. Jones worked his way through piano, drums, and cymbals at Koontz Junior High, then played violin, tuba, baritone horn, E-flat alto horn, and trombone before he finally got to trumpet, his destination instrument, at the age of twelve. He had no private instruction, save some general pointers about music handed down by Eddie Lewis, a Bremerton barber whose son, Dave, later became an important figure on the Seattle rock scene. Jones, for whom arranging would become a more passionate concern than "chops"—instrumental prowess—did get inspiration from Joseph Powe, a local school music teacher who had a dance band.

> *I used to get butterflies when I stood in front of that band. They had real music, written by hand, with numbers on it, and copied out, not like the stock music that's printed. That was like big-time stuff, because that's what Woody Herman had. That's what Basie had. I used to baby-sit for [Powe]. I'd look at his Glenn Miller arranging books and it was just like walking into fantasy land, just to be able to look at those things with the trombones and how they worked. How you put the saxes and trombones and stuff together. I was just hooked on it. I must have been about thirteen. It took over my life.*

Just before the end of the school year, in 1947, Jones' family moved to Seattle. As soon as Quincy got to Garfield High School, he gravitated toward Charlie Taylor, who, like himself, was a natural leader.

"Charlie was an only child," remembers Jones, "and came from a family where he was well-raised, so to speak, and he was well-loved as a child. He had a lot of high self-esteem. He was a big influence."

Both Jones and Taylor played in the Garfield concert band, directed by Parker Cook, a teacher who was supportive of their extracurricular ambitions and who would answer their questions about theory, songwriting, and arranging. The two also took lessons from Frank Waldron. Jones was not an exceptional instrumentalist, but he had a fantastic ear for harmony.

"Quincy had his lesson from Frank Waldron right before I did," says Ron Pierce. "Frank would say, 'Quincy, play me an augmented flat nine scale here.' He'd play it. 'Okay, play me a thirteenth scale.' He was very impressed with Quincy. Quincy was a good student."

Quincy agreed to join Charlie's band. Taylor then continued recruiting, this time going to two musicians whose lineage, like his own, dated back to Seattle's first jazz generation—alto saxophonist Oscar Holden, Jr., and pianist Grace Holden; their father was Oscar Holden, Sr., the veteran pianist from the 1920s. The rest of the chairs were filled by Eddie Beard, another Waldron student who Quincy says played the best tenor saxophone version of "Stardust" in town; Quincy's stepbrother, Waymond Miller, on drums, shortly succeeded by Harold Redman; and Billy Johnson on bass. Tommy Adams, later an innovative local drummer, did vocals. Says Jones:

> *The first job we ever played was at the YMCA on 23rd and Madison, in 1947. We got seven dollars apiece. We played all of Louis Jordan's things and a little bebop. We used to rehearse at Charlie's house, in the basement, every day. We listened to records. We were very conscientious. I still have the minutes. We had a president, vice president, and a secretary/treasurer. All that stuff. We were really organized dudes. We used to have fines for drinking. If you were late, this happened, and so forth. I couldn't believe how organized we were as kids. We were really serious about it.*

At first, Taylor's band played Garfield noon dances and the spring talent show. As the group moved on to gigs at Fort Lawton and other outlying areas, Grace Holden bowed out, supplanted by Van Lear Douglas. Major Pigford joined on trombone. Harold Redman replaced Waymond on drums. Billy Johnson started playing bass. Sometimes they were joined by a guitar player named Booker Martin, a seaman who was older than the kids and was into playing Charlie Parker solos on guitar.

Oscar Holden, Jr., was soon replaced, as well, by Buddy Catlett, another student of Waldron's who was also in the Garfield school band. Catlett is known as a bass player, but in his youth he played alto saxophone. He was the premier instrumentalist in the Taylor group. Catlett, who, like Taylor, was a Seattle native, joined by serendipity. Recalls Buddy:

*The alto player was a basketball player and he didn't show up for rehearsal. I dropped by Charlie's basement and they asked me to play. I had my tenor and I transposed the part. Charlie thought that was fantastic. The tunes were fairly simple and I'd heard both of them anyway. So I got hired. Oscar was six-foot-three or -four. My first uniform . . . they cut the sleeves off and that was all. I looked like Pee Wee Marquette!*

Catlett's idol at the time was Johnny Hodges, whose warm, full tone he imitated. That tone, and Taylor's chutzpah getting jobs, soon had the Charlie Taylor band playing for functions all around Puget Sound. One night, Bumps Blackwell heard the band at a dance at Lake Sammamish. Blackwell had lots of connections and one of the only organized sets of written band arrangements in town. Knowing a good thing when he heard it, he offered to expand the band's bookings if the kids would change their name to the Bumps Blackwell Junior Band and give him a percentage. Taylor and his friends agreed.

Robert A. "Bumps" Blackwell, who later pioneered the careers of Little Richard and Sam Cooke, became an influential figure in the lives of his young protégés. Born in 1918, he was a Garfield graduate who had little musical training as a youngster but adopted the airs of a conductor, dressing and acting the part. Like many swing-era bandleaders, he could barely play his putative instrument, the vibraphone.

"Everybody that was around Bumps, overall, was a better musician than Bumps was," Ray Charles comments. "But that didn't matter, because Bumps had the gig."

Bumps was the kind of man who always tried to make something dramatic happen, and often did. Before he attached himself to Quincy and his friends, Bumps single-handedly mounted an original musical, *Ceremony in Swing*. He had tremendous energy. Father figure, promoter, manager, uncle, counselor, and bandleader, he tirelessly promoted the Junior Band around the region, particularly at white society gatherings where black leaders had not ventured before. A whole generation of white Seattleites grew up listening to Blackwell's various bands—at fraternity and sorority parties, for the cotillion in the exclusive, walled-in neighborhood of Broadmoor, for dances in Leschi and Madison Park, at the Seattle Tennis Club, and at fancy resorts out of town.

"Bumps Blackwell could talk his way into anything," remembers trumpet player Floyd Standifer, who arrived on the scene in the late 1940s. "Sometimes he talked his way out the other side, but he really was a showman. He had an inventive mind. This guy would never take no for an answer on anything."

In addition to the Junior Band, Bumps led a Senior Band and a group called the Big Band that combined personnel from each. Blackwell would send different combinations of musicians out on four or five gigs in one night, all under the Blackwell aegis, then drive around town to check up on them, like a booking agent. Elmer Gill, a pianist who sometimes worked for Bumps, didn't think much of his methods.

*He'd call any three things to play together. I remember one time he called me and we were playing out at the Knights of Columbus Hall. I got there—now, this was a formal dance—and it was me to play the piano, Dick Thorlakson to play trombone, and somebody else playing the guitar! That was it. Piano, trombone, and guitar. Bumps came in with a white jacket and a great long baton. Man, I went out the back door! He was standing up there with his baton, directing a trombone and guitar! No drums, no bass! And all these people in long dresses and tuxedos.*

Blackwell kept his ad hoc music agency afloat from his butcher shop on 23rd and Madison, within shouting distance of the Savoy Ballroom and the Washington Social Club. Remembers Floyd Standifer:

*On any given day, you could walk over there and there'd be a whole bunch of people, most of them musicians, standing around at the meat counter. You might find young Ernestine Anderson. Quincy would be there. I was there a few times. Major Pigford. All these guys standing around waiting to hear about rehearsal plans and things like that. Bumps lived right around the corner, and everybody rehearsed at his place. He was kind of like a magnet. If you were at all any kind of a performer with any kind of pizzazz,*

*Bumps had to attract you. He was really Mr. Show Business, as far as Seattle was concerned.*

For a time, Blackwell had a virtual music monopoly, according to Billy Tolles: "If you wanted to work, you were working in one of Bumps' bands. He would come and collect the money off of each gig, and pay you what he wanted you to have. He had the thing locked up."

The Charlie Taylor band thrived under Blackwell's sponsorship. Blackwell coached the youngsters to be total entertainers. They not only played, they danced, they sang, they did routines—they could put on a whole floor show. Jones recalls:

*At the Seattle Tennis Club we played all the schottisches. Then we'd play at ten o'clock till about one at the black clubs, where it would really loosen up, and get down and go into stuff like Eddie "Cleanhead" Vinson's "Kidney Stew Blues," and Roy Brown's "Good Rockin' Tonight." We had comedy acts. I used to sing "Run Joe" with a big hat. We had the stock arrangements on "Room Full of Roses," we'd sing "Blue Moon." And we also had all the stuff that Dizzy was playing.*

The band's first gig under Bumps' baton was at the Civic Auditorium, playing opposite no less a figure than Cab Calloway. The band wore white jackets with no lapels. The date went over so well Blackwell approached Lemuel Honeysuckle to reopen the Savoy Ballroom, which had been converted into a skating rink. Honeysuckle complied, and the Junior Band played there every Sunday. Blackwell also got the Junior Band gigs at county fairs in Yakima and Puyallup, at the Pacific National Exposition in Vancouver, British Columbia, at nearby

**The Bumps Blackwell Junior Band at the Trianon Ballroom, March 14, 1949. Left to right: Billy Johnson, Harold Redman, Charles Taylor, Buddy Catlett, Quincy Jones, Bumps Blackwell, Major Pigford, Tommy Adams.**

**Courtesy of Charles Taylor**

The 41st Infantry Division Band, Washington National Guard, directed by Warrant Officer (j.g.) Robert A. "Bumps" Blackwell, Camp Murray, Washington, 1947–1948. Far left: Bumps Blackwell. Five columns, left to right, looking front to back: 1) Billy Johnson, Charles Taylor, George Brown, Quincy Jones, Harold Redman; 2) Major Pigford, unknown, Harold Hardy, Eddie Beard, unknown; 3) "Butch," unknown, Andrew Guyong, unknown, unknown; 4) unknown, Clayton Harold, unknown, Clark, unknown, unknown; 5) Buddy Featherstone, Oscar Holden, Jr., Buddy Catlett, unknown, unknown.

resorts on Shadow Lake and Angle Lake—even a regular weekend engagement at Island Lake Resort, near Bremerton. Jones still teases Ernestine Anderson about the night in Vancouver she squeezed into a shake dancer's skirt and shimmied onstage.

Blackwell was on the lookout for the moral character of his young charges, offering them friendly guidance in the ways of the world. Recalls Taylor:

> *He took on the role of being a father to us. He would be telling interesting stories about [how] you got to watch this, and watch that, and make sure that you look at her bra strap—if it's dirty, don't have anything to do with her. He had all these little tales. He gave us lectures on dope. He would get upset if he thought we were smoking pot. And he would always point out all the people that had gotten into music and then gone down the tube by getting caught up in all the things that were peripheral to it. He spent a good deal of time on that. It didn't take much to turn the shoulder, you know. I remember I got in the cab with Bird once, on my way to the Social Club—it just happened we were in the same cab together—and I remember that he was incoherent. It wasn't hard to see what [Bumps] was talking about. It wasn't an abstract thing.*

Blackwell's caution was perhaps warranted. One night, after a gig at Island Lake, on the way back to the ferry the band was pulled over for driving too slow, and the police discovered a joint in somebody's pocket. Taylor insists the incident was a "setup," but the band spent the night in jail. The charges were later dismissed.

Another depressing object lesson in the perils of the jazz life came on March 5, 1949, the night the Junior Band found itself backing up Billie Holiday at the Senator Ballroom. Though most of the young men felt proud to be playing behind Lady Day, they vividly recall how incapacitated she was. "She could barely talk," says Jones. "I remember she didn't show up for rehearsal."

The following year, Billie's accompanist, Bobby Tucker, came back with Billy Eckstine and requested the same backup band. "That was very, very important in terms of building confidence," remembers Jones. The Junior Band also opened for Nat Cole at the Civic Auditorium, and worked the same stages as Mel Tormé and another important musical model, Louis Jordan. Blackwell units also traded sets with a parade of early rock groups that had started to come through the Washington Social Club: Bull Moose Jackson, Pee Wee Crayton, Joe Liggins, Roy Milton, and Lucky Millinder. Sammy Davis, Jr., and Clark Terry also offered Quincy and his pals time and guidance. Says Quincy:

*We'd hang with Sammy. Worry him to death! All day long. He had all these records—"Lemon Drop" and "Early Autumn," all this bebop, with "Birth of the Cool" and Miles and all that stuff. It had a tremendous influence. He was the first guy that had earphones and a record player. I had never seen that before. We used to play hookey and go down to the Palomar Theater. We dressed like we were old, so we could get in. We'd take our bags and go in there and pretend like we were part of the band. Clark Terry was [there] with Count Basie. I used to ask Clark, "How do you do this?"*

After the Bumps Blackwell Junior Band had been together less than a year, an odd turn of events brought together many of the area's young white and black jazz musicians in an unlikely setting that is still a source of amused pride for all concerned. The armed forces were segregated during the 1940s, but times were changing. The Washington National Guard decided to form a unit including blacks. Charlie Taylor got wind of this through a friend of his mother's and went to visit Bumps.

Thus was formed, in October 1947, the 41st Infantry Division Band, Washington National Guard, with fifty-six musicians under Warrant Officer (j.g.) Robert A. (Bumps) Blackwell—temporary quarters, the Field Artillery Armory at Camp Murray. The band included Quincy Jones, Buddy Catlett, Major Pigford, Charlie Taylor, and just about anybody else in the neighborhood who could hold a horn. Trumpeter Floyd Standifer, who was attending the University of Washington, was also recruited. The members were issued free instruments (a big motivation for many of the kids) and uniforms, and they started to learn to march. "Not one of them could blow their nose," Blackwell later exaggerated affectionately. "I ended up bringing in men out of my big band."

One of the professional additions was Ish Dotson, a tenor saxophone player who had worked in Al Pierre's big rehearsal band. Another was Ron Pierce. Soon, white musicians Al Pace, Dick Thorlakson, Bruce Ford, Dave Tuttle, Ken Boas, and a whole batch of others just out of high school, whom Bumps had been using in his various bands, also joined the unit. The National Guard band survived three summers at Camp Murray, running the telephones and communications and playing for retreat parades and dances. The band was a boon for many kids, but it was also a firsthand preview of how badly the jazz life mixed with military regimentation, particularly when the guys tried to play gigs in town. As Jones recollects:

*We all had staff-sergeant ratings. We came back to camp late one time, and we all got busted. Including Bumps. I couldn't believe it. They were* pissed. *They said, "Good to see you, Sergeant, do you have any answer for this?" I said, "No." They said, "Well, Corporal, go over there." We'd been demoted. It got to the place where we were privates.*

*I was supposed to be company bugler. I had to play reveille in the morning. We stayed out all night and I didn't get up until about 11 o'clock. The who-o-o-le base overslept. They were so pissed off at me they made me sleep with the MPs after that, so I'd get up with them and wouldn't oversleep.*

Eventually, Blackwell was replaced as leader of the National Guard band by sweet-band leader Jackie Souders, but not before he mustered out the kids to protect them from being sent to the Korean conflict.

Bumps Blackwell, who died in 1982 having achieved little national recognition, cared a great deal for the young musicians he nurtured in Seattle, and afforded them many opportunities. Regrettably, as some of his protégés became famous, he exaggerated the magnitude of his influence on them. It was not uncommon for him in later years to boast that he had "given Quincy Jones his start," or led a big band with

Jones, Ray Charles, and Ernestine Anderson. In fact, Blackwell's contribution to Jones' career was minor and he never led such a band—at least not on any but the most sporadic basis. Musically, Blackwell was neither an innovator nor even a quality bandleader. But he made his claims on Jones often enough that people came to believe them. Even Buddy Catlett, who remains a close, lifelong friend of Quincy's, surmised that Jones was inspired by Blackwell's take-charge attitude and dramatic sense of leadership, a notion that surprised Jones: "No. Not at all. Not at all! I was much more influenced by Charlie [Taylor] than by Bumps. But, you know, people write whatever they want. You tell them about Frank Waldron and they put down Clark Terry. You put down Charlie Taylor, they put down Bumps Blackwell."

If Charlie Taylor was Quincy's personal inspiration, Ray Charles was his musical one, since it was R. C., as he was then called, who fired up Quincy's arranging ambitions. The meeting of Quincy Jones and Ray Charles on Jackson Street is one of the most important moments in the story of Northwest jazz. It began a lifelong musical relationship that has had a lasting influence on both men. With all the millions of dollars that pass through their offices, Jones and Charles still work together without a contract. Neither seems to remember exactly how or when they met, but it was soon after Charles' arrival from Tampa, Florida, in the spring of 1948. Quincy's first recollection of Charles is at the Elks Club, where Charles was singing on the stand: "Ray seemed o-o-o-old. He was so mature. And he was only two years older than I was! He was sixteen and I was fourteen. He had his own apartment, his own suits, and everything. Oh boy, did I look up to him. He was just so wise."

"Quincy tells lies!" Charles laughs out loud, upon hearing this quote repeated back to him during a Los Angeles interview:

> *You know why he says that about me, though, because I had my own apartment. I had a girlfriend that stayed with me and all this kind of stuff. I had a piano. I had a hi-fi. And my old lady, we were keeping house. He was a kid in school, so I guess I did seem like an old man.*
>
> *Quincy was playing trumpet, but he really wanted to write jazz. So he asked me how to do it. He was a very enthusiastic fellow. Not only enthusiastic—you see some people that are extremely attractive, and that's the way Quincy was with me when we were youngsters. I was very, very attracted to him. Our chemistry just clicked.*
>
> *You remember, we used to work from one o'clock till five in the morning and I didn't get to sleep till six-thirty. Quincy was the kind of a guy, he'd wake me up at nine. He wanted to learn how to write music. He liked things like "Emanon," with Dizzy Gillespie's band. And it just turned out that I knew how to write music. I had*

**Billie Holiday performing at the Eagles Auditorium on March 5, 1949, with the Bumps Blackwell Junior Band behind her. Sidemen in rear, left to right: Billy Johnson, Harold Redman, Charles Taylor.**

**Courtesy of Charles Taylor**

*been writing music since I was maybe ten, eleven, twelve years old. So he would come over and I would show him things. I'd show him how to voice for saxophones, how to voice for the trombones and the trumpets, what the chord structures were, like a B-flat augmented eleventh, with an added thirteen, things like that, you know? And from that, he started to write.*

Jones echoes the story, remarkably remembering the exact same chord:

*I must have been fourteen years old and I wanted to write so badly. I used to listen to Billy Eckstine's band, "Blowing the Blues Away." I couldn't figure out how eight horns—four trumpets and four trombones—could play together at the same time and not play the same note. So Ray hit a B-flat-seventh in root position and a C-seventh, which is a real Dizzy Gillespie kind of sound. They always had that eight notes or seven notes [in the chord]. And bang! He just hit that thing. When I saw that, it was like that whole world just opened up. Everything from then on made sense. Just that one chord started to let me know.*

After the *bang!* of that chord, Jones and Charles were inseparable, hanging out, comparing notes, staying up all night or playing together at the Washington Social Club.

"I remember Quincy being so excited about this new thing that R. C. had shown him," says Ernestine. "All these new changes and the new chord structure . . . he was just so knocked out about R. C. and his music. Ray just sort of took him under his wing."

It's not difficult to surmise why the relationship between these two men ran so deep. They shared a lot. They were teenagers when they met, they were both going through formative, sensitive periods in their lives, and they got their first "breaks" at around the same time. Both were alive to the musical possibilities exploding around them, and both were extremely ambitious.

Says Charles:

*A lot of people don't understand Quincy and my relationship. And I'll tell you something, if you look at Quincy, as a side note, and you look at me, you probably would never understand how we could be brothers, close to each other as we are, because our personalities are so different. I'm very—almost introverted. Some people think I'm antisocial. Whereas Quincy is more open, he's more around people. He enjoys that, and people love him. We're very opposite in our styles, and yet we are very together in our feelings.*

*We don't work for each other. That's number one. I can't afford him! [laughs] He calls me and says, "Ray, hey, lookahere, I want to —," and I say, "Okay." And that's it! No contract, no nothin'. If it's something Quincy Jones wants me to do. He tells me. I do it. And it's the same thing. If I call him up and say, "Hey, Q, I want you to—" [claps hands] That's it. Finish! So that's why we are the way we are today. This is not like all of a sudden we have got ulterior motives or we're looking for something, you know, it ain't that kind of thing. It's a true, genuine friendship, man. And it has lasted now for some forty-three years. That's a long time. I'm just thankful, because I love him so much, ever since we were kids. He's like my brother, and I really mean that sincerely. He's always been that way with me, until this day. If I got a dime, he's got a nickel. Honest to god.*

"Ray and I are the only ones that have been in touch all the way through," confirms Jones. "We've been working right up until now. As we get older, we're getting more sloppy and sentimental about our relationship. Before, we used to be kind of cool about it. There was always love, but you turned around and be cool. But now it's gushy and mushy and we just hug and hang out as much as we can."

From the start, Jones had been more interested in composition and arranging than in the trumpet, but when he met R. C., a whole new world opened up. Jones' growing arranging skills attracted the attention of a young music teacher at Seattle University, Gus Mankertz, who recruited the young trumpet player for a progressive, seventeen-piece "jazz workshop" band. Mankertz was an oboist who had studied jazz and composition at the College of Puget Sound (later renamed the University of Puget Sound). For his workshop band, he raided the Jackson Street clubs and Garfield High School, bringing in Quincy, Buddy Catlett, Tommy

Adams, Floyd Standifer, tenor saxophonist Rollo Strand, and trumpeter Don Smith. The workshop band was ultra-modern, performing the hippest new bebop arrangements by Stan Kenton, Woody Herman, and Dizzy Gillespie.

While playing for Mankertz during his senior year in high school, Quincy composed his first major piece, *Four Winds Suite*. On May 9, 1950, a month before Jones graduated from high school, the suite was performed by the workshop band. Don Smith, who would later join Kenton, played lead on the premiere. Rod Levitt, who would later distinguish himself as a composer, played trombone. Floyd Standifer, who also played trumpet on the piece's debut, recalls that from this moment on, Jones' reputation as an arranger began to soar: "With Quincy, you said to yourself, 'This cat, he doesn't play all that well, but man, he can sure write.'"

Besides learning to arrange, the other consuming passion for Jones at this time was to leave town with a name band. "Ernestine was our idol," he recalls. "She was out with Johnny Otis and those bands before anybody. Everybody was in awe of anybody that had gone on the road with a professional band. 'I'm on so-and-so's band,' 'I'm on so-and-so's band.' That was really hot." As it turned out, the arranging skills Ray Charles passed on to Jones would be Quincy's ticket out of town, though not quite as fast as he had hoped. The story of how Quincy left Seattle with Lionel Hampton after auditioning backstage has been told and retold—and embellished—but what really happened is known by only a few.

Hamp was in town. The year was 1950. As usual, Quincy had found a way backstage at the Palomar. He introduced himself, sat down at the piano, and played an excerpt from *Four Winds Suite*. Hampton was knocked out. He invited Jones into the band on the spot. However, Hamp failed to clear his invitation with the band's business manager—his wife, Gladys. Jones recounts:

> *I wanted to go with that band so badly. I never wanted to play with a band so much. Hamp had all these guys! Jimmy Cleveland and Benny Bailey and Betty Carter and Jimmy Scott and Sonny Parker and Porter Kilbert. Jerome Richardson. Incredible band! It was just like, "God!" you know, just "Please!" I wanted to leave home. I was dying to leave home. I just wanted to go. I didn't want to finish school or anything. So when Hamp said, "You're with the band," I didn't want to take a chance! I just got on the bus. I had one of those little bebop things, the little leather cases. I was ready to go. I was gone. I wasn't even going to ask anybody. I didn't even want anybody to notice I was there, so they'd just leave town and I'd be with them. Then Gladys got on the bus and she said, "No. Get that kid back to school. Get him off the bus." I was so hurt. So hurt. I just wanted to go so bad.*

For the time being, Jones had to settle for a scholarship to Seattle University, where he continued to play for Mankertz. He became a local celebrity. An article in the school newspaper—"Quincy Jones, Musical Prodigy, Studies at Seattle University"—captures the intellectually cool, button-down–collar image the young Jones had picked up hanging out with touring professionals:

> *Though this is his first year here, freshman music major Quincy Jones made his debut in SU music circles last year when his descriptive suite, "The Four Winds," was played at the spring concert. He plays the trumpet and the piano. The same arrangement of "The Four Winds" is scheduled to be played by Lionel Hampton at "Bop City" in New York in the near future.*
>
> *When asked his plans for the future, he replied, "I would like to study at Westlake Music College in Hollywood, and later to write serious studies for the movies—mood music, they call it. . . . I appreciate the good in all classes of music, from boogie on up to the classics. However, at present I have a leaning toward popular dance music."*

Jones spent only one semester at Seattle University. In the spring of 1951, having sent his *Four Winds Suite* ahead as an audition manuscript, he left Seattle for Boston, to attend the Berklee School of Music.

"I liked Seattle University, because Gus Mankertz had this band there," remarks Jones. "But it was just a little bit square, that's all. I just really wanted to get out of town. I wanted to get away from home and get back to Boston

so I knew I'd be close to Bird and Miles. And get me to New York. That's all I cared about. I knew I would never be home again. Never."

Jones had been in Boston but a few months when Lionel Hampton came through town. Janet Thurlow, the hip singer from Seattle, was with the group. She reminded Hamp he had once unsuccessfully tried to hire Quincy in Seattle. Hamp renewed the invitation. Jones needed little prodding to drop out of classes and jump on the band. This time—with Gladys' blessing—Quincy was allowed to stay. As the new kid on the block, Jones at first met with resentment from older band members. But his unique arranging talents soon won over the skeptics. By May, he was recording with the band. The following fall, his name was on the marquee of the Trianon Ballroom, with Hampton's and Thurlow's. Most of the fans who came to see him that night thought he'd been hired right out of Seattle, knowing nothing, of course, of the incident with Gladys or of Janet Thurlow's role behind the scenes.

Once Jones left town—in fact, even earlier, when he entered Seattle University—the Bumps Blackwell Junior Band began to disintegrate. Charlie Taylor enrolled at the University of Washington and married a woman who discouraged him from pursuing music. Buddy Catlett contracted tubercular pleurisy and was hospitalized. Bassist Billy Johnson moved to Los Angeles, where he became a successful professional musician. (He appears on an album with Roscoe Weathers.) Tommy Adams remained in Seattle, working with Billy Tolles as a drummer and becoming the most important single force in early Seattle rock 'n' roll. Major Pigford continued playing, then dropped out of music for over a decade, pursuing biology and accounting, only to come back to his trombone in the 1980s.

The Charlie Taylor/Bumps Blackwell Junior Band lasted less than three years, but Jones has intense affection for the days he spent with it. "It was one of the magic times in my life," he says. "We were finding out what makes sounds work and listening. Everybody was always trying to pick up new tunes and just learning and growing. All we cared about was getting better."

And getting ahead. It's clear that raw ambition played a large role in Jones' youth. Charlie Taylor remembers sitting around in his basement with Quincy practicing how they would sign autographs after they became famous. Jones himself idolized bandleaders like Billy Eckstine and Duke Ellington, men who were not only great musicians but successful entrepreneurs. At a time when racism barred most African Americans from basic free enterprise, black bandleaders were an attractive role model.

Jones' ambition may also have been a veil for his desperate unhappiness at home, a way of focusing his attention on something other than his difficult family situation. His parents had recently divorced—a stigma in those days—and his stepmother brought her children from a previous marriage to live with the family. During his high school years, Jones stayed away from the house as much as he could. Quincy would often fall asleep in school, having been up until all hours the night before at the Washington Social Club. The image of the intense, heavy-lidded Jones, carrying his trumpet in a cloth bag, is conveyed by old friends in a tone that implies that Jones was, like most geniuses, eccentric in his intensity and single-minded in his devotion to music.

"I think about sitting in the attic of that little house," says Jones, who sometimes practiced his scales and arpeggios in a closet, for privacy and protection from criticism.

And yet, if an unhappy home helped launch Jones into the world, it is also true that the middle-class life his family enjoyed in Seattle in the 1940s nurtured him. Jones himself has said that had he grown up amid the violence of the Chicago ghetto, he probably would not have made the choices he made. "I came stone out of the ghetto in Chicago to Washington and it was just the antithesis of that whole thing. That really struck me early. I was lucky that I got a chance to deal with people one-on-one, and not by the road signs."

By "road signs," of course, Jones means racism. Though there was much about race relations that needed to change in Seattle, Jones had the moral support of a strong black middle class whose roots went back to that turn-of-the-century Edwardian community established by Powell Barnett, Horace Cayton, and others. The result was that when push came to shove, Jones had Charlie Taylor for a role model, Frank Waldron for a music teacher, and Bumps Blackwell as a booking agent (a ticket into white social life), not to mention the whole neighborhood support system that allowed the Junior Band and the various nighttime exploits he undertook to happen without incident. Had these strong figures and solid supports not been there, many of his experiences—the bust in Port Orchard, for example—might have had entirely different results.

Jones was not the only Seattle musician of his generation to be ambitious and well-cared-for. Pianist Patti Bown, hailed as a prodigy at Seattle University in the same year as Jones, grew up in the heart of Seattle's upwardly mobile black community, too. Though she was not officially part of the Bumps Blackwell/ Charlie Taylor band, Bown hung out with the guys, and her career converged with Quincy's on several important occasions after they both had left town.

Patti Bown is an outrageous character, one of the great eccentrics in contemporary jazz. An enormous woman who wears broad-brimmed hats and speaks in page-long sentences, Bown can hold forth on contemporary composition, spiritual healing, cosmetics, geopolitics, and the music business—and often does, all in the same breath. As a pianist, she is an oddity—a technical virtuoso who hews to no stylistic camp yet combines an utterly individual approach with broad entertainment values. At her best as a soloist, she can entertain a cocktail crowd at New York's Village Gate, as she did for several years, without sounding cloying or pandering to bad taste. She can also hold her own with the best of the beboppers, "free"-jazz improvisers, studio pop musicians, or even rock 'n' rollers. Whitney Balliet, jazz writer for *The New Yorker*, once described a Bown solo on John Coltrane's "Giant Steps" as "an eight-minute lesson in how to make a piece of improvisation so tight and complex it would supply a dozen soloists for a week."

Bown's parents settled in Seattle's Central District in 1921. Ten years later, Patti was born and the family moved to an old-fashioned, two-family house on 22nd Avenue. The Bown household was a center of social and cultural activity, where visiting black artists such as Marian Anderson and Roland Hayes sometimes boarded overnight, because they were not welcome in white-owned hotels. Neighborhood musical gatherings were common.

> *We had the whole ground floor of this big, old-fashioned house, with a big backyard and a lot of fruit trees. It was really a beautiful place, lovely flowers in it. Saturday night, we would have "at-homes." My mother and father were exquisite chefs, so they would cook unbelievable food. The bread was always homemade. There was fresh cake, dill bread, homemade booze. There would be music and people reading poetry and painters coming there to visit. Morris Graves named all his dogs after one of my sisters!*
>
> *My mother really encouraged us into the arts. We always had dance lessons, tap lessons. We were considered poor, [but] my mother always found money to take us to all kinds of concerts. We went to the museum every Sunday after Mass. Our mother used to paint. She took us to see Arthur Rubinstein, Marian Anderson, and Katherine Dunham.*

The Bown girls were sent to Immaculate Conception School. The first to take up music was Edith Mary. A piano prodigy, she made her New York debut at Town Hall in 1950 and later studied at Fontainebleau with Robert Casadesus and Nadia Boulanger. When two of Patti's other sisters also got piano lessons, and her sister Florence started to dance, Patti was jealous. She began to teach herself to play.

"I discovered that when they were going to school, I had the piano to myself," says Patti. "So all day long I could get these little goodies off the radio. I'd just make them up, and play games in my head. My mother had taught me the alphabet when I was about three, so I just started a form of writing on a piece of paper, where I would draw lines, to make myself remember where my melody was."

Bown started formal piano lessons when she was six. By the time she was eight, she, too, was being touted as a prodigy. She performed for Danny Kaye at the Overseas Press Club and got a job playing hymns in a funeral home. Like Billy Tolles, she also found her way into the Syvilla Fort studio—not as a dance student, but as a rehearsal pianist. Recalls Bown:

> *Syvilla Fort was every Saturday morning. They had a little place where they had dance classes, and she always did improvisational dance. So it gave me a chance to make up original music. Which meant that every Saturday morning I had a chance to improvise jazz for the dancers to exercise and dance to. She'd count out a rhythm of how fast she wanted and I made up original music for it.*

As with so many budding jazz pianists, improvisation—the freedom to create one's own melodies—was already important to Bown. Privately, she had begun to take apart her classical lessons and "swing" them. Her rebellion from classical music and her mother's middle-class proscriptions were already underway. Her father took her to see Count Basie at the Trianon Ballroom. She skipped out of school early to hear Percy Mayfield at the Palomar Theater. Bown's sisters brought home records of Glenn Miller's "Slow Freight" and Duke Ellington's "Chelsea Bridge." When they put on a record by Will Green, "In the Dark," their mother, who played "pretty fair" blues piano herself, objected to it as "dirty" and "suggestive."

> *My mother was still living out that old script from* The Jazz Singer*—"I want a concert pianist, I don't want you to go in those clubs"—that whole middle-class thing. Jazz was evil, jazz was the work of the devil. It was the music of gangster movies. My mother figured I was going to be a drug addict or an alcoholic if I stayed with jazz because people who took classical music went into nice halls and they had prunes in their mouths. It was like a higher-class thing, a prestige thing. She was very socially conscious, you know? I naturally rebelled.*

As it had for Ernestine Anderson, the neighborhood along Madison, where the Savoy Ballroom and the Mardi Gras stood facing each other, provided a ready temptation.

"When I walked home from school, I passed the pool parlor and the Mardi Gras," she recollects, "and they always had jazz playing. It was like, my mother was saying, 'No!' but the music was sensuous and it said, 'Yes, come here!' It was too exciting to pass."

The teenage Bown was soon making up stories to get out of the house, peeking into speakeasies in Chinatown and along Jackson Street. By the time she was thirteen, she was working with Pops Buford on the sly at the Officers' Club at Fort Lawton. Some of her mother's worries about drugs and jazz proved to be well-founded.

> *I was singing and playing piano. Wearing rhinestone earrings and strapless dresses. Showing all my female pulchritude. It was on Sunday afternoon. The colonel would pay me the money at the end of the gig and he always gave me a bag of smoke. Yes. The guys in the band were delighted. I didn't get high because I was a kid. We rode back from Fort Lawton in a convertible Cadillac. I probably got a contact high, for all I know. They were smoking away. My mother didn't know I had this job. Eventually, I told her. We had some pretty rough periods there.*
>
> *I tried to look older, so I could get in a lot of places. That's funny when you think about it, the nerve you have. But when I think back on it, it was the only way I could learn my craft. Today, the kids have the advantage of jazz programs in the schools. We didn't have any of those things. To learn your craft, you had to get around other musicians and learn.*

The adult atmosphere Bown was entering intimidated her, but she put up a bold front.

When a friend brought Dizzy Gillespie over, Patti recalls being high-handed even with the king of bebop. "I got to the house before they brought Dizzy back," recounts Bown. "I was in the bathroom and Dizzy knocked on the door and I said, 'Who is it?' He said, 'It's Dizzy Gillespie.' I said, 'Well, I'm Patti Bown and you'll have to wait.' Honey, I had a real attitude. I was shy underneath, but I had to act like I was ready."

In the summer of 1949, Patti won a music scholarship to Seattle University as a concert pianist. In 1952, she performed with the Seattle Symphony and transferred to the University of Washington, where she studied with August Werner, an authority on German lieder, and worked as a rehearsal pianist for opera singers. But by this time, she had emotionally given up the idea of a classical career. Her sister Edith Mary had already made her debut, so some of the pressure from her mother was off. For the next four years, Patti played concert music in the daytime and jazz at night, soaking up the best of both worlds, sometimes mixing the two. She worked with her old friend Billy Tolles, who led her to Ray Charles, saxophonist Floyd Franklin, Emmett Lewis, Jabo Ward, Vernon Brown, and Al Pierre—anywhere she could pick up another bit of knowledge. The club scene, with its stars and sessions, was dazzling to the young pianist.

"Being in Seattle in those days was like seeing this great movie that never ended," she says. "I'd be playing the piano like this, never looking at my fingers, and looking out, scared I'm going to miss something!"

Two of her first mentors were Vernon and Wanda Brown: "I learned how to go out onstage from Wanda, and how to talk to the audience. I learned how to be calm, how to have fun. Wanda always made the audience feel good. Vernon would have a deep laugh in the background, sort of re-emphasizing the words she'd say as the emcee. They would guide me. People like that were very good to me."

So was Ray Charles, whose jam sessions at the Washington Social Club with Billy Tolles, the Charlie Taylor gang, and visiting musicians such as Dexter Gordon were another proving ground.

*That's how I learned to comp. Ray Charles and Dexter Gordon and Billy Tolles would have a tenor battle. They might play one tune an hour and a half or two hours. They would tell me, "You're all over the keyboard, girl! You have to learn how to put those chords. Leave some space!" Telling me, showing me. There was no books. You had to learn by doing it. Those rhythmic licks, trying to figure what they're doing, how to feed a soloist, stay out of his way, give him space, do a little nice, rhythmic pulsing thing to give him encouragement.*

Another early confidence-builder was Myrtle Francois, a woman from New Orleans who owned a nightclub on the corner of 12th and Yesler and played drums and sang in her own house band, in the window of the club. Francois billed herself as the "Personality Girl" and later worked with pianist Melody Jones in an act called "Melody and Mirth." Female drummers were far more unusual in 1949 than they are today. Seeing a woman instrumentalist was encouraging for an aspiring girl pianist. Francois' club also afforded Bown an unusual chance acquaintance.

*One night, this man came in. He sat down in the back and ordered dinner. They had New Orleans food in there and it was kind of late, about eleven-thirty or twelve. I was playing Billy Strayhorn's "Lush Life," and he came up to me and said, "Did you like that tune you were playing?" And I said, "Yes, you know Billy Strayhorn is a genius." "Oh, well, why is he a genius?" "Because he knows how to write simple melodies that singers can sing and very complicated harmony on them." He looked at me and said, "What's your name again? I'm Billy Strayhorn." He was there because Duke Ellington's band was in town.*

When Count Basie came through, Bown impressed his trumpet man Thad Jones at a cutting session at the Blue Note.

*Thad Jones looked around the room and he said, "We're going to play a blues in B-flat, and every chorus, we're going to raise it a half step." Then he called an impossible tempo, like "Dang!Dang!Dang!"—real fast—and everybody's all over the keyboard. It got to the key of B, and some people dropped out. Finally, it was just me playing by myself, me and Sonny Payne. Thad dropped out. Everybody dropped out. They asked me what my name was and said, "When you come to New York, you're going to do something."*

Like Quincy Jones, Patti had stars in her eyes.

*When they would take me to see Katherine Dunham or Marian Anderson, in my mind that meant, "These people are from New York!" It was like in Never Never Land. Little girl me, about four, five, six years old, off I would wander. My mother would be talking to somebody, I would let go of her hand, say I'm going to the ladies' room or something, and keep on going until I got backstage. Get an autograph. Look at the person, they'd say, "It's nice, this sweet little girl." I'd say, "Take me to New York." I always thought of myself as being a star. Even when I was a little girl, I had hitched my wagon.*

In 1955, Bown made her move, joining her sister Edith Mary in the Big Apple. The first trip proved to be little more than exploratory, but by the following year, Bown had become a permanent feature on the New York scene. It was a struggle at first. She sat in at Birdland, did gigs for a talent agent who sent her to businessmen's bars where the men pinched her on the rear, wrote commercial music for CBS television, and got a duo job playing with English bassist Peter Ind.

"In Seattle, I had never learned how to ask for a job, because everybody knew that I could play. I was shy. I learned to open my mouth and carry on a conversation. I was so poor I had to make two audition dresses. For a while, I lived in Harlem. That's where I wrote "G'wan Train" (a rhythmically propelled, churchy tune she later recorded with the Quincy Jones Orchestra).

Patti was helped in her effort to break into the New York scene by her old friend Quincy, whose reputation as an arranger with Hampton had enabled him to start making a living as a freelancer in New York, beginning in 1953. One of the first things Quincy did when Patti got to town was to set up a recording session for her. It was a much-needed break. Nevertheless, she immediately ran into gender prejudice.

*Quincy brought me on this date because he was forming a band. He had a choice of anybody he could want. We went in the studio, and Ernie Royal—bless his heart, he's dead now—yelled real loud, "Oh, a B-I-T-C-H is going to play the piano." He said the word, and all the guys cracked up. I felt weird, because I was looking on them as heroes. Why were they doing this chauvinistic thing to me? Quincy came over and he put his arm on my shoulder and he said, "Why don't you just go on over there to the piano and warm up a little bit." So I went over and I started playing, and when I finished warming up, the whole room started clapping. Then they stood up and they just kept clapping. I was so embarrassed I couldn't figure out what they were doing. They were coming up to the piano and shaking my hand and putting their arm around me, "Say, baby, you can cook. You can blow. I'm going to get you some work."*

In New York, Bown came under the stylistic influence of Horace Silver. In 1958, she made her first album as a leader, *Patti Bown Plays Big Piano*, a knockout of eclectic jazz piano that included "G'wan Train" as well as "Nothin' But the Truth," "Head Shakin'," and "Waltz de Funk." A year later, Jones invited her to join a special project in Europe that would involve two other Jackson Street veterans—Buddy Catlett and Floyd Standifer—and also would have disastrous consequences for almost everyone concerned.

In 1959, Jones had been invited to put together a big band for an unusual new Harold Arlen musical, *Free and Easy*. The path leading to this invitation had been one of frenzied activity for the young trumpeter-arranger, who in six years had risen from a section trumpet player in the Lionel Hampton band to one of the new stars on the transatlantic jazz scene. His reputation had begun in earnest with an arrangement he'd done for a small group in Europe, with Hamp, on the tune "Stockholm Sweetnin'," subsequently recorded by Clifford Brown. This had led to projects with, among others, Dinah Washington, Art Farmer, Jimmy Cleveland, and Clark Terry, as well as the leadership of two big bands for Dizzy Gillespie—one for a recording in 1954 and another for a State Department tour to the Middle East. (The latter included an old Seattle University pal, trombonist Rod Levitt.) Jones had also made an eighteen-month detour back to

France under special assignment for Mercury Records, working as musical director for Barclay Disques in Paris throughout 1957 and much of 1958. While there, he conducted a fifty-five–piece orchestra for Frank Sinatra at Grace Kelly's annual benefit party at Monte Carlo's Sporting Club and studied theory and composition with the great French teacher Nadia Boulanger.

Now, in 1959, Quincy hooked up with his old Seattle friend Ray Charles, who had broken into the mainstream market with his infectious blues piece "What'd I Say," and together they produced one of the best albums of both of their careers, *The Genius of Ray Charles*, a jazz big-band effort that pulled out the stops on soul, jazz, R & B, and rock.

Just as he was producing *The Genius* and writing scores for half a dozen other musicians, Jones was approached by the producers of the Arlen show. *Free and Easy* was one of the only big failures of Quincy Jones' career. The show itself had been tossing around New York for some time. Originally called *St. Louis Woman*, it had begun as a pastiche of old Arlen tunes, but over the years it had evolved into an experimental musical featuring jazz recitative (sung dialogue), stylized pantomime, and a full jazz band onstage in acting roles, an idea credited to Jones himself. The story was about a turn-of-the-century New Orleans jockey, Augie, and his love interest, Della. (Singer Patti Austin, then seven years old, was part of the cast.) It was hoped that after the show completed its European tour, Sammy Davis, Jr., would take the part of Augie. An opening was scheduled in Europe for December 7, 1959. To skeptics who feared that a show with jazz musicians acting onstage would never work, Quincy replied, "We're either going to rock the boat or sink it."

His bravado was prophetic. The show opened in Paris on January 15, 1960, at the Alhambra Theatre. At about this time the Algerian crisis erupted, and France's attention was turned to politics. Ten days later, *Free and Easy* closed; Quincy had eighteen jazz musicians on his payroll with nowhere to play. He called a meeting of the band and announced that anyone who wanted to go home had a ticket waiting for them. If they wanted to stay, he would book the band for a European tour. "It was a nightmare," he recalls.

*It was one of the hardest things I ever did in my life, because I jumped into some water I didn't understand. I didn't have a manager. We had no agent. I was twenty-five years old. I didn't understand about the business at all. I felt a tremendous pressure. Guys like Clark Terry had left Duke Ellington to come with my band. At one point, Clark got a call from the Johnny Carson band. I said, "Go. Do it, man. We're over here scuffling."*

Desperate to keep the band working, Quincy patched together bookings from one week to the next in Yugoslavia, Sweden, Denmark, Portugal, Spain, Holland, France, and Austria. Patti was often featured as a soloist to warm up the audience. Patti and Buddy Catlett went into the studio with Bill Coleman, the expatriate swing trumpet player, and made an album. The whole band recorded for Barclay Disques.

At one point, Jones booked a thirteen-city tour of one-nighters on the *Orient Express*, in remote towns in Eastern Europe. Catlett remembers:

*I went to sleep in an empty car. When I woke up, we were going into Transylvania. It was a gray morning, it had been raining all night, and there was one of those twisted trees on a big cliff and there was a river down there and it looked just like Dracula was coming, like one of those old 1930s movies.*

"When we got to Cannes," says Bown, "there were no hotels because it was the height of the season. I had to sleep on top of the grand piano." Catlett adds, "We flew from Denmark to Rome in one of those English two-motor jobs. The plane was loaded down. We flew *through* the Alps, not over them. Nonpressurized. My ears stayed plugged up for three days."

"Near the end," Bown remembers, "we had a bus with cellophane windows. Rain was on the floor this high. Everybody was coughing on the bus. People got sick."

After nine months, the pressure got to everyone, including Quincy: "I finally got to Finland and I just ran out of energy. That's the only time in my life I ever thought about suicide. I never saw the sun shine. I was upstairs, trying to figure out how do we survive the next week. We need new uniforms, we got to have new bandstands, we got to do this, we got to do that. I was just so tired."

In the fall, he booked passage home, on the USS *United States*. For a while, the group worked in New York as the house band at the Basin Street, but by 1961, the project fizzled. Quincy must have known that in 1960, big bands were economic dinosaurs. But he had grown up wanting to do what Basie, Hamp, and Duke had done. It's a shame that his big band didn't last. Many musicians on the scene, including trombonist Jimmy Cleveland, say that in terms of swing, drive, solo power, and sweetness of arrangements, Quincy was giving Basie a hard run for his money.

According to Cleveland, "Basie came over there. We were playing a theater in Paris, and they were standing in the wings and we came off and he said, 'I don't know what you all are trying to do, but it looks like you're trying to put me out of business!' And there wasn't a smile on his face. This band was smokin'! And we didn't care who knew it."

A rare live recording of the band as it was constituted in Paris, *Live at the Alhambra '60*, was made just two weeks after *Free and Easy* closed. This is Quincy Jones at an all-time peak, with the knockout punches of Basie combined with open voicings for French horn and flute riding over big, airy chords with baritone sax at the bottom. "Walkin'" features a fourteen-chorus solo by Buddy Catlett, a booming, entirely credible outing that came about, Catlett laughs, "because the band wouldn't come in." Patti Bown offers an appealing and novel chorus, as well, with odd, angular intervals.

But by far the most polished and representative recording of the band is *I Dig Dancers*, recorded in Paris after nearly a year on the road. The band made every tune in one take, and breathes as if it were a single player speaking perfectly articulated, laid-back swing. Three more recordings were made back home (with slightly different personnel, and excluding Standifer): *Newport Live*, *Birth of a Band*, and *The Wide World of Quincy Jones* (subsequently re-released as the two-record package *Birth of a Band*).

The *Free and Easy* tour was a personal disaster for many of the musicians involved, including Jones. Musicians came home nearly penniless to wrecked families and detoured careers (Jimmy Cleveland described it as an "alimony band"). Catlett's plans to attend Juilliard did not materialize. Standifer came home to a new child who didn't recognize him. "Everything we had at home disappeared," recounts Buddy. "Wife, kids. Not only me, Floyd just made it back on time."

For Patti Bown, however, the exposure to Quincy's troupe of heavyweights turned out to be a catapult into the heart of Manhattan jazz. She became musical director for Dinah Washington, toured with Sarah Vaughan, and appeared at the Newport Jazz Festival with Quincy Jones. She was invited to record with George Russell, Roland Kirk, Benny Carter, Nina Simone, Charles Mingus, Sonny Stitt, Duke Ellington, and Aretha Franklin. She composed dance music for Joseph Papp's West Indian musical, *Tijean and His Brothers*, and fed tunes to Basie, Jones, and others. She also started "ghosting" in the studio, playing for a variety of projects, including rock records by Ben E. King and Little Anthony & the Imperials; Aretha Franklin's early, pre-rock album, *After Hours* (produced by Quincy); and the soundtrack of Norman Mailer's film, *Tough Guys Don't Dance*, which features her famous belly laugh at the end of the film. The Duke Ellington Society presented a Patti Bown Night in 1982. In 1985, she became a member of the New York Jazz Repertory Orchestra, and the Mary Lou Williams Foundation gave her its Award for Excellence in 1986. She has been a guest on Marian McPartland's radio program, *Piano Jazz*.

For Jones, the *Free and Easy* disaster was a turning point, too—one that, bit by bit, steered him away from jazz and toward a more eclectic, commercial approach. Over the next five years, Jones learned the music business from top to bottom. In 1962, he became the first black executive of a major record label when he took the job as vice president for artists and repertoire at Mercury. One week, he was producing hit records by bubblegum-pop artist Leslie ("It's My Party") Gore; the next week, it was an album with Count Basie, the classic *One More Time*, or Basie and Sinatra, *It Might as Well Be Swing*. On *Genius Plus Soul*, he paired Milt Jackson and Ray Charles. *The Great Wide World of Quincy Jones* initiated a sequence of albums under his own name that would establish him in the role of leader/presenter for which he is known today.

Back in his Garfield High School days, someone had given Jones a copy of Frank Skinner's *Underscore*, a classic treatise on writing music for films. He had often spent entire weekend afternoons watching films at downtown theaters, sometimes closing his eyes to see if he could guess who the composer was. Music had always been a visual experience for Jones, anyway. "Even now," he told a reporter for *Life* magazine in the 1980s, "I think of primary and secondary colors first, and shapes and densities, before the sound comes."

Jones broke into movie scoring with a jazz soundtrack for *The Pawnbroker* in 1964, and never looked back. *In Cold Blood*, *In the Heat of the Night*, *Cactus Flower*, *MacKenna's Gold*, *The Lost Man*, *The Anderson Tapes*, *The Wiz*, and twenty-five other films followed, earning Jones and his record albums nineteen Grammy Awards.

Jones' gigantic success and his move away from an all-jazz program angered many of his colleagues, who felt he had sold out to commercial interests even as they were struggling on the artistic front lines for jazz. His 1974 move to no-holds-barred funk music, with gold records for the Brothers Johnson, and his subsequent best-selling album of all time, for Michael Jackson, *Thriller*, added fuel to the fire. But Jones stoutly defended his choices. "It always surprises me when I run into these beboppers and they're talking about, 'You sold out!'" says Jones hotly. "I've been playing this music all my life. A whole life. Everything. Concert music, swing things, rhythm and blues, gospel. I'm happiest that way because I got a chance to enjoy the best of all music."

Jones entered an even wider public imagination when he scored the music for the television series *Roots* and produced the gospel-inspired, all-star album *We Are the World*, to assist with famine relief in Africa. After those projects, he became a kind of American institution. He has been memorialized in a series of *Doonesbury* cartoon strips and received numerous public honors. He has been able to use his money, power, and influence in ways of his own choosing. For those specialists who would disparage his contribution to jazz, they have only to look at the work he did as an arranger for Hampton, Basie, and Clark Terry, the small group records he did with everyone from Oscar Pettiford to Dinah Washington to Jimmy Cleveland, and his own albums from the fifties and sixties. If populism or commerce—or perhaps a bit of each—has prevented him from being an advocate for jazz in and of itself as an art music, separate from other black traditions, then it must also be said, in fairness, that Jones has made more people aware of black traditions generally than most of his detractors.

In all this, Jones has remained true to his Jackson Street roots. He regularly visits old friends and colleagues in the Northwest—particularly Charles Taylor—and makes time for birthdays and special occasions, despite a schedule that perpetually has him hopping from one continent to the next. A miraculous recovery from a double aneurysm in 1974 made him even more conscious, he says, of maintaining the "warm and fuzzy" things in life.

# 7
# WHITE BOPPERS and ivy leaguers

The transition from swing to modern music is associated with a switch from big bands to bebop combos, but there were big bands playing modern music in the forties, too. The Dizzy Gillespie group that Quincy Jones had so regretted missing in Seattle was a good example. So were Woody Herman's Second Herd, organized in 1947, which specifically addressed the new music, and Stan Kenton's orchestra, which aggressively marketed its "modern" sound. These groups, which ranged from seventeen to twenty-five pieces, looked like swing bands, but their music was aimed at hip listeners rather than ballroom dancers. In this, they held a card in common with the bebop quintets, and like the boppers, they also occasionally outreached their audience's grasp.

"Progressive jazz" bands, as they came to be called, exercised an enormous influence on young players all over the country in matters of both musical and personal style. The boppers brought black pride to the black community; the progressives brought a new image of the cool and crazy hipster—or "beatnik"—to the white community. Seattle and Tacoma, for some reason, seem to have spawned more than their share of "wild men," some of whom are legendary in regional lore.

The first Seattle group of wild and crazy progressives coalesced around Ronnie Pierce in 1946. Pierce, recall, had gone to Roosevelt High and played with the Noteworthies in 1943; he'd also played in Stanton Patty's Chevaliers. Pierce was a white player fascinated with black culture who operated easily on both sides of the color line. He had studied with Frank Waldron, hung out on Jackson Street, and played with Bumps Blackwell at the Washington Social Club. He was also—and remains—a fast-talking, eccentric fellow who loves excitement and anything slightly loony, a sort of Spike Jones character with a grand sense of the absurd.

Raised in the carnival business in Puyallup and Seattle, Pierce was already playing after hours while in high school—with Bud Storm, at the Havana Club. (The bassist was Red Kelly; the pianist, Kenny Kimball; and the drummer, Don Manning.) In 1946, Pierce formed a band that tackled modern sounds—a brassy, ambitious bebop group with five trumpets, four trombones, French horn, five saxophones, four rhythm, and two singers. The roster was a virtual insiders' list of the best-known and best-loved white jazz musicians in the area. In the sax section were Pierce, Freddie Greenwell, Milt Price, Jimmie Shevenco, Irwin Adler, and Dick Sanders; trumpets were Marv Thomas, Dave Nelson, Walt Chamberlain, and Jim Freng; on trombone were Don Anderson, Dave Tuttle, Danny Reff, and Harold Spohr; Lowell Richards played French horn; Keith Purvis or Vernon Brown was on drums; bass was Red Kelly; piano, Kenny Kimball; and guitar, Glenn Thompson.

Local aficionados will immediately notice trumpeter Marv Thomas, who later owned the Seattle jazz club Parnell's, and whose son, Jay, is among the finest jazz musicians ever raised in the Northwest. Also of historical note is French-horn man Lowell Richards, who later played tuba in Seattle Dixieland groups and worked in the short-lived Norm Bobrow Little Big Band in the fifties, and whose wife, Phyllis Richards, became Seattle's first jazz critic, writing freelance under the name Maggie Hawthorn. Jimmy Shevenco and Don Anderson were top-notch studio musicians who became pillars of the 1950s scene, as did Dave Tuttle. Keith Purvis made a contribution in Dixieland. Freddie Greenwell became one of the top four or five players ever to come out of the Northwest. And bassist Red Kelly became a legend in his own right, perhaps the wildest of the Seattle-area wild men, during his many years with the Harry James and Woody Herman bands.

For a year or so, Ronnie Pierce's band had steady work, playing high school proms and such venues as the Palladium Ballroom and the Civic Auditorium, but as Pierce says, "The band was geared more for the ears than the show." After a deal fell through with Sonora Records in Chicago, the band dissolved. It had been a brave experiment.

"I guess you could say it was the dream jazz band of that era," says pianist Kenny Kimball. "You've got to give credit to Ronnie Pierce for trying to do in Seattle what Stan Kenton was doing in Balboa Beach about the same time. God, what a band that was! Great charts, marvelous charts!"

Pierce went on the road shortly after the "dream band" broke up. For a while, he played third alto with a comic, Spike Jones–style nine-piece, in Billings, Montana, then in 1948 played in the pit at Seattle's Palomar Theater and with Frankie Roth's dance band at Dick Parker's ballroom, on Aurora Avenue. In 1959, Pierce helped bring music back to the Pioneer Square area, working in a "funny hat" comedy band at the Blue Banjo and playing with Skinny Malone and the Hot Bananas at the World's Fair. Pierce went on to become one of Seattle's most colorful rock entrepreneurs, running a legendary go-go club called the Vault, at Second and Union Street.

Pierce's drummer, Don Manning, also played with Frankie Roth, which indirectly, in 1946, led to Seattle's first white bebop jam session, at a downtown place called the Players Club, at Seventh and Pike. Manning remembers:

> *[Frankie Roth] called me from a place called the South Seas. His group was real commercial. At the same time, they open a place upstairs and call it the Players Club and make it a hot jamming joint. I was the leader at first. [Red Kelly and I] hired two guys that were older, [pianist] Jimmy Beuttner and [tenor saxophonist] Norm Hoagy, who was just out of the service. Guys would come and sit in, whoever came through town, like Harry the Hipster [an early Los Angeles bebop pianist and comedian].*

Tacoma trumpet ace Neil Friel confirms the importance of the Players Club. "I date my whole Seattle experience from the time I went on a jam session with Les Brown's guys at the Players Club," he says. "That's where I heard Freddie Greenwell jam. The Players Club had acoustical qualities that just made a horn player feel like playing. You felt like you had gone to heaven."

Bassist Red Kelly, at the time just out of Queen Anne High School, calls the Players Club a "milestone," noting that Purvis, trombonist Dave Tuttle, clarinetist Rollie Morehouse, and California bassist Willie Cain also made the Players scene. Norm Bobrow, who had revved up his Metropolitan Theater concerts, sang at the Players from time to time, recruiting musicians for concerts, and eventually became manager of the place, renaming it the Stage, Screen and Radio Players Club. But the club soon succumbed to milder stewardship, as the wild men, Manning and Kelly, were forced out by the very sidemen they'd hired—Hoagy and Beuttner.

"They fired us," says Manning. "Can you believe it? They said we were endangering their livelihood and they were really concerned because we were so wild." Part of the problem was hard drugs, which were beginning to infiltrate the Seattle bebop scene.

"It was common knowledge that heroin was present there," says Friel. "It was in the form of caps. I think they called them number two caps and they sold for as little as three dollars. Being a seaport town, Seattle had a reputation for having good-quality heroin."

Drummer Dave Stetler, who had come up in the kid bands, recounts:

> *You know, when Parker and Diz broke on the scene, I knew a lot of young musicians around Seattle who were quite a bit younger than me, just out of high school, [who were] very impressionable. Charlie Parker had been on heroin, so they said, "If this guy's a genius, then we'll be able to play like that." Next thing you know, four or five of these kids are strung out so bad you can't believe. Some of those kids are dead.*

Hard drugs were just one symptom of social change in a world that had gone from pre-atomic to post-atomic in one August day. The Cold War had begun, and the Seattle-Tacoma area was one of its military-industrial nerve centers. Everyone had the jitters. Seattle saxophonist Aaron Davis went mad trying to find the "atomic note" in his horn. One player after another succumbed to drug addiction,

The New Chinatown, corner of Sixth Avenue South and South Main Street, 1937.

Courtesy of the Washington State Archives

alcoholism, or madness. Major Pigford captures well how the atomic nightmare related to the musical mood:

> *Bop was frantic, ending on notes that people were unaccustomed to hearing, phrases and melodies that were kind of strident. There's an uncertainty about bebop. Your ears are satisfied with it, but it's not like the old Tin Pan Alley songs, where you usually knew where they were going. . . . To me, this reflected the hecticness and the uncertainty of the world we were in. We didn't know what was going to happen. Nothing was certain.*

Given this emotional turmoil, it is not surprising that rebellious behavior became almost normal. "Outlaw" musicians such as trombonist Dick Thorlakson and trumpeter Bob McDermid competed with each other to see who could drink, shout, and burn more violently than the night before.

Musicians like Thorlakson and McDermid were quite at home at Danny Woo's New Chinatown, on Sixth, up the hill from Jackson, an occasionally rough place patronized by sailors and prostitutes. A plain upstairs joint with a wall of concrete blocks behind the bandstand, the New Chinatown had a restaurant downstairs with a raging bootleg business that served the nightclub on the second floor, at the top of a very steep and long flight of stairs. Owner Danny Woo later became a pillar of the Asian community—a park across the street from his old club now bears his name—but in his salad days he was one of the biggest bootleggers in Seattle. For five dollars, you could walk up the stairs to the New Chinatown with a bottle purchased on the premises.

"It had this huge kitty in the shape of a cat," recalls Buddy Catlett, who worked the New Chinatown with Terry Cruise. "A real kitty. It looked like Sylvester. Red nose. Sitting on the floor. It was almost as big as you are. You dropped money into its mouth."

The kitty wasn't always full. Kenny Kimball recounts:

> *Sometimes it got really lonely and we'd spend our time on the bandstand just shooting the breeze, but most of the time we went through the motions of playing sets and taking intermissions, just as if we had an audience. When the fleet was in, the place would occasionally get crowded with sailors and chicks, mostly prostitutes, and we'd be so thrilled to have someone there, even though they were mostly making boozy love in the booths and not listening to us, that we'd trot out our best tunes and try to play really inspired solos. Since we were an after-hours joint and didn't even begin to play until 1 a.m, we'd have other musicians drop by after their gigs to socialize.*

The bouncer at the New Chinatown was "Big Dave" Henderson, who also played piano. Musicians have described Henderson as a remarkable player whose sparse, natural style reminded them of Thelonious Monk's. Nearly every musician seems to have a drinking or brawling story about the New Chinatown. One perhaps apocryphal tale has the bouncer (not Henderson) throwing an obnoxious patron down the steep stairs to his death.

Jimmy Shevenco, a hard-drinking clarinetist who moved to Seattle from Universal Studios in Los Angeles and then played in Ronnie Pierce's "dream band," led a group at the New Chinatown during and just after the war. Shevenco became notorious for drinking whiskey on the bandstand from a one-quart milk bottle.

Into this rather seedy atmosphere, with its case of musical nerves, briefly ventured a white teenager from Wenatchee who would become the most notorious Northwest bebopper of them all—Don Lanphere. Though Wenatchee, at the eastern foot of the Cascades, was far from the Jackson Street hub, Lanphere kept in touch with the action while growing up, thanks to his father, who drove him over the mountains to Seattle every week for saxophone lessons with Johnny Jessen, and to the Trianon to see the great swing bands. By the time Lanphere was twenty-one, even Miles

Davis knew where Wenatchee was.

One night, the story goes, Lanphere was sitting in a club listening to Miles, who came off the stand and sat down next to Don at the bar. Lanphere was awestruck, but did not tell Miles he was an aspiring saxophonist from rural nowheresville. They made small talk for twenty minutes. When Miles got up to return to the stand, he asked, "Where are you from?"

"Oh, nowhere you've ever heard of—Wenatchee, Washington."

Miles paused. "Say hello to Don Lanphere."

Being recognized by Miles Davis came as a pleasant shock to a young kid who just a few years earlier had been listening to 78s of the new bebop in his father's music store. Lanphere started playing when he was eight, after discovering his dad's saxophone in the attic. At thirteen, when the Lunceford band came through Wenatchee, Lanphere played his version of Coleman Hawkins' solo on "Body and Soul" and made Willie Smith and Joe Thomas smile.

As a youngster, Lanphere collected 2,000 jazz records, buying them in big batches through his father's store. Jazz writer Doug Ramsey, who grew up with Lanphere, vividly remembers intense listening sessions with Don. "That's where I first heard Miles," Ramsey wrote in a liner note to a Miles Davis album.

In the summer of 1944, the sixteen-year-old saxophonist got permission from his parents to live alone in Seattle. Working at the Olympic Hotel with Wally Anderson's tenor band, Lanphere lived in a downtown hotel and explored the after-hours scene.

"I got introduced to life there," he recalls. "The war was still going on, so the Club Maynard was servicemen all night long. And yet, walking there at one o'clock in the morning at the height of the war, carrying my horn with a smile on my face, nobody ever bothered me."

In 1945, Lanphere graduated from high school and headed for Northwestern University in Chicago, with the intention of becoming a school music teacher. He was soon soaking up the sounds of Sonny Stitt, Jimmy Raney, and others on the scene. When Claude Thornhill had an empty alto/clarinet chair, Lanphere filled in for a few days. Other opportunities followed. Charlie Ventura needed a sub, and Don found himself playing in a band with trombonist Kai Winding. Another player who would later work in the Northwest showed up, as well—pianist Betty Stitt (no relation to Sonny), who was also attending Northwestern and studying with Lennie Tristano. The two recorded an acetate.

For a while, Lanphere, trombonist Jimmy Knepper, and saxophonist Joe Maini roomed together. Maini had started to make illicit recordings of Charlie Parker at the Regal and Pershing ballrooms. Lanphere caught the bug and joined the crowd of "Bird Watchers"—or "Ornithologists," as they would be memorialized in a later song title—who would make important recorded "sightings" of Parker throughout his career. Lanphere and Knepper joined a bebop septet led by swing bandleader Johnny Bothwell, which after three months took them to New York, into the Baby Grand, in Harlem. Lanphere dropped out of school; the year was 1948.

The first night the septet played at the Baby Grand, a beautiful, dark-haired girl named Chan Richardson walked in with Bothwell. She left with Lanphere. The next day, the jealous bandleader gave Lanphere notice. Chan was a hip follower of the new music who lived in an apartment above 7 West 57th Street. Musicians playing the clubs downstairs would come up during their breaks to get away from the crowds. Chan was another "Bird Watcher" and was good friends with Ross Russell, who was recording Parker on his label, Dial, and would later write a Parker biography.

"One night Ross Russell came in with Chan and said, 'Be at this place on a Friday at such-and-such a time and bring your horn,'" Don remembers. "So I walked in and I saw Max Roach and Fats Navarro, and I'm supposed to make a record. It was a bit of a shock!"

This was Lanphere's first record date in the Apple, November 29, 1948—a vocal session led by Earl Coleman. The group waxed the very first recording of Denzil Best's new tune, "Move," which would shortly become a "cool jazz" classic. Lanphere learned "Move" on the set, soloing after hearing Fats run through it once.

After the date, trumpeter Navarro befriended Lanphere. The saxophonist was invited to do his own album for Bob Weinstock's New Jazz label, a subsidiary of Prestige. "Bob asked me who I wanted in my band," says Don, "and I said, 'Bird's rhythm section and Fats Navarro.' Of course I was joking. He said, 'All right.' In September, Lanphere went into the studio

with Fats, Al Haig (piano), Tommy Potter (bass), and Max Roach (drums), and recorded four sides, including a tune Don had written on the changes of "Pennies from Heaven" titled "Stop." These records are early bebop classics.

Between these two recording sessions, Lanphere did three months on the road with clarinetist Jerry Wald, then went out with Woody Herman's Second Herd. Lanphere was in the thick of the most exciting musical happenings in jazz. Jimmy Knepper and Joe Maini rented a sub-basement in a building on 136th Street and Broadway and fixed it up as a jam-session pad where Lanphere, Bird, Bill Crow, Gerry Mulligan, Warne Marsh, Bob Dorough, Seattle drummer Buzz Bridgeford—and even Lenny Bruce—would come by to play, at any time of the day or night. On one session, taped by Lanphere and later issued as *The Apartment Sessions*, Bird and Lanphere performed together. Another famous Bird "bootleg" album, *Bird at St. Nick's*, was also the result of a Lanphere recording session. "Playing with Bird was like lesson time," recalls Don. "He was very generous in showing us stuff and making little explanations."

Joe Maini started a jumbo-sized rehearsal band to showcase the arranging of Gene Roland that included Lanphere, Al Porcino, Red Rodney, Jimmy Knepper, Charlie Parker, Al Cohn, Zoot Sims, Joe Bushkin, and Tiny Kahn, among others. The group never performed, but it can be heard on the recording *The Band that Never Was*.

As Lanphere was soaking up the sounds of this extraordinary environment, he also was unfortunately absorbing some of the more deadly aspects of the bop lifestyle. He had already been exposed to heroin in Chicago. By the time he went to New York, he was an addict. To make matters worse, Chan Richardson had left him and moved in with Bird. Lanphere began to lead an increasingly reckless life. In 1951, he was arrested on the street in Detroit for scoring drugs and ended up in the county jail. He was twenty-two.

Lanphere spent the next six years back in Wenatchee, working in his father's music store, trying to get his life back together. In 1956, he and his childhood friend jazz writer Doug Ramsey produced a two-day jazz festival in Wenatchee, bringing over pianist Paul Neves, bassist Larry Rockwell, drummer Gerald Frank, Patti Bown, and trumpet player Chauncey Locke from Seattle. The following year, he headed back to the East Coast with renewed confidence. For eight months, he lived in Boston with Paul Neves. The following summer, he rejoined Woody Herman. More tours and recordings followed, with Charlie Barnet and Claude Thornhill. But in 1961, Lanphere's lifestyle caught up with him again. He was arrested for possession of marijuana in Oklahoma. His parents bailed him out again.

For the next twenty-three years, Don Lanphere's horn lay nearly mute. In 1969, Lanphere was reborn a Christian, and he finally found an anchor to his life. By 1982 he felt he wanted to try to revive his career. "[My wife] said, 'You're sixty years old. If you don't do it now, you're never going to do it,'" he says. Lanphere took her advice, and the jazz world has been the better for it.

The saxophonist started out with a few local gigs in Seattle, then got booked into the West End Cafe in Manhattan, and his career took off again. Since then, he has recorded ten albums, beginning with *Out of Nowhere*, utilizing a nexus of Northwest musicians that usually includes Jon Pugh on trumpet, Jeff Hay on trombone, Dean Hodges on drums, Marc Seales on piano, and Chuck Deardorf on bass. He has also released collaborative albums with guitarist Larry Coryell and vocalist Jay Clayton, who has lived and taught in the Northwest since the early 1980s. Lanphere has toured Europe and Britain, played at the North Sea Jazz Festival, and now performs regularly in clubs around the country. He has a large clientele of improvisation clinics at school jazz programs. Don Sickler, a Spokane native who makes a specialty of publishing jazz tunes, transcribed Lanphere's bop lines, published by Jamie Aebersold as *Lanphere Lines to Aebersold Tracks*.

In the nineties, Lanphere is still a tough tenor whose swaggering, sinuous improvising bristles with the excitement of swing-to-bop discovery. His lowing tenor tone is an extremely personal one, plaintive and hollow, through which the chuffing warmth of his swing-era roots still bubbles. Since his religious renewal, Lanphere has taken up soprano saxophone, which he plays with extraordinary sensitivity on ballads. Like most old boppers, Lanphere is in love with speed, and loves nothing better than to flip expectations, such as in his recording of "Take the 'A' Train" as a waltz, or his speedy "Cherokee" takeoff, "Noble Indian Song Pt. 2," which doubles back on itself with tricky rhythms that are nearly impossible to play.

Lanphere says he's having a lot more fun now than he was back in his frenetic 52nd Street days, when he was driven by competitiveness: "I'm thoroughly enjoying this, because I'm not trying to impress anybody anymore."

At one of Lanphere's all-night jam sessions in Manhattan, he had hooked up with Wayne "Buzzy" Bridgeford, the drummer who had played with Curt Sykes at the Trianon. Bridgeford was another great Seattle swing-to-bop–era musician. Buzzy was from Olympia, where his father, a prominent doctor, had worked for the state government. Friends and admirers paint a picture of the young Bridgeford as a sensitive Chet Baker–type who had many advantages growing up, among them the unfortunate one of getting his fingers into his father's pharmaceuticals. As a youngster, Bridgeford was playing in Brad Bannan's commercial swing band in Tacoma, then graduated to Curt Sykes' group. After the war, he became a savvy hipster whose sense of rhythm was matched only by his sardonic sense of humor. Don Manning, who idolized the drummer as a guru and became his informal student, recalls the first time he saw Bridgeford, about 1944:

> *The word went out that Buzz was going to take [the drummer's] place in Curt Sykes' band. There's this knock at the door and he walks in. I couldn't believe it. Here's this little guy. He had long hair almost like a girl. He was so frail. He acted real strange, a real hepcat. Buzz, he's gritting his teeth and frowning, listening to everything, you know. He's looking down at the floor and he's going just like a Kerouac character. He's wigging out. I'm hanging on his every word. What's he gonna say? What's he gonna do? And the music stops and he says, "Don, goddamnit, if I ever overplay the band like that I want you to tell me." And he walks out and slams the door. The next day, he comes in and plays all the arrangements like he's already studied them.*

"He was a real natural, amazing player," according to Red Kelly. "Those guys, like Shadow Wilson, and Art Madigan, they'd hit a cymbal and it'd sound like a painting, Van Gogh or something. . . . Buzzy could do that." (A private 1955 recording of Bridgeford with a Seattle quartet bears Kelly out. Buzzy's cymbal sound was luxurious.)

Bridgeford enjoyed turning on other musicians to music and to his philosophy of life. He told Manning early on he had to decide whether he wanted to be a drummer like Gene Krupa—the aggressive, bashing type—or like Jo Jones, the subtle, understated power beneath the band, using shading and dynamics as well as force. Buzzy had already made his choice.

**Buzz Bridgeford, Tupper Lake, New York, summer 1950.**

**Courtesy of Bill Crow**

Morehouse tells of a night on the road with Curt Sykes, when the bandleader asked Buzz to put a little more backbeat into his playing, to make a particular tune a little more danceable: "I looked up and Buzzy was back there with a saw and a board, sawing on the afterbeat!"

"Buzzy would get so frustrated with the people that wanted to hear corny stuff, the same old commercial tunes, like 'Tea for Two' and 'Ace in the Hole,'" remembers Kenny Kimball, who worked with Bridgeford in 1950. "I remember one night Buzzy jumped out from his drums and he kicked the bandstand—BANG! BANG! BANG! He was so frustrated he couldn't stand it any longer."

Bridgeford left Seattle with Jan Garber, a commercial bandleader, played in trumpeter Jimmy Zito's band for a while, along with Seattleite Fred Greenwell, then joined Randy Brooks. For a couple of years, Brooks' sizzling modern big band—a good example of a swing unit taken over by young, bebop-hungry soloists—captured the imagination of jazz aficionados, scoring sixth in the 1947 *down beat* poll for Best Swing Band. Bridgeford rode the critical wave, placing No. 15 in the Best Drummer category. At some point, he became Brooks' manager, in which capacity he got into a severe car accident while driving the bandleader's Cadillac, which prompted a return to his parents' home in Olympia to recuperate.

Bridgeford was a fast talker and a born hustler. In Seattle, when he met and fell for the astounding Lennie Tristano student Betty Christopher (whom Don Lanphere had known in Chicago as Betty Stitt), Buzzy decided he had to play music with her. Christopher had come to Seattle with an all-girl orchestra. Bassist Bill Crow, who was attending the University of Washington at the time, remembers:

> *Buzzy couldn't believe what he had found here. In the first place, he had eyes for her, and in the second, she was somebody who played very good piano and didn't know anything about anything except Lennie Tristano. Since he loved to hip people, he started hipping her to Bird and to Bud [Powell] and all these wonderful things. She was just sopping it up like a sponge.*
>
> *Buzzy manufactured a job at one of Russian John's clubs, the Filipino Veterans of Foreign Wars. I think they had some kind of Hawaiian band in there. Buzzy talked to the owner. "Look," he said, "you've got a rounders' club here. This is where all the high rollers and the pimps and the hookers and everybody that's hanging out after hours [goes]. You're supposed to have jazz in a club like that. This Hawaiian music isn't it." The guy said, "Yeah, maybe you're right." So he put a band together with Betty, Doug Goss on bass, and Freddie Greenwell on tenor. I used to take my valve trombone and bongos down.*

In Tacoma, Bridgeford promoted a gig at a beer joint on Ninth and Pacific called the Pirate's Cove, easily the best white bebop band assembled to that date in the Northwest, with Freddie Greenwell on tenor saxophone, Don Ober on guitar, Hollis Sulser on piano, and Paul Binnings on bass. As Greenwell recalls:

> *That was really one of the best jobs I ever played in the Northwest. We had a real good swing bebop band there. We played blues and rhythm and blues and jazz. That piano player was absolutely one of the best piano players you'd ever want to hear in the world. He was like Hank Jones. He was really a gasser. That was quite a jazz experience down there. It was just really inspiring to play a steady job with Buzzy.*

Like Lanphere, Buzz Bridgeford was into playing very fast. Dean Reilly, a bass player who also worked on the Tacoma scene, remembers bassist Traff Hubert and Bridgeford having "speed contests": "Buzz would say, 'Okay, here we go.' Just the two of them. I remember Neil Friel and Buzz and Traff once played 'Cherokee' for five or ten minutes as fast as it could go—it was breathtaking."

Bridgeford played at the Black Hawk in San Francisco with Stan Getz in 1951. Later, he traveled east with bassist Bill Crow and played in a group with vocalist Dave Lambert. But his drug abuse was getting progressively in the way. He eventually came home in a shambles. Dave Stetler remembers filling in for Buzz at the Union Club when the sick drummer was sent home in a cab. Bridgeford died in 1956, one of the first of the drug casualties on the Seattle bop scene.

Hollis Sulser, the pianist on the Pirate's Cove gig and the leading bebop pianist in Tacoma, later went to Hollywood, where he joined Bobby Sherwood's big band. Tragically, he died young in an automobile accident in Tacoma in the early sixties. Bassist Paul Binnings left town and became a professional musician in Reno. Don Ober was a Charlie Christian–style guitar player who wore a big hat and pinstriped suit and smoked a cigar. In the seventies, he became a regular sideman at Red Kelly's club, the Tumwater Conservatory, and died in the mid-eighties.

When Buzz Bridgeford left the Pirate's Cove, the job had gone to one of the most unlikely, underappreciated underground musicians ever to work in the Northwest, trumpet player Neil Friel. An obsessive and zany character with a precocious enthusiasm for many of the themes adopted by the beat generation—Eastern mysticism, fringe therapies, and drugs—Friel is universally acknowledged as one of the best bebop musicians to emerge from the Northwest. A bent imp of a man today, whose face has aged beyond his sixty-two years, Friel is a gentlemanly, warm individual who possesses a gift for storytelling and a wry sense of life's ironies. Tracked down in Manhattan for an interview, Friel recounted his early years this way:

*I was born in the Black Hills of South Dakota, on February 27, 1930. My father, Monte Friel, played violin, trumpet, clarinet, and drums. When I was nine, he came west with a band led by Dale Fitzsimmons. They had their sights on the big time. They had four nights a week at the Crescent Ballroom in Tacoma. With one break or two, one way or another they could have made it.*

*My father wouldn't hear of anything else but that I should become a swing trumpet player. Bunny Berigan was his absolute idol. When I was nine, I started practicing. Within a few months, I was solo cornetist with the all-city orchestra. I had to practice two hours a day. I wasn't even permitted to think of anything else. My father used to take me around to hear black jazz trumpet players. I heard one named Leon [Vaughn] and another named Herman Grimes. Then, one Sunday, it came like a full-blown transcendental revelation. My friend Whitey Collier put on a record by Louis Armstrong one Sunday afternoon. I would always listen politely to the notes as they transpired and they meant nothing to me. All of a sudden, Louis Armstrong took this jazz break, improvised, and what he said in that break just illuminated me from the bottom of my spine. I lit up like a fluorescent tube! From that moment on, I've never wanted to do anything else in my life but play jazz trumpet. I think I was fifteen. I would run two miles home from Bellarmine High School at lunch hour in order to play Sonny Berman's trumpet chorus on "Sidewalks of Cuba."*

*Neal Ely and I worked with Brad Bannan at Five Mile Lake during the summer. Brad Bannan had the best band around. Louis Grenier played at the Top of the Ocean for thirty years. If I hadn't been so imbued with star eyes, I probably would have just stayed there and had quite a comfortable little middle-class career.*

*Then I saw Charlie Parker. It was 1948 at the Jazz at the Philharmonic show, down at the Moore Theater. It was pure distilled magic. I decided I wanted to go to New York to see Bird and Diz and get in on the bebop. But there was another reason. One of my chief mentors at that time was Neal Ely, who had promulgated this system of Reichian analysis. He was worried about my becoming heavily neurotic. And there was no doubt about it, I had a little persecution complex going. It's obvious, looking back, to see what brought it all on. I was wearing long hair before it was popular. I ran into all kinds of heat, was called various names. I developed a hell of a chip on my shoulder. So Neal thought I should go through Reichian analysis. I was all for it. My family had been going through an internal scene that was just utterly unpleasant.*

*The Reichians had an approach dealing with life energy, which in terms of Indian mysticism and yogi teachings is the same thing they have known for centuries in the East as* prajna. *Wilhelm Reich was the Charlie Parker of psychiatry. Neal got an orgone accumulator. The first time I got in one, I didn't know one was not supposed to do yogic breathing in there and I just passed right out, within thirty seconds.*

*I went to a Reichian analyst in Brooklyn named Dr. Chester Raphael. Dr. Raphael said, "Yes, you need help my son, and the sessions are fifty dollars an hour, minimum." In 1950, that was just hopelessly out of my range. He did give me some hope, some group therapy, but I wanted that one-on-one vegetotherapy. I thought it was going to unlock my personality. . . .*

*New York was like being thrown into a bathtub of great music. Right across the street from my little room on 53rd and Broadway, every night at nine o'clock, the Tito Puente Orchestra would open up and play their theme song till hell wouldn't have it. It was an immensely exciting time. I got to meet Sonny Stitt. Don Lanphere was there. He was already a famous player. He had recorded with Fats Navarro. Music was coming out of the skyscrapers themselves.*

When Friel returned from his first trip to New York City, in 1950, at age twenty, he was one of the few musicians in the Northwest who had actually jammed on 52nd Street—Fred Greenwell was another—and the only one who had picked up on the nascent "beat" movement. He immediately began to spread the word. Quincy Jones recalls:

*Neil had a big influence on me philosophically, because he was real far out. We were dealing our little homemade orgone emulators, out of tin foil and stuff. And we were enlightening the teachings of the masters of the Far East. We were into L. Ron Hubbard, Dianetics, and all that stuff. Fourteen and fifteen. There were about four or five of us who were into this real spiritual quest.*

Friel and Jones became friendly competitors:

*Quincy was further advanced than me when it came to writing. Trumpetwise, we seemed about even. We were both into playing bop. We played together in this one band and he and I still talk about it. It was Fourth of July. We went out to this lake and that band did not do anything but swing, à la Dizzy Gillespie's Orchestra, right from the get-go.*

Friel hung out on the Tacoma and Seattle scenes for a year or so, playing after hours and with various commercial dance bands, when his pal Charlie Johnson, another avid bebop trumpeter, gave him a call to join Darryl Harpa, a debonair Latin bandleader with whom Red Kelly and Don Manning had left town. Harpa was Seattle's mambo man throughout the late 1940s and gave nearly a dozen local jazz musicians their first taste of the road.

Originally from Los Angeles, where he had led a floor-show–style rumba band, Harpa had started working at Seattle's El Rancho, on Aurora Avenue, in 1947. He billed his band as "Musical, Both Americas," a reference to the group's two sets of arrangements, one Latin and one swing. His bongo player was Desceito (David) Niego, a showboat Cuban who danced in front with Harpa's wife, Myrna. Pianist Eddie Diamond, a Hawaiian who worked in Seattle in the late forties, wrote the band's Latin book. Pianist Jim Gilles, who worked with Harpa in 1950, says he learned authentic Latin style in the band, but Red Kelly characterized Harpa as a "con artist" who "didn't know anything about music."

Kelly was right about the "con artist" part. On his Midwest tours, Harpa never played the same hotel twice, because of the gambling debts he left behind.

In early 1951, Harpa was playing in Washington, D.C., and he needed both a trumpet player and pianist. Friel and Gilles took off like two bullets aimed at their dreams. As Friel remembers it, "Jimmy Gilles and I rode across the country on a Greyhound and joined the band at the Wardman Park Hotel. Darryl taught us all we know about Latin music." On the road, Manning and Kelly defected from the band, but Friel stayed on, recording a tune with Harpa in 1952 called "You and the Night and the Music," with Marana Page on vocals. After the Harpa tour, Friel spent some time in Los Angeles, working as a copyboy for the Associated Press during the day and jamming at night wherever he could, including sessions on Central Avenue with Wardell Gray, Sonny Clark, Frank Morgan, and Max Roach. Friel also began a laborious reconstruction of his trumpet embouchure and technique in Los Angeles, studying with symphony player Louis Maggio.

When Friel came back to Tacoma, he hired bassist Traff Hubert and pianist Jimmy Gilles for the gig at the Pirate's Cove, on Pacific Avenue. Friel was still having trouble with his trumpet embouchure, so he took up drums. His trio, called the Cosmos, toured the Northwest throughout 1955. Friel then got a show job as a drummer in Great Falls, Montana, and switched back to trumpet for a gig with a group called the Fabulous Woodsons.

By this time, Neil felt he was ready to go back to New York to try to get on with a name band as a trumpet player. Returning to the Apple in 1960, he got a call from Billy May, a bandleader who was making a career of reviving the big-band sound with some integrity. For the next ten years, Friel worked with plenty of name bands—not only Billy May but also Woody Herman, Les Elgart, Charlie Spivak, Jimmy Dorsey, Glenn Miller, and Claude Thornhill. In 1965 he recorded with Sy Zentner, and in 1967 with Woody Herman at the Monterey Jazz Festival, getting off a dizzy trumpet solo on Bill Holman's "The Horn of the Fish."

Friel drifted from one band to the next, getting fired and rehired, as he alternately got straight and fell off the wagon. Eventually, in 1971, he left the fray and moved to the Catskills. He played at Grossinger's in a show band for over four years. In 1976, Friel came home to Tacoma, where he played at Seattle's Roosevelt Hotel with pianist Johnny Lewis. In the early nineties, he was living in the small village of Jamestown, New York.

Looking back on his career, Friel is poignantly honest: "The traveling and doing one-nighters with a big band—that was all we ever wanted. Once I had reached that, I didn't have any other goals. I had never thought of myself as becoming a jazz star. All I ever wanted to do was just play for a big band."

"Neil was his own worst enemy," remarks white saxophonist Chuck Stentz. "He never got his personal thing together. But he played great. And he played very warm."

In spite of his failings, Friel survived the era's accelerated lifestyle. So did Fred Greenwell, whose career bears striking parallels to both Friel's and Buzz Bridgeford's. All three came up as swingers, then turned to bop. They all played in some of the hipper post-war big bands, and all were diverted from music by drugs and alcohol. They are also among the top ten musicians ever to come out of the area. One solo by Fred Greenwell could stand by itself as justification for a book about Seattle jazz.

Greenwell is a burly, soft-spoken man who counts among life's great pleasures music, large mugs of tea with sweetened milk, purebred cats, and the close, shrouded environment of the rainy Northwest. Fred lives in a tranquil neighborhood on a hill near Green Lake in Seattle, and likes to look out his window at the soft contours of the city, with its evergreen trees and constant cloud cover. It is an image that matches his playing, which has the soft and swirling attack of his contemporary Stan Getz, but with a slightly acidic edge.

Few players elicit the unqualified endorsement Fred Greenwell does from his contemporaries. Says drummer Dave Stetler:

> *Now there's the giant of the saxophone. When I first heard that guy play, I was fortunate enough to play in a session with him. He would take a chorus, then he'd take another chorus, and then another one, and every one would get more beautiful than the last. He would just take you on a trip, have you sailing on the clouds. He was so full of soul, this guy, you couldn't believe it.*

Greenwell was born in Wilmington, Delaware, in 1924. His parents were both musicians. During his youth, he went to all the shows coming through Wilmington at the black Odd Fellows Hall—Duke Ellington, Cab Calloway, Andy Kirk, Earl Hines, and Count Basie. Black swing was his passion.

"I used to have to walk past the black ballroom to get to high school," recalls Greenwell. "I'd go in early and watch those guys set up. I was eighteen years old and studying the clarinet real hard. This was really an education, that style of music. I had a lot of desire to be in the field of modern music that those guys represented."

When the war broke out, Greenwell was accepted into the Navy music school, where he received conservatory training and wound up in bandleader Claude Thornhill's detachment. (Seattle clarinetist Rollie Morehouse was also in the band.) Thornhill was one of the progressive bandleaders introducing the sounds of modern classical harmony to the white big bands. Greenwell toured the South Pacific with Thornhill for a year, then was stationed in New York. He naturally got into Manhattan as often as he could to hear the boppers on 52nd Street. (Hanging on Greenwell's wall today is a picture of him jamming at the Spotlite Club

Fred Greenwell sitting in with Charlie Parker at the Spotlite club, 52nd Street, New York, 1946. Left to right: Stan Levey, Leonard Gaskin, Sir Charles Thompson (partially hidden), Charlie Parker, Greenwell.
Courtesy of Fred Greenwell

with Charlie Parker. Another shows him in a tenor duel with Wardell Gray.)

After his Navy stretch, Greenwell moved west. His mother, who had been born and raised in Prosser, Washington, had moved back to Seattle and started a successful music studio, where she taught piano and violin, in the Greenwood neighborhood. Rollie Morehouse had also encouraged Greenwell to come to Seattle. Fred entered the University of Washington music department, but soon dropped out. To keep cash flowing, he joined Morehouse in the Curt Sykes band, but, he reports, Sykes' commercial arrangements "bored me out of my skull." A six-nighter with the celebrated Texas trombone player Jack Teagarden made life more livable. So did Greenwell's discovery of the few like-minded souls in Seattle who were hip to what he'd heard on 52nd Street; these were the friends who introduced him to the after-hours joints where the real music was happening. He became an instant regular.

*As soon as I could get through at the Trianon, I would go down to Jackson Street, which was just roaring. You couldn't get in the Rocking Chair very easily at all. That's where Ray Charles worked. He never seemed to want to let anybody sit in, but I would still try to do it, because I knew he was really good. I enjoyed being able to play at least along behind him. Milt Garred [Charles' bassist] would talk Ray into letting me play. They always had good music. If you were known, you could get in as a white. But most white people wouldn't want to even go there. They're not interested in really relaxing and having a good time and being up at that time of night. They're out running the banks.*

Though Greenwell had absorbed the latest licks in New York, his goal at this time was to learn more tunes so he could make a living playing with commercial combos. He set about getting an education on the street.

*I made an effort to go to a lot of different places where I knew they were going to play some different tunes. I found you could always get ten dollars out of playing "Ace in the Hole." Another one was "Squaws on the Yukon," and if you can sing it, even better. I learned ballads that later guys would say, "Where'd you ever hear that?"*

Greenwell soon became an in-demand player, welcome everywhere—except, of course, by other tenor saxophonists. Al Hickey, tenor man with the Jive Bombers, recalls:

*One night, Paul Quinichette came to town. He said, "Hickey, get your horn and let's jam." We played at this club for a half hour and then we'd go to the next club and jam and the next club, and then we got to the Rocking Chair and Freddie Greenwell was up there. I said, "You go and get your horn out and I'll be right up there." Boy, he got up there with that Freddie Greenwell and I thought that cat was about ready to throw away his tenor. He said, "What you doin'?" I said, "Look, I have to deal with this every night!"*

What knocked out other musicians about Greenwell was not only his natural ability but his individual voice, something all jazz musicians strive for. Like Dick Wilson before him and white saxophonist Denney Goodhew after him, Greenwell is a Seattle saxophonist who plays in a personal and completely accomplished style of his own.

Chuck Metcalf, a bassist who as a young man worked in the Bobrow Little Big Band, today adds perceptively: "The tenor saxophone players [in Seattle] sounded different from one another. Gerald Brashear and Billy Tolles had markedly different styles, and Freddie Greenwell had another different style. He was a highly evolved, Les Young–style player of those first kind, like Herbie Steward and Stan Getz and Zoot Sims. One of the highlights of my career here was first hearing Freddie Greenwell play."

When Fred wasn't knocking out other musicians at concerts, he worked casuals with Vern Mallory and sat in wherever he could, including a blues joint near 12th and Yesler where Palmer Johnson's old drummer, Punkin Austin, and pianist Dave Henderson worked.

After a couple of years on the Jackson Street scene, Greenwell was picked up by Jimmy Zito, a hot Les Brown trumpet man who had started an eleven-piece big band and needed a third alto player who could also play good clarinet. (Bud Shank, who would move to the Seattle area in the 1980s, was playing lead alto and flute.) The band recorded with vocalist Helen O'Connell for Coast Records and toured San Diego, Albuquerque, and other points close to Hollywood, where most of the players were based. For several months, Buzz Bridgeford played drums.

Greenwell was based in Los Angeles for about a year, where he played with Wardell Gray, scat singer Leo Watson, and Zoot and Ray Sims, and did some occasional studio work. But

Fred Greenwell and Wardell Gray. Jack's Basket Room, Los Angeles, 1948.

Courtesy of Fred Greenwell

Greenwell was uncomfortable in the laid-back southland. In 1949, he found a ticket out with Alvino Rey, the electric-guitar pioneer. After two or three years touring with Rey, Greenwell was hired by Buddy Morrow, an excellent bandleader who eventually became extremely successful in Hollywood. Greenwell made twenty or thirty records with Morrow (playing in section, not soloing), including *One Mint Julep* and Morrow's monster hit, *Night Train*.

Throughout the 1950s, Greenwell moved back and forth between Seattle and New York. His itinerary is sketchy. Like Bridgeford, his personal habits were beginning to catch up with him. In 1950, he was in New York, where he shared one of the notorious bebop lofts: musicians would pool ten or twenty dollars each to use an apartment to jam twenty-four hours a day. This was a "very constructive" period, says Greenwell, in which he played with Zoot Sims and Herb Geller, worked weekend casuals, and hung out with Don Lanphere. Greenwell also subbed in the Artie Shaw group, "before Artie fired the whole band," and rehearsed with the Benny Goodman band for two weeks.

In 1951, Greenwell came home for a spell, playing with Buzzy Bridgeford, Ken Kimball, and bassist Bill Crow in Seattle. When Crow and Kimball left for New York, Freddie joined them. The following year, Fred was back in Seattle, where he joined Norm Bobrow's Little Big Band.

In 1954, because he thought a change of scenery might help him stop drinking, Greenwell moved to Tacoma. The band he worked with there, at the Pirate's Cove, was the legendary Tacoma bebop ensemble that also featured Buzz Bridgeford. Greenwell and the men were so inspired by one another that after the gig, they would drive out to the countryside and continue playing. "We'd pile into two or three cars at one-thirty or two o'clock in the morning and we'd go out to the Straits, way out in the fields—no homes, out in the forest, the great green, wet Northwest—and we'd have our instruments, and in the middle of fields we'd play. Far out, boy. We had some wild times."

During the fifties, Fred hung out a lot with the other great bebop tenor saxophonist from Seattle, Gerald Brashear.

*We usually took the bus to my house, just about dawn. I usually had long hair and it was real kinky. Once Gerald told me, "You know, one time we were coming out here, Sunday morning, the two of us were sitting in a bus that was pretty empty, and these two blue-haired ladies were going to church and they were looking at the two of us and they looked at me and they said, 'He's one of those white black guys.'" Gerald thought that was good.*

*We'd go down to my basement room and just sit around. We never would drink or carry on, just try to be quiet. I'd play him some of the things I'd been listening to. I really liked him. He was really good. He had that kind of sound and feeling in his playing—alive, alert, swinging.*

In 1956, Red Kelly got Greenwell onto the Woody Herman band for nine months, but Fred didn't get along with Woody or pianist Nat Pierce, who was running the band. It was to be Fred's last road trip. He spent the next two decades fighting the monkey on his back, moving first to Charleston, South Carolina, in the sixties, then to Dallas in the seventies, still working parties and country clubs but having put ambition aside. In 1980, after pulling himself together, he says, he came back to his beloved Seattle. "I've always liked the natural environment here," he says, looking out his window. "I think it's there, in people's playing."

Greenwell still plays casuals and makes the occasional festival appearance, but not nearly often enough to satisfy an older generation of listeners who know he is one of the greatest musicians ever to arise from the Northwest.

When Red Kelly learned there was to be a book about Northwest jazz including him and Fred Greenwell, the bassist said, "I want this to go on record. I think Freddie Greenwell is the greatest living jazz saxophone player. Period. I don't think there is anybody that comes close. Not even remotely close."

Kelly is probably best known to Washingtonians as the whimsical, red-faced, publicity-prone prankster who, in the grand tradition of Vic Meyers, started a tongue-in-cheek political campaign in 1972 that wound up garnering the largest minority vote in Washington history. On a lark, Kelly and a couple of politico friends submitted an official slate of jazz-musician candidates. Kelly ran for governor; his wife, "Fast" Lucy, ran for secretary of state; pianist Jack "Clean as a Hound's Tooth" Perciful, another

Harry James alum, ran for state treasurer; guitarist Don Ober was on the ballot as commissioner of public lands; and trumpeter Floyd Standifer ran for Congress on the OWL Party ticket (Out With Logic, On With Lunacy).

But Kelly is more than a political clown. A Queen Anne High School kid from Seattle, he has worked on the road with some of the best big bands in the business, including Harry James, Stan Kenton, and Woody Herman, and his locomotive bass is legendary among drummers and sidemen. "Red" was born Thomas Kelly in 1927, in Shelby, Montana, and moved to Everett, a mill town just north of Seattle, when he was six months old. During the Depression, Red's parents were forced to place him and his brother in an orphanage in Great Falls, Montana. Kelly's first exposure to playing music came from there.

> *I found out if I could get in the drum-and-fife corps I could get out of working in the laundry. It's amazing the talent you develop overnight with that incentive. I found that it came easily. When I came here [to Seattle] to go to high school, there was a bass at Queen Anne and nobody played it, so I just took it home. That way, I could play in the band. I never had a lesson.*

Kelly saw very quickly that the life of a professional musician was a way out of the regimentation and poverty he had experienced at the orphanage.

> *I didn't want to get up at eight o'clock in the morning, ever. I don't ever want to get involved in an environment that's remotely like school. Ever since we got out of the caves and somebody invented something we can see in the nighttime, I don't see why we got to get up the minute the sun comes up. We got light, you know?*

Musically, Red was what jazz musicians call a "natural." Without knowing the first thing about music, he made his way into the business through chutzpah, a great sense of time, and a phenomenal ear. "I remember watching him start to figure it all out," recalls Don Manning, who knew Red in high school. "We were sitting in my car and the radio was playing and Red starts singing the low tone and he realizes that he's got a gift, that he can find the notes. He always knew something that would fit underneath."

When he was sixteen, Kelly was recruited by a Dixieland band playing at the China Pheasant, the prosperous roadhouse out by the Duwamish River (near the present-day Boeing Developmental Center) where Dave Stetler had worked in Bob Harvey's band. In the time-honored jazz tradition of passing on the music hand-to-hand, Kelly learned to play bass on the job. He couldn't have had better teachers. Joe Darensbourg, Seattle's jazz pioneer from the 1920s, was the clarinetist; Johnny Wittwer, a veteran of the Kid Ory and Wingy Manone organizations and one of Seattle's most remarkable musicians, was on piano; Tacoma doctor Neal Ely, who'd introduced Neil Friel to Reichian therapy, was on saxophone; Evan Humphrey or Pete Carraba played trumpet; and Keith Purvis was on drums. The gig attracted the attention of a national magazine, Art Hodes' *The Jazz Record*, which praised the band for its authentic revival of New Orleans jazz.

Joe Darensbourg describes Kelly's first night on the job:

> *We held the rehearsal and this big redheaded, freckle-faced kid came out there. He had a nice smile and plenty of enthusiasm. Johnny said, "Now we got a bass player, we gonna start our rehearsal. Are you tuned up, fellers?" So Red says, "Tuned up? What do you mean, tuned up?" We nicknamed him Jimmy Blanton, after the greatest bass player in the world. He got the biggest kick out of that.*

The China Pheasant was a classic roadhouse—a huge place parked in the middle of a cow pasture by the river, complete with a rickety back porch, where musicians slipped out for a swig or a toke, and an elaborate casino concealed behind the kitchen. White bandleader Bob Harvey, who had worked as an arranger for Ted Weems, led a society band there throughout the forties and fifties. National acts such as Johnny Otis and the Wardell Gray/ Howard McGhee sextet worked there on occasion. The club eventually became the spearhead for Seattle's Dixieland revival.

Owner Harry Lew was a Chinese operator who played a continuous game of cat and mouse with the authorities; the club was raided often. Reporter Johnny Reddin recalled one botched, slapstick bust when "three carloads of sheriff's deputies . . . [broke] down several doors, arrested the proprietor and two employees, and . . . confiscated the most complete assortment of gambling paraphernalia to be found this side of the ornate establishments in Reno and Las Vegas."

Kelly thought it was all good fun, but after working at the China Pheasant for nearly a year, he was soon swept into the national maelstrom of swing. "Red was the first to go," says Manning. "He was just gone, overnight. This is the way it was then. They'd stop a guy on the street, some kid coming home from school with a music case: 'Say kid, you wanna go on the road?'"

Kelly's departure with bandleader Tiny Hill was the beginning of a lifelong career on the road, a cascade of names and places and one-night stands that all ran together in Kelly's mind as he hopped from town to town, band to band, and hotel to hotel. Kelly toured with Hill a few months, then got a telegram from Ted Fio Rito, on Manning's recommendation. Don Trenner, the pianist who would later lead the band on Steve Allen's television show, was in the band; so were trumpeter Doc Severinsen and alto man Ward Swingle, who later created the Swingle Singers. This was 1945.

One night on 52nd Street, Kelly played with Charlie Parker. Apparently, Bird approved, because Kelly got a good "review":

*I remember the first tune we played was "Slow Boat to China," and I thought, "Boy, oh boy, here I am and Bird's playing, wowee!" So I played and that night we went up to Joe Maini's house and I walked into the apartment and Bird was there. Bird looked up—he was talking to somebody—and he got up and came over, gave me a big kiss on the cheek and hugged me and then went back and sat down.*

When the war was over, Ted Fio Rito's band broke up and Manning and Kelly returned to Seattle. Kelly took a commercial gig with Wyatt Howard at the Town and Country Club and played with Curt Sykes. Then Buzz Bridgeford called from New York.

*He said there was an opening in Randy Brooks' band. So I went back to New York. Then I got a telegram that said, "Be in Brooklyn tomorrow night. Sam Donahue needs a bass player." Sam Donahue was the white Jimmie Lunceford, right? Oh, shit, that was a band! It would knock your hat off, that band.*

The stint with Donahue led to one of Kelly's most exuberant musical experiences, playing with the legendary Chubby Jackson, who had turned from playing bass with Woody Herman to leading his own band. Of all the shrill, frenetic big bands that rose and fell with bop after the war, Jackson's best communicates the sizzling intensity of the genre. Kelly fit right in. As a bassist, he was in the vanguard of a new wave of big-band players who replaced the four-four "thump" of swing with a more complex, sinuous feel that complemented bebop rhythms. When Kelly joined the band at the Royal Roost, in New York, all the bass players in the audience—including big names like Eddie Safranski and Oscar Pettiford—wore red to honor his arrival.

*I got out my bass and right in front is Eddie. I thought, "What in the hell am I doing here?" We worked all the black theaters. There were only two ballads in the book, so everything was just a screamer. It was powerful as hell. Twelve-piece band—three trumpets, two trombones, four saxophones. It was just astounding. That was really my entrance to the wild, great, frenetic, marvelous jazz band. Chubby played out-and-out jazz music. But there isn't much else you can do with that kind of a band. It was about 1949, and the dancing, the frenetic jitterbugging and all that, was over. Everybody kind of wanted to sit back and get over the war.*

Like Ronnie Pierce's local "dream band" back home, Chubby Jackson's group succumbed to a lack of bookings. Kelly joined Herbie Fields, a hot saxophonist who had been with Lionel Hampton and had formed a septet. Red worked with Fields around the Midwest for about six months, then replaced Eddie Safranski in Charlie Barnet's band.

*That Barnet band was where the expression "We saw the big man tonight" came from. Which meant that you go into that thing where it was so powerful that you don't even know what your name is or what the tune is. It's just one big instrument, it's not a bunch of guys there. "We saw the big man tonight." Now once you do that, you spend the rest of your life trying to do it again. And you do, maybe once or twice a year. If there's a religion, that's mine.*

Kelly left Barnet and toured to Hawaii with one of the era's historic small groups, the innovative Red Norvo Trio, with vibist Norvo and guitarist Tal Farlow. But big bands were his first love; he was replaced in the Norvo trio by Charles Mingus.

*I don't know if that was the wisest move, looking back. It would have done more for my career had I stayed with Norvo. [But] I got homesick for horns. One night in San Diego, I got drunk with Barnet. It was his wedding night. We went out on a boat, and Barnet invited me to join a new band he was forming. Woody says if it ever gets to where it's not a hobby, you don't want to do it.*

Music apparently became less than fun for Charlie Barnet, too; he abandoned his new band. Kelly returned to Seattle, where he shared an apartment on Capitol Hill with Fred Greenwell. The peripatetic bassist was soon back out on the road, this time with Darryl Harpa. In a Nashville bar one night a Woody Herman sideman told Kelly that Claude Thornhill was looking for a bass player. "I loved Claude," says Kelly. "He had a whole book full of Gil Evans, long before Miles Davis ever thought of getting into that stuff. The band was just one continuous party."

Kelly toured with Thornhill a year, rejoined Woody Herman's Third Herd, jumped off Woody's band in Seattle, and went to work with Norm Hoagy at the Showbox Theater.

*Woody kept calling, but he would replace me with Chubby anytime Chubby wanted the job back, so I said no. Finally, Woody called and said, "Okay, the job is yours from now on." Somehow, I got the dates screwed up. I was supposed to meet him in Knoxville, Tennessee. A saxophone player and myself were out celebrating my imminent departure. Somehow, we lost track of the days. Somebody said, "You're supposed to be playing when?" I said I'm supposed to be playing the night of the 20th or whatever it was. Tomorrow night. Well, this is the 20th. Holy Christ. So [he] said, "Go back by plane." So I just throw a bunch of stuff together and grab my bass and go out and I jump on the wrong plane. I wound up in Minneapolis. Fortunately, I did leave a day ahead of time. So they ran me down to Chicago and stuck me in a hotel. Right downstairs there was a joint where a bunch of guys were playing. I went down and got loaded with them and sat in and, you know, the next day I got to Knoxville and walked into the lobby and there's [Bob] Brookmeyer, and he says, "What are you doing in Knoxville?" I said, "I'm going to join Woody," and he says, "Well, so am I."*

By this time, Kelly had had enough of the road, at least for a while. After playing with Woody, he returned to Seattle, where he worked at Norm Bobrow's new nightclub, the Colony, and at the Lake City Tavern in a group called Don Anderson's Seattle Rhythm Kings. In 1956, Kelly got a call from saxophonist Med Flory, who was working with Maynard Ferguson. Red worked with Maynard awhile, then went with Stan Kenton for two years. Afterwards, he tried doing studio work, but he missed the camaraderie of the road and the big bands. He worked briefly in 1960 with Les Brown ("Kind of Boy Scout," he says); then Harry James called—twice.

"I kept thinking every time I heard his band, he always had one of those really white-sounding bass players. Really short notes and really stiff rhythms. I like Jimmy Blanton, with that big ring. So I figured Harry ain't gonna like me. But it turned out he did like me and we had a lot of fun." That's an understatement. Kelly worked with James for the next fourteen years. Every other month, they played the Flamingo Hotel in Las Vegas and three weeks in Lake Tahoe. Pianist Jack Perciful, who had grown up in Idaho and settled in Olympia, and Corky Corcoran were also in the James band.

Kelly worked with Phil Harris' band for a while, in Las Vegas, and jumped off the James band from time to time to work shows in Lake Tahoe and Reno with Sonny and Cher and others. It was during this period that he took up the electric bass, using a special instrument made for him by Ampeg, a "Red Kelly" fretless bass with more resonant pickups than a

Fender. The idea was to sound more like an acoustic bass.

In 1974, Kelly finally left the road and opened his own club, the Tumwater Conservatory, near Olympia, the staging ground for the revival of Ernestine Anderson's career as well as the site of the OWL party's genesis. In the 1980s, he opened another club—Kelly's—in Tacoma. Musicians all over the country know about Kelly's, but for most musicians, the bass player's name will always be associated not with a nightclub, but with one of jazz music's most famous "road stories." Known affectionately as the "Red Kelly Story," the "Red Kelly Dog Story," or the "White Room Story," it goes like this: One night, Kelly was invited to visit a wealthy woman whose home was furnished all in white—white carpets, white furniture, white walls. During the course of the evening, Kelly got drunk, and at some point wandered off to find the bathroom. On his way, he bumped into a writing desk and spilled a bottle of black ink all over the rug. His attempts to clean it up only made the mess worse, and eventually he fled from the house, leaving a trail of black footprints. The next morning, he woke up and felt so guilty he decided to go back to the house and offer to pay for the damage. A maid answered the door. She asked him to sit down while she went to fetch the lady of the house. Kelly sat down to wait. He heard a sickening yelp beneath him. Inadvertently, he had smothered the woman's little dog. Completely undone, he hid the dog in the grand piano and ran away from the house, never to return.

This story has been repeated by musicians on the road thousands of times. Northwest novelist Tom Robbins even borrowed it for his book *Still Life with Woodpecker*. Of course, as Bill Crow explains in his entertaining collection *Jazz Anecdotes*, as with other "urban legends," the Red Kelly dog story never happened. In fact, Seattle trombonist Mike Hobi originally told Kelly the story while driving to a gig; Kelly, always fond of a humorous tale, started telling it to everyone he met. Over the years, musicians began to associate it with Kelly until he became the protagonist.

As Kelly told Crow, "Total strangers would come up and say, 'Are you the guy that sat on the dog?' After years of going through this, it got to where I finally resigned myself. . . . I didn't even deny any complicity in it at all. People would come up to me in Florida or someplace and say, 'Are you the guy with the dog?' 'Yeah, that's me.'"

As Crow also points out, it's the kind of story that *should* have happened to Kelly, and that's why it stuck. A fellow who started out joining the fife-and-drum corps in an orphanage to get out of doing chores, who took his first gig without knowing how to tune his bass, yet wound up traveling around the world with Woody Herman, probably has a right to think the world is just a trifle upside-down.

Kelly is still laughing at life, in the darkest corner of the room behind the bar at Kelly's. Though his road days are over, whenever sidemen from the modern big bands come through town—Herman, Kenton, James—they always drop by Kelly's and pull out their horns. After the music, they pour themselves a drink and tell all the old war stories. It's an education for the listener, and it's the closest you'll ever find Red Kelly to a school.

Kelly's accomplice in the James gang, Jack Perciful, is another white "renegade" whose career touched on Jackson Street. In *The Swing Era*, Gunther Schuller lists Perciful as one of James' "outstanding" soloists, along with Kelly, Corky Corcoran, Buddy Rich, and Willie Smith. Perciful's credentials as a Pacific Northwesterner date from his Idaho days and a brief stint around Fort Lewis during the war years. The pianist was born in 1925 in Moscow, Idaho, a small university town just six miles across the border from Pullman, Washington. After taking classical piano lessons, Perciful started to learn jazz and pop from a college student who rented a room from his parents. "He got me into the college band," Jack says. "I got into playing a lot of boogie-woogie. Albert Ammons. Pete Johnson. Jay McShann."

When Perciful enrolled at the University of Idaho, he had already been playing with the school band for three years. He was drafted out of the university in 1943, which brought him to Camp Roberts, where he worked in a combo behind Red Skelton. After the service, Perciful returned to Moscow to complete his degree. For most of 1949, he toured the West with a funny-hat band called the Jay Makers, led by Red and Jeanne Thompson. (Red Ingles, who later did most of the vocal sound effects in the Spike Jones band, played with the Jay Makers as well.) Perciful completed his degree in classical music and theory, then worked in a trio out of Spokane for a year and a half. As he remembers it, "The leader, Howard Robins, kept telling me, 'Don't go down there to L.A., they'll eat you alive, you'll never make it.' I got tired of hearing that, so I said, 'Howard, find a new piano player. I'm going to L.A.'"

This was November 1952. Perciful immediately found work in the California Club, a black night spot in East Los Angeles. After the gig, musicians hung out at an all-night barbecue place. "That was the greatest learning process in the world, education right off the street," says Jack. During this period, Nat Cole and Spokane native Jimmy Rowles were Perciful's biggest influences: "Jimmy still is a big influence. I think he's the most creative player there is right now. Whenever I get depressed, or I just get stale or I'm bored, I just put on some Jimmy Rowles and listen to it for about an hour and I feel great." Perciful counts Jess Stacy, Teddy Wilson, Fats Waller, Dodo Marmarosa, and Bud Powell as other influences.

Jack stayed in Los Angeles until 1956, then went to Las Vegas to play with Milt Hirth, an old-time organ player from the thirties. After five months, he was just getting ready to leave the gaudy city in the desert when Harry James' manager asked if he would audition. Convinced that auditioning was for beginners, Perciful refused.

> *I sent a demo record. Harry liked it and called me back. They sent me a plane ticket, which I cashed in because I was broke. I took a bus to L.A. I was scared to death. I went to the first rehearsal at the Palladium. Harry says, "Jack, you just got here, so you don't know, but be at Capitol tonight at 6 p.m. We're doing an album." It was my first recording of any kind and I was with my heroes. I was twenty-eight, had no idea what I had gotten myself into. I had no intention of staying with the band. I was married and had two kids still in Vegas. But we went on a six-week tour and got a Fourth of July three-day shot at the Flamingo Hotel in Las Vegas. That gig was so successful they hired us for ten years.*

Perciful worked for James for the next eighteen years, ten of which were at the Flamingo Hotel, three to six months a year. During the rest of the year, the band toured the world—South America, Japan, Europe. One of the best musical moments came around 1964 in Lake Tahoe, when he, Buddy Rich, and Red Kelly were the rhythm section. Gary Moore, the comedian, was doing his television show in Tahoe and had brought in his whole crew.

> *Our band was hot. Harry laid about an hour-and-fifteen-minute set on them and they were just in tears. . . . The highlight of the James era was the five years with Buddy Rich on drums. This affected me musically more than anything in my whole life—harmonically, lyrically, professionally, attitude-wise.*

Perciful wrote charts for the James band, including "James Gang," recorded on the *Double Dixie* album, and can be heard on twenty-five records with the bandleader. His favorites are *Double Dixie* and *The Relaxed Mood*, a sextet album.

Perciful left James in 1974, but stayed on good terms with him, playing in the band in 1980 and 1981 in South America and, later, on a Texas tour. He also did cruises with the James ghost band, as well as a public-television special. He says he misses the travel and camaraderie, but "musically, it wasn't that great near the end. I can't really put my finger on it, but it had deteriorated. Harry knew it, but didn't do anything about it."

While Perciful and Kelly were playing with James, they became roommates and fast friends. When Jack left the band, he joined Red at the Tumwater Conservatory. When the Conservatory folded, Perciful got a job at the Capitol Bar and Grill, in Olympia, playing solo piano. Five years in Olympia gave way to a job with trumpeter Fred Radke (who became leader of the James ghost band) at Seattle's Four Seasons Hotel. In the early 1990s, Perciful was playing with Olympia vocalist Jan Stentz and with the excellent Buddy Catlett Trio at the Thirteen Coins, a lounge near Sea-Tac International Airport.

The wild men—and women—of Seattle's bebop era were not the only white musicians to embrace the new music. While Perciful, Kelly, Greenwell, and the rest were taking their knocks out on the road, another school of beboppers was forming in the ivied halls of the University of Washington. Many of the musicians who were part of this scene—Chuck and Joni Metcalf, Bill Crow, Kenny Kimball, Chuck

Mahaffay—forged significant relationships with musicians on Jackson Street that would become the crucible for the jazz culture of the next decade.

More than four decades after he wrote it, clarinetist and drummer Mahaffay's article in the July 15, 1949, *down beat* still serves as a fine introduction to what came to be known as the Annex Sessions:

> *In the last few months, the staid atmosphere surrounding the older buildings on the University of Washington campus has been somewhat shaken by a series of flatted fifths and fast choruses of "How High the Moon." Although these sounds do not carry too far, many students walking through the campus have stopped and wondered if the music they heard was coming from a small building that houses practice rooms for University musicians. Every Friday afternoon, when the rooms are usually empty, a group of campus jazzmen move in and make the most of two or three hours of freewheeling, modern jazz.*
>
> *The sessions were started early in January. . . . Since then, however, they have become a gathering place for the best musicians on the campus who like to hear and play bop. Those that come have a genuine appreciation for each other's ideas and ability and, as a result, some of the finest modern jazz in the Northwest is being played by this unique group of university students. . . .*
>
> *A typical Friday meeting starts about 4 p.m. when pianist Kenny Kimball arrives*

**The "Annex sessions" at the University of Washington, 1948. Left to right: Dick Mandle, Bill Crow, Bill DeMenthe, Kenny Kimball (piano), Dick Nelson, Bernie Bursett.**

**Photo by DeWayne Sharp**

**Courtesy of Chuck Mahaffay**

*and starts playing a few warm-up choruses. . . . He started the original sessions in January, and has since penned three or four of the bop tunes that the boys use for material.*

*Since the start of the weekly sessions, attendance of both musicians and interested onlookers has greatly increased. This in itself serves to keynote the rising trend toward more bop and modern jazz in the Seattle area as well as on the University campus. . . . One of the more worldly listeners at a recent session remarked, "These guys are the young pioneers of Northwest bop."*

Musicians who participated in the Annex Sessions included Chuck Metcalf, bass; Dick Mandle, trumpet; Bill Crow, valve trombone; Ed Jenkins, trumpet; Bernie Bursett, tenor saxophone; Joni Swartz (who would later marry Metcalf), piano and vocals; Floyd Standifer, trumpet; Ernestine Anderson, vocals; Gerald Brashear, saxophone; Bill DeMenthe, a bassist who later went on to become a leading dream scholar at Stanford University; Armand Boatman, bass; Bob Dyke, piano; Jim Giles, a tenor saxophonist who became a psychiatrist and still plays in local big bands; Al Pace, piano; Kayo Shelton, guitar; Rod Linden, trombone; Rod Levitt, the arranger who would later work with Quincy Jones on Dizzy Gillespie's Middle East tour; and Mahaffay himself, on clarinet. Of these participants, Metcalf and Standifer would become the most important players for the region, but Kimball was the innovator of the Annex scene.

Kenny Kimball had come up through the kid-band circuit with Ronnie Pierce, in the Noteworthies, and went on to study piano and composition at the University of Washington. While he was leading the Annex Sessions, Kimball also took casual gigs downtown. One day, he wandered into Al Siedel's record store and met the great go-between, Janet Thurlow, who introduced him to Ray Charles, as well as Quincy Jones, Ernestine Anderson, and the rest of the Jackson Street crowd. The pianist fondly recalls leaving the Washington Social Club one night in his 1934 Plymouth with Quincy, Ernestine, and Charlie Taylor in tow. As he became a Jackson Street habitué, Kimball picked up the beboppers' lingo. He says he had to remember not to talk too "hip" at home.

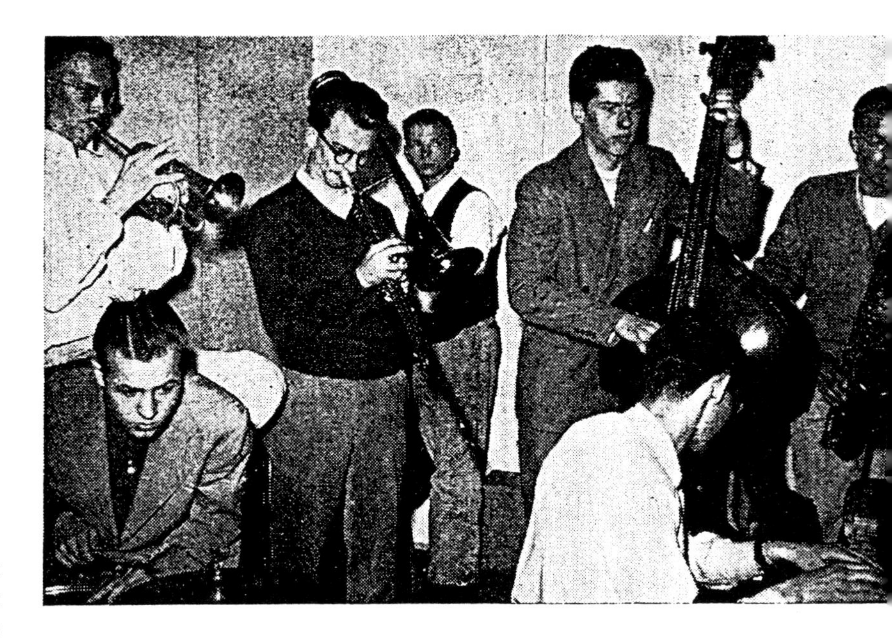

Recalls Kimball:

*I led a Jekyll-and-Hyde life. In the daytime I was a full-time student at the university. Then at night I'd go on into the jazz world and I'd talk a different language. I had to keep them separate. One of the expressions we had then was that when something was really great, it was "gone." One night I forgot myself at the dinner table at home and I said to my dad, "This pie is gone, Dad." And he said, "It is? I thought we had plenty."*

Besides being initiated into the night world of jazz, Kimball also had the opportunity to learn an authentic Cuban piano style working with a group at the Olympic Hotel led by Darryl Harpa's former percussionist, Desceito Niego. When Kimball sat in with another Latin bandleader, Raymundo Val, Val asked him to go on the road, which he did, but Kimball soon tired of playing commercial dance music night after night, and returned to school.

Kimball graduated in 1952 and began pursuing a master's degree in music, but was drafted the following year. He was assigned to the cryptography room of NATO, in Paris—a move that allowed him to fulfill a lifelong dream of studying with the great Parisian composition teacher Nadia Boulanger. As it happened, Quincy Jones had also moved to Paris. Kimball spent an idyllic year (1954–1955) in the French capital, cracking codes, studying composition, meeting the woman he would later marry, and hanging out with his old friend "Q."

*We went to all the great little clubs. I got a chance to hear Lucky Thompson and all these other marvelous players I'd always heard about. They would sit at the table and talk to Quincy, you know, basking in his glory. I was able to go down and jam at places like the Ringside Club, which I wouldn't even have known about otherwise. I owe an awful lot to Quincy.*

That summer, Kimball and his fiancée married in England and came back to the United States by way of New York. Quincy, who was now working for Mercury Records, was on hand to host him again. Ernestine Anderson was in the Big Apple, as well.

*I remember us walking down Broadway. Quincy had this big coat on, with fur lining just around here [the neck]. I thought, boy, this is real living. All these guys were playing that I'd worshipped all my life. Like Art Farmer, Kenny Dorham, Lennie Tristano, Horace Silver. Art Farmer was going with Ernestine in those days. She was singing at a place called the Page Three down the street in the Village. Quincy and Art took Audrey and me down there to see Ernestine. That was a thrill. Oh, it was just a marvelous night.*

Kimball returned to Seattle, finishing his degree at the University of Washington in 1955. The same year, he took a job teaching music at Centralia College, from which he retired in the early nineties.

One of the other lucky university musicians to be initiated into Jackson Street by Janet Thurlow was bassist Bill Crow. Crow, who was playing valve trombone at the time but would later record as a bassist with the Gerry Mulligan Quartet, was, like Kimball, a native Washingtonian. Crow grew up in Kirkland, a small bedroom community across Lake Washington from Seattle. He'd gone to high school with trumpeter Dick Nelson, who also played on the Annex scene. Crow started on piano, switched to trumpet, then to baritone horn—a small, tuba-like brass band instrument—which he played through the end of high school. He discovered bebop, and the valve trombone, in the Army. In 1949, he decided to enroll at the University of Washington, but soon discovered that "the only thing I was interested in was the jam sessions that were going on after school."

As students, Crow and drummer Dick Mandle shared a houseboat on Lake Union, which became another key site for the Annex crowd. "Our routine for a while was to get up in the morning, somebody would put the coffee on, and we would start playing while we were still in our pajamas," recalls Crow. "We would play until everybody had to go to class."

Sometime during this idyllic collegiate period, Crow, like everyone else, ran across the hip lady behind the counter at Al Siedel's Music:

*I was looking through the Charlie Parker records, and the girl that was working behind the counter came over and said, "Are you a musician?" I said, "Yes." Her name was Janet Thurlow. She asked me if I had ever been up to the Washington Social and Educational and if I'd met Bumps and if I'd met Ray Charles and if I'd met Quincy. Of course I hadn't, so she took me right up there and introduced me to everybody. Ray Charles was sitting at the piano playing kind of like Bud Powell. I had no idea there was something as good as that going on in Seattle. There was a good band on the stand. Everybody was laughing and dancing and carrying on. I thought, "My god. There's a world here that I never knew about."*

*Quincy was nice. He said, "Oh, man, we got this big band that I'm writing for. Bumps got a couple of gigs for it. Why don't you come over and rehearse? We need a trombone player." So I came over and I think I was the only white guy on the band. It was the first band like that I'd ever worked with. It was sloppy and out of tune, but there was this strong musical impulse. Everybody had the phrasing down. As soon as I came, Quincy wrote a new chart that had a trombone solo in it on my part. It was like, "Welcome to the band." It was funny. Everybody in Seattle felt like if you were a musician, you were automatically a member of a secret society and everybody should know everybody.*

In 1949 or 1950, Crow and Kimball got a gig with saxophonist Paul McCrae's quartet at the Cirque Club, a large venue on Madison and

Broadway. At one point, Duke Ellington's vocalist, Ivie Anderson (who recorded "It Don't Mean a Thing If It Ain't Got That Swing") worked with them for a week. Crow then joined a band with his first great mentor, Buzzy Bridgeford.

*Buzzy was the one who showed me the difference between just keeping time and swinging. I didn't know there was a difference. He danced it out for me one night while playing me some records. It was just like these scales fell from my eyes. I saw what the whole idea was. I have a soft spot in my heart for Buzzy because he really turned my musical life around. He couldn't believe that I had never heard the Basie big-band records with Lester Young. He got out all these records and played them for me. That really added to my education tremendously. He showed me what the rhythm sections were doing. He showed me what Jo Jones was doing, how Shadow Wilson did it differently, and showed me what different drummers did about kicking certain figures. Those were issues that had never occurred to me before.*

One night, Buzzy turned to Crow and said, "Look, if you want to be a musician, you got to go where the music is. Let's go to New York."

"I think I only had about fifty dollars cash, my trombone, and a small suitcase full of clothes," says Crow. "We got on the Greyhound bus and came to New York. January, 1950."

In New York, Bridgeford introduced Crow to his friend Dave Lambert, who later started the great Lambert, Hendricks and Ross vocal trio. Buzzy found them a summer job in upstate New York with trumpeter Gene Roland and pianist John Benson Brooks. (Fred Greenwell came out from Seattle and also joined the band.) Crow started out on trombone, then switched to bass.

Later that year, Crow moved to New York City and entered the mainstream of jazz history. Stan Getz hired him in 1952 and they recorded some excellent sides; Crow went on to work for Claude Thornhill, Terry Gibbs, Marian McPartland, and Gerry Mulligan, with whom he stayed from 1957 to 1965. It's a neat coincidence that Mulligan's famous quartet came to feature Bob Brookmeyer on valve trombone, since Crow had started out on that unusual instrument at the Annex sessions. Crow recorded several excellent albums with the Mulligan Quartet, including *Live in Boston at Storyville*, *Newport Jazz Festival*, *What Is There to Say?*, *Live at the Village Vanguard*, *The Gerry Mulligan Quartet*, and *Night Lights*. When work slowed with Mulligan, Crow settled down to the life of a jazz and pit-band musician in New York City, playing five years with trombonist Kai Winding at the Playboy Club and eight years in the pit of the Broadway production *42nd Street*.

Today, Crow is well-known not only as a world-class bassist, but also as a jazz writer. His monthly humor column for *Allegro*, the journal of Local No. 802, led to the publication of a hilarious and critically well-received compilation, *Jazz Anecdotes*.

Crow's style as a bassist is light, accomplished, swinging, and melodic—qualities that clearly attracted Mulligan and Getz to him. It's tempting to link Crow to the "West Coast" style associated with those saxophonists, given Crow's dues-paying in Seattle, but it would be a misleading connection. Neither the Annex players nor the Jackson Street scene at that point was influenced significantly by the "cool" school. The Seattle scene was steeped in tradition, not in experiment. For Crow, however, the stylistic influence of Seattle is less poignant in his memory than is the milieu of the jazz life generally.

*Seattle was where I first began to realize that there was a community of musicians that were supportive of each other and would teach each other stuff and were looking for the fun in the music—a wonderful grapevine of information about jobs and the music itself. It was really the springboard that got me going. It seems ironic that I spent so much time during my school years in the thirties and forties wishing I could be on the jazz scene in New York, when there was so much going on right across Lake Washington that I never knew about.*

One of the ironies of the Annex scene was that, although it unfolded on-campus, few of the musicians involved were music majors. One of its most important figures, Chuck Metcalf, was studying architecture. Metcalf points out perceptively that for him as well as for others in his circle, it was almost a matter of principle *not* to become a professional musician.

"Everyone seemed to think they didn't want to make music their career," recalls the bassist, who did not become a bona fide professional himself until 1960. "And if you wanted to be a star, that was bullshit. I never, ever practiced. This is the absolute truth about me, I never practiced the bass until age thirty. That was my idea about my life, that I was going to be an architect in the daytime and a musician when it suited me."

For a guy who started out not wanting to be a professional musician or a star, Chuck Metcalf has traveled a rather remarkable distance. A veteran of both Dexter Gordon's and Anita O'Day's groups, and a first-call bassist in San Francisco during the seventies, Metcalf wound up as one of the dozen or so Seattle musicians to be recognized by anyone but locals.

Metcalf was born in 1931 in Grand Rapids, Michigan, and moved to Pasadena when he was six. As a teenager, he attended the historic Gene Norman concert that included Corky Corcoran's "Stardust" solo. His parents, both public-school music teachers, moved to the Northwest in 1946. Metcalf started on violin and piano as a youngster.

"When I was eleven or twelve," he says, "I discovered boogie-woogie piano—Meade Lux Lewis and Albert Ammons."

*My mother used to come in from the kitchen and say, "Charles, come to a cadence!" She couldn't understand those unresolved dominant sounds! When Bird's records came out, I was fifteen. I went up to the record shop and I heard it and immediately it was as if Charlie Parker captured my soul. Stan Kenton was on the charts then, so I started listening to that stuff—Woody Herman and Dizzy Gillespie —and I was off into it. Bebop caught my ear right away.*

Metcalf started to play the bass that year, taking lessons from his mother. At Highline High School, south of Seattle, he played in the school orchestra and in a swing dance band. In 1948, he entered the University of Washington and immediately fell in with the bohemian crowd around the Annex. A trip to San Francisco that year, during which he sat in on piano at Bop City, gave him a vivid and enticing image of *la vie bohème*.

"Hey, I was a beatnik in college," he says.

*I was dap. I had my Mr. B collar and my peg pants, a flannel suit with wide rolled lapels and my wide knit tie with a Windsor knot. I was cool. I meant business. I had a pad at 3809 Brooklyn which was actually one of the scenes in the fifties. I had the whole Stan Kenton band over to my pad in 1951 or '52. It was a building dated from Victorian times, probably from the Alaska-Yukon Exposition. It had a [defunct] grocery store in the first floor and an apartment up on top. I just cleared all the shit out, finally put a toilet in the back. The meat locker, I turned into a giant clothes closet for myself. I put foreign newspapers all over the walls and ceiling and I had apple boxes as a divider. It was kind like a Mies van der Rohe, beatnik-style thing. I moved a piano in. The people upstairs were kind of intellectual types, so they didn't mind the music. We used to have sessions. Lee Konitz was with the Kenton band when they came up.*

Meanwhile, Chuck met Janet Thurlow, who sent him to the YMCA, where the Brashear brothers were playing.

*You can't imagine any more green, naive seventeen-year-old, out of the suburbs, never been around any black people, totally enthralled by the actual shit happening right in front of his very ears. They let me sit in. They told me not to rush and so I got some of my early training. I knew the tunes and I could play the right notes and that was a rarity among bass players at that time. A bass player that actually played the right notes, the roots of the chord, and knew what they were. Pops Buford, Mike DeFillipis, Traff Hubert, and Floyd Standifer—those four in particular really became role models for me. I just admired them tremendously and found them to be very warm, extremely intelligent, and hip, you know. Almost immediately, I was in demand. I was playing gigs. I quit my job as a busboy at the Roosevelt Hotel because I was making so much more money, and pretty soon I was putting myself through college as a musician. I was having a ball.*

In 1951, Metcalf got one of the choicest gigs on Jackson Street—Friday, Saturday, and

Sunday at the black Elks Club, with pianist Paul Neves and drummer Jimmy Raymer. The music at the Elks was on the cusp between bebop and swing, less fiery than East Coast bop, but bluesier than California jazz.

"See, the black people could dance to the up-tempos," Metcalf explains. "The rhythm sections were basically going 'chug-chug-chug-chug-a-chug,' [but] a lot of the tunes were actually bebop." (A 1947 live recording of one of Norm Bobrow's concerts illustrates Metcalf's point nicely. As Pony Poindexter flies over lines inspired by Charlie Parker, drummer Chris Tull plods along in straight swing time.)

As a bassist, Metcalf developed quite differently than Bill Crow. The fat tone and raunchy swing attack of club players such as Milt Garred and Al Larkins were Metcalf's main influences, with the recordings of Jimmy Blanton following a close second.

> *They were playing by the Pops Foster method, which was [to] grab with your whole fist for each note, and go for it. [As for] left-hand technique, I didn't bother with it, because I saw that they weren't. I knew that was the "correct" way, but I was in revolt against classical music, because my parents came from an extremely uptight scene. It was only later that I realized that I really should have taken stuff out of it.*

While he was at the University of Washington, Metcalf fell in love with Joni Swartz, a singer/pianist who had attended Lincoln High School in North Seattle and entered the university in 1949. Swartz was studying music—classical voice—and had been playing jazz and pop piano since she was a teenager. She started to fall by the jam sessions at the Annex. For many years, Chuck and Joni Metcalf's "pad" in the University district—with its grass mats and grand piano—was the center of the scene, and for many Seattleites this couple was what local jazz was all about. Joni's reminiscence of those idyllic college years appeared as a handwritten prose poem on the back of one of her locally produced albums. It evokes the feeling and spirit of the times better than any press clipping could:

> *There were jam sessions every Friday at the U of W HUB. Who could resist? Kenny Kimball and I crawled through an unlocked window in Meany Hall one nite and gave a concert from the darkened stage. Bob Dyke shocked everyone at faculty-student parties with his wild improvisations. I sang over KUOW on a weekly air show produced by Chuck Mahaffay. Ray Charles was working in a small club downtown, and we called him R. C. then. Everyone was digging the Cecil Young Quartet. One night a bass player sailed on Green Lake on his aluminum bass. Jack Korsaw had wild-wild parties on his houseboat every Saturday nite. I married Chuck Metcalf. Our "honeymoon cottage" was an old abandoned store in the "U" District.*

Joni Metcalf's mention of Ray Charles—as yet an obscure lounge pianist—and her own subsequent success as a jazz-inspired cocktail vocalist are a reminder that in the forties and fifties, jazz wasn't just a matter of bebop quintets and dream bands. As the wild men and women of the beat movement and their Ivy League cousins at the university pursued the frenetic muse of bop, working musicians on Jackson Street also beat time to a more subtle, accessible culture of commercial trio music. Often, their music had as much jazz content as its more obviously jazz-oriented relatives. Ray Charles, among others, forged his early career within that culture.

# 8

# "STRAIGHTEN UP AND FLY RIGHT"

## Ray Charles and the Nat Cole influence

Bebop and blues drove the imaginations of musicians after World War II, but another influence equally as mighty shaped post-war music, and that was the piano trio. As Pete Barrington suggested, a demand for intimate, romantic music—particularly with vocals—rose after the swing era, perhaps to accommodate soldiers who had come home to their wives and girlfriends. Technology played an important role, too. Finally, after years of thumping along in the background, the bass could be heard through a microphone as a melodic instrument, and the amplified electric guitar could soar above a big band. Early piano trios featured either bass and guitar or bass and drums. With all the instruments clearly audible, a new orchestral sound could be created by just three players.

The most influential piano trio of the 1940s was led by Nat Cole. Though Cole later became known as a crooner, he started out as a jazz pianist and virtually invented the piano trio during the period of 1939 to 1944. His trio featured the great Oscar Moore on guitar and Wesley Prince on bass. Moore raised the ante for guitar players by employing sophisticated, "open" voicings, leaving just enough notes in a complex chord to suggest the harmony. The interplay between Cole, Moore, and Prince captured the ears of musicians everywhere. A November 1943 hit record, "Straighten Up and Fly Right," captured the public. By the 1950s, Cole would be an international pop star with his own television show.

Cole's influence over the next twenty years of jazz history has been oddly underplayed, probably because disappointed jazz critics became sidetracked over his defection to pop music. But the issue never was Cole's popular success, it was his ensemble innovation, which, while it has encouraged its share of corny cocktail pianists, also spawned a new genre that has lasted half a century. Piano trios inspired by Nat Cole flourished in post-war Seattle. Pianist and vibraphonist Elmer Gill led one of the most durable, helping to define intimate, small-group jazz locally.

ELMER GILL — an outstanding pianist now at the ITALIAN VILLAGE.

Gill came to Seattle in 1946 and played there through the end of the fifties, establishing one of the most important venues in town, the Ebony, along the way. Guitarist Milt Green, a friend of Cole's who had come to Seattle from Minneapolis and later played with Gill, led another prominent trio. A third Nat Cole imitator, R. C. Robinson, also came to Seattle as a youngster to hone his nightclub skills. Robinson was later known as Ray Charles.

Elmer Gill was such an accomplished Cole imitator that Quincy Jones' crowd sometimes referred to him, affectionately, as "Char"—short for "charcoal," the tone of Nat Cole's complexion. Like Gerald Wiggins, Gill came to Seattle after being discharged from Fort Lewis. A short, stocky man full of sparkling energy and a continuous line of talk, Gill speaks in a quick, halting clip, with a hint of a lisp. He grew up in Indianapolis, a few blocks from the Montgomery brothers (Wes, Monk, and Buddy), studied piano from the age of nine, and attended the Cosmopolitan School of Music. He formed his first band as a senior in high school and enrolled as a chemistry major at Indiana State University in 1942. Erskine Hawkins on the jukebox, big bands on the road, and church music filled the gaps in his musical education. He recalls:

> *Some of the first experiences I remember with something that swung [were] in a vacant lot about five blocks from our house. They would set up one of those "holy roller" churches in a tent. Boy, we'd go down there, my brother and I, they'd be inside of this church and they'd have tambourines and everything. The preacher would be preaching, man, and they would be swinging like you wouldn't believe. You felt like telling them to take another chorus.*

Gill had no intention as a youngster of becoming a professional musician, but two years in the Army changed all that. When he found himself unemployed in Tacoma in May 1946 with two other ex-service musicians, bassist Johnny Warren and saxophone player/vocalist Jonas Weir, the three formed a trio and got a job at the newly opened Rocking Chair Club, on 14th just off Yesler. Later, they added vocalist Juanita Cruse. Before they knew it, each of the band members was making $100 a week in tips.

"I started in playing there and I've been in the music business for forty-two and a half years," laughs Gill. "The first fifteen years, I wasn't out of work six weeks."

The Rocking Chair was owned by "Big Lewis" Richardson and Herb Coleman. Richardson was an old friend of Count Basie's who had been running clubs in Seattle since the late 1920s, when he'd had the Blue Rose, around the corner. When Basie was in town, he and his men would often drop by the Rocking Chair after hours. It was a very exclusive place. Situated in a tall house with a fake-brick exterior and a tall chimney, the tiny club had a small bandstand with an upright piano. The decor was red and black, with leather-upholstered booths and an elegant bar. Customers dressed up. Downstairs was a bar, kitchen, and bandstand; upstairs, a card room. (The building was torn down several years ago to make way for Bailey Gatzert elementary school.) The club ran from midnight till morning and was hard to get into, unless you knew someone. You had to pass through two doors to get in.

At the door, "Cabdaddy" would hail taxis and watch for police. If there was a raid, the doorman pressed a button under the carpet. "It would make all the lights flash inside in the bar," according to Gill. "They'd pour all the whiskey down the drain and everybody would be drinking Coca-Cola when they'd get in there."

The Rocking Chair crowd loved the blues.

"Sometimes," Gill remembers, "we'd start in playing the blues at twelve o'clock, and at four o'clock in the morning we were still playing the same blues. Everybody would come up and take their turn singing or playing. In those days, man, we just played for the playing. There wasn't any categories like they're having now. People played from their soul."

Gill stayed at the Rocking Chair until August, then went back to school in Terre Haute, Indiana. When he realized he could make more money in a weekend playing music than college graduates were earning in a week, he got more serious about becoming a professional musician. After returning to Seattle in 1947, he worked in Portland with guitarist Al Mitchell, then was back in Seattle at the Sessions Playhouse, first with Al Hickey and Al Larkins, and later with Johnny Warren and guitarist Buster Coates. Gill then took a steady job after hours at the Black and Tan for ten months. The tips were so good, he never even opened his pay envelope.

Gill had a knack for finding good jobs. He also refused to fall in line with a system that kept black musicians working after hours for tips, while whites earned steady wages at decent hours. For the next two years, he ensconced himself at the Spinning Wheel, downtown on Second Avenue, in a group called the Question Marks, with Bob Braxton (alto saxophone and vocals), Duke Moore (drums), and Milt Price (guitar). By this time, Gill was playing marimba and vibes as well as piano, and had turned into an all-around entertainer, doing vocals, leading the band, and writing arrangements. *Billboard* magazine reported, "Braxton's . . . billing as 'Seattle's Billy Eckstine' is not unwarranted. He's better than good."

In the summer of 1952, Gill was lured to Anchorage, Alaska, with Al Hickey and Duke Moore, in hopes of earning big wages. The pay was excellent, but Gill disliked the cold weather and raw pioneer edge of the town. He gave notice and flew back to Seattle. With cash in his pocket, no commitments, and nowhere in particular to go, he bought a car, filled the gas

**The Elmer Gill Quartet at the Rocking Chair, 1946. Left to right: Juanita Cruse, Elmer Gill, Johnny Warren, Jonas Weir.**

**Photo by Al Smith**

The bar at the Rocking Chair, late 1940s. Third and fourth from right (seated at bar) are Bruce Rowell, who worked for Noodles Smith, and Bob Frazier, a club bouncer.
Photo by Al Smith

tank, and headed for California. In San Francisco, he jammed with Pony Poindexter at Jimbo's Bop City, then continued down the coast.

*I drove to Los Angeles. I was just driving down the street and I looked up at the Paramount Theater and here was a sign that said Lionel Hampton's orchestra was playing there. I knew Quincy was with the orchestra, so I wheeled into the parking lot and I go backstage to the theater. The band was out on the stage, playing. I waited until they got off, and I spoke to Quincy. Quincy told me, he said, "You know, Milt Buckner's just left the band. If you think you'd like to have a gig, I'll introduce you to Hamp." So Hamp had them bring his vibes back. He had a little piano back there and he asked me would I play "Tenderly." I played "Tenderly" and he hired me right then! I put on a uniform and played the very next show with them, at the Paramount. . . . I stayed with them the next year and a half.*

Ernestine Anderson joined Hamp while Elmer was still with the band. Quincy, Gill, and

Ernestine all played for Dwight D. Eisenhower's presidential inauguration. In New York, Hamp decided to take the band to Europe; however, the terms of the tour were so fuzzy that Gill and Ernestine decided against the trip, fearing they might get stranded abroad. Gill returned to Seattle, where he would be instrumental in the struggle to integrate the black and white musicians' unions.

When Gill was playing at the Black and Tan, another jazz trio, led by guitarist Milt Green, also was becoming known around town, at the 908 Club, Doc Hamilton's old stomping grounds. Green grew up in Minneapolis in the same neighborhood as pianist Julian Henson, where he had also known Leon Vaughn. Green was a light-skinned, fine-featured fellow who had blue eyes and sometimes passed for white. "He modeled himself on Charlie Christian—real crisp, and trying to keep it melodic," recalls Vaughn. Green arrived in Seattle in the late thirties. Guitarist Al Turay remembers jamming with Green and Junior Raglin; others remember Green playing with saxophonist Tootie Boyd. In 1944, Milt was with Vaughn's band at the Basin Street. The following year, he persuaded Henson, who had returned to Minneapolis, to come out and form a trio for the 908 Club. It turned out to be a good move. Says Henson:

"He and I and [bassist] Bob Marshall formed a trio and got a Nat 'King' Cole–type sound, the three of us. Milt sang like him. We went to work at nine o'clock and very rarely got off before four or five. One night, we made fourteen hundred dollars in the kitty."

The 908 Club had changed since Doc Hamilton had gone to prison for his dice games. Sometime in the 1940s, the club had been bought by Dick Ruffin and Nixie Smith, who toned down the gambling, but kept the refined atmosphere.

"The 908 Club was one of the finest," recalls Henson. "They had the old dining-car waiters and a chef in the kitchen called Honeysuckle that could make a piece of cardboard taste fine. Steaks and chicken, you never tasted anything like it in your life. Fine service. And they had these nice, dark lights. We played nice, soft music. It was a nice atmosphere."

In this lounge-style ambience, which was to set the tone for the 1950s, Ruffin and Smith catered to rich whites and celebrities, just as Doc Hamilton had. Dave Beck, leader of the Teamsters union, was a regular. Judges and lawyers came by frequently. Diana Barrymore had been seen there. So had many entertainers—including Nat Cole himself, whom Henson met at a concert one night:

> *Nat Cole came to Seattle and the microphone went wrong, so he went down underneath the stage and I followed him in there. I asked him if he wanted a drink and he said, "No, but my bass player needs one real bad." We told him where we was working at, so from that time, he'd come out to the 908 Club whenever he was in town. He was a real gentleman, a sophisticated, nice person. With no advertising at all, it was unbelievable, he would come to the club and it would be just packed. I don't know how it got around! He was gracious to people. He would play.*

**Elmer Gill collage with Lionel Hampton band, 1952. The band featured several Seattle musicians. Center circle, Elmer Gill (left), Lionel Hampton (right); bottom center, Ernestine Anderson; left side, in trumpet section, second from right, Quincy Jones, and below trumpet section, Monk Montgomery.**

**Courtesy of Elmer Gill**

Sometimes Cole would socialize after the gig. "When King Cole came to Seattle, after the show, he came out to Milt's house," says Leon Vaughn. "I can kick myself now for not having recorded King Cole all night long with the songs that he sang and played, as we were drinking and telling lies and stuff about our one-night stands."

Seattle's early lounge trios broke up and regrouped over the years. Julian Henson moved to Portland in 1948, where he pursued a successful career as a lounge player. Green stayed at the 908 for seven or eight years. Between 1952 and 1958, he worked R & B social-club dates with tenor saxophonist Floyd Franklin and opened a pool hall, Milt's Recreations, at 12th and Jefferson. Green was a regular on Norm Bobrow's extravaganzas, and often worked with Elmer Gill, first at the Spinning Wheel, then at the Caballero, on Sixth. Gill, Bob Braxton, Duke Moore, and Green played in Vancouver, British Columbia, at the Pacific National Exposition in 1951. Green died in 1983.

The lounge era affected the focus of solo piano players as well as jazz groups. There had always been a market for "singles," as they are known in the business—Oscar Holden and Palmer Johnson were good examples—but early solo pianists were all-around "piano professors," playing a variety of material from Tin Pan Alley tunes to light classics. After the war, a new, "mellow" style of cocktail pianist/singer emerged, in the style operative today in hotel lounges. Though the majority of the players who worked in this vein were, and continue to be, purveyors of pianistic clichés, there were a few local singles with jazz backgrounds.

**The Question Marks at the Spinning Wheel, c. 1952. Left to right: Elmer Gill, Bob Braxton, Duke Moore, Milt Price.**

**Courtesy of Chuck Mahaffay**

One of the most important was Ernie Hatfield, a delightful swing-era pianist and vocalist who worked two years with Ella Fitzgerald and performed at the Seattle Tennis Club into the 1990s. Hatfield, among many other accomplishments, has the honor of being one of the first musicians ever to appear on television. It was 1940, and he was working with a vocal quartet called the Four Keys, which would later back up Ella Fitzgerald.

"There were only 300 [television] sets in the whole country," states the affable, remarkably fit seventy-seven-year-old pianist. "It was a station in Philadelphia—WPTZ. It was so hot under those lights it wasn't even funny. The monitor they had was a huge cabinet with about a six-inch picture."

Hatfield, who was born in Chester, Pennsylvania, formed the Four Keys with his classmates the brothers Bill, Slim, and Arthur Furness. The group became well-known in the Philadelphia area and had a weekly radio program featuring spirituals. Says Hatfield of the era:

> *At that time, there were lots of trios—the Andrews Sisters, and so forth—then all of a sudden they became quartets—the Mills Brothers, the Ames Brothers. Slim wanted to get this real deep and close quartet harmony, like the Modernaires were doing at the time. After about three years we had a call from New York because Chick Webb had died. Ella had been with Chick's band. They put her with the orchestra after he died, but the men in the band didn't respect her, so now they were looking for something to put with her. So we went up there and the man said, "Just sing something." So we sang, "I've Got It Bad and That Ain't Good," and everything just blended right together. Moe Gale—he was the manager of the Ink Spots—said, "That's it!" and he pulled the bottle out of his bottom drawer and sealed the deal.*

Hatfield and the Four Keys worked with Ella two years, 1942–1943, touring the eastern seaboard and making eight records for Decca, among them "I'm Gettin' Mighty Lonesome" and "Mama Come Home." Ella still performs "Fuji Boo," a song she and the Four Keys composed spontaneously while driving to a gig in

Detroit. Hatfield has fond memories of those years in New York, including an evening when Jay McShann accidentally introduced the group as "Ella Keys and the Four Fitzgeralds." Hatfield worked with Clyde McCoy's band and at the Onyx Club, on 52nd Street, on the same bill as Billie Holiday.

The Four Keys disbanded in 1943 and Hatfield was drafted. After three years in the service, he returned to play piano around Philadelphia in a quartet called the Dial Tones. One day he received a call from drummer Jimmy White, who had been working across the street from him in Atlantic City.

> *Jimmy said he was putting together an act to come out west because he'd married a girl from here. They guaranteed us fifty weeks out of the year. We piled into the car —it was a brand new Buick Roadmaster, so I knew we wouldn't have any trouble getting out here—all three of us, and drove out in three days.*

Hatfield found the musicianship in Seattle stood up pretty well to New York's and Philadelphia's, but, like Roscoe Weathers before him, was appalled by requests from customers for country music. "You don't find anybody in Pennsylvania that goes for western music. Nobody." The Jimmy White Trio—with White, Hatfield, and Duke Johnson on bass—worked all over Washington, Montana, and Colorado, and up and down the West Coast. When White decided he wanted to take the band to Southeast Asia, Johnson went to Hawaii, instead; Hatfield was stranded. "I had to get a job," he says. "I had just written to my wife and six-month-old baby to come out, so I went down to Boeing and got a job as a mechanic." Two and a half years later, Hatfield got on as an evaluator with the State of Washington, where he stayed until retiring in 1977.

Like so many other musicians trying to make ends meet, when Hatfield finished his day gig, he changed clothes and went back to work. One of the first players he met was Stan Payne, an outstanding tenor saxophonist who had recorded several sides in 1939 with Billie Holiday, including "Them There Eyes," "Strange Fruit," and "Fine and Mellow." Hatfield and Payne started working at Fort Lawton every Sunday at the Officers' Club, then moved to McChord Air Force Base. Hatfield also worked with Payne and drummer Myrt Francois (Patti Bown's inspiration) at Coe's Tavern. During the 1980s, he was the senior member of a swing-to-bebop group, the Inner City Jazz Quartet, with Jabo Ward (tenor saxophone), Terry Morgan (bass), and Peter Madsen (drums). In the early 1990s Hatfield was working at the Seattle Yacht Club two nights a week and occasionally playing casuals.

Melody Jones at the Showbox Theater, 1947–1948.

Courtesy of Melody Jones

One of Hatfield's favorite musicians in Seattle was another "single" pianist, Winfield King, the son of LeEtta Sanders King, an important early piano teacher who had moved to Seattle from Yakima. King, who was playing in Seattle groups by the late thirties, sometimes subbed for Al Pierre. Pops Buford remembers working with King for several years during the sixties. In Pops' opinion, King was one of the best musicians in the area. King died in the 1970s.

The other important piano single in town was Derneice "Melody" Jones, a Seattle institution who worked regularly in the early 1990s in the foyer lounge of Lofurno's Italian restaurant, one of the last places where the old Jackson Street flavor persisted, until it closed in 1993. A heavy-set, modest, but tough woman with a still-cute voice and a wonderful sense of humor about life, Melody has been around the block more than a few times. Her life is a slice of jazz history that can be heard through her fingers.

Jones was born in Chicago in 1907 and moved to Harrisburg, Pennsylvania, as a girl, where she started piano lessons when she was seven. After graduating from high school, Jones moved to New York City, where she lived with her aunt in Harlem. She learned to play Bach on the organ and to accompany movies on the Wurlitzer, at the Alhambra Theater. She also played at the Lafayette Theater, where Fats Waller was featured. (When Waller went on a binge, Melody sometimes sat in for him.) After the stock market crash of 1929, Melody began to get "hands-on" lessons, literally, from Waller, at Harlem "rent parties."

*Mr. Waller used to play house-rent parties. He would book five or six of them and have me and other piano players go and keep the music going until he could get there. The house-rent party usually ended up with some kind of jam session sometime during the course of the party. A man like Waller, who knew a lot of musicians, would draw big crowds. He used to put out a card that said, "Talk, Mr. Rabbit; Skip, Mr. Bear; and Mr. Thomas Fats Waller will positively be there."*

*Fats called me "Baby Sis." People thought we were some relation, because we were both so fat! He took my hands in his and showed me the walking bass and how to play tenths. One of his hands was as big as my two together. He told me, "Pay strict attention to your left hand, but whenever you play your right hand, let your melody stand out."*

*Fats taught me one or two of the tunes that he had written so that if people asked for them, I could play them. Many were double-entendre tunes. In those days, in the cabarets they always featured one singer who did what we called the dirty songs, the double-entendre songs. While the orchestra and the show were resting, we moved the piano up to the side of the table where there was a party that wanted to hear something like that, and we would play and sing just for them. They had a piano with a short keyboard. They called us "floor girls."*

When Roosevelt was elected president, Jones got work with federal theater projects as a rehearsal pianist and accompanist. In 1941, she worked with USO shows up and down the Atlantic seaboard and all through the South. The following year, she entertained troops in the Far East, working in the Philippines, New Guinea, Indonesia, and the South Pacific. In the Philippines, Jones met a warrant officer from Seattle who asked her to marry him. He also gave her her nickname: "When he heard me play the piano, he said, 'You sound something like Fats Waller.' I told him what Fats had said about playing the melody and he said, 'That's just the name for you—Melody.'"

When the war was over, Jones' fiancé suggested they move to his beloved hometown of Seattle. Melody was unenthusiastic. She had been there on her way to the Far East, and hadn't been impressed.

*I got here at the time of year when it was rainy season. They had a camp down there in the middle of Fourth Avenue called Camp Jordan. Our building was at Jefferson Park, which was a mud puddle. We had to make fires in open stoves, with wet wood. We tried to heat the water to take our baths so that we could do the shows. We worked in three feet of mud and rain. When I met my husband and he told me he was from Seattle, I said, "You couldn't give me a telegraph pole in Seattle."*

Reservations aside, Melody made the move and things turned out better than expected. Her husband's uncle, it developed, was Gus West, who owned the black Elks Club, on Jackson Street. Gus introduced Melody to Al Pierre, who hired her to play pipe organ afternoons at the Showbox Theater, before the band came on.

The Showbox gig ended early. Afterwards, Melody and some of Pierre's men would occasionally work after hours at the New Chinatown. Other nights, Melody subbed for Elmer Gill in Johnny Warren's group at the Black and Tan. Despite abundant local work, Melody and her husband shipped out again, to the Far East. From Japan she broadcast "foxhole shows" over Air Force Radio to Korea and played in Pusan for the Air Force. The Far East stint was followed by four years in Europe. In 1956, Jones settled in Seattle for good.

By the time she'd come back, piano bars had come into vogue, and Melody, a swing-era player with a Harlem-stride background, found work in hotel lounges, among them the Mayflower, on Pine Street. Sometimes, she worked in a combo with Al Larkins and Milt

Green; she also played with white drummer Dave Coleman and Pony Poindexter at the Ebony. Jones counts Larkins as her biggest influence in Seattle. "I had known [pianist] Ellis Larkins in New York, so when I met his brother out here it was like sort of a reunion," she says. "Al Larkins introduced me to the musicians. Just before he died, we started giving jazz concerts in schools. He was teaching at Franklin [High School]."

As part of her concerts, Jones also lectured the Franklin kids about the struggles she experienced as a woman instrumentalist in jazz. Until recently, women usually have been relegated to the "girl singer" role. Jones has been in the trenches for five decades fighting that stereotype. Jones also pointed out that dark-skinned girls like herself were shunned in show business, even by blacks. Promoters preferred "high yellows," the light-skinned black women favored as chorus girls at the Cotton Club and elsewhere during the 1920s and 1930s. In Seattle, however, she says she found neither racial nor gender prejudice to be as deeply ingrained as elsewhere. She also found several strong women players here.

> *There had been a girl here who played with Bumps Blackwell [probably Patti Bown]. She had done quite well. Then there was another girl named Elise Blye, who lives now in Portland. She was a very fabulous woman pianist. I worked also with this girl Myrt Francois. She played the drums. We formed a team one time and called ourselves Melody and Mirth. We worked all through Montana. Ruth Rhymer was a drummer who came to the Washington Social Club with Elise Blye. At times, Ruth would work for Terry Cruise. And Bea Smith worked at the Colony for a long time. Beatrice Smith. She was a great blues singer.*

Although Jones is held in high regard in Seattle, one of her most important contributions to Jackson Street has gone unacknowledged. In 1948, while working at the Black and Tan, Jones was indirectly responsible for the arrival of the greatest Nat Cole imitator of them all, Ray Charles. Jones recounts:

> *One night, a fellow named Garcia McKee came into the Black and Tan. He told me that he was looking for work and he was a guitar player. I was getting ready to leave [for a USO job in Germany]. I said, "There's plenty of work here. I could give you four or five spots if you could get a piano player." Garcia said, "I have a friend who's a marvelous piano player. He imitates King Cole, but he plays beautiful piano and he sings well." I said, "He would do well here. Can you get him? If you can, I'll pass this job that I'm working on over to you." So he got in touch with his piano player. I loaned him the money and Ray Charles came up here on a Trailways bus.*

Thus began a new era in Seattle music. Nine months after Quincy Jones moved to Seattle, and four years after Ernestine Anderson came up from Texas, in March 1948, Ray Charles embarked on a project that would turn the world of American popular music upside down. Blind, ambitious, and a mere seventeen years old, Ray Charles spent just over two years in Seattle, making many close alliances, both musical and personal, as well as making his first appearances on radio and television and recording his first single. Though he wasn't yet performing in the rock style that he would invent and become famous for, Charles would exert a profound musical influence on the Seattle scene, and, likewise, the city's high-rolling nightlife gave him the opportunity to develop into a well-rounded musician.

Ray Charles Robinson was born in 1930 and raised by his mother in a country shack in Greenville, Florida, near the Georgia border. He was not born blind. His sight was claimed by glaucoma, a deteriorating disease that could have been treated had he been raised in different circumstances. By age seven, he was totally blind. Charles learned Braille and how to play the piano and clarinet at the Florida State School for the Blind, in St. Augustine. He spent summers at home, where his mother prepared him well for independence, treating him as a sighted child, teaching him to chop wood, haul water, and do chores. In his autobiography, *Brother Ray*, Charles says he even rode a bicycle around the countryside; once, for the sheer thrill of it, he started up a tractor in the school parking lot.

When Charles was fifteen, his mother died, and the young man then struck out on his own. He moved in with friends of his parents in

Jacksonville, then spent two difficult years on his own, scuffling in blues and jazz bands, at one point going on the road through the South. Even at this early phase in his career, Charles was an eclectic, versatile player, comfortable with gospel, blues, swing, and commercial crooning. In the fall of 1947, he moved to Tampa and worked in a seven-piece, Louis Jordan– style band led by Charlie Brantley.

It was in Tampa, in 1947, that R. C. met guitarist Garcia McKee, in a summer rehearsal band at Florida A. & M. University. The band included in its ranks bassist Sam Jones and alto saxophonist Julian "Cannonball" Adderley. Charles and McKee played together as a duo at Drew Air Force Base for about six months. McKee had worked up an imitation of Oscar Moore's complex harmonies and steady beat and R. C. was singing as close to Nat Cole's crooning as he could. Says Charles in *Brother Ray*, "During all these years I was imitating Nat Cole. To me, it was practically a science. I worked at it, I enjoyed it, I was proud of it, and I loved doing it. He was a guy everyone admired, and it just made sense to me, musical and commercial sense, to study his technique."

The club owner at the base was impressed by the young duo and encouraged them to take their act out of town. But Charles was skeptical: He had just moved in with a girl named Louise, and he didn't want to leave her behind. He was also somewhat apprehensive about leaving the South for points unknown—a not-uncommon attitude for southern blacks at the time, even more understandable for a blind teenager. However, Charles eventually agreed to leave town with McKee. "I told Ray Charles," says McKee, "I said, 'Listen, let's get away,' and he says, 'Where?' and I said, 'Well, I'll get a map!' and I went and got a map and we decided we wanted to go as far away from Tampa as we could go, so we wouldn't know nobody!" Together, they found a town in the upper left-hand corner of the map—Seattle—which seemed faraway and exotic.

"I didn't know anyone living up there, and I hadn't heard a thing about the town," explains Charles. "It just seemed like a reasonable place to go. All mystery and adventure. I also liked the fact that it was way on the other coast—real far away. That term—West Coast—was appealing to me. I came from the woods, and the idea of heading west was enticing as hell."

McKee left first. As soon as he got to Seattle, he went to the Black and Tan, where he met Melody Jones. Melody's uncle Gus booked a room at the Coast Hotel for Charles and loaned McKee $100 to bring Ray out. Garcia left a message for Ray at a Tampa pool hall. After five days and nights on the bus, the hot, sweaty, tired seventeen-year-old arrived at the depot, unannounced. He had no idea how to find McKee. Always the survivor, Charles called the police department and several radio stations, asking them to broadcast McKee's name, and to say that his friend R. C. had arrived. McKee remembers:

> *A guy who had seen me around told me, "You know, there's a blind guy down at the bus station looking for you." So I went down to the bus station and they said [they] had told him I lived at the Coast Hotel. I went on back there and that's when I found him, sitting down, waiting for me. I let him get some sleep, we went and ate at a little place up on Jackson Street that was open twenty-four hours. Then I took him down to the Black and Tan that night . . . because Melody told me that's where she was going to be. Elmer Gill was playing piano, Johnny Warren was playing bass, and a Caucasian boy was playing guitar [probably Mike DeFillipis]. Nice group. Melody introduced us to all the people and asked us to play. We went into our act. This is the very first night. We played all these pretty tunes, didn't need nothing behind us. That's how we got the job at the Elks Club.*

"We were astounded at how young he was and how well he played," recalls Melody.

Charles and McKee played as a duo at the Elks Club for several months. It was a popular place. The local black chapter of the well-known fraternal order, it was situated on the north side of Jackson, between Maynard and Seventh, upstairs. The ornate white building, one of a pair with a series of little cornices, is still standing. The club was open at least as early as 1938, when the Gene Coy band played there. A large, smoky, low-ceilinged establishment peppered with cocktail tables, the black Elks offered people a place to socialize in an atmosphere where they could also drink. The kitty was a cigar box. A huge elk's head that musicians used to duck behind to smoke joints was mounted near the piano. The place could accommodate about two hundred people, and was known for its excellent barbecue sandwiches and as a place where name entertainers often dropped by after their gigs; the clientele was cool enough not to make a fuss over them when they did.

The Elks Club had a running card game; other vices could be satisfied there, as well. Leon Vaughn remembers being introduced at the Elks to *yen pah*, a concoction made from the scrapings from an opium pipe, which were then poured into a drink or put on the lip and sipped with coffee. The crowd at the Elks was racially mixed, but mostly black.

"The lady that did the cooking at the Elks Club was named Georgia Kemp," recalls Melody Jones. "Ray used to sing that song to her, 'Georgia.' She liked him very much. I rented a room at Mrs. Kemp's house. I was leaving, so Garcia asked me, 'When you leave, Mrs. Jones, can we have your room for Ray?'"

Charles moved into Kemp's house on 20th Avenue, near Madison. She had a grand piano, and she enjoyed letting musicians rehearse on it. She also liked to take care of players who were down on their luck. She was from the South and frequently cooked one of Charles' favorite southern "comfort" foods, red beans and rice.

Comfortably ensconced at Georgia Kemp's and secure with his new gig, Ray played with Garcia McKee at the Elks Club throughout the spring of 1948. The young Floridian soon convinced his girlfriend, Louise, to come out and live with him. Life was good. R. C. Robinson began a youthful idyll in Seattle, working one of the best jobs in town, "keeping house," as he puts it, with Louise, and making friends with local musicians. Charles has recorded his first impressions vividly:

> *The entertainment business was in something of a boom. Competition was fierce. Many cats had just left the armed-forces bands—and don't think those outfits couldn't play. In one respect it was just like Tampa: There were lots of musicians roaming the streets who'd blow your ass off the stand if you gave 'em half the chance. . . . Cat called Bumps Blackwell had a well-known combo around Seattle. . . . And there was also my good friend Gerald Brashear. . . . There were a lot of faces around Seattle, and I tried to make mine familiar so I could keep working. The McSon Trio [Charles, McKee, and bassist Milt Garred] played all over—Fort Lawton, Kirkland, Tacoma, and places in Seattle like the Washington Social Club or the 908 Club. . . . I could see that in a city like Seattle—a place which was more sophisticated and open than what I was used to—my act was going to pay off.*

The black Elks Club, 662 Jackson Street.

The nightclub was on the second floor of this ornate building, which is still standing. Ray Charles played his first regular gig here, and the Cecil Young Quartet dominated the room for almost a year.

Courtesy of the Washington State Archives

Nearly everyone from the period remembers Charles as a versatile musician and a playful, remarkably independent person. "Everybody liked him," says Elmer Gill. "He didn't make any special deal about his being blind. He was just one of the boys. He'd walk all over town, never had a cane. Never used a dog or nothing. He'd come in always smiling and carrying on."

"I'd see him walking downtown," remembers Sonny Booker. "He'd be by himself always—and he'd walk right alongside of the curb, just as fast as anybody else, just—boom! boom! boom!—there'd go Ray. And you'd say, 'Hi, Ray,' and he'd say, 'Hi, how're ya doing?' and he'd just keep on going." Buddy Catlett adds, "We went on for about a year before we knew that he was an orphan. He'd keep saying his parents were on vacation. He wouldn't tell anyone he was taking care of himself."

In the summer of 1948, Charles landed a regular job at the Rocking Chair. As Elmer Gill had discovered two years earlier, the crowd there demanded raucous music. Charles and McKee hired a bass player to drive the group. Milt Garred was twenty-four years old, a friendly, round fellow who had moved to Seattle from West Virginia. A monstrous swinger with a huge, booming sound, Garred became an immensely important figure on the Seattle scene. Fred Greenwell describes him as

The Maxin Trio, 1948. Left to right: R. C. Robinson (Ray Charles), Garcia McKee, Milt Garred.

Courtesy of Melody Jones

"the Seattle Wilbur Ware . . . gigantically talented," and Traff Hubert, bass player and longtime connoisseur of jazz history, counts Garred as his "favorite bass player of all time." Charles agrees. "He was a real funky bass player. He had that old nasty sound. Milt was a very strong player. I would say that Milt was the glue of the trio, I really would, honestly. I was the quote, star, unquote, of the trio, but Milt was the glue."

After Milt joined, the group changed its name to the McSon Trio—a combination of the musicians' names, McKee and Robinson. (Later, the name was changed to the Maxin—then the Maxim—Trio.) The ensemble played at the Rocking Chair for most of the rest of 1948. It was a plum gig, one of the only regular-paying jobs in town where the salary was worth as much as the kitty. "All the rounders, pimps, and the working girls would come and throw the twenty-dollar bills for us to play 'Nature Boy' and 'To a Wild Rose' to the women," remembers McKee.

In addition to blues and progressive numbers in the style of Nat Cole, one of the McSon Trio's specialty numbers at the Rocking Chair was a version of Frankie Laine's "Mule Train," a novelty number that featured the rhythmic "snap" of a whip against the hide of a mule. Recounts McKee:

> *Ray Charles got him a cap pistol and we got a belt, and whenever we would play "Mule Train" he would take the belt and hit on the piano like it was the horses and he would take the cap pistol and shoot it. That was our act. But [one day] Ray was out of caps, and instead of asking me to get them for him—he was so independent, he wanted to do it himself, and he never did use a cane or a dog, never did in his life—he went downtown and he was waiting for the bus to come along and he had the pistol in his hand, and the police came along there and told him to "Get back up against the wall!" The guys who were standing there, they said, "Man, that guy's blind!" And of course they were red-faced.*

*And he said, "That's just a cap pistol. I wasn't attempting to rob that place. I just need some ammunition. Yessiree!"*

Charles continued to add new tunes to his repertoire at the Rocking Chair. The house singer, Juanita Cruse, and another Rocking Chair vocalist, Bea Skaggs, introduced him to some of the material he would later become famous for, including "Just for a Thrill."

Charles says he doesn't remember Skaggs, but everyone remembers the smooth and sexy blues Charles himself added to his repertoire, in honor of the club—"Rocking Chair Blues." Charles and McKee both claim authorship of the tune, though neither seems to care enough to argue about it. The lyrics are mostly generic, and the fictional characters, such as "Dubonnet Judy" and "Gin Fizz Flo," bear no relation to the actual people who worked at the club, though there's one line that pegs the blues in soggy Seattle: "If you don't have your rubbers, take a taxi down." It's fitting that Charles commemorated the Rocking Chair with a blues, because the McSon Trio is largely remembered for shaking the rafters there with house-rocking music.

The new demand for shuffle tempos and "down-home" blues reflected the demographic changes occurring in Seattle, as southern blacks moved north. An informal sample by the Seattle Urban League from the period showed that the majority of blacks living at the Delridge Housing Project were from five southern states—Texas, Louisiana, Oklahoma, Arkansas, and Missouri. For a while, there was friction between the older black community and the new arrivals. "I was quite ashamed of them," confesses LeEtta King.

*They looked so bad. Dungarees weren't worn on the street by women, but these women would be wearing them. Their big shapes—and their heads tied up with a handkerchief. I was so ashamed. And they were noisy. I just tried not to see them. . . . [Before they came] we could eat in any restaurant we wanted to. . . . The parks were always open and the theaters were open. You bought a seat in the theater and it didn't matter where you sat. . . . There was a feeling of the people that were here of resentment against them.*

Others, like Powell Barnett, were simply condescending. "I actually saw a man eating watermelon on the street curb," he recounts. "But I felt that was all the more reason to extend a helping hand and help these people adjust to western ways."

**Political cartoon, the *Northwest Enterprise*, September 5, 1943.**

**The arrival of thousands of rural African Americans from the South and Southwest in the 1940s caused friction in Seattle's black community.**

**Reprinted from the *Northwest Enterprise***

Though no one dared speak publicly of it, there was also an issue of skin tone within the black community. The new immigrants, largely from the Southwest and the South, were not only more rural, less educated, and "ill-mannered," they were also darker-skinned. "They used to call us 'cotton-pickers,' and 'sharecroppers' when we first came to Seattle," recalls Leon Vaughn, the trumpet player who came to Washington from Nebraska in the early 1940s. "The only people that were any good were those that had been here for years and years and years, the light ones that could fit in."

Buddy Catlett's family had been in the area for half a century before the great migration started, so he understood why older, established families were upset: "You don't want to see so-called ignorant people coming in your domain, because that means the whites you have to deal with are going to look at you in the same manner. When you get halfway cool, you don't want nobody to come around and rock the boat."

On the other hand, Catlett saw that the people who came up from the South actually put him in touch with his own culture.

*We were fortunate; [before they came] we were isolated. I mean, it's the people in the fields that bring this culture value, that bring the spices to the stew. That made jazz what it was. A lot of people resent the harshness of the blues, an intrusion on the values they already got set up. The Army, the war, the shipyards, Fort Lewis brought the culture up here. That's why you had so many musicians that could play. We're fortunate. We'd just be non-white whites, in a sense [if it hadn't happened].*

The division between North and South, urban and rural, created a double bind for African Americans, who on the one hand needed to stand together against discrimination from whites, but on the other felt culturally divided. Nowhere was this cultural split more evident than in music, where the new styles of the southerners and southwesterners—house-rocking blues and sanctified church music—were as new to most Seattle blacks as they were to whites. "I didn't know what Ray Charles was doing," declares Al Hilbert, the bartender at the Basin Street club. "But I liked it. I took him down to this place that a friend of mine owned to see if he would hire him. He just laughed. The guy that owned the place, he was from Memphis. He said, 'Yeah, people don't know anything about that kind of music here.'"

Buddy Catlett tells another story that suggests Charles knew that his accent and brash, in-your-face southern style embarrassed northerners. Catlett says R. C.'s idea of a good joke was to start playing some gutbucket blues, real loud, over at Catlett's house just as a girlfriend would call—or worse, just as her parents answered the phone—and he was trying to impress her with his best uptown English. "He'd try to f--- your act up," laughs Catlett.

The whole issue of blues brings up the question of whether Charles was performing in his signature, gospel-inflected style—the way he later sounded on "I Got a Woman" and "What'd I Say"—while in Seattle, or if he was still just an imitator of Nat Cole and a so-so jazz pianist.

Bill Crow, the ex–Gerry Mulligan Quartet bass player who grew up in Kirkland, Washington, observes:

*When I heard him at the Washington Social, I thought, "Well, he sounds like a fairly decent imitation of Bud [Powell], but he doesn't really have it down." Then everybody was saying, "Ray, sing the blues! Sing the blues!" So finally Ray sang the blues and he tore my head off. I never heard anything like that in my life before. When I met him later, I said, "Ray, how come you don't do that all the time?" And he said, "Oh man, you can't make a nickel singing like that."*

In *Brother Ray*, Charles writes that his looser vocal style, which wedded the gospel sound of Clarence Fountain with the rolling beat of Kansas City blues, definitely had not jelled in his Seattle days. Many of the recordings of the McSon Trio, such as "Rocking Chair Blues," "Honey, Honey," "Ain't That Fine," and "What Have I Done?" bear him out. As a singer, Charles was still imitating the smooth stylings of Nat Cole and the restrained blues inflections of Charles Brown. However, two cuts Charles recorded in 1947 in Tampa, "Walkin' and Talkin'" and "I'm Wonderin' and Wonderin'," and his 1951 Los Angeles recording "Kissa Me Baby," show unmistakable trademarks of his later style, complete with aching gospel inflections and cries, suggesting that Charles may have been singing occasionally in his mature style even in Seattle.

According to Buddy Catlett, Charles had already come up with the germ for this style, without even knowing it. "It wasn't until after he went to Los Angeles that he began that gospel style that he has now," he says. "Here, he would only do that for fun. I mean, gospel was involved in church. It was sacrilegious. So he would like poke fun at it. I didn't know he was serious!"

"I was surprised when he really *made* it doing the blues, [because] it was always like a joke," confirms Sonny Booker. "We'd say, 'Ray, do your thing,' you know, and he'd do his fun thing—joke thing—going into the blues, which really made him famous."

The notion of the young Ray Charles privately "gospelizing" tunes in Seattle as a joke, then discovering later that this was what people wanted to hear and that this was his truest musical self, is an appealing and plausible one. One 1958 review of "What'd I Say" noted that "many of Charles' gospel blues songs are virtually parodies of gospel songs." Ray Charles has a puckish sense of humor. Things tickle him. It's easy to imagine him getting a kick out of the attention his southern accent and sanctified vocalizing would evoke from a Northwest audience. As Albert Goldman has perceptively pointed out in his (otherwise unpleasant) biography of Elvis Presley, there was an element of parody in the best early rock 'n' roll, which set it apart from the blues proper.

Charles, a guarded, private soul who maintains a firm first line of defense between himself and the public, was inconclusive about this notion. Sitting on a stool in his huge, private studio on the second floor of his South Central Los Angeles offices, mug of tea and whiskey in hand, he laughed, "I don't know. When you're that young, you just do things, especially when you're around musicians. . . . I'm sure that they are right . . . so I'm sure I could do takeoffs. . . . [But] if you were to say to me, 'Ray, could you give me specifics?' I can't remember that. . . ."

Pinpointing the origins of Charles' style may be chronologically slippery, but there is no disputing that he was a fairly accomplished bebopper in his early years. Traff Hubert, a bass player who worked with Cecil Young, recalls being mightily impressed by Ray Charles one night in 1949 at the Tuxedo Club, across the street from the New Chinatown:

"I thought he was the best piano player I had ever heard. He played piano, bass, drums, and sax, and he really did it. He'd demonstrate a different guy—'This is Bud Powell. This is Tatum. This is whoever.' Then he'd say, 'This is me,' and he'd play the blues. This was 1949."

Says Buddy Catlett:

> *Ray sounded like Bud Powell. He was a bebopper. Except he was always commercially minded. He liked to play saxophone and when he'd come off his job somewhere, working someplace with a small group, he'd come up to where we were working after hours at the Washington Social Club and he'd always grab my horn—"Let me play your horn!" I walked into Birdland once and Roscoe Weathers, Floyd Standifer, Ray Charles, Milton Garred, and a drummer named Jimmie Rodgers were playing. That was really a good bebop group.*

Charles also began to work on another musical innovation on Jackson Street—the use of electric keyboards. In 1948 or 1949, he bought a tinny electric piano made by Wurlitzer, the same company that made jukeboxes, and began to experiment with the sound. Floyd Standifer remembers this well: "He just beat all the keys off it, he played it so hard."

Contemporary musicians use electric keyboards for convenience and as replacements for live instrumentalists, but Charles says he bought the electric piano strictly because he liked the sound, not to take to work. His fondness for his little Wurlitzer led to a revolution in music, beginning with his hit record "What'd I Say," which helped to popularize the instrument. Charles chuckles now to think how even fellow musicians laughed at him when they saw his little keyboard. "Later on," he says, "when I got to Atlantic, the people were laughing. 'What you going to do with that little piano, man? That little toy?' They used to call it a toy. Then I made 'What'd I Say' and everybody got one of these little 'toys'!"

The most important personal connection Charles made on Jackson Street was with Quincy Jones. It was a musical relationship that had a lasting influence on both men, particularly on the young and impressionable Quincy. The relationship survives to this day. Their most recent collaboration is "I Be Good to You," on Jones' 1990 hit album *Back on the Block*, but they've produced many others over the years, including *The Genius of Ray Charles* and Jones' *Black Requiem*, for symphony orchestra, dedicated to Charles.

When Ray Charles and Quincy Jones first met in Seattle, both young men were hungry for knowledge and success. But whereas Jones had to go east to find his big break, success came courting Charles on Jackson Street, first in the form of a radio show, then with a primitive television appearance, and then—prize of prizes—a record deal.

A few short months after the McSon Trio started at the Rocking Chair, the group was offered a fifteen-minute "pay-to-play" spot on Saturdays for KRSC radio. ("We gave Garcia's phone number over the air in the hopes of finding some gigs," Charles recalls.) Soon afterward, the trio was asked to perform on KING television, on what must have been one of the earliest live broadcasts in town. Though it was a one-shot deal, it brought attention to the group, which was subsequently asked to play when United Nations dignitary Ralph Bunche came to town.

But more important for R. C. was that all

over the country, independent labels were beginning to record the new styles of black music that had cropped up after World War II. In Los Angeles, Specialty, Swing Time, Modern, and Black and White were just some of the labels capturing the new sounds. Just as they had in the twenties, these new "race record" labels sent out scouts to find and record new talent. Unbeknownst to Charles, a Los Angeles record executive named Jack Lauderdale had heard about the McSon Trio from saxophonist Jack McVea a couple of months after the group started at the Rocking Chair. When Lauderdale offered the trio a record date, they thought he was putting them on. McKee recollects:

*Ray and I got together and said, "This guy thinks we damn fools!" I told Ray Charles, "This guy is talking about records." Ray says, "Oh, man! He's full of bull!" And I thought so, too. We didn't know he was serious, because we didn't know nothing about recording. He kept on persisting, and persisting, and finally he got us down to this station and then that's when we did our first tune. We had about three or four days to get these things together. We recorded them downtown, at a studio, down around Second or Third.*

"You know," adds Charles, "when something comes along that you've been wanting and you really have a strong desire for it, and somebody just sort of puts it in your lap, you don't quite believe your good fortune. We just couldn't believe that—we're going to get to make a record and we're going to make it in Seattle."

The trio made two sides, "Confession Blues," by Charles, and "I Love You, I Love You," written by Charles' friend Joe Lee Lawrence. The session occurred in late 1948, only six months after Charles hit town, and the record, a 78, was released in early 1949. Though "Confession Blues" was not a hit, it sold respectably enough that Lauderdale brought the trio down to Los Angeles to record again. Several records were waxed, including "Ain't That Fine?" "Honey, Honey," and "She's on the Ball." Within a year or so, Lauderdale's Swing Time sessions would lead to R. C.'s first national hit on the black charts, "Baby Let Me Hold Your Hand," a languid, Charles Brown–style number.

The Los Angeles sessions would also lead to the breakup of the trio. Lauderdale, who was interested only in Ray Charles, let bassist Garred go. Recounts McKee:

*The second [trip to Los Angeles], Jack Lauderdale didn't send Milt a ticket. I think Milt faulted me a little, but I couldn't do nothing about it. While we were down here making the second batch of records with another guitar player and a drummer, he gave me enough money to buy a car. I bought me a '49 Chevrolet, and Ray Charles and I drove all the way back up to Seattle. We almost froze to death, because we didn't have no heater. But we had transportation! We got back to Seattle and Georgia Kemp loaned me money to buy a heater in the car.*

It was around this time that McKee also anointed Charles with his first pair of sunglasses, which would become one of his signatures. Oddly, in the first promotional picture showing Charles wearing shades, the glasses are drawn in, like a bad cartoon. McKee explains:

*Once the guy recorded us, we had to have a professional picture taken. I had some pictures taken at the radio station where we were paying to play, but I didn't know what I was doing and they weren't good enough. What happened was, they drew the sunglasses on that one when I sent the picture to Jack Lauderdale. They are drawn on him on that picture. Right after that, Len Brooks [Seattle pianist and photographer] said, "Let me take some pictures," and I said, "Let's put some [actual] glasses on him."*

Despite tensions created by Lauderdale, the Maxin Trio remained together through 1949, moving from the Rocking Chair into the Washington Social Club, where it played intermissions. McKee saw to it that the trio had gigs at the university, playing fraternity parties, socials, and dances. In June 1949, Charles played an unusual novelty show at the Trianon Ballroom, inspired by the musical shenanigans of Slim Gaillard and probably produced by Bumps Blackwell, who, if indeed he produced the show, billed himself as "Julius MacVootie." Called "French and Be-Bop," the program featured Ray with the brothers Brashear (Gerald and Buddy), Floyd Standifer, and Al Larkins; the ads claimed that MacVootie would sing

"French Jazz. See you hipsters Sunday. . . ."

But the trio was starting to break up. When Jack Lauderdale recorded Charles with guitarist Oscar Moore and other top-flight studio musicians, McKee began to get the picture. Sometime in early 1950, the guitarist headed for Great Falls, Montana, where many entertainers were finding work on the "silver circuit" in Las Vegas–style nightclubs run by the mob. McKee connected with bassist Eddie Cole—Nat's brother—and they formed a comedy and music group called Three Loose Nuts and a Bolt, which, says McKee, transformed him into an entertainer. In Great Falls, McKee also met his future wife, actress Lillian Randolph ("Amos and Andy," "The Great Gildersleeve"), with whom he formed a family band that played Hong Kong, Honolulu, and Army bases all over the world. The act worked on cruise ships for a while, and McKee eventually turned away from entertainment, becoming master chef for a cruise line. McKee is now retired, and he and Lillian live in Los Angeles. If there were any hard feelings in the breakup between McKee and Ray Charles, the two musicians mask them well. "We wasn't mad," McKee recalls. "No, no, no, no . . . Because next time I saw him, he was doing good with his blues, and had his band, in Philadelphia, and Lillian and I had our family act. We felt good about it. It was the best thing to do."

Charles agrees. "It wasn't anything bitter or angry. The trio thing just wasn't happening, and Milt and Gosady [Garcia] ran out of bread. . . . Jack was primarily interested in me."

Charles had other reasons for leaving Seattle. His girlfriend, Louise, had returned to Florida. At about the same time, the police had begun to crack down on the drug trade in Seattle, too. One of the sorrier legacies of Ray's Seattle period was the beginning of his heroin use. Charles describes his early addiction openly:

> *Didn't take me long to figure out that before a gig, the cats might be doing something besides smoking reefer. Or if we were at someone's house, I'd hear them doing something in the kitchen. Before long, I discovered that they were cooking up "horse," and I wanted to try some for myself. . . . There wasn't no pusher hanging 'round the back alley who enticed me into it. . . . I wanted the shit bad enough so I found a way to get it. I went back to bugging the other musicians. . . . One of the cats finally said, "Give the kid some shit just to keep him quiet." . . . And that was how I got my first hit.*

Buddy Catlett remembers the change that came over Charles when he started using hard drugs:

> *Ray moved to an apartment on 12th and Jackson. I went by to see him there one day. He had a record on and he was sitting in a big, overstuffed chair. He had slumped to the floor and he was just sitting there—listening, scratching. I could see where that euphoria that dope gives you just lightened his whole load. He could then focus on what he wanted to do, and do it. In his case, it seems, the ends seemed to justify the means. But he could afford it. He didn't have to go to the street to find it.*

Charles remained addicted to heroin for several years. Perhaps because of the addict's perennial fear of being busted, he seems to have been prepared for a swift departure from Seattle at any time. Ernestine Anderson says, "He told [his group], 'One of these nights, I'm just going to disappear. I'm going to get on a train and I'll be gone.' And he did. He just left in the middle of the night and nobody knew."

"Things got a little hot, as you may have heard," comments McKee. By February of 1950, two years after he had arrived, Ray Charles left Seattle and started working in Los Angeles.

In April, Lauderdale put Charles out on the road with label-mate Lowell Fulson, the great Los Angeles blues man. Through working with Fulson, and traveling as a single through the South for the next two years, Charles found his true voice, which came from his rural blues and gospel roots. In 1952, Charles signed with Atlantic Records, where the promotional genius Ahmet Ertegun guided him to success. The Atlantic deal was R. C.'s first honest contract in the music business: In the three years he had worked with Lauderdale and Swing Time, he never earned a nickel in publishing royalties for his songs. Charles is philosophical about this:

> *Jack Lauderdale, [to] my mind, is a great man, to this day, because he provided for*

*me the one thing that I felt I had been wanting ever since I knew what music was, and that was to record a record. This was the ultimate in life, I thought, at that age. So who in the hell knew anything about royalties and stuff? And Jack Lauderdale was not any different from most record companies. They didn't pay no artist no royalties. A lot of record companies, what they would do for artists is go buy 'em a car. But then in the end, they would still take the money out of their royalties.*

The rest of the Charles story is well-known. Along with Lowell Fulson, Pee Wee Crayton, Guitar Slim, Jay McNeely, Roy Milton, T-Bone Walker, and others who played the Washington Social Club, Ray toured up and down the West Coast and throughout the South, continuing the fusion of jazz, blues, and gospel that would become contemporary rhythm and blues. Eventually, in 1954, that fusion would result in the groundbreaking record that announced to the world his gospel-rocking signature—"I Got a Woman." Five years later, "What'd I Say" put him over to white audiences and the nation in general.

Ernestine Anderson vividly recalls hearing those records and trying to square them with the R. C. Robinson she had known in Seattle:

*Ray left first. When he resurfaced again a few years later, it was a different Ray Charles. It was the Ray Charles that we know now. The style was totally different. He had added this gospel thing to it. It was like a whole different person. It was like, "He had that in him?" I was just so awed! Amazed at the difference. I knew he was going to be bigger than life, as soon as I heard it. Yeah, this will fly. He was the first person to do that. He was the originator. The pioneer.*

Ray Charles was a pioneer in another sense, too, in that he never bought into the then-popular misconception of the blind as dependent. On the contrary, he seems to have taken delight in shocking people with his ability to function normally, enough so that some Seattleites became convinced he wasn't blind at all.

Sonny Booker once saw Ray sitting on the floor, repadding a clarinet, an intricate task that involves gluing tiny, button-sized pieces of fiber onto the underside of small metal keys. Ernestine Anderson also had her doubts: "One time, he had the radio all taken apart on the floor. He said to me, 'Watch out. Don't step on that!' and I'm—'Can he see, or what?'"

Both Anderson and McKee swear that on different occasions they each watched Charles, alone, drive a car. Says Anderson:

*I saw him drive a car in Houston. With my own eyes. At a motel where the drive was a round kind of thing that went around in a circle. There was a big thing in the middle with flowers and cement and curb. Fathead Newman had just bought a car. Ray got into the car and drove it around this circle. I'm standing there in the doorway watching the whole thing. I saw it. I saw it.*

Leon Vaughn and bassist Bill Crow, among many others, report that Charles always knew where he was when he was being driven somewhere, and would audaciously tell drivers when to turn right or left. Continues Anderson:

*Ray used to have his checks sent to my house. One night, when he called to let me know he was coming, my dad got up and was standing on the landing to watch for when he came in, because he was going to go out and help him. We were both standing there, looking out the window. You could see the street clearly. Ray got out of the cab, a Yellow Cab. The cab did not park where you could just walk straight up the walk [to the house]. Ray walked along the curb and then got to the walkway, turned, and came into the house. We were both standing there with our mouths hanging open. He came up on the porch and we opened the door. So everybody used to think he was putting us on. My dad, he just [said], "Nawwww, he's not kidding me. He can see." But he couldn't.*

Emmett Lewis, the agent for Local No. 493, tells a similar anecdote:

*I used to tell my wife that he could see. Because when I come in the door, he would say, "There's the business agent coming in from 493. Get your money ready." At the Eagles Auditorium, I saw Ray Charles leave the piano on the bandstand, walk out the front, and go right straight up the aisle. Didn't hit nobody, and got in a cab and went home. The first intermission. Got him a cab when he got through, come back. Walked straight back through the crowd, got on the bandstand. Sit down at the piano for the next three, four hours. Now, there's no way to prove that if you hadn't seen it, but I was there. The other two guys with me is dead. I used to tell him about it and he'd laugh and say, "Oh, will you stop kidding me."*

Charles explains most of these tales away in his autobiography. For starters, he admits he has always had a near-suicidal attraction to motor vehicles. On summers off from school, a neighbor taught him to drive. He also asserts that he would meticulously go over familiar routes on foot, listening for variations in the sound of his footsteps, so that later he could walk back over the same route at a confident clip. As for giving drivers directions to his house, many blind people use the same technique: memorizing bumps in the road—or sounds that come from certain corners—so they always know where they are.

Garcia McKee, who ought to know more than anyone about Ray during this period, states categorically and emphatically that Charles was "stone blind." What's more interesting than raising questions about Charles' blindness is that in the process of proving he could take care of himself, he slighted McKee, the man who gave him so much over the years. For it was McKee—not Charles himself, as he claims in his autobiography—who auditioned at the Black and Tan and got them the job there. It was McKee who first came out from Tampa on the bus. It was McKee who borrowed the money for Ray's bus ticket. And despite the amazing independence that Charles displayed as a teenager in Seattle, it was again McKee who looked out for him during their stay there.

"He knew that I was going to see that he was taken care of, no matter what," says the guitarist. "Even though he was alone, he had that confidence. He knew I was there. No matter where he was, he knew I would be there."

Leon Vaughn is less equivocal: "Everywhere he went, Garcia went."

Ray Charles, like Quincy Jones, is now a millionaire several times over. A canny businessman as well as an ambitious and talented man, he has become a national hero, part of American folklore. He recently signed a three-record deal with Jones' label, Qwest, and has been one of the few African-American musicians to crack the lucrative television-commercial market with his ads for Pepsi-Cola. Looking back at his Seattle days, after warming to the subject, and hearing again of his experiences as a struggling teenager, making his first record, meeting Quincy Jones and Ernestine Anderson, Charles became philosophical, even sentimental:

*What do they call this—bar mitzvah?—where you come out as a man? I think Seattle was kind of like that for me. The reason I put it to you that way is because in Seattle, at that point, all of a sudden I had to become a man. I started keeping house—like Quincy says—I had an apartment, a piano, a big radio, hi-fi set, telephone. Cookin'. There ain't no doubt about it. I became a man.*

# 9
# JACKSON STREET GLITTERS then goes dark

The year 1950 exploded on Jackson Street with the debut of the most successful bebop unit ever to grace the neighborhood—the Cecil Young Quartet. Young's group took Seattle by storm, enjoyed a regional hit record, then traveled to New York, where it played Birdland. Folks lucky enough to have seen the quartet witnessed Jackson Street at its very best.

**Cecil Young, c. 1950. Courtesy of Traff Hubert**

Young was a vaudeville entertainer from New Haven, Connecticut, who came to town on a Palomar Theatre date, part of a thirty-week series that featured Sarah Vaughan, Billy Eckstine, and other stars. The Palomar was a living testimony to Seattle's historic passion for theater—the last vaudeville house in town, it ran four shows and a movie daily, until 1956. The ebullient Norm Bobrow was hosting the series.

"One of the acts that came through was called Young and Williams," he recalls. "The guy that was the dancer out front was Williams, and Cecil Young, a young guy, quite balding, was his stand-up piano player, who would mug. We hit it off, Cecil and I. He says, 'You know, I want to break away from this ridiculous vaudeville act.' So he stayed and I became his patron."

Cecil Young was like no one Seattle had ever known before. A short, stocky man with a wicked sense of humor, Young was a hipster and a hustler who spoke with a rabbity stammer. He was also the genuine item—a modern piano player with East Coast fire. Young spent two years at Yale's School of Music and lived for a while at the Cecil Hotel, in Harlem, where he met and jammed with Charlie Parker, Dizzy Gillespie, and other early beboppers. Cecil had a white girlfriend who drove a Bentley and used a Vassar vocabulary. He liked to put people on. Continues Bobrow:

> *Cecil was "fly"—you know, an old synonym for hip. He was one of those "fly cats" from the East Coast. Cecil was a guy who just out-hipped the world—a very, very bright man.*
>
> *Sometimes he would affect a little mintiness. I remember once someone called me to ask if he would play a private party in the Highlands [a fancy neighborhood in North Seattle]. I said, "I think that Mr.*

*Young would like to look at the place in advance." So we went out there, and indeed it was beautiful. Cecil was dressed in a gray flannel suit and he was carrying an umbrella. It was a sunny day. The only thing that would have added to that image would have been if he were wearing a derby. And he's walking like this [affects strut]. We get in there and there's this huge living room with French windows that open out to the terrace lawn. And in this huge room there's statuary, almost like a Venus de Milo kind of thing. So Cecil is standing there leaning on his umbrella, and he says to this woman, maybe in her fifties or so—"I think that statue ought to go."*

Chuck Metcalf considered Young one of his most important "gurus." Cecil turned on the impressionable bassist to Jimmy Blanton, but also to such exotic musical influences as Ravi Shankar and Edgar Varèse.

Once Young decided to stay in Seattle, his first move was to drop by the New Chinatown, where Dave Henderson, the bouncer/pianist, had recently played. Cecil got the gig. He assembled a quartet, drawing on tenor saxophonist Gerald Brashear, who had been around since the Savoy Boys days and was now sounding a bit like a young Sonny Stitt; white bassist Traff Hubert, a new kid on the block from Tacoma; and Jimmie Rodgers, also new in town, a slick drummer originally from Detroit. The gig skidded, but the quartet took flight, securing a slot at the Elks Club, where Ray Charles had made his start. Once the word got out, the Elks became the place to be. "They were hanging from the rafters," describes Hubert. "Billy Tolles and Ernestine Anderson came by to sit in. It really took off."

"The band was the number one turn-on of any musical group that I've ever heard," asserts Norm Bobrow categorically. "Nothing has been more exciting in this town."

As a pianist, Young played in a sparse but nervous, harmonically hip style, a combination of Basie and Horace Silver. But what made the group so extraordinary was its rhythm section. This was the New York heat that hadn't yet appeared on the local scene. Young's "comping" was legendary. So were the tempos he and the quartet undertook. "Cecil Young's quartet would play some tempos faster than the fastest thing recorded by Charlie Parker, if you can imagine that," recalls Neil Friel, who sat in with Young at the Elks. "Jimmie could just sit there like nothing could give him pause."

One night, Nat Cole dropped by the Elks. "Cecil's quartet was on the stand," remembers Bobrow. "We're having some drinks, just the two of us, nobody bothering Nat. A little bit into it, Nat grabs me by the belt buckle and he says, 'Norm, that drummer's *walkin'*! He is *walkin'*!' Oh, Jimmie Rodgers was a bitch!"

Bobrow promoted Cecil Young relentlessly on his radio show and eventually became the group's quasi-manager. The quartet played Spokane and Yakima, then Bobrow approached 908 Club owner Dick Ruffin about bringing in the group. Ruffin agreed. The Cecil Young days were a golden period for the 908. Bobrow hosted the place as if it were his own living room. The menu sported a woodcut of the

**The Cecil Young Quartet, c. 1951.**

**Left to right: Jimmie Rodgers, Traff Hubert, Gerald Brashear, Cecil Young.**

**Courtesy of Traff Hubert**

quartet, etched by Bobrow's wife, Pat Ward, and life-size caricatures of the musicians along one wall, also drawn by Ward. In the shell of Doc Hamilton's speakeasy, Seattle had the beginnings of its first modern jazz temple, where hipsters and bohemians, night people and nomads, came to listen—instead of dance—and talk about Zen and Camus, all in an atmosphere of reverence and cool.

"We used to close the place at five o'clock," says Norm, "and go to the 411, where Ernie Lewis and Pony Poindexter and Ernestine Anderson played a breakfast show, which started at seven o'clock, six days a week. We always went there for breakfast, then we went home to bed."

As the group gained notoriety, Bobrow began to book Young as a headliner in theaters. The quartet brought a sense of razzmatazz to Bobrow's concerts that tickled the New York impresario and bowled over audiences. Young was a total entertainer, a tap dancer and clown who excelled at barn-burners such as Dizzy Gillespie's "Salt Peanuts" and "Oop-Pop-A-Da." With Young doing his show-biz routines, Gerald Brashear playing congas as well as saxophone, and both Brashear and Young scat-singing, the group was a sensation.

"When you went to their concerts," says Ernestine Anderson, "you came away feeling just really elated. They put so much into it, so much energy."

Gerald Brashear's conga-playing was no small part of the act. Brashear had taught himself to play in the style of Dizzy's Cuban drummer, Chano Pozo. Buddy Catlett says Brashear "played like a Cuban," he was that good.

The bass player in the Young quartet, Trafton "Traff" Hubert, originally from Puyallup, Washington, was an unusual character who had transformed himself from fan to musician, seemingly overnight. Hubert confesses:

> *I was a "jitterbug" originally. I was obsessed with jazz. I had about three thousand 78s. When Dizzy Gillespie and Charlie Parker first came out, I almost went crazy. I thought that was the greatest thing I had ever heard.*

Traff was avid. In 1945, when he heard Charlie Parker was playing at Billy Berg's, in Los Angeles, he drove south, where he saw Bird and met Harry the Hipster, who would later appear at Seattle's Players Club. "I asked him, 'Is it true that you take Benzedrine all the time?' He said, 'No, man, only when I can get it.'"

Back in Seattle, Traff was initiated into the local scene by—who else?—Janet Thurlow, whom he'd met at—where else?—the record store. Janet introduced him to bassist Adolphus Alsbrook. Traff started playing.

"I had some friends in Tacoma who had a band and they didn't have a bass player, so I rented a bass from George Greenwood at Tacoma Music and bought a Bobby Haggart bass book and taught myself how to play."

"He just decided he was going to play bass," recalls Traff Hubert's childhood chum, Dean Reilly, also a bassist. "He didn't know anything about music, was never in a band or anything like that. But he had a great record collection, so he knew what was supposed to happen."

Hubert jammed with locals, ventured out to after-hours clubs on Tacoma's Broadway, then went on the road for five months with a group with the unlikely name of the Wen Shu Orchestra, led by a German. When Hubert came home, he was a seasoned road bassist. He hooked up with Billy Tolles, who got him onto some rhythm-and-blues gigs at Fort Lewis;

then, again through Tolles, Hubert broke into the Seattle scene, working after hours with Billy and Jimmie Rodgers. Traff also worked at the New Chinatown with Dave Henderson. Gerald and Cecil heard him there: thus was born the Cecil Young Quartet. The group was known for its comedy as much as its music, particularly when Young and Brashear went on a tear. Says Ernestine:

> *Gerald had a dry sense of humor. The two of them together were just craziness on the loose. Cecil was always playing crank jokes on people. A prankster. We used to wonder when he slept—he'd always be doing something, no matter what time of day or night it was. He reminded me of an overgrown kid. He never grew up, in that respect. You had to laugh when you were around these two people. I mean the Marx Brothers was nothing compared to these guys.*

Recalls Neil Friel:

> *Cecil would go into his gay act— "Gerald, you bitch, you stop that!"—and Gerald would pretend to be very embarrassed and raise his eyebrows. And Cecil just wouldn't let up on it. And always with a smooth front. I never saw him up a tree. He was one of the wildest operators I have ever known.*

As funny as he was, Cecil Young was deadly serious about making it big in the music business. When Sid Nathan, president of King Records, came to town looking for Ray Charles (who was in Los Angeles cutting sides for Swing Time), Cecil convinced Bobrow to pitch the quartet. Bobrow agreed, and in one of his greatest gambits whipped up a Tuesday-night crowd at the 908.

"This Sid Nathan had never seen anything like this where he'd come from," remembers Hubert. "Jumping so heavy on a Tuesday night!"

Tapes of the quartet had been made earlier at the Ladies Musical Club (which now houses the Harvard Exit movie theater) and the Metropolitan Theater by Bert Porter, a local sales representative for Ampex and stereo-recording pioneer. Porter played the tapes for Nathan at a party and the record exec decided the quality was high enough to master a 10-inch album and ten 78s.

The Cecil Young Quartet album, released on King in 1951 as a 10-inch LP under the title *Concert of Cool Jazz,* was the first local record since the Maxin Trio's to make an impact outside of Seattle. The quartet's influence reached even further when Los Angeles promoter Gene Norman released the crowd-pleaser "Who Parked the Car?" backed with "Jumpin' with Symphony Sid," as an EP. The Norman record showcased Gerald Brashear and so impressed San Francisco jazz critic Ralph Gleason that he encouraged local disc jockeys to play the cut, writing that Brashear's scat solo on "Who Parked the Car?" was the best scat solo ever recorded.

Gerald's solo is incontestably in a class by

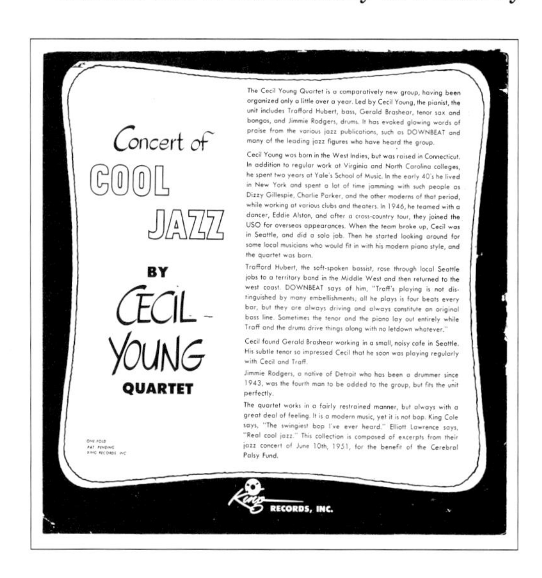

Concert of COOL JAZZ BY CECIL YOUNG QUARTET

The Cecil Young Quartet is a comparatively new group, having been organized only a little over a year. Led by Cecil Young, the pianist, the unit includes Trafford Hubert, bass, Gerald Brashear, tenor sax and bongos, and Jimmie Rodgers, drums. It has evoked glowing words of praise from the various jazz publications, such as DOWNBEAT and many of the leading jazz figures who have heard the group.

Cecil Young was born in the West Indies, but was raised in Connecticut. In addition to regular work at Virginia and North Carolina colleges, he spent two years at Yale's School of Music. In the early 40's he lived in New York and spent a lot of time jamming with such people as Dizzy Gillespie, Charlie Parker, and the other moderns of that period, while working at various clubs and theaters. In 1946, he teamed with a dancer, Eddie Alston, and after a cross-country tour, they joined the USO for overseas appearances. When the team broke up, Cecil was in Seattle, and did a solo job. Then he started looking around for some local musicians who would fit in with his modern piano style, and the quartet was born.

Trafford Hubert, the soft-spoken bassist, rose through local Seattle jobs to a territory band in the Middle West and then returned to the west coast. DOWNBEAT says of him, "Traff's playing is not distinguished by many embellishments; all he plays is four beats every bar, but they are always driving and always constitute an original bass line. Sometimes the tenor and the piano lay out entirely while Traff and the drums drive things along with no letdown whatever."

Cecil found Gerald Brashear working in a small, noisy cafe in Seattle. His subtle tenor so impressed Cecil that he soon was playing regularly with Cecil and Traff.

Jimmie Rodgers, a native of Detroit who has been a drummer since 1943, was the fourth man to be added to the group, but fits the unit perfectly.

The quartet works in a fairly restrained manner, but always with a great deal of feeling. It is a modern music, yet it is not bop. King Cole says, "The swingiest bop I've ever heard." Elliott Lawrence says, "Real cool jazz." This collection is composed of excerpts from their jazz concert of June 10th, 1951, for the benefit of the Cerebral Palsy Fund.

King RECORDS, INC.

itself, Eddie Jefferson and Jon Hendricks notwithstanding. Frenzied, articulate, witty, and dazzling, it is a nine-chorus tour de force that includes quotes from *Flight of the Bumblebee* and the *Hungarian Rhapsody No. 2*, a perfectly in-tune recitation of the cycle of fifths, and a comic, conversational call-and-answer between high and low ranges that Clark Terry later used with great success.

"Who Parked the Car?" was reissued in Seattle on a 12-inch LP titled *Jazz on the Rocks* (Audio Lab), which featured four cuts from the King album—"Race Horse," "Stompin' at the Savoy," "The Campbells Are Coming," and "Jumpin' with Symphony Sid" (retitled "Tribute to Al Benson")—plus four others. It is a West Coast classic that cries out for reissue. Its bebop intensity, hip wit, and classical and avant-garde allusions epitomize what the early fifties were all about. Brashear weaves curlicue Lestorian solos with an appealingly dry, woody tone, fluid, fleet phrasing, and spitfire tonguing. Cecil blows cool and clear, with even-noted melodic ideas and ironic classical allusions, going "out" with a sonic landscape, à la Varèse, at one point, with variations on a drone followed by dense block chords. Jimmie Rodgers keeps light, swift time, and Traff follows suit.

On the strength of the album, the Cecil Young Quartet was signed to the William Morris Agency and booked on a national tour, playing Birdland in New York, Chicago's Blue Note, and Boston's Hi Hat. "As far as I know, we were the only band to go directly from Seattle to Birdland," comments Traff.

At Birdland, they played on the same bill as Sarah Vaughan and "Wild Bill" Davis; Hubert and Jimmie Rodgers accompanied Vaughan. The quartet members were ecstatic. In Chicago, they worked beside Sarah, Teddy Wilson, and the Delta Rhythm Boys and stayed at the Pershing Hotel, where Hubert remembers hearing an unknown pianist named Ahmad Jamal playing in the lounge. Because the group was racially mixed, the members often had to stay in black peoples' homes. Hubert, the only white musician in the band, says, "I learned to eat hot soul food and learned about the illegal black cabs called 'jitneys,' who would act as your personal taxicab. It was an education. Some black people asked me, sincerely, if I was crazy. I said, 'I'm here because I like the music.'"

Ernestine Anderson heard the Cecil Young Quartet play at Birdland while she was on the road with Lionel Hampton. "They were hot," she recalls. "We would hang, you know. It was a good feeling. They really made it big, and fast. Maybe a little too fast. As soon as this record was released they just [snaps her fingers] took off like a rocket."

Unfortunately, the New York trip proved to be no more than a tease. The quartet's record never caught on nationally. Work dried up, and the members became impatient and discouraged. Some fell into drug use. According to Wanda Brown, who married Gerald Brashear after Vernon Brown died, the New York trip was devastating to the saxophonist: "He was disappointed. He thought that they were so great they were going to knock New York dead. And it didn't work like that. He didn't want to come back. Some friends back there bought him a bus ticket and put him on it and told him, 'You go home. This is not the place for you.'"

The quartet soon disbanded. Cecil Young never came back to the West, though he apparently continued to play until his death, in the 1970s. Jimmie Rodgers died young after succumbing to the street culture around Times Square. Hubert played for a while with Elmer Gill and Neil Friel, but gradually moved into work as a deejay and record distributor. Brashear came home and continued to contribute to the local scene. As fast as it had risen, the Cecil Young Quartet fell.

Cecil's white-hot but short-lived Seattle career turned out to be a last hurrah for Jackson Street. Over the next five years, a variety of forces conspired to scuttle the scene, and the action began to shift downtown and to the North End. The initial cause for the change was a drastic liberalization of state liquor laws that rendered the after-hours clubs almost obsolete. Shifts in popular taste, the rise of R & B, and, perhaps most importantly, the integration of the black and white musicians' unions also contributed to the district's demise.

All through the late forties, the state Legislature had been edging toward legalizing hard liquor. With the war years, it had become obvious to everyone that there was a demand for public social drinking. The population had become more diverse and sophisticated, and the pioneer generation of anti-saloon reformists had died off. In March 1949, Initiative 171 legalized hard liquor by the drink, and 235 establishments in Washington legally began pouring vodka, gin, whiskey, and rye over bars where spirits had been served illegally for years, if not decades. The police and the state liquor board began to work together with a reform-minded Jackson Street Community Council to stamp out the "bottle clubs."

Club patrons and owners had seen the writing on the wall for years. Even before Initiative 171, the Seattle police department had relentlessly pounded the after-hours clubs. In 1947, the police raided the Yukon Club five times. The Clover, Beaver, Sessions, Breakers, Rocking Chair, Owls, and 83 clubs were hit the same year. The Clover Club fell to the baton and the axe again, as did the White Hat Club and Club Lido. In 1948, there were still more raids. On January 12, ninety-two people were hauled away from the Basin Street. The club was padlocked and remained dark forever. In May, the military got into the act, declaring the entire district "out of bounds" for troops stationed at Paine Field, in Everett. On October 8, 1948, in the largest arrest ever made in a Seattle speakeasy, 166 people were herded down the long flight of stairs of the Washington Social Club, packed into paddy wagons on Madison Street, and booked. After Ray Charles left the Rocking Chair in 1949, its doors never opened again. An era was ending.

The attack on the Jackson Street "joints" was motivated by greed as much as it was by a desire to uphold the law. Liquor was an extremely lucrative business. Once it was made legitimate, the bottle clubs were not only illegal, they were competition to legitimate operators. The state had no intention of sharing the spoils with the old speaks.

The city fathers were enthusiastically supported by the Teamsters union in the effort to stamp out the competition, as the union recruited bartenders into the hotel-and-restaurant-workers local. Since the new law allowed only restaurants and hotels to sell hard liquor, it was in the owners' and union's best interests to make sure they maintained a monopoly on liquor sales. On the street, this meant a shift in the action from black-owned Central District joints to Italian-owned—and union-controlled—cocktail lounges. In the 1950s, jazz fans began to find themselves in downtown clubs with names like the Italian Village and Rosellini's Four-10.

To many blacks, this shift of venues had the air of discrimination, particularly since the

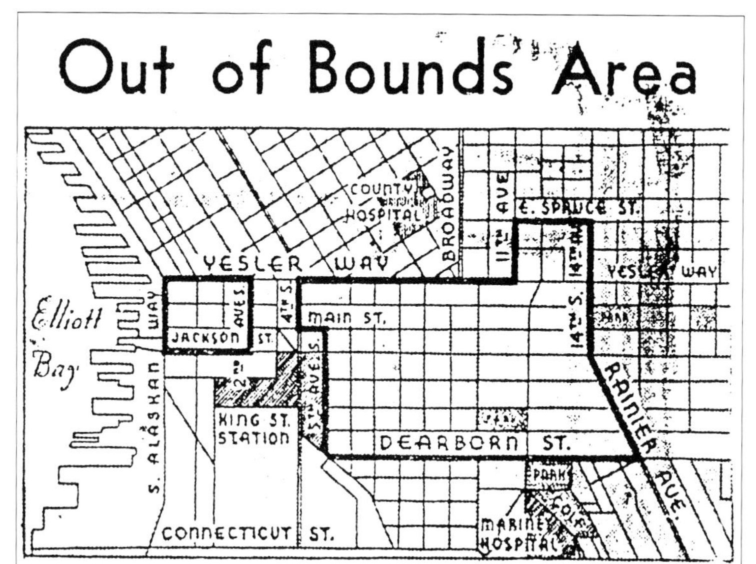


HEAVY BLACK LINES on this map show areas in Seattle's "South End" which have been declared 'out of bounds" for soldiers from Paine Field, army air base near Everett. Three uptown hotels are also out of bounds.

new lounges continued to engage in other illegal activities, such as gambling. (As late as 1968, gambling rackets constituted one of the largest industries in the state, with profits of fifty million dollars a year.) The payoffs continued, via an amended and relocated tolerance policy; so did raids on the black clubs. After the massive arrests at the Washington Social Club in 1948, the veteran establishment was formally abated in 1950. The big neighborhood club, where so many of the great figures of the forties had cut their teeth, became a tangible focus for community outrage. Owner Sy Groves took out a full-page advertisement in the *Northwest Enterprise*, addressed to prosecutor Charles O. Carroll, asserting that the establishment was a legitimate enterprise employing twenty-two people and was being singled out because it was a black business. Citizens of the Central District signed a petition to keep it open. Not everyone in the Central Area sided with Groves. The Republican editor of the *Northwest Enterprise*, Prentice Frazier, took out a reply ad, arguing that there had been many complaints about the Washington Social Club and that the prosecutor was "entirely free of bigotry." In the end, Groves lost. Mabel Williams re-opened the establishment for a while, but by 1951 the Washington Social Club was gone. The black Elks Club followed in December 1952, when 117 people were arrested

The Norm Hoagy Orchestra at the Showbox Theater, 1951–1952.

Left to right: Sal Carraba, Dave Stetler (lower), Red Kelly, Jim Weaver, Norm Hoagy (piano), Wayne Saxe, Dave Tuttle, Stan Keen.

Courtesy of Dave Stetler

there. Prosecutor Carroll, for his part, was later convicted of accepting bribes.

Unhappily for jazz musicians, the change in Washington liquor laws also coincided with profound shifts in musical taste that contributed to a severe shortage of work. In the early 1950s, popular music entered a bland stage that featured such vapid songs as "How Much Is That Doggie in the Window?" and catchy tunes by scrubbed, "girl-next-door" goddesses like Patti Page. Hot swing was dead. Even nationally, the biggest name bands were having trouble staying on the road. Duke Ellington was wracked by the departure of Johnny Hodges and several other important sidemen (though Ellington did record an album in Seattle in 1952, *The Seattle Concert*, on RCA). Count Basie disbanded for the only time in his career, and Charlie Barnet threw in the towel. Crowds stopped coming out. A 1954 booking of the Dorsey brothers, who in the forties had drawn 6,000 people to the Civic Auditorium, sold fewer than 500 tickets. Local swing bands began to fall apart, as well. Al Pierre couldn't draw a crowd at the Showbox; neither could commercial tenor saxophonist Norm Hoagy, the bandleader who succeeded him. Bob Harvey's band at the China Pheasant started to cut back its hours.

Swing's stylistic successor, the complex and

demanding bebop, wasn't accessible enough to take up the slack. Roscoe Weathers' refusal to play "Wreck on the Highway" for a drunken customer had turned out to be a harbinger of the growing isolation many jazz musicians would feel as they strove to assert their status as artists rather than entertainers. Ray Charles, always alert to the marketplace, had noticed this development in Seattle even before 1950:

> *The one thing which bothered me about some players I met around that time was their strange attitude: They'd say to a crowd, "This is my music. If you like it, cool. If not, fuck it!" I thought that was wrong. People give you their bread and are entitled to some kind of musical return on their dollar. I don't mean you got to give them exactly what they want. But you do have to keep them in mind.*

Whether or not one agrees with Charles' conclusions, his recognition of the situation was on target. In the new, lounge-oriented climate of the 1950s, Seattle jazz musicians would either have to adjust to the new audiences or find somewhere else to play.

White musicians who made the adjustment often managed to create lounge jazz with some verve and integrity. One of them was Norm Hoagy, a Kansas City saxophonist with a strong tone and sinuous, swing-era phrasing, who moved to Seattle in 1946 and for years headed a six- to eight-piece band at the Magic Inn, at Sixth Avenue and Union Street.

Gene Sargent, Gene Boscacci, and Frank Sugia also stood out on the lounge scene and remained well-respected by jazzers. Sargent had played guitar in Woody Herman's famous Second Herd, the bebop ensemble that made Stan Getz and the Four Brothers famous. Gene Boscacci, who was playing at the Washington Athletic Club in the early nineties, is a pianist and vibes man who found a niche playing jazz accordion, which enjoyed a faddish vogue in the late 1940s.

Frank Sugia, who started playing piano and accordion in Seattle in 1935, held forth at the Italian Village, on Fifth Avenue, during the 1950s and became popular playing with violinist Joe Venuti and Floyd Standifer at Sugia's club, the After Five, in 1968. This group also became known to locals as the Dickensian, top-hatted gentlemen who played Christmas music for the now-defunct downtown department store Frederick & Nelson. Sugia sometimes played at another lounge where jazz was welcome—Norm Bobrow's large supper club, the Colony. The Colony opened in 1955 at the corner of Virginia and Fourth and was a Broadway sort of place, where jazz musicians backed up quality singers. Many of the area's finest white players worked at the Colony, including Red Kelly, Walt Tianen, Al Pace, Bud Schultz, Dave Stetler, and Don Conway. Conway, who had worked in Bobrow's Little Big Band, was an excellent alto saxophonist in the feather-toned, Lee Konitz manner.

The downtown lounge scene was a viable compromise for white musicians, but as long as the unions remained segregated, black jazzers had to make do in the vestiges of Jackson Street. Two of the clubs that hung on for a while included the Elks Club and the old Local No. 493 clubhouse, the Blue Note. At the black Elks, Cecil Young was succeeded by a young musician from Boston, Paul Neves, regarded as the best jazz pianist in Seattle during the 1950s. Neves had studied in Boston with Madame Chaloff, the famous music teacher and mother of saxophonist Serge Chaloff, one of the original "Four Brothers" from Woody's Second Herd. (Neves' brother, John, achieved some notoriety as the bassist for pianist George Shearing.) Paul Neves was a quiet man with a sweet disposition and a natty wardrobe. Bassist and tenor saxophonist Gary Steele remembers him as the first person he ever saw in Seattle wearing a porkpie hat, Lester Young's trademark. Neves, who originally came to Washington courtesy of the Air Force, enrolled in the early fifties at the University of Washington as an English major. While going to school, he worked after hours at the Elks in the trio with Chuck Metcalf and white drummer Jimmy Raymer.

In August 1955, Neves played at the Lake City Tavern with Fred Greenwell, Buddy Catlett, and white drummer Bill Kotick. Neves also worked often with Pops Buford. Tenor saxophonist Chuck Stentz remembers working with Neves at the Congo Club, in Tacoma, in 1955.

Neves' work impressed locals as particularly advanced, a stylistic step or two beyond Cecil Young. Private tapes of Neves' playing from the mid-1950s reveal him as a cool, linear bopper with a light touch and great time, with flashes of harmonic daring and a sense of when to leave open space in a chord.

At one point, Neves' advanced harmonies cost him a job with saxophonist Coleman Hawkins, who found him too far out. "Paul was before his time around here," says Buddy Catlett. "He would be perfect for today's music." Neves left Seattle in the late fifties, roomed for a while in Boston with Don Lanphere, and moved to the Bahamas, where he became musical director of a hotel. He died in the late 1980s.

After Neves left town, the piano chair in the Raymer group went to Jimmy Gilles, a Tacoman who had jammed with Cecil Young at the New Chinatown and worked off and on with Billy Tolles. Of these rocky times in the early 1950s, Gilles recalls:

> *The principal job that kept me [going] was the colored Elks Club. It would start about eleven or twelve and go to four or five. Then we all wandered up to the [New] Chinatown and got out of there about eleven or noon. It was a four-piece band. Pops Buford played tenor. Pops was a neat guy. I just loved Pops. The rest of the band there was white guys, which was unusual, because this was a black joint. We were probably the most swinging, most hip band in town at that time, except Billy Tolles.*

After a stint on the road with Darryl Harpa, Gilles returned to Seattle in 1953. He worked with bassist Traff Hubert in a duo for a time, but jobs were scarce. The black Elks Club had closed. "Things had wound down a little," he says of the time. "Everybody had scattered." Gilles eventually went to Montana with Hubert in 1956, then on to Las Vegas and Los Angeles, where the pianist moved into rock and commercial music. During his Seattle rock 'n' roll days, he was known as "Mandrake," because of his pointed beard.

The other mainstay for black musicians during this difficult period was the Blue Note at Jefferson and 13th. Union hall, night spot, and social club wrapped into one, the Blue Note was a hub of fraternal camaraderie, hosting sessions on Friday and Saturday nights. Every member of Local 493 had a key to get in and was allowed one guest. Drinks were twenty-five cents, and there were no union agents around to stop the jamming, because the club *was* the union. Next door was a little restaurant where you could have a T-bone steak after the gig for $3.95. Name players showed up often, not only to jam, but also to hang out, relax, and meet the locals. Floyd Standifer recollects:

> *That's where I first met—and heard—Johnny Hodges. That's where I first met Thad Jones. This was 1950. These guys would come in and they'd know a few people in town already and they'd just be so happy to walk into a joint where it was, "Hey, man, Hodges is here, how you doing, man? Say, I want you to meet Johnny Hodges. Oh, man, I've admired you for a long time. Say, bartender, give my man a double." They weren't on a star trip, no. They were on the road. All that was beaten out of them. They were among friends. You talk about fraternalism, those guys brought new meaning to the word.*

"All the guys would come around there," says Elmer Gill. "Sonny Criss, Lee Konitz, Thad Jones, anybody that happened to come through town. They used to have some sessions in there that would be fantastic. We used to stay there all night long, walk out the doors and the sun would be shining bright, nine, ten o'clock in the morning. That was a great place."

In the 1980s, the Blue Note became a modest lunch counter named Debbie's. On the tile floor, you could still make out a faded pattern of blue tiles in the shape of an eighth note.

The Mardi Gras, one of the first legitimate, black-owned taverns in town (it had opened in 1943), also continued to present jazz during these lean years, and remained open well into the sixties. Part of the reason for its success was that it presented rhythm-and-blues–influenced organ trios, part of the "funky" trend of the fifties. Bob Braxton led a group there in 1954; Pony Poindexter, Gerald Brashear, Jabo Ward, and Billy Tolles played the Mardi Gras, as well. One of the star attractions at the club was Gerald Frank, the best drummer in town after Jimmie Rodgers died. Originally from Detroit, Frank drifted from music in the sixties into a go-go girl operation in Pioneer Square, then into a lucrative real-estate business.

But despite their convivial spirit, the Mardi Gras, the Blue Note, and the black Elks could not sustain a jazz scene by themselves in a period that was increasingly being referred to by musicians as a "jazz drought." As club after club closed, and the music in the lounges became more watered-down, musicians began to pack their bags or take other jobs to supplement their incomes. In 1950 and 1951 alone, Al Hickey, Ray Charles, Ernestine Anderson, Janet Thurlow, Quincy Jones, Cecil Young, Bumps Blackwell, and Al Pierre all left town. Dave Stetler, Floyd Standifer, and Jabo Ward took day jobs. It was a desperate period for jazz. It's no surprise that this was also the bleak era when many jazz musicians turned to hard drugs. In 1954, Stan Getz and fellow tenor saxophonists Zoot Sims and Wardell Gray were working their way up the coast with a Seattle rhythm section (drummer Bill Kotick, white pianist Bob Alcivar, and bassist Larry Rockwell) when Getz attempted to rob a downtown Seattle drugstore for morphine. Getz was taken to jail, where he downed sixty grains of barbiturates in a suicide attempt. Charlie Parker, too, brought his problems with him, performing in 1953 at the Metropolitan Theatre in a drugged and drunken stupor. Parker, who had spent the whole day drinking, in one of his periodic attempts to kick heroin, was discovered backstage, before the show, getting a "fix" from Pony Poindexter.

Ironically, just as the bottom dropped out of Seattle jazz, Tacoma's Pacific Avenue, a sailor's strip along the dark edge of town by the water, exploded with bebop clubs catering to soldiers being shipped back and forth between Fort Lewis and Korea. The Pirate's Cove, where Buzz Bridgeford had played, plus the New Yorker, the Tiki, the 1306 Club, the 1515, and the 1518 all hosted jazz. In South Tacoma there was the Hi Hat and the Players; elsewhere were the Towers, the Congo Club, the Broadway, Ping's Gardens, and the Union House Club.

"There was a lot going on around Tacoma in those days," remembers white saxophonist Bill Ramsay. "Good Seattle musicians would come to Tacoma for sessions after their gigs." The atmosphere was sometimes rougher than in Seattle's after-hours clubs. In Ramsay's words:

*There was quite a bit of Mafia control in those days. A lot of the clubs were owned by the families. The godfather of the Northwest was a Tacoma resident by the name of Vito Catone. Many times I remember playing at the New Yorker and it was like some B movie, where the place would be full of people and a couple of Vito's boys would come in and clear the place out. They'd lay a long table right in front of the band. Then Vito and his family'd come in and we'd end up playing "Come Back to Sorrento" all night long.*

Among the Tacoma players who moved freely between the two cities on the Sound were Ramsay, Chuck and Jan Stentz, Dean Reilly, and Gary Steele. Ramsay, who later went on to work with Count Basie, was one of the best. A huge, imposing man with a big voice, alert eyes, and driving energy, he chews phrases off his saxophones—alto, tenor, and baritone—with the gritty energy of bop players who have swing flowing in their veins. A native of Centralia, Washington, about 100 miles south of Seattle, Ramsay taught himself to play saxophone as a youngster and learned to play jazz while he was stationed at Fort Lewis, from 1948 to 1952. The young saxophonist gained early experience at the Evergreen Ballroom outside Olympia, working with Art Doll (the saxophonist who had done the brilliant Lunceford transcriptions for the Men About Town), saxophonist Chuck Stentz, Traff Hubert, Buzzy Bridgeford, Neil Friel, and white bassist Paul Binnings. He worked at Tacoma's 1306 Club for a year, then moved to the 1515, while Fred Greenwell and Buzzy were down the street at the Pirate's Cove.

Like so many swing-to-bop musicians, Ramsay played in combos but yearned for the power and punch of a large group. In 1958, he put together a short-lived "dream band" that knocked progressive-jazz fans on their ears. In 1979, Ramsay got a call from saxophonist Buddy Tate, asking him to sub in the Benny Goodman band. Five years later, Ramsay was offered the baritone saxophone chair with Count Basie. The thrill of that assignment gave way soon enough to fatigue, however, particularly after Basie did three coast-to-coast round trips in six days. Ramsay quit in 1985.

He has continued to enjoy an active musical career in the Northwest and on the road. In 1991, he recorded a CD, *Entre Nous*, with ex–Basie saxophonist Frank Wess. (Mel Tormé's *Night at the Concord Pavilion* also features the Wess band.) Ramsay occasionally performs in a monster saxophone group, Tenor Dynasty, with Olympian Chuck Stentz and Seattleite Denney Goodhew, and leads his own band.

Chuck Stentz is another musician who entered the local imagination during the Tacoma boom of the early 1950s. For two or three years he worked at the New Yorker club with Art Mineo and every Sunday with Paul Neves, Buzz Bridgeford, and Floyd Standifer at the Congo Club in South Tacoma. A no-nonsense "musician's musician" who describes himself as "a born sideman," Stentz is a self-taught musician who joined the Air Corps after high school, then used his GI Bill to attend the New England Conservatory, working and studying with pianist Nat Pierce and saxophonist Charlie Mariano.

Stentz toured New England with Pierce, Johnny Bothwell, and Shorty Sherock. In 1949 he returned to Olympia. For a while, he played in a big band at the Evergreen Ballroom that included hot, white Tacoma trombonist Art Mell. In the mid-1950s, Stentz went to work at Yenney's Music Company in Olympia, which he later bought and turned into a musicians' hangout. Stentz plays with more of a beboppish rhythmic edge than Ramsay, but still has a vestige of the hollow, woody sound of Lester Young's disciples. In the late 1980s, he developed a generation-crossing collaboration, called Bebop Revisited, with white saxophonist Bert Wilson, a remarkable California avant-gardist who moved to Washington's capital in 1979.

In 1955, Stentz married one of the area's top vocalists, Jan Stentz (née Swenson), a romantically charged balladeer who swings with the light touch of such jazz singers as Lee Wiley and Chris Connor. Like many women, Jan put her career aside when she had children, but in the mid-1970s, she started singing again, at Red Kelly's Tumwater Conservatory. Stentz then began a long musical relationship with Olympia pianist Jack Perciful; in 1981, she worked with another local white piano man, Barney McClure, at Port Townsend's Manresa Castle. Stentz recorded a sparkling album for McClure's BAM Records, titled *Profile*. In 1989, she worked briefly with the Harry James band but found she was no more fond of the road life than her husband was. Stentz continues to work locally with Jack Perciful.

The Tacoma scene also nurtured Traff Hubert's friend bassist Dean Reilly, who first surfaced nationally in recordings by the Vince Guaraldi Trio. Reilly had put in a short stint with Jimmy Beuttner at the pioneering Seattle bebop haunt the Players Club, before enrolling at the University [then College] of Puget Sound, where he studied for two and a half years. In 1950, Dean joined Neil Friel and Jimmy Gilles on the road with the Darryl Harpa band, which took him to San Francisco. Since then, he has worked there as a first-call sideman with everyone from Georgie Auld to Helen Humes and has recorded with guitarist George Barnes, Earl Hines, and Cal Tjader.

Gary Steele, the small-town kid who was so knocked out by the Dizzy Gillespie big band in Seattle, is another important Tacoma bopper. Steele is known in Seattle as the stalwart electric bassist who plays behind his wife, vocalist Patti Summers, at their cozy basement nightclub at the Pike Place Market, but in his Tacoma days he was a tough tenor saxophonist. Steele worked his way through Tacoma's University of Puget Sound, playing gigs at night, then spent two years in a Seventh Army Special Services unit. When he came home in 1956, he started playing bass in a lounge trio with Bud Schultz, an excellent pianist/vibist who used to show up on the Annex scene and later worked with "mood music" maestro Martin Denny.

Many other strong players worked in Tacoma, including "Sonny Red" Norman (tenor sax) and white musicians Bill Baty (trumpet), Bob Schlicte (tenor sax), Dick Morehead (drums), Ford Collier (trumpet), and Shelby Zollman (piano).

One of the ways Tacomans got experience was by playing with seasoned black musicians stationed at Fort Lewis or McChord Air Force Base. The most important of the soldier/musicians was Eric Dolphy, who would later become an avant-garde innovator and introduce the bass clarinet to modern jazz. Dolphy was stationed at Fort Lewis from 1950 to 1952, having joined the Army in Los Angeles with his friend Walter Benton. While in the Northwest, Dolphy played clarinet and bass clarinet in the Tacoma Symphony, jammed on the local scene, and often showed up in the back room at Tacoma Music, where owner George Greenwood kept a "jam room." Dolphy was a master technician, even then.

Steele remembers:

*The first time I heard Eric Dolphy play was at the NCO club out at McChord Field. The tune was "Idaho." You had to really know what you were doing to get through the tune. It was usually done at some kind of ferocious tempo. I walked in and Eric's playing it. You could hear horn cases slamming shut all over the room. No way would anybody get up there with him.*

Bill Ramsay, who rehearsed some legitimate woodwind compositions with Dolphy, says he was an unusual player even at this early stage of his career, with a penchant for playing notes "outside" the normal chords and scales. Steele reports that because the Tacoma scene was racially regressive, he and Dolphy—and other black musicians—could not play regular gigs together in the same clubs: "Black musicians and the whites had to come out to the college to play, where there were practice rooms where you could jam, or you had to go out to the NCO club at McChord. Eric and I got thrown out of places."

Official racism notwithstanding, there were some great jam sessions in those days at the Congo Club and at Ping's Gardens. The great pianist Sir Roland Hanna, also stationed at Fort Lewis, was known to show up, as was Wilbur Hogan, the cooking drummer Ray Charles would later hire for his big band. Granville T. Hogan, another drummer who later worked with Bud Powell, also came by. So did Walter Benton, Dolphy's childhood friend and an excellent "groove" tenor saxophonist; Leo Wright, the keen-toned alto saxophonist and flutist who worked many years with Dizzy Gillespie; pianists Earl DeWitt and Ernest Crawford; and white trombonist/composer Tom McIntosh.

While bebop had a burst of glory in Tacoma, the scene continued to deteriorate in Seattle, in part due to the growing popularity of rhythm and blues. Still confined at this stage to an African-American "race" market, R & B nevertheless was making its way into the hearts of teenagers like the ones who had been hypnotized by swing a generation earlier. This is the period when Roy Milton, Jay McNeely, and Amos Milburn, among others, were thrusting the double shuffle of Lunceford and the amusing backbeat of Louis Jordan into a new dance genre, which after a few years would cross over to the white market and be dubbed "rock 'n' roll."

The jazz musicians who had the biggest hand in bringing rock to Seattle were Billy Tolles and Tommy Adams. "When I got back from college," recalls Tolles, "nobody was popping the sock cymbal two-four."

*They were all just kinda leading their sock cymbal, hitting it a lick or two. Back East, boy, they were popping that sock cymbal. I got [Tommy Adams] doing that, and that brought a whole new thing of drums to Seattle. I brought that from back East. That's what set everything on fire! That tight backbeat, man. We kicked ass right from the beginning. We were playing those heavy shuffles. Tommy Adams had such a raw sense of rhythm, boy. He'd be chopping wood, and there'd be wood all down up under the snare drum, where he'd been hitting that rim stick.*

In what would become a harbinger of things to come, Tolles' little rock 'n' roll combo won a "battle of the bands" at the Eagles Auditorium against the best jazz groups in town.

*We were all raggedy-looking, and the rest of the bands were all dressed up. Cecil Young was on that thing and Elmer Gill and they were so sophisticated and intellectual, and so on, and we came on there with that blues and that "Flyin' Home" and just walked off with that one-hundred-fifty-dollar prize.*

Tolles formed his first rock 'n' roll band in 1951. He worked at the 908 and at dances organized by "social clubs," such as the Esquires, which sprang up to fill the void left by the closing of the Washington Social Club. In 1951 and 1952, one of the hot spots for these black dances was a room on the second floor of the Chamber of Commerce building, on Marion Street between Second and Third avenues. The atmosphere was essentially unchanged from that of the old bottle clubs. People brought their own liquor. Sometimes the dances were held at Washington Performance Hall, at 14th Avenue and Fir Street.

Billy Tolles presented a showcase quintet sometimes known as Billy Tolles and the Four Tolls, a funky, hard-driving rhythm band in which the front line later sang hits like "Sh-boom, Sh-boom!" and did dance steps. As Tolles remembers:

*I was playing the style that I learned with Louis Jordan. He made everything just happy, you know, playing those little shuffle rhythms and the blues and keeping it comedic and high-octane. I went and got Floyd Standifer, Buddy Catlett, Tommy Adams, and Elmer Gill, and we formed a singing group that set Seattle on its ear. If I could have six pieces, I would use Floyd Standifer and Rod Levitt. Then I started using another white boy playing trombone, Dick Thorlakson. That band survived for several years. We were singing songs like "Mother in Law" and the Mills Brothers. Me and Floyd Standifer fell out about something, so I brought Jabo Ward into the band, and he'd sing Floyd's parts.*

In 1955, Tolles streamlined his R & B concept to a trio, using Tommy Adams and keyboard man Mike Taylor. The following year, he and saxophonist Floyd Franklin moved into Ayer's Cafe, at 12th and Yesler, Myrt Francois' old place. White students from the University of Washington flocked to the neighborhood. The Sessions Club (which had become Sessions Playhouse) was two blocks away, and the Esquires Club found a home around the corner. The streets were rocking.

"I could just honk," Tolles recalls, "and walk through the joint, jump from tabletop to tabletop, honking on my low B-flat, walk the bar, [go] outside and come back in the back door, and all that kind of stuff. That really got us over. Those white kids, they'd be in there clamoring for that."

While Tolles was at Ayer's, Dave Holden, Oscar Holden's son, replaced Mike Taylor on piano. Dave was just out of Garfield High School and attending Everett Junior College on a basketball scholarship. He started using an electric keyboard called the Organo, playing a walking bass line with the left hand and a honky-tonk riff with the right. With Adams' drums and Holden's electric piano, the new trio quickly became a local attraction, working at the Mardi Gras and Dave's Fifth Avenue. As Tolles threw himself more and more into rock, many of the local jazz players turned away from him, regarding his forays into dance music as rank commercialism. Tolles, who could blow most of the jazzmen out of town at their own game, bridled at their comments.

*Everybody was ridiculing us. I was the best jazz player in town, but here I was, playing rock. They were saying, "Oh, man, you playing that funky butt stuff." But boy, we had the joint packed, jammed up, man. And we were getting grand-theft money. Everybody was coming, them included, because they'd be getting off their jobs early because all the people would be at our jobs. I said, "To hell with what you think." When I was doing dance music, I played rhythm and blues, and when I was jazz, I was all jazz.*

Not only did Billy play Seattle's first rock, he was one of its first major promoters. Between 1952 and 1955, he booked T-Bone Walker, Earl Bostic, Fats Domino, Pee Wee Crayton, Jay McNeely, and James Brown, among others, at the Eagles Auditorium, the Trianon Ballroom, and the China Pheasant. Sometimes his own band opened the shows. In 1952, he presented T-Bone Walker at Birdland for one of the first editions of the annual city-wide celebration known as Seafair. Walker played a street dance on the corner. Tolles didn't forget his jazz roots. He also brought up James Moody, his old friend from North Carolina, who had just come out with his hit "Moody's Mood for Love." "I had Moody at Birdland and Earl Bostic at the Eagles Auditorium the same weekend," he boasts.

Deejay Bob Summerise and club owner Wilmer Morgan also promoted R & B shows in the early fifties. Morgan owned three clubs—Birdland, the Mardi Gras, and the China Pheasant—where he booked Percy Mayfield and Amos Milburn. Summerise, an ardent jazz fan who also owned a record store at 12th and Jackson called World of Music, was the first local jock to play R & B, on Bremerton station KBRQ, in 1947. Seattle musicians and fans grew up on the intelligent mix of R & B and jazz on his "Cool Breeze" show. His theme song was "Tonsillectomy," by Boyd Raeburn, but he'd often follow a jazz cut with a tune by the Spinners or the Ravens. Summerise promoted several jazz concerts and also wrote a column for the *Northwest Enterprise*, in which he touted new sides, chatted about the local scene, and sometimes waxed philosophical about music. Summerise felt, as Tolles did, that jazz and rhythm and blues were part of the same tradition, and needn't be at war.

Nevertheless, the money was increasingly in rock, and Tolles went for the gold. In 1956, his promotional talents led to a television show for

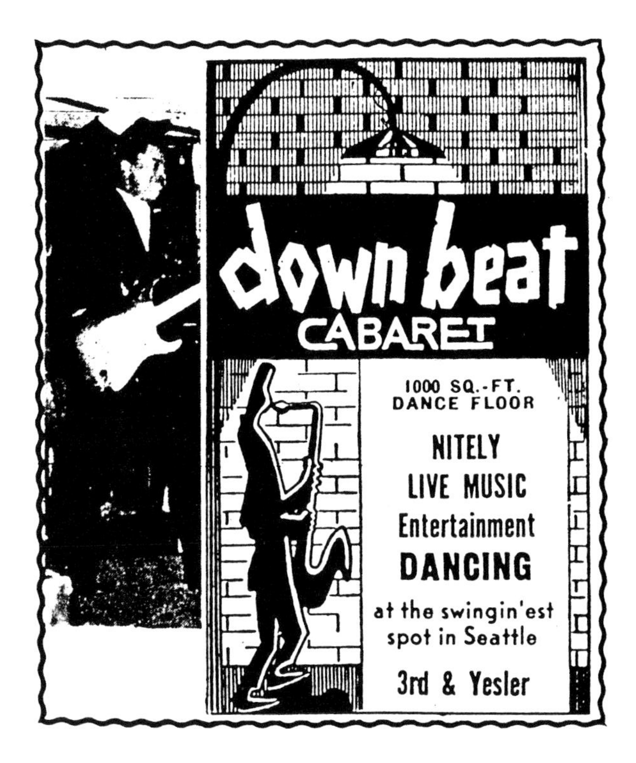


teenagers, "Rock 'n' Roll Party," on Channel 13. The show was a local version of "American Bandstand," live from Parker's Ballroom. Dave Lewis, a keyboardist who had become popular by this time at Birdland, and the Frantics, a twanging R & B group that included white keyboardist Jimmy Manolides, were two of the popular acts on the Channel 13 show.

Tolles eventually decided to give up booking and go south with his trio to get in on some of the action. The Tolles Trio, with Tommy Adams and Dave Holden, played first in Santa Clara, then in San Francisco and Las Vegas. While Billy and Tommy and Dave were playing the El Morocco in Vegas, Dave's younger brother, Ron, hit the rock 'n' roll jackpot with a single, "Love You So." (The record reached No. 7 on the 1960 *Billboard* charts.) Dave left Tolles to join his brother on the road. Tolles continued working in Las Vegas with Earl DeWitt, the keyboard man he had first met at Fort Lewis, making periodic trips to Seattle to work at the Mardi Gras and the Downbeat, a new club in Pioneer Square at Third and Yesler that later became the Pink Pussycat. During the 1962 World's Fair in Seattle, Tolles tried to open a club in Pioneer Square, but it never got off the ground. In 1966, he went to Denver to visit DeWitt; he has lived there ever since, except for a period when he toured the world as a regular for the Playboy Club circuit.

Tolles' pioneering drummer during this period, Tommy Adams, did not fare as well as Billy. Tales about Adams' behavior have circulated among Seattle musicians for years. Many of the stories are true. Most people do not know, however, that Adams' erratic antics were caused by the onset of diabetes, which for many years he did not know he had.

Born in 1930, Tommy Adams was a natural musician who came up in the swing-to-bop era, first as a singer in the smooth manner of baritone Billy Eckstine—performing with Quincy Jones in the Bumps Blackwell Junior Band—then as a drummer in a manner all his own. Adams and Billy Tolles had been friends since the old days at the Washington Social Club, when they had jammed with Bumps' bass player, Billy Johnson. In 1950, Adams also played briefly in the Gus Mankertz workshop band at Seattle University. His hard-driving backbeat style marked the local transition from jazz to rock. Describes Dave Holden:

*All the drummers in the area would come to hear Tommy. Tommy had one high hat and one cymbal and a snare drum. That's all. None of these other cymbals. Tommy was a swing drummer, but he was a swing-shuffle drummer. He gave swing a new feel, because he'd shuffle through every swing piece. He influenced all the drummers that ever heard him in the Seattle area.*

Slim as a young man, in the fifties Adams began to put on weight, earning the nickname "Fat Daddy." Adams loved to cook, and enjoyed feeding his bandmates rich, fattening foods, probably the cause of his eventual diabetes. On edge, Adams began to get into fistfights, shout hysterically in clubs, and play so ferociously that it scared people. Sometimes he would jump up and down on his drums, run around the club, and tear his shirt off. He acquired a fetish for Indian regalia, donning a war bonnet, feathers, and a sash. At first, people put up with Adams' behavior, labeling it simple eccentricity, but in time, owners became leery of hiring him. The end came with a nasty incident in South Tacoma, near Fort Lewis, when he was playing with Dave Holden and Gerald Brashear. By this time, Adams had learned that he was sick; a doctor had put him on a severe diet, and he had lost eighty pounds. Recalls Holden:

*The last night, Tommy started jumping up and down and running around and pushing people out of his way and running through the crowd and doing a "whoa-hoa-hoa"–type Indian thing in the middle of 450 people, in a beer tavern. This was a military place in South Tacoma, right down the street from Fort Lewis. Jam-packed. It got so bad at that point that we couldn't handle it. Nobody could handle it. He was gone, mentally. The owner called the police because they had to restrain him. Tommy was down on the ground with handcuffs and they took him off to jail.*

Adams was taken to the mental hospital at Steilacoom. When he realized where he was, he ran away. Adams died in 1965 while living with his mother in Detroit, after another severe bout with his illness.

Rhythm and blues cut severely into the market for jazz—later, rock would hit jazz even harder—but the most significant change affecting Jackson Street in the 1950s had nothing to do with musical style: It was the merger of the black and white locals.

By 1955, integrated bands were already working at the Lake City Tavern and at the Flame in the North End. "Mixed" bands were tolerated at the black Elks Club as well, because they were under the jurisdiction of Local 493. But Local 76 still did not tolerate integrated contracts in the lucrative downtown clubs north of Yesler, the unofficial "color line." The 1950s would be the decade in which, finally, there'd be some changes made.

No one was more ready to start making these changes than pianist and club owner Elmer Gill. Gill bitterly resented the way legalized racism had held down black entrepreneurs, and how the terms of the racial discussion were consistently shifted by whites to tolerance and integration, when the issue for blacks was also money—the ability to make a living and succeed. More clearly than anyone else on the scene, he seems to have understood that while black musicians might earn $100 a night in tips at the Black and Tan, Jackson Street was still an economic ghetto.

Gill had first run into racial discrimination in the music world when he worked in 1952 with the Question Marks at the Spinning Wheel on Second Avenue, just north of the "color line." As he remembers it:

*The Spinning Wheel was a white-only place. I didn't know that at the time that I went in there. This friend of mine and their whole party and his wife came down there and they were standing at the door. I was up there playing and I could see that there was something going on. After a while, this guy came out from behind the bar and he says, "Uh, Elmer, [there's] some friends of yours back there and they want to come in. You go back and tell 'em," he says. "Tell them what?" I said. "Uh, you know the score!"*

*I caught on right then what he was trying to do and I went back there and I said, "Hey, man! What you doing standing out there! Come on in!" The guy almost fainted. From then on, when I played in Seattle, I used to put in my contract that anybody, regardless of race, creed, or color, as long as they were acting in accord with the place, and the policy of the place, and so forth, then they could come into the place while I was playing. You'd be surprised at the number of people that wouldn't sign that contract.*

Gill's first solution to racial discrimination was to open a room of his own. In 1953, he bought part ownership in the Ebony Cafe, on Jackson Street just east of Fifth Avenue. Though it was just a block away from the shuttered Elks Club, Gill made an all-out effort to dissociate himself from the now-discredited after-hours scene, if not completely from the public that had made it lucrative. He wanted his place to be considered "legit," and aimed for a "classy" image in the new atmosphere of legalized liquor. He built a small stage and moved in a grand piano. The kitchen served full dinners and drinks. To this day, tellingly, Gill is sensitive when anyone refers to it as a "club."

"It was a *restaurant*," insists Gill. "It wasn't a club at all. It used to make me mad. People would come in and they'd say, 'Where's the gambling?' We used to have a terrible time trying to make people drink up the drinks: 'Oh, this is Jackson Street, you don't need to be worried about that. You go all night here, don't you? Where's the back room?'"

For the Ebony, Gill formed an excellent, Nat Cole–style trio, hiring Al Larkins on bass and Al Turay on guitar. Larkins, whose brother, pianist Ellis Larkins, is one of New York's finest café jazz players, was one of Seattle's two or three best bass players in the 1940s and 1950s. An accomplished tuba player and a solid swing bass man who could play intricate solos with a bow, Larkins played for a long time with the Rainy City Jazz Band, a Dixieland group, and eventually became a math teacher at Franklin High School. For his service to the community, the city named a park at 34th Avenue and Pike Street after him when he died, in 1984.

Gill's choice for guitar, Al Turay, is known mostly to Seattleites as a teacher who runs a guitar studio in Wallingford, but the mild-mannered, lanky bassist/guitarist had been kicking around Seattle since the late thirties, when he used to jam with Milt Green and Junior Raglin. Since that time, Turay had worked on Alaska cruise ships for a couple of years with white pianist Art Barduhn and white drummer/vibist Jimmy Sutton in a group called the Rhythm Rascals, followed by a gig at a downtown club called the Forty and Eight. After the war, he was in a jazz trio with Al Pierre's bassist, Bill Rinaldi, and pianist Jimmy Beuttner at the Roll Inn, a downtown tavern on Eighth, near Pike. Turay also did a stint with Norm Hoagy at the Magic Inn.

Turay was working early hours at the Colony when he happened to drop by the Ebony to check the place out. He sat in, and one of Seattle's most popular groups from the 1950s was born.

*That thing jelled right from the start. That was strictly a jazz thing. We used to have them lined up halfway around the block to get into that place there. I think I enjoyed that just about as much as any gig I played. We had a good feeling. We could sense what each individual was going to do.*

As the black Elks Club had been before it, the Ebony became the hottest spot on the street, running successfully until 1957 and reopening in 1959 with another trio that featured drummer Dave Coleman. Touring jazz musicians dropped by after their gigs, among them Dizzy Gillespie, Oscar Pettiford, the Modern Jazz Quartet, and Ben Webster.

One of the reasons celebrities came was to check out a strange gimmick Gill had come up with. A few months after the Ebony opened, perhaps out of a perverse reaction to those customers who kept asking where the "after-hours" action was (or because the liquor board forced clubs to stop selling booze early), Gill started to present jazz on Saturdays—from 6:00 to 9:00 a.m.! He titled the sessions "Jam for Breakfast." The concept was a smash. Recounts Gill:

*It always bothered me that they always wanted people to play music from nine o'clock to one o'clock in the morning. So I told these people, "Look, you can sell booze starting at six o'clock in the morning. Why not on Saturday morning?" They thought I was absolutely crazy. But I was so sure [it would work], I paid the musicians myself. The thing immediately took off. We did that for almost two years, every Saturday morning. There'd be a line out in front. We'd get people before they would go to the golf course, or maybe doctors and nurses that had been working all night long. You had people that would come all the way from Vancouver, every week. Make a day of it, go shopping and everything.*

"Jam for Breakfast" was such a success that other clubs started imitating the concept, and Gill eventually was forced to copyright the name to protect himself from unfair competition.

But having a successful concern on Jackson Street did not satisfy Gill, as long as the downtown lounges were still closed to blacks. In 1956, he decided to challenge the whole rotten system of union segregation. The climate was ripe. Two years earlier, the U.S. Supreme Court had forcibly integrated schools in Little Rock, Arkansas. People had watched televised reports of fire hoses beating back demonstrators. Though many black musicians struggled for equality in Seattle, Gill's story is worth singling out—first because he pulled in a musician from outside who would later have an enduring love affair with the Seattle jazz public, but also because the likable and popular Gill was so forthright and organized—yet disarming—in his demands. To Gill, it just seemed obvious that he should have the same opportunity to play downtown as anyone else, just as it had seemed obvious that he should sell alcohol at six o'clock in the morning if the liquor board prohibited selling it at one o'clock.

In August, recruiting his Ebony trio mates Larkins and Turay, Gill offered to play in the upscale Brigadier Room of the New Washington Hotel, a downtown establishment on Second Avenue and Stewart Street, a bastion of the white union local, just a block from the Bon Marché department store. The hotel was owned by Gene Autry's Doric Hotel chain. No black group had ever played there before. When the management discovered that not only did Gill intend to bring a racially mixed trio into the lounge but that his contract specifically stipulated the management could not refuse entry to anyone on the basis of race, creed, or color, they balked. Remembers Gill:

> *This guy called me. He was the manager of the hotel. He whispers to me, "What they're worried about is it's gonna [bring in] the 'Jackson Street element.'" I said, "Well, I don't know what you're talking about the 'Jackson Street element,' but if this is a first-class place, a bum is a bum. It's no more than getting the Skid Row element from First Avenue. If he's a bum, then that's not in accordance with the policy of your place." I knew what he was trying to say, but I wasn't going to let him. So they called a meeting of the board of directors in Los Angeles.*

The board of directors was somewhat more progressive, it developed, than their Seattle managers. They took a look at Gill's proposal, shrugged, and stamped their approval on the contract. After all, Nat Cole had been on television with his own show; blacks were demanding their rights. Besides, this was good business. Gill had a popular trio. The board said it thought Elmer Gill's integrated group would be just fine.

Shortly after Gill's landmark invasion of white territory, his achievement took on new luster when Larkins and Turay, who didn't like the restrictive atmosphere of the Brigadier Room, went back to the Ebony and Gill replaced Larkins with Monk Montgomery, the electric bassist he had worked with in Lionel Hampton's band. (Milt Green took Turay's place.) Elmer and Monk were both from Indianapolis, and while they hadn't known each other there, they had the same attitudes about music and the need for improvement in the racial situation. Indianapolis was particularly backward at the time, so Montgomery had been anxious to leave. "When Elmer called me," recalled the bassist, "it sounded like music to my ears. I was very depressed."

"We were the first black group to play in a first-class hotel downtown in Seattle, the first one," boasts Gill. "Len Brooks played solo piano down at a place that's now the Moore, but there wasn't any other."

Gill's "outlaw" contract at the Brigadier Room went counter to the unwritten policy of segregation at Local 76, but, in fact, negotiations were already underway to integrate the two unions. By the time the trio finished its engagement at the Brigadier Room, Seattle's segregated unions would be history.

Previous attempts by the black union to force amalgamation, in 1936 and 1950, had been brusquely rebuffed by the American Federation of Musicians, but with Little Rock pushing a new national agenda, the national leadership had begun to promote mergers rather than resist them. Ernie Lewis, the bandleader from the Basin Street who had reestablished Seattle's black union local in the 1940s, had risen in the national union's ranks and was now assistant to the AFM president, delegated to represent black locals in all merger proceedings. At a 1954 meeting in Chicago aimed at bringing the unions together, Lewis worked with Local 493 delegate Powell Barnett, the man whose determination to join the white local in 1909 had inadvertently given rise to the black union in the first place. Barnett came back with a plan. Each Seattle local was to form an amalgamation committee to consider the issue, then present it to their membership for a vote.

Perhaps surprisingly, the majority of white musicians favored the merger. Though some feared for their jobs, most musicians saw the move as a positive social step. Tiny Martin, Gay Jones' former bassist and then a member of the Seattle Symphony and president of Local 76, endorsed the effort of the amalgamation committees. An unsigned editorial in the December issue of *Musicland* (probably penned by pianist John Wittwer, who was on the amalgamation committee) appealed to local pride and moral uprightness:

> *Not only can we steal a march on our 'Frisco friends by desegregating now, we can join in a sweeping nation-wide trend which gives the lie to the white supremacy bilge prevalent throughout much of our ethically decadent and crassly ignorant South. . . . On December 11th, let us give our resounding approval to the efforts of the two committees, to our own long*

*history of tolerance among musicians everywhere, and to that precious principle: "All men are created equal."*

Emmett Lewis, president of the black local, contributed a mild but firm statement: "Generally, the Negro musician has proved no exception to an accepted pattern and for years his best source of livelihood was in the least desirable places. . . . We feel that joining your local will benefit both unions as a group, our members and their families, and the community as a whole. . . ."

On December 15, 1956, the black union voted unanimously for the merger. The white union followed suit, passing the issue with a large majority. It took a little more than a year for the details to be hammered out. On January 14, 1958, Lewis deposited a check with Local 76 and all members of the black union became members of Local 76. Lewis was elected to the board of a new, integrated local. Local 493 was no more.

The Seattle merger was part of a groundswell around the country that quickly integrated musicians' unions everywhere. In 1955, Ernie Lewis had had fifty-five black locals to service. By 1957, the only segregated union on the West Coast was San Francisco's, which soon followed Seattle's lead. Between 1960 and 1966, the AFM merged twenty more locals. By the end of the decade, union segregation was a thing of the past.

The effects of amalgamation on the Seattle scene were complex and took some time to play out. The rationale behind the merger, of course, had been fairness. When the unions joined, Local 493 had 101 members, of whom perhaps 80 or so were active (Ray Charles and Quincy Jones, long gone, were still on the official list). The new, racially mixed union, it was hoped, would open the best-paying jobs in downtown lounges and theaters to those eighty players, who had been barred from them for more than half a century. In practice, however, this did not always happen. For while their membership in Local 76 made blacks technically eligible for jobs downtown, there was nothing in the new rules that forced the lounges and hotels—or, for that matter, white bandleaders—to hire blacks. For many black musicians, the post-merger world was, sadly, in some ways worse than the pre-merger one. As the years went by, many black musicians felt hoodwinked; a sour wake of bitterness developed. Tenor saxophonist Jabo Ward says:

*At our own local, they called us. When we went into 76, we got crumbs. We didn't get the show jobs—like when the Ice Follies came, they didn't call black musicians. Didn't call us for certain artists coming in town to play the background music for them down at the theaters. No, we didn't get those jobs. We had our own buildup of clients that we dealt with, but 76 didn't do anything for us. Just made us pay more money into another local. It hurt. I'd say it hurt, yeah.*

Chuck Metcalf agrees.

*I think it turned out to be a bummer for the black musicians because they didn't get any more work, but they had to pay higher dues. . . . Okay, so Floyd Standifer . . . started to get calls to play in some big bands. But guys like Milton Garred wouldn't be hired by white musicians. Or Jabo Ward. The social patterns had already kind of congealed. There was a certain group of white musicians that went to play with black musicians and that stayed the same. But there was a certain group of white musicians that had just never played with black musicians and it wasn't that they were racist or anything, it was just the way the scene was at that time. They didn't know them as friends. They had no reason to hire them, and so they didn't.*

The problem wasn't only with the ingrained patterns of white bandleaders. Hotel managers and club owners often resisted integrated groups. Recalls Elmer Gill:

*The Sorrento Hotel used to have a place up at the top. The guy came down to the Ebony and he wanted Turay and Larkins and I to play. He offered me a good deal, more money than I was making down there. I went to talk to him about signing the contract and we were sitting at the bar talking and as I got up to leave, I was shaking his hand and thanking him, and he says, "Oh, one more thing. By the way," he says, "you got to get rid of the guitar player."*

Gill eventually became so fed up with the American racial situation that he moved to Canada. In the early sixties, he began to divide his time between British Columbia and Basel, Switzerland, where he played in a four-star hotel.

It's a pity Gill did not stick around to enjoy the legacy of his labors. With his "Jam for Breakfast" and early-hours jazz dining concepts, he successfully broke the local stereotype that jazz had to be played in an after-hours atmosphere or a cheap tavern, thereby gentrifying the context for jazz and closing the door on its old bootlegging-and-gambling image. Ironically, he had done this right on Jackson Street. The clubs that emerged downtown in the modern era from the ashes of Jackson Street—integrated, upscale, and catering to hip listeners—owe much to Gill's efforts.

Unfortunately, the new social attitudes that allowed these clubs also drove a stake into the hearts of the old ones. Without a black musicians' union, there was no support system for the most lucrative work black musicians had ever had—in the Jackson Street venues. The first blow had been thrust by the Legislature in 1949, when it legalized hard liquor. The second had come from the neighborhood itself, which had sought to squelch the clubs in the name of respectability. The third had come from changes in popular taste, which created markets for lounge music and rock 'n' roll. Now, finally, in 1956, the very social structure that had made the whole scene necessary—segregation—was caving in.

One by one, the black "bottle clubs" succumbed. Even diehard joints that had cut new deals with the police began to close. Mayor Gordon Clinton, in a fit of gratuitous moral reform, had his picture taken in front of the 908 Club, holding an axe. It closed in 1956. The Blue Note, where Local 493 convened, trickled on for a spell, some say until 1959; the New Chinatown lasted into the 1960s. The last after-hours place to close, according to Dave Stetler, was the 605 Club (at 605 King, formerly known as the Kun Ming). "It went for quite a few years," says Stetler, "and I really don't know how."

"As long as there was 493," explains Floyd Standifer, "there was a center. When 493 disappeared, it took away the focus for jazz. People began to spread out. Instead of having someplace to go, where you could find all the musicians in town at any given time, there was no place for this sound to be concentrated anywhere."

**YOU'VE BEEN A GOOD OLD WAGON**
**(But you've done broke down)**
**Please omit flowers!**

# 10
# AFTER THE BOTTLE CLUBS CLOSED

When Jackson Street collapsed, it did not spell the end of jazz in Seattle, nor did all the great musicians who had been nurtured there hang up their horns. On the contrary, Seattle jazz experienced another golden period in the late 1950s and early 1960s, as new, legal nightclubs sprang up and a fresh, young audience came to patronize them. As the best musicians moved from the bottle clubs into the new, racially integrated venues, elements of the old underground were absorbed into the "overground" culture at large. Floyd Standifer, the musician whose career best represents this transition during the 1950s, explains:

> *Musicians black and white began to filter together. There became this great interchange. People began to spread out—and rightly so, you know, rightly so, because that other scene was built on something that was socially improper and intolerable. The jazz scene began to benefit.*

As Standifer points out, amalgamation was progressive socially—however, like all assimilations, it involved losses. With integration, the music moved away from its roots in the community, as nightclubs relocated from the black district to downtown. Audiences changed. The mood of performances shifted from comfortable neighborhood affairs to commercial exchanges. On the other hand, the clubs were no longer raided, wages were regulated by the union, working conditions were (usually) improved, and—perhaps most important of all—a great musical tradition was made accessible to a wider spectrum of American society. The music played in the new clubs was more sophisticated than what had been offered on Jackson Street, as well. Local players improved their command of bop, and the new styles of modal jazz and hard bop became a part of the regional vocabulary. National touring acts began to stop over on a more regular basis. By 1962, with the coming of the World's Fair and the establishment of modern jazz clubs such as Pete's Poop Deck and the Penthouse, Seattle—and Seattle jazz—would become thoroughly cosmopolitan.

Many Jackson Street musicians enjoyed their most productive years after the district's heyday. Ernestine Anderson, Pony Poindexter, and Buddy Catlett left town and forged important careers in the national mainstream. Floyd Standifer, Jabo Ward, Chuck Metcalf, and Elmer Gill worked throughout the fifties in a handful of venues that were the prototypes of the modern jazz club, where people came to listen to the music rather than to dance or socialize. Two of the most important clubs—the Flame and the Lake City Tavern—opened in the North End, where the audiences were mostly white. Elmer Gill's Ebony Restaurant, on Jackson, continued to draw a mixed crowd of professionals and working people. The short-lived but influential Northwest Jazz Workshop, in the University District, tried to fill the void left by the closure of the Blue Note. By the end of the decade, the energy from these hubs would, in Standifer's words, "filter together," and a new jazz flowering would replace the old Jackson Street scene.

It's useful to look briefly at how this transition occurred, since Jackson Street was not some exotic, ahistorical event, but an era whose characteristics have profound links to the present. It would also be a disservice to leave unfinished the stories of those players whose careers blossomed after the decline of the Jackson Street era.

Buddy Catlett, who had started out with the Charlie Taylor band in the forties, is a case in point. Having a musician of Catlett's caliber in a town the size of Seattle is one of the rewards of being a jazz listener in the Northwest. Catlett has a round, firm acoustic-bass sound, the type that can only be achieved by plucking

with real force against a string braced high above the fingerboard. Catlett's sense of time is the standard against which that of all other local bassists is measured—so are his walking blues lines and his note choices in a ballad. He sometimes gets unfairly typecast as an "old-fashioned" player—indeed, his roots are in Basie—but anyone who listens carefully to his solos knows that he is every bit as versed in modern harmonies as bassists who succeeded him on the scene. A short, stocky man, Catlett masks a deep, analytical intelligence behind his amiable smile.

A good sense of humor about himself and life's vagaries has always been a hallmark of George James "Buddy" Catlett. Though he was born in Long Beach, California, Catlett comes from a Washington pioneer family. His first musical memories are of his mother Natalie's wide-ranging record collection, which included Basie, Lester Young, and Nat "King" Cole; only later did he discover that his father played passable stride piano. The first live music he recalls hearing was at a picnic near Black Diamond, a small town in the foothills of the Cascades.

*A guy named Banjoski [Adams] played guitar and Joe Darensbourg played clarinet. I was about eleven years old. They were really good players. The first big band I ever saw was Count Basie. My grandmother took me to it. They had dances every Thanksgiving here at the Civic Auditorium. I almost fell out of the balcony. J. J. Johnson was in the band, Illinois Jacquet, Shadow Wilson, Lucky Thompson—I never heard nothing like that in my whole life.*

Catlett learned to dance first, then took up cornet, on which he mastered a Louis Armstrong blues. When he was twelve, Catlett moved from trumpet to tenor saxophone, purchasing an instrument with money he'd earned as an usher at a Ballard movie theater. Lessons from Frank Waldron put him in touch with an early jazz style that would later prove valuable when he played with Armstrong himself.

Catlett played alto saxophone in the Charlie Taylor Band; in 1950, however, he was struck with a severe case of pleurisy that doctors feared was tuberculosis—common at the time, and also incurable. The doctors instructed him not to play saxophone under any circumstances: blowing into the horn might make him sicker. For a teenager who sounded like Johnny Hodges and whose whole identity was wrapped up in music, this was devastating. Catlett was forced to spend his last two years of high school in and out of the hospital.

*When I got out, I still wanted to play music. I had decided that in junior high school. But I'd lost the momentum and I was scared of it, really. I approached Elmer Gill about taking lessons from him. Then the bass player Billy Johnson went into the Air Force and his bass was at home. I knew his parents. They said, "Well, Billy's bass is here, you want to use that?" That's when I started playing bass. I took lessons from Tiny Martin. I started playing with Billy Tolles, Freddie Greenwell, Paul Neves, and Buzz Bridgeford.*

Catlett got his first gig as a bass player at an after-hours spot called the Aurora Country Club, where Floyd Standifer led the band. Buddy worked days at the university bookstore and jammed after hours, "going over those things over and over again," as he puts it, "until it starts to make sense and you can hit it from any angle." One musician remembers seeing Catlett at the Lake City Tavern in those early years, playing "until his fingers bled." In the early hours, he played the Lake City with Paul Neves; after hours, he worked in Billy Tolles' rhythm-and-blues band at the 908 Club. Catlett could have stayed in town and made a good living playing rock 'n' roll with Billy, but when veteran bandleader Horace Henderson (Fletcher's brother) scouted the 908 one night, Catlett promptly signed up. That was May 1956.

Horace Henderson was a jazz pianist, arranger, and bandleader who made some forays into R & B; he has been described by Gunther Schuller as "one of the most talented yet most neglected and enigmatic of figures in all of jazz." Catlett worked with Henderson until the spring of 1957, doubling as a copyist and teaching himself some of the principles of composition and arranging. The tour wound down in Denver, where Henderson was based, and Buddy, who had since married, joined his wife in the Mile-High City.

Denver had a thriving jazz scene in the

1950s, and Catlett immediately found work in a band playing opposite Art Blakey at Sonny's Lounge. The group featured saxophonist Booker Ervin. Buddy also worked in Denver with Johnny Smith, the great guitarist. In 1959, California vibist and drummer Cal Tjader hired Catlett, an experience that gave him a chance to learn Latin music from Tjader's sidemen Willie Bobo and Mongo Santamaria:

"Willie and Mongo helped me a lot to understand Latin rhythms, which I didn't understand then at all. I had to go by Willie's place every night because I was playing the conception of Latin music all wrong. I was playing swing music. That perpendicular feeling was just too bad!"

Catlett was willing to take seriously any music put before him. But like many jazz musicians of his generation who had missed formal training, he had come to realize that to grow, he needed to acquire musical tools only available from a conservatory. When Quincy Jones invited him to Europe, one of the reasons he went was so he could attend the Juilliard School, in New York, after the tour:

*Learning on the bandstand is one thing, but it leaves a lot of gaps, when it comes down to important music. What I wanted to do was stop and practice and study someplace. But I couldn't. When we came back, we were supposed to go on Broadway, and that would give me a chance to go [to Juilliard] or Manhattan [School of Music] in the daytime. But none of that took place. I stayed on the road.*

When Buddy got to New York, he made his first recording, *Under Paris Skies*, with Jones and Andy Williams. While the *Free and Easy* band was in rehearsal, Catlett also worked in Harlem with the great pianist Red Garland.

After the European tour, which lasted ten months, Catlett did return to New York. But instead of going to school, he went right to work with pianist Junior Mance, followed by stints with Chico Hamilton, Eddie "Lockjaw" Davis, and Johnny Griffin. When Count Basie needed an anchor man, Quincy recommended Buddy. By this time, Buddy had been around long enough to know most of the players, so while it was an honor to get on the band, he was no longer in awe of them. Catlett also knew the music, inside and out.

*I had listened to Basie since I was old enough to walk. I knew what it was supposed to sound like. There was a guy that lived in West Seattle, he's a retired ferryboat captain. We went to a Basie concert ten years before and we taped the whole concert at the Civic Auditorium. I had that tape for ten years, so I knew every tune they had. I knew it like I could do it upside down. So when I started, it was great. [People thought] "Wow, he's reading his ass off!"*

While Catlett was with Basie, the band recorded an album with Frank Sinatra, *With Rose-Colored Glasses*, and appeared on television numerous times. But the moments he remembers as highlights were when the band hit an ineffable groove:

*We were doing a Polish dance on the North Side of Chicago one night. We were playing "Little Darlin'" so slow that it actually would stop if you played it any slower. And the whole band was doing it. For everybody to function at that level was really an incredible feeling. The whole band, the dynamics of the thing—just diamond perfect. I think that's the most memorable time. Oh, there was one other time, on an arrangement called "Mama Devil." That was the first time I ever felt a band that large just get up and sit up off the ground. I mean, you feel it, it's like your hair stands on end when that happens. You're not even playing anymore. The whole thing has taken on a life of its own.*

Buddy stayed with Basie until the first part of 1965, then settled down in Brooklyn, where he played with the Maynard Ferguson band awhile, then with Coleman Hawkins. One night at the Five Spot he looked up and saw Paul Neves and Norm Bobrow. "They were sitting there with their arms folded," he recalls, "like 'The jury is out.' It was quite a pleasant surprise."

Working with Hawkins was "like a sociology course. You could tie up what you heard your parents talk about—the past. You could see how things were and how they were changing. To me, that was the important thing about it. Just playing the licks is superficial."

After working with Hawkins, Catlett

formed a group of his own, at Birdland, then was hired by Louis Armstrong. It would be Satchmo's last regular group, and Catlett stayed with Louis until the trumpeter died, in 1971. Louis' combo consisted of Billy Kyle (followed by Marty Napoleon), piano; Buster Bailey (followed by Joe Muranyi), clarinet; Danny Barcelona, drums; and Tyree Glenn, trombone. The Armstrong band toured Europe once a year and even played Tunisia.

For twenty years Catlett had been fighting a losing battle with alcohol. When Armstrong died, Buddy's personal problems, combined with the scarcity of work brought on by the rock revolution in the sixties, finally brought him to a halt. He worked around New York for a spell, playing Beatles tunes in lounges, but got disgusted and lost his heart for music. For several years, he stayed home and took care of his and his second wife's new baby. Catlett remembers spending a lot of idle time in those days, sitting on the terrace of their Brooklyn home, drawing sketches, not knowing what to do next. In 1973, he left New York to live with his brother in Connecticut. An offer from Dizzy Gillespie to go to Europe slipped by. Catlett drifted. In 1978, when he moved back to Seattle, he didn't even have a bass.

It was a call from a commercial contractor that got Buddy to pick up his brother Bobby's electric bass for a gig. Remembering that he enjoyed playing more than anything else, he decided to put music in front—and leave alcohol behind. For a while, he worked in a funny-hat band with Ron Pierce called the Salmon City Seven, as well as for swing bandleader Mickey Martin. Since the early 1980s, Catlett has been the sideman of choice for out-of-towners, from Eddie "Lockjaw" Davis to Art Farmer. In the early nineties, he was working regularly in a trio with Jack Perciful at a hotel and at Lofurno's, and had toured Europe a couple of times with Elmer Gill.

Catlett has never stopped studying music. He practices clarinet and bass every day and gives lessons to a variety of students in a small studio in the back of his house. A blown-up photograph of the Bumps Blackwell National Guard band looks down over him. Along with Bumps, the ghost of Catlett's childhood saxophone teacher, Frank Waldron, is probably staring down, as well. As old Frank listens, leaning over to sip his vodka, he's probably saying severely, "Buddy, keep on practicing and you'll be with Duke Ellington." Old bald-headed Frank called it pretty close.

Another Jackson Street veteran whose career has taken her around the world and back to Seattle is Ernestine Anderson. After the Johnny Otis tour that brought her home in a shambles from Los Angeles in 1949, Anderson went back to California for a second shot at fame. Marriage and motherhood soon interrupted her career. Based in Seattle, she worked in Fairbanks, Alaska, for four months on a double bill with tap dancer Emily Foster. But when Stan Kenton offered her a job in 1951, she realized that her next child, daughter Shelley, would have been born in the middle of the tour, so she turned Stan down. When Lionel Hampton came to town the following year, Ernestine's husband encouraged her to go. She recalls:

> *My husband at the time had heard that Betty Carter was leaving Hamp's band and Lionel was looking for a singer. He told me to go audition. I didn't want to go, because our children were young. But he kept encouraging me: "I think you should do it, because I don't want you years from now going to bed thinking or wondering, 'What if . . .' If you're going to do it, I think you should do it now."*

Anderson set off to Georgia Kemp's house on Madison and 20th—Hamp's home away from home in Seattle—for an audition. Ray Charles' trio, which rehearsed at Georgia's house, backed her up. Guitarist Garcia McKee remembers the afternoon well:

> *She auditioned with "Body and Soul." She sounded beautiful. He hired her on the spot. The only thing we laughed about was that "Body and Soul" is written in five flats [key of D-flat] and she said she wanted to sing it in B [five sharps]. [But] she wasn't nervous. She was a young girl so, naturally, once she started singing, that professionalism came out. Just a young girl, but she could sing.*

This was in the fall of 1952. Ernestine spent the next fifteen months on the road with Hampton, "paying her dues" with her first real name band. Any loneliness or road blues the young singer may have felt were soon mitigated by the circle of friendly faces from Jackson Street: Quincy Jones was in the trumpet section, Elmer Gill was on piano, and Pony Poindexter was playing alto saxophone. She also got to know Monk Montgomery.

Still, there were some bad times. On the way to Indianapolis, Anderson was thrown out of an equipment truck; her severely broken arm required a metal plate and a two-week hospital stay. Later, Hamp's band was booked to play Dwight D. Eisenhower's presidential inauguration, which led to a famous incident. After the inauguration, the band played in a park along the Potomac, on the site where the Kennedy Center now stands. There were three acts—Louis Armstrong, Illinois Jacquet, and Hampton. As Ernestine remembers it:

> *Since Louis was on first, Hamp was worried about getting upstaged, so he told Illinois Jacquet not to play "Flyin' Home," and it made Jacquet mad. "I'm the one that made 'Flyin' Home' famous," said Jacquet. "I'll play it whenever and wherever I please." [Jacquet] goes out there [and plays "Flyin' Home"], so by the time Lionel came on, none of his stuff worked. He jumped up on top of the drums. He did his sticks—he caught them and he clapped his hands. But it was over.*
>
> *Monk [Montgomery] told Quincy, "Now, when we play 'Flyin' Home,' I'm going to jump into the Potomac." He said, "I'll hand you the bass," or something. So sure enough, Monk went. Lionel looked up, and if you could have seen the look on his face—"What the hell is going on?" But when he did that, the crowd went wild! From then on, Lionel was like, "Yeah! Yeah, yeah!" Like it was planned. He didn't say nothing to Monk about that. In fact, I think he was really grateful, because he thought Monk did it to save the day. He had no idea what was going on behind his back.*

When the band got to New York in the late fall of 1953, Ernestine, along with Elmer Gill and several other musicians, balked at a proposed trip to Europe. The trust level between Hamp and his musicians was low. Gill, Anderson, and some of the others presented a petition to Gladys Hampton, the band manager, requesting that the itinerary be pinned down to a specific timetable, pay scale, and return date, and that passage home be guaranteed. According to Anderson, Lionel responded by calling an old friend in Chicago, a union boss, who threatened the mutineers with revocation of their union cards. Several band members defected. Quincy traveled to France—an influential move in his life that eventually resulted in his job at the French record company Barclay Disques.

Ernestine, for her part, returned to Seattle to raise her children, at least for the time being. In a touching article in the *Seattle Post-Intelligencer*, previewing an appearance at the Metropolitan Theatre, she told columnist John Voorhees, "I had a postcard from Quincy. He said they'd be playing in Paris this weekend." Anderson's wistful tone, along with her decision to come home, speaks well to her profound ambivalence about pursuing the limelight. Throughout her career, Anderson has repeatedly made thrusts into the national arena, only to walk away from the business a few years later. The issue for Anderson does not seem to be one of confidence, as it is with so many musicians who find the national scene frighteningly competitive, but rather some basic "homebody" spirit that constantly pulls her back to the house where she grew up, as if her sister, Josephine, were still calling her name from that windowsill. It is an issue she would not resolve until much, much later, after suffering a good deal during her first, remarkable successes in the 1950s.

For while Ernestine told the *Post-Intelligencer* in 1953 that she had come home to raise her family, she had, in fact, already decided to go back to New York. Her first job there was at a gay nightclub called the Page Three, where vocalists Sheila Jordan and Morgana King were also starting out. Anderson made her recording debut during this period, in November 1955, on two tracks of an album with Gigi Gryce, *Nica's Tempo*. Art Farmer, Oscar Pettiford, and Art Blakey played in the band. After a couple of years of struggling in New York, Ernestine took an offer to tour Sweden with Swedish trumpeter Rolf Ericson. She wound up staying there six and a half months, recording an album for Metronome with Harry Arnold. When Metronome sold the masters to Mercury,

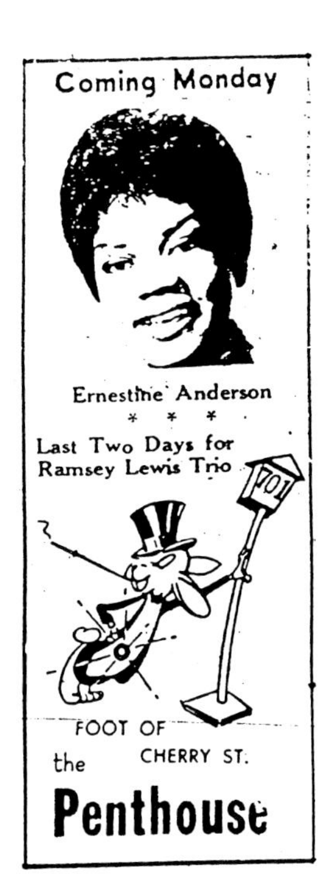

Ernestine assumed that she would come home to the release of her first American album. It wouldn't be quite that simple.

Ernestine spent the early part of 1957 working in Seattle, waiting for the record to come out. She sat in with her old Hampton bandmate Monk Montgomery at a new Seattle club, Dave's Fifth Avenue, in a promising new group called the Mastersounds. Soon afterward, she moved south to San Francisco with Monk's new group, where she caught the avid attention of San Francisco jazz critic Ralph Gleason, the same writer who had raved about Cecil Young and Gerald Brashear. Wrote Gleason in the *San Francisco Chronicle*: "Well, for me, she is the best new jazz singer in a decade. She has good diction, time, an uncanny ability to phrase well, great warmth in her voice, a true tone, and, on top of all that, she swings like mad." Gleason got Ernestine booked into the very first Monterey Jazz Festival, that fall, and began to pressure Mercury to bring out her album. The pressure worked. Record-company representatives began to offer deals. The ever-supportive Gleason stepped in again, advising Anderson to hold out for the best contract. In early 1958, Ernestine, who by now had moved to Los Angeles, signed a deal with Mercury, where Quincy Jones was working as an executive. *Hot Cargo*, her first record under her own name, was finally released.

NORM BOBROW
presents
FRI. OCT. 2nd.
METROPOLITAN
8:30 P.M.
COLUMBIA RECORDING STAR
DIRECT FROM LIONEL HAMPTON
ERNESTINE
ANDERSON
WITH
ELMER GILL
JOHNNY LESTER QUARTET
FEATURING
FLOYD STANDIFER
WITH BUDDY CATLETT
AND
KENNY SMITH
BOB DYKE DUET
WITH
CHUCK MAHAFFAY
PLUS
JAZZ STARS!
FREDDY GREENWELL
PONY POINDEXTER
DAVE TUTTLE
BUZZ BRIDGFORD
MICHAEL DE FILIPPIS
ADDED ATTRACTION
SENSATIONAL
TOMMY HART
HIS RECORDED SONGS
OF RUSS COLUMBO!

This Design by
Granderson Russell
of Cole and Redmayne

The response was tremendous. John S. Wilson of the *New York Times* wrote, "Miss Anderson is a singer who disdains mannerisms, who respects both tune and lyrics and who seems to feel that a melody should fall pleasantly on the ear. . . . She displays an approach in ballads that in warmth, directness and sensitivity invites favorable comparison with Ella Fitzgerald." Twelve years after Norm Bobrow had been chastised by a local critic for making the same comparison, the Seattle promoter's enthusiasm had been vindicated.

John Tynan, writing for *down beat*, followed suit: "She's good, darn good, and stands head and shoulders above the covey of cool-ies who have gained exaggerated prominence since June Christy set the style."

On August 4, 1958, Ernestine's picture appeared on the cover of *Time* magazine. The article inside described her as "the best-kept secret in the land" and "the best new voice in the business." The journalists were not exaggerating. *Hot Cargo* is an excellent album, and particularly instructive for listeners who know only Anderson's later work. Though the record is decidedly a period piece, featuring lush, stagey ballads with strings and alto flute that in the 1950s would have been quaintly termed "mood music," Anderson's pure tone, true pitch, artful dynamics, and control of her instrument are downright startling, on a par with Ella Fitzgerald, Sarah Vaughan, and Carmen McRae. Her relaxed vocal control is even more impressive on her fourth Mercury LP, *Moanin' Moanin' Moanin'*. It's interesting that Tynan thought to compare Ernestine to June Christy. The Stan Kenton songbird had recently popularized an erotically stripped-down, "cool" ballad style that was setting the pace in the marketplace. To that minimalist environment Ernestine brought a firmness of intention and earthiness that must have set listeners on their ears. On *Hot Cargo*, Ernestine's voice is lighter—the drawling, molasses-like quality isn't there, except perhaps as a hint of sexy amber in the lows—and there is an ingenue quality, an innocence. Her treatment of "Autumn in New York" features a fetching turn that has vanished from her style; there is a sense of deep conviction on "Little Girl Blue."

For a couple of years after *Hot Cargo* was released, the public couldn't get enough of the singer from Seattle. At the end of the year, she played a successful engagement at New York's Village Vanguard, following a two-week stint at Bobrow's Colony club. The *down beat* critics voted her New Star of the Year in 1959, and the next year she was running third only to Ella and Sarah in the magazine's Critics Poll. Ronnie Scott, the prominent British saxophonist, recruited her for opening night at his posh new London club. Ernestine took a second apartment in New York, dividing her time between there and Los Angeles, then settled in Manhattan in 1959. Mercury continued to release new albums—she made six, in all—and she continued to tour. But the record-buying public is fickle, and Mercury never could find the right formula to keep her records on the charts. Her popularity started to slide. When the Beatles began to transform the record business into a rock 'n' roll monopoly, says Ernestine, "most agents didn't want to know you. It was either sing rock or don't sing at all."

Anderson decided to take her chances in "swinging London," the new rock capital. For a moment, she flirted with pop, recording a dreadful album called *The New Sound of Ernestine Anderson*, but soon she returned to jazz. For a while, she was successful in Europe. She toured the Scandinavian countries, Spain, and Germany. But this was the beginning of a prolonged disillusionment with the music business. Discouraged by Mercury's failure to push any but her first album, and by the bleakness of the jazz scene in general, she dropped out for two years, from 1966 to 1968. A last-ditch foray to Los Angeles to give it one more try was a bust.

> *I just couldn't get going. I tried a few gigs and it was like my heart wasn't in it. I did not feel it. I had nothing more to say. I was just dry. So I thought, "It's time to hang it up." I didn't really know what I wanted to do, but I knew I didn't want to sing anymore. I didn't have anything more to say. It was a bad time of life all around. For some reason, it got to me, kids taking dope and dying, all that. I had reached the point where I just wanted out.*

Anderson fell into a deep depression. Afraid to go out on the streets or into a crowd, she retreated from the world. She would do her supermarket shopping only late at night. At about this time, four friends told her, independent of one another, about the healing qualities of Buddhist chanting. She took it as a sign, and attended a meeting. "I wanted to get in touch with myself. Find out who and why and what I was all about, as a person. Which I had never done before. I'd always been too busy concentrating on a career, ever since I was thirteen years old."

That was in 1969. Anderson began to chant morning and evening as a regular practice. It would be several years before she felt ready to perform again, but in 1974, the jazz critic for the *Post-Intelligencer*, Maggie Hawthorn, coaxed her out of retirement, escorting her to Red Kelly's new club in Tumwater. The following year, Elmer Gill invited Anderson to sing at a "Jazz Weekend" on Vancouver Island. Ernestine reconnected with her old friend Ray Brown, who offered to produce a record for

**Ernestine Anderson's first album, released in 1958 on Mercury Records.**

her on the new label he was recording for, Concord Jazz. In 1977, Ernestine was back on track with a new career, debuting with a fine album, *Hello Like Before*.

"Before, there was a war. I couldn't put the two together—the homebody and the show singer. This Buddhism has allowed me try to find out who I am, what my relationship is to the rest of the world. There's more to me than show business. I'm a mother, a daughter, a sister, a friend—I'm even a grandmother."

Anderson has released eleven albums on Concord, earning Grammy nominations for two of them—*Never Make Your Move Too Soon* (1981) and *Big City* (1983). She has also rekindled her career to a worldwide heat that includes annual tours of the United States, Europe, and Japan. The contemporary Ernestine has a more rambunctious, raunchier style, put to particularly good use on her superb album of blues, *When the Sun Goes Down*, though she can still mesmerize an audience with the breathtaking purity of a tune like "Old Folks" or Hoagy Carmichael's "Skylark." Her signature song has become a long, talking-blues version of "Never Make Your Move Too Soon," a worldly-wise poem that reflects her own maturity, wit, and wisdom.

Like Ernestine Anderson and Buddy Catlett, little Pony Poindexter, the alto saxophonist who had first come up from Oakland with the Ernie Lewis band to play at the Basin Street, also found success after his Jackson Street days. In 1947, Poindexter joined Billy Eckstine's orchestra—whose personnel also included Miles Davis. Poindexter made his first record in San Francisco during this period, coincidentally with Seattle bassist Red Kelly backing him up. In 1950, Poindexter joined Jack McVea for a tour to Salt Lake City, came back to San Francisco, and went to work with Dexter Gordon at Bop City. In early 1951, he played around the Bay Area with Vernon Alley before joining Lionel Hampton. While on tour with Hampton, Poindexter recalled jamming at the Club Alabam in Los Angeles with Dexter Gordon, Wardell Gray, Hampton Hawes, and Ernestine's old lookout, Shifty Henry. Like many musicians at this time, Poindexter also started injecting heroin.

"Pony used to get so high, man, he couldn't get away from the microphone," laughs Quincy Jones, who got Pony into Hamp's band. "Bless his heart. He was a legend in his own mind."

Pony left Hampton in 1952 and returned to San Francisco, where he traded sets with Bird at the Say When and played at Bop City with no less than three great trumpeters—Dizzy Gillespie, Miles Davis, and Kenny Dorham. At about this time, Poindexter and Dorham came up the coast and hung out together in Seattle for several months, staying at Billy Tolles' place. This was the period when Tolles put together his remarkable group with Dorham and Poindexter, which won the "battle of the bands" contest in 1952 at the Eagles Auditorium.

Neil Friel recalls running into Poindexter and Dorham one morning at a breakfast session. The two brilliant young musicians told him they were on their way to Alaska to seek work as bricklayers. "I stopped them," Friel recounts. "I showed them an article in the newspaper telling unskilled laborers not to come to Alaska."

Pony continued to gravitate back to Seattle year after year. Part of the attraction was a woman he had met, his future wife, Marie, but he also came back because he thought Seattle was a "cool" place for addicts, where the police didn't bother you as much as they might in, say, San Francisco and Los Angeles. It was an assumption that would nearly prove to be his undoing.

Poindexter's Seattle arrest and subsequent prison term in the Monroe Reformatory are recounted in his autobiography, *Pony Express*. It is a bizarre and dream-like tale in what is, overall, a fanciful, angry, and bitter book—so bitter, in fact, that it is hard to know how much of it to believe. According to Poindexter, he had just gotten off the road with T-Bone Walker and was living in San Francisco when he discovered that his name mysteriously had become part of a federal "secret indictment" list. He decided to flee to Seattle. On his way, he stopped to play a gig at the Swing Club in Portland with trumpeter Bobby Bradford; he wound up staying there, until February 1954. Next, Babs Gonzales, the vocalist who composed "Oop-Pop-A-Da," invited Pony to Seattle for a gig with saxophonist James Moody and vocalist Eddie Jefferson at the University of Washington. Poindexter claims that one night, following a jam session in a roadhouse that sounds like it might have been the China Pheasant, he was arrested in a motel room for being there with a white woman, brutally beaten in an elevator by the police, and taken to jail. Poindexter was sent to Monroe for fifteen months, for what he calls a trumped-up charge of grand larceny.

The Seattle Police Department was not known for racial tolerance in the 1950s; Poindexter may well have been beaten. And he definitely spent time in Monroe. But it was not for integrating a motel bedroom and it didn't happen when he says it did. In fact, Poindexter had already been convicted of second-degree burglary in Seattle—likely for one of the thefts he committed in search of drug money —and had been paroled in 1954. The incident he describes in his autobiography most likely is a glamorized version of an arrest for breaking parole. Whatever the details, Pony was sent to prison in October 1956, where he remained until at least the end of the year, possibly until the spring of 1957. While there, he played in a jazz group—and also kicked his heroin habit. Paul Gonsalves and Ray Nance, then of Duke Ellington's band, also paid him a visit.

When Stan Getz was arrested in Seattle, his story made front-page news. Pony Poindexter's catastrophe barely rated an item. That the press cared more about white musicians than black was nothing new. Such things were not supposed to happen to nice, white Jewish boys, even if they did play jazz, while the arrest of yet another black musician was perceived as routine. In the 1950s, however, such racial bias took an ominous twist that was particularly exasperating for black bebop musicians. The roots of the conflict went back to 1949, when Miles Davis recorded *Birth of the Cool*, an album inspired by the arranging of Gil Evans and Claude Thornhill, who in turn were having great influence on other white musicians working in Los Angeles, such as Gerry Mulligan and Shorty Rogers. At the same time, a young composition student at Mills College, in Oakland, named Dave Brubeck was beginning to come on strong. When Brubeck, Mulligan, and Rogers began issuing a slew of even-edged, carefully arranged, dynamically "cool" jazz records in the early 1950s, the movement called "West Coast jazz" was born.

Though never really a school, the concept nevertheless caught on with the press and public, particularly college students. Dave Brubeck made the cover of *Time* magazine. Whites, who had left swing behind but had been perhaps confused or turned off by bebop, embraced jazz again.

There was only one problem. As the term "West Coast" took on stylistic as well as geographic meaning, the media ignored anything from the West that wasn't "cool," or else assumed that if music came from the West, it must be cool. Black bebop pioneers in the region—like Pony Poindexter—suddenly became invisible. Perceiving the cool school as a racial conspiracy to rip off blacks, Poindexter became angry and paranoid. He accused Neal Hefti, who had written a musical homage to the saxophonist, "Little Pony," of stealing his lick for the tune. He also claimed Brubeck appropriated his "special arrangement" of "How High the Moon." Spending over a year in jail did not improve his mood. When he was released, he went to work at the Mardi Gras, the soul lounge on Madison that had been keeping the Jackson Street spirit alive, but complained that he was ill-received.

"The black musicians in Seattle were mostly cold," writes Pony in his book, "but I overwhelmed them with sheer talent. Of course, most of them thought that I'd just go back to using skag right away and go back to the prison. Some of them sent dealers to me, offering free skag, which they had paid for. But I froze. Much to their surprise."

Poindexter makes no mention here of his wife or of Pops Buford, who had loaned him his horn, or of any other Seattle musicians. Pony played at the Mardi Gras off and on throughout the latter half of 1957 and early 1958 and, once he cleaned up his act, headed into the most fruitful period of his career. He returned to San Francisco, where he worked with Cal Tjader and Dizzy Gillespie, played on poet Kenneth Rexroth's famous "Poetry and Jazz" shows, and recorded with both Wes Montgomery (*Beginnings*) and Jon Hendricks (*A Good Git-Together*), who liberally featured his New Orleans–style singing and soloing.

"The following week," he writes, "I did another album with Wes, his brothers and Harold Land called *Montgomery Land*. Because of the West Coast jazz movement, I hadn't been able to buy a record date for nearly ten years. And now, in less than two weeks, I had made two albums with some of

Dope-Craving Saxophonist Foiled in Robbery Attempt

Jazz Man Collapses In Jail Cell

the best musicians in America—all black musicians."

Poindexter notes with glee that soulful, black-oriented "funk" music by Cannonball Adderley had finally started to supplant cool: "That marked the official end of West Coast jazz. Cannonball and his group had put the nails in the coffin. I was a delighted pallbearer at the funeral."

Pony enjoyed a flurry of albums under his own name and others', plus dates at Carnegie Hall, the Newport and Monterey jazz festivals, and every major jazz club in the country. His album *Pony Express* and his work with Jon Hendricks on the landmark *Evolution of the Blues* secured him a niche in jazz history as a lively original who successfully incorporated New Orleans roots and bluesy entertaining skills into a bebop imagination. In 1964, the combination of an established reputation and depressing racial tensions at home catapulted Poindexter to Europe, where he worked and recorded successfully for fourteen years, returning to the Bay Area in 1977. An album for Inner City done the following year, *Poindexter*, suffers from a poor rhythm section, but Pony's tone is still fierce, his articulation Bird-like, and his humorous "ditties" fully in place. He moved back and forth between the Bay Area and Europe until he died, in 1989.

Why does one musician turn to the road and another stay at home? The knee-jerk response is that those who reach for recognition are better musicians; only the mediocre stay home, where life is safe. But as anyone knows who has spent time listening carefully to a local scene, such a simplistic answer is often misguided. Issues such as family, economics, and temperament often lead excellent players to work on a local scene. In Seattle, several of the best musicians stayed put, including Floyd Standifer, Jabo Ward, Chuck Metcalf, Elmer Gill, Jerry Gray, and Dave Coleman. Their refusal to leave home had a salubrious effect on Northwest jazz that still can be felt. Working through the 1950s in a handful of local venues, these musicians and others pioneered Seattle's modern jazz scene.

Floyd Standifer in many ways is the quintessential Seattle bebop musician, capable of hot and furious chromatic improvisation of the first order, but also influenced by the steady and evenhanded shapeliness of Fats Navarro and Miles Davis. With his fat sound, absolute control, and sly sense of timing, the mature Standifer arrived at a bag that was part Art Farmer, part Carmel Jones, and part Lee Morgan—a hard-bop modernist with a cool undersurface.

Standifer was born in 1929 in Wilmington, North Carolina; he came to Portland as a child in 1936. Though his father had a comfortable income as an African Methodist Episcopal–Zion preacher, with the Depression on, the Standifers wound up picking strawberries three years later. Floyd's father bought a farm about five miles outside of Gresham, Oregon. Standifer grew up learning solid values and respect for the land, milking cows, slopping hogs, and walking two and a half miles to school if he missed the bus. He and his father plowed with a mule, planted fruit trees, and cleared land with a grub hoe.

Back in 1939, there wasn't much jazz around Gresham, though there was all kinds of black music at home:

> *My father sang and played guitar. He loved Josh White. Leadbelly. He'd have that guitar around the house and he'd sit around and do what he called "frammin'"—just grab something and play. My mother was a schoolteacher. She did church singing. I told her on two or three occasions, "Mother, you sound just like Bessie Smith," and she said, "Oh pshaw, go away from here, boy, that's blues, that's trashy music."*

Like Elmer Gill, Standifer counts his experience in the AME-Zion church as his first exposure to swing.

> *I'm talking about swinging singing. Hand-clapping, shouting. I got so I could tell when they were getting ready to shout, because that beat would start getting insistent. It would build, just like a good jazz set. You could feel the intensity. I was hip enough at the age of three or four to understand. I'd slide up under Mama because I knew somebody someplace was getting ready to shout. When you come up in that kind of atmosphere, swing used to be second nature.*

Floyd was first exposed to instrumental music in 1937, when he played drums in a

WPA kid band in Portland led by a teacher named Bert Turner.

Standifer had no other formal training. He plinked out melodies on the piano at home, imitating Basie, and took tunes off the radio. In high school, Standifer was interested in the trumpet, but because his music teacher thought he'd never make it on that instrument, the young musician was assigned the tuba. Meanwhile, Standifer taught himself to play a friend's alto saxophone. He finally got a trumpet of his own in his mid–high school years: "I used to play it in the fields. It was a beautiful echo. There was about a two-second delay. You could play and then the note would come back. This was on a hillside. You'd play a scale and then you could hear whether or not you played it right."

Radio brought the sounds of swing into the Standifer home—Harry James, Glenn Miller, Count Basie.

> *We had this one long room. My mother and father slept at one end, my baby brother slept next to them, my two sisters slept in this bed, and my middle brother and myself slept over here. At dinnertime, I would ask the family to be quiet so I could listen. There'd be these remotes coming in from L.A. Frankie Laine was brand new on the scene. People from Jantzen Beach and Portland. There was a western band that came there and they were bebopping.*

Floyd soon found a group of peers at Gresham Union High School, and they formed the Hot Club of Eastern Multnomah County. Exchanging precious copies of *Bandstand* magazine, they listened to records by Basie, Tommy Dorsey, Bunny Berigan, and Joe Thomas. Standifer remembers reading a story about young Corky Corcoran getting picked up by the Harry James band. Standifer worked in a cannery, stacking 500-pound barrels of frozen strawberries, to earn enough money to buy a secondhand turntable that would hook up to the family's Atwater-Kent console radio. The purchase led to his discovery of bebop. A friend brought him a Charlie Parker record, and from then on, Dorsey and Berigan were supplanted by Dodo Marmarosa and Miles Davis, Roy Eldridge and Anita O'Day, the Gramercy Five and Nat Cole. A friend dragged Floyd into Portland for a Coleman Hawkins all-star show in 1945, where they heard pianist Thelonious Monk.

The boys in the Hot Club of East Multnomah County were clean-cut achievers. Standifer was vice president of his class, and college-bound. His father had been recently transferred to Seattle; the family was to follow the next year. In 1946, Floyd headed for the University of Washington — and his future.

Standifer's father had a little white church with green steps at 23rd and Olive, a stone's throw from the YMCA where Ernestine Anderson had first sat in with Gerald Brashear in 1944. Standifer soon fell in with the same crowd. As he remembers:

> *One afternoon, I was walking down Madison. I had my horn with me. Right on that corner was a little restaurant, and right next to it was something that used to be a skating rink and was eventually called Birdland. I was walking past this, and in this building there was this group playing. I said "Man, that sounds just like that stuff I heard off those records." I stuck my head in there and I listened. It turned out to be Gerald Brashear and Buddy Brashear, on drums. I don't know who the piano player was. But they were playing bebop. I introduced myself to them. I said, "I'm going to school and man, this is the first time I've ever heard anybody play that stuff like on records." Gerald laughed.*

Gerald took Floyd over to the YMCA near his father's church, and Floyd started to jam there on Saturday nights for the kids' dances. They earned ten dollars a night apiece. It was there that he met Ernestine, Quincy, Buddy Catlett, Major Pigford, Charlie Taylor, Bumps Blackwell, and everyone else on the scene. For the next six years, Floyd worked with just about everybody in town, including Quincy, Billy Tolles, Bumps, and Ray Charles, plus musicians on the Annex scene. Throughout, he tried to keep his studies together, primarily at the University of Washington, then at Seattle University, then back at the UW. Stylistically, he says, the years 1947 to 1950 were the ones that formed him. Rhythm-and-blues shuffles with a bebop accent, played with fellows at the YMCA, were his foundation, followed by the influence of Fats Navarro, on records.

The Fats Navarro style, which applied an

elegant, even pressure to all registers of the trumpet and emphasized continuous eighth-note scales (unlike Dizzy's flamboyant, angular melodies) would become the dominant trumpet style of the 1950s, associated with the "hard bop" movement. Navarro's style was popularized by a young virtuoso named Clifford Brown. Standifer remembers Kenny Kimball calling him from New York, excited about Brown: "He said, 'Hey, man, there's a cat out here that sounds like you.'"

"Floyd Standifer was on a very high level," assesses Chuck Metcalf. "Floyd was a bebopper. Stone Fats Navarro, right away, highly evolved."

Being a more complex music, bop required not only fast reflexes and a sensitive ear, but also a working knowledge of theory and harmony. Standifer never studied theory, per se, but he gradually figured out what was going on. Many swing musicians at the time were still untutored, able to improvise in only three or four keys, at best, and not hearing the extensions and relationships between chords the beboppers used. Beboppers played in all twelve keys, and no chord progression was too complicated—or at least that was the goal. Standifer remembers when he noticed that he had reached this level:

*[We] were rehearsing "Valse Hot," by Sonny Rollins up at Birdland. And these cats pulled this new tune. I listened to it the first time, because I didn't know it. Somebody played the first solo and then they looked at me. Well, I had long ago figured out that if you could separate two-five-ones, you can convert that back to the scale, so you don't need to know the chords. So it was the same old two-five-ones. I just played it. Then I got arrogant on the second chorus and I decided I'd do a third one, just for the hell of it.*

Standifer emphasizes that despite the superior standards of the boppers, Seattle's music scene remained open to many levels and types of players. The kinds of tensions that developed between beboppers and swingers in other cities, for example, and between jazz musicians and commercial players, though they existed, were much less pronounced, possibly due to the smallness of the scene.

*If you played R & B, the cats still dug you. Cats like Al Hickey were considered to be good jazz players. "Big Jay" McNeely would come and we used to laugh, because he used to wear gloves with fluorescent lights and stuff like that. But we knew it was a show. Once you got Big Jay into the light, took off those fluorescent gloves, Big Jay could get out and play you some horn. He could flat play, man. Just because a guy played commercial, we didn't knock it.*

Standifer wasn't above taking a little commercial work himself. In 1957, he played on Seattle's first rock record, "Rock 'n' Roll Radio," with a group called Joe Boot and the Fabulous Winds. Pianist Ernie Hatfield and drummer Kenny Smith were also in the band. Standifer's willingness to play in all situations led him to most of the spots on Jackson Street, and the tight corners they sometimes led to. He has a warm, humorous memory of the after-hours scene:

*The weekend started on Thursday and it didn't stop until Monday morning at about eight o'clock. There was the Sessions Club. A guy named Jimmy Linegan ran that. This cat would play E-natural all night long. He kept a pistol on top of the piano. Later we'd go in there and play for people like Zenobia, or George Bernie, a cat who'd dance on tables. Pick tables up with his teeth. After these little acts, they'd "chase" the act off with "Lester Leaps In." That's why they call it a "chaser." Variety entertainment.*

*The first thing I learned, don't ever stand next to anybody in a raid. Keep your hands in your pockets. Don't take them out until you're told to. And when you do, make sure nobody's next to you, because you never know what'll end up in your pocket. Those were the days when I started carrying my horn either in a shopping bag or something light, because you could always keep it under your arm when you were running.*

*There was a camaraderie, a fraternalism, that doesn't seem to be here anymore. That's when unionism was really a fraternal thing. Then, if you played any kind of jazz at all, you were a member.*

The fraternalism whose passing Standifer laments would never really return. It was a

THE NORTHWEST JAZZ WORKSHOP PRESENTS
1956 SEAFAIR JAZZ FESTIVAL
MOORE THEATRE
Sunday, August 5th, 8:30 P.M.
No. 710

product of the special circumstances created by the black musicians' union and Washington's peculiar alcohol laws. In 1955, a group of enthusiastic musicians, including Floyd and Chuck Metcalf, briefly attempted to fill the void left by the demise of Local 493 and its "clubhouse" by banding together in an organization they called the Northwest Jazz Workshop (NWJW). In an old house on Roosevelt, north of 45th, they taught lessons, ran rehearsal bands, jammed, and staged concerts. The NWJW also produced a gala, locals-only concert at the Moore Theatre, tied in with Seafair, then a five-year-old, fledgling citywide summer festival. Dubbed the Seafair Jazz Festival, the concert took place on August 5, 1956, and featured Don Anderson's Dixielanders, the Paul Neves Quartet, Jimmy Glover's big band and Afro-Cuban septet, the Signatures, the Highlanders (a Renton youth quartet that sang on a locally produced television show, *Sheriff Tex*), Patti Summers, Don Lanphere, and Floyd Standifer. Eight hundred people attended.

The NWJW persisted for a couple of years, even broadcasting a live weekly radio show, on KUOW-FM, courtesy of Chuck Mahaffay, from the old Annex crowd. The workshop folded, says Mahaffay, because Paul Neves, who was a prime mover in the effort, went back to Boston.

Though the old 493 era could never quite be recaptured, as the fifties wore on, quality local jazz musicians such as Standifer and Metcalf began to form bonds in a series of new clubs that made the transition from the old Jackson Street scene to a more modern one. One of these transition venues was Elmer Gill's Ebony. Another was the Flame Tavern, an unpretentious brewery at 110th Street and

**The Norm Bobrow Little Big Band, c. 1952. Center photo, Norm Bobrow. Clockwise from upper left-hand corner: 1) Floyd Standifer; 2) The Signatures; 3) Mike DeFillipis; 4) Don Conway (seated, alto saxophone) and Fred Greenwell (tenor saxophone).**

**Courtesy of Fred Greenwell**

Above: Cathi Hayes.

Roosevelt Way with a horseshoe-shaped bar and a big fireplace.

From 1954 to 1959, Standifer made the Flame his home base, thanks to a call from keyboard man Milt Price. Standifer was still trying to put himself through school, undecided as to whether he wanted to study physics or music. He also had taken a day job, with the Military Sea Transportation Service. With the birth of his first son, in 1953, he began to get eyes for a steady "six-nighter"—a commercial gig where the check would be steady. One day, Price got hold of him:

> *Milt was playing organ and guitar out at the Flame Tavern. He'd heard me play saxophone and he asked me if I'd come play. I said, "Sure." I went out to the Flame in December of '54, middle of the month. That's the greatest Christmas we ever had.*

For three years, the power-jazz trio of Milt Price, Dave Stetler, and Floyd Standifer kept the fires alive at the Flame, blowing nearly every instrument known to jazz. Standifer doubled on saxophone; Milt Price was a multi-instrumentalist who played piano, alto and tenor saxophone, flute, guitar, and drums. He had grown up in Chicago with Ralph Davis, the drummer who had worked in the Jive Bombers. In Seattle by 1946, Price worked with Darryl Harpa, Bud Storm, Elmer Gill, and Billy Tolles. Price had a deep blues background and liked to play hard and funky.

Drummer Dave Stetler, for his part, had been making a smooth transition from swing to bop. Since his days with the "kid bands" and his 1945 trip to New York, he had put in time with Harpa, Wyatt Howard, and a variety of jazz combos at the New Chinatown, the black Elks Club, and the 908. In 1951, Stetler was at the Showbox with Norm Hoagy; right about this time he played on a fluke local country hit, "Navy Hot-rod Boogie." The slow scene in the early fifties forced him to take a day job at the Bellevue Post Office, where he stayed for fourteen years. He leapt at the chance to play real jazz with Floyd and Milt at the Flame, a period he counts as among his most musically satisfying:

> *We had one grand time. It was one of the most fun jobs I ever played. Even as tired as I was when I was playing at the Flame, I had more inspiration playing there and more fun, just straight-out, stretched-out, hard jazz, as hard as we could play, every night. We brought it up from somewhere. We were all tired, but we went ahead and did our thing and went home and collapsed. I had more fun with those guys than I've ever had with any musicians in my life.*

Price, Stetler, and Standifer had a good time, but they also played advanced modal bop. Discussing how the new approach mystified some of the old swingers, Standifer says, "This was the era when Corky [Corcoran] would come by and he'd say, 'How come you guys are playing all them scales?' Those were the days when we were searching. We were starting to get away from bebop and finding that hard modal-bop thing. Started to slide off into the Dorians and Phrygians. . . ."

Deejay Bob Summerise did a remote broadcast on KRSC from the Flame Tavern, helping to bring in the crowds. "I used to tell people they were only ten minutes from downtown," laughs Standifer. "I had guys coming in waving speeding tickets in my face."

Milt Price left the Flame in 1957 to form a more lucrative "one-man band" that would herald the canned music of lounges in the 1960s. Standifer continued at the club until 1959, with pianist Ernie Hatfield and, after Stetler, moved over to the Colony, with drummer Kenny Smith. Stetler continued his career into the nineties, backing up touring stars, playing casuals, and working in Dixieland groups.

Standifer joined Quincy Jones for the *Free and Easy* jaunt to Europe, where he subbed for Clark Terry on Paris club dates. When he returned in 1960, he "walked the bar" for a while, playing rock 'n' roll tenor saxophone with drummer Gerald Frank and pianist Dave Holden at a "go-go" dance club called the Pink Pussycat, on Yesler and Prefontaine. Working in 1962 with Norm Hoagy at the World's Fair, Standifer composed a beautiful jazz liturgy, *Postlude*, an open-voiced suite inspired by the sonorities of Quincy Jones and Gerry Mulligan. Standifer then supplemented work in the Cornish Jazz Sextet with lucrative commercial jobs in groups led by Frank Sugia and white violinist Joe Venuti. From 1965 to 1970 Standifer taught at

Cornish College of the Arts, followed by six years as an instructor at Olympic College, in Bremerton. By 1990, Floyd was leading his own group at the New Orleans Restaurant and working as the dean of humanities at the Northwest School.

The Flame held on to its jazz policy through the early sixties. Ernie Hatfield took the gig for several years, and in 1961, Gerald Brashear had a trio there with drummer Gerald Frank, whose group at the Mardi Gras was so popular. While the Flame Tavern was at its peak, another important transition venue sprang up in the North End as well—the Lake City Tavern. A barn of a place on the corner of 130th and Lake City Way, where students carried pitchers of beer to other college kids sitting at long picnic tables, the club was opened in 1955 by two University of Washington law students.

It spawned a variety of memorable groups. One of the best-loved among them was the Signatures, an upbeat white ensemble inspired by the hip, close harmonies of the Hi-Lo's, and featuring Bob and Ruth Alcivar, Lee Humes, Cathi Hayes, and Gus Mancuso. Hayes and Mancuso, a multi-instrumentalist and vocalist, also put together an innovative white jazz band at the Lake City called Gus and Us, with drummer Dave Coleman, tenor saxophonist Joe Romano, and pianist Jerry Gray.

Traditional jazz enjoyed a revival at the Lake City Tavern, too. Seattle's Rainy City Jazz Band, formed in 1946, played there often. The original members were Gordon Greimes (clarinet), Boots Houlihan (cornet), Jack Sheedy (trombone), Lowell Richards (tuba), Dolph Bleiler (drums), and Barry Vye (piano).

A less strictly traditional white group also formed at the Lake City Tavern—the Seattle Rhythm Kings, named with tongue-in-cheek bravado after a classic early jazz band, the New Orleans Rhythm Kings. The group was led by trumpeter Don Anderson, who was from Yakima, but had worked for years in the MGM studios in Los Angeles and played in the original Spike Jones Orchestra. (Anderson, who died in the 1970s, is not to be confused with the other Seattle Don Anderson, a trombonist who grew up in Seattle and played in Dixieland groups such as the Island City Jazz Band.) In addition to trumpeter Anderson, the Seattle Rhythm Kings included Rollie Morehouse, clarinet; Mike Hobi, trombone; Red Kelly, bass; John Wittwer, piano; and Dave Coleman, drums.

John Wittwer spent some time in San Francisco, where he played intermission piano for Earl Hines at the Hangover Club. He also became friendly with Kenneth Patchen, who along with Kenneth Rexroth, had started a vogue for reading poetry to live jazz. This and other beat-era styles moved north to Seattle and became major ingredients in the modern jazz clubs that opened there. Jerry Rosen, a San Francisco–based author (*Blues for a Dying Nation*, *The Carmen Miranda Memorial Flagpole*) who spent a year in Seattle as a young man in the late fifties, has written a novel set in Seattle's beat scene in which he captures with Kerouac-like verve the quality of feeling suddenly at large during that era. As

**Floyd Standifer at the Trianon Ballroom, summer 1948.**

**Photo by Harold Kaminske**

**Courtesy of Chuck Mahaffay**

he walks into a Seattle jazz club, Rosen's protagonist says:

> *Jazz clubs were the only institutions in America in which I did not feel alienated at that time. The jazz people were my nation, the clubs our temples. . . . Jazz was not, for many of us, simply another form of entertainment, but it constituted rather a last sanctuary, our only hope, the underground religion of a racially integrated sub-culture, where blacks and whites could engage in the ceremonies of welcoming each other to the new color-blind society which we felt was coming into existence before our eyes . . . .*

**Dave Coleman.**
**Courtesy of Noreen Coleman**

Pete's Poop Deck, the Penthouse, and Dave's Fifth Avenue were the first Seattle nightclubs to fulfill the sacred function Rosen describes and as such were the city's first true modern jazz clubs. Dave's Fifth Avenue was opened by Dave Levy in 1957, across the street from where a new city landmark would soon be erected for the upcoming World's Fair—the Space Needle. At Dave's, fans gathered to hear Billy Tolles, Ernestine Anderson, and occasional touring acts such as Jay McNeely and Cal Tjader. Stars like Miles Davis and Dexter Gordon dropped by to jam. "The rest of Seattle was out on their boats," says Rosen, "and we were inside this dark tavern on a sunny afternoon, listening to jazz. We felt like we knew about something everyone else had missed."

One of the most important "inside" events at Dave's was the birth of the Mastersounds, the best-selling jazz group ever to come out of Seattle. The Mastersounds was the pet project of bassist Monk Montgomery, who had left Elmer Gill's gig at the New Washington Hotel. The quartet featured Monk, his brother Buddy on vibes, plus Indianapolis drummer Benny Barth and Montana pianist Richie Crabtree.

The Mastersounds opened at Dave's Fifth Avenue in January 1957. The group was an instant success, holding the crowds for three months. Mixing jazz tunes such as "Dexter's Deck" and "The Chase" with standards and songs from Broadway shows, the group opened each selection with an arrangement that carefully melded the sound of piano, vibes, bass, and drums. The sound was mellow and dynamically controlled, but the emphasis was still on swing, unlike that of the Modern Jazz Quartet or the Dave Brubeck Quartet.

A local engineer named Joe Boles brought his equipment into Dave's Fifth Avenue and recorded the Mastersounds live. Monk drove south and sold the tapes to Pacific Jazz Records, which released them in 1957, as *Jazz Showcase*. Between 1957 and 1960, the group made a series of extremely popular albums, the most famous of which was *The King and I*. (Broadway jazz albums and original cast albums had become a fad, as the musical comedy enjoyed a comeback.) The Mastersounds disbanded in 1960, but not before introducing the world to guitarist Wes Montgomery, who played on several of the albums and went on to revolutionize jazz guitar.

The Mastersounds left their mark on Seattle by introducing the college crowd to modern, arranged jazz. Before the Mastersounds, there had been the arranged trio music of Elmer Gill and Ray Charles and Milt Green; there had been the big bands of Al Pierre and Bumps Blackwell; there had been the raucous jazz-jamming of groups such as Floyd Standifer's at the Flame; and there had been the burning tempos of Cecil Young's bebop. But there had been nothing like the Mastersounds, a modern, four-piece group that incorporated the latest developments in jazz into listenable, swinging music of the highest caliber. Part of the beauty of this was that the jazz listeners in Seattle knew the group had been spawned on their own ground. It gave them a sense of participation and ownership in the national jazz scene they had never experienced before. As a jazz town, Seattle was growing up.

Seattle jazz took another leap forward when Pete's Poop Deck opened in the Pioneer Square district at the foot of Main Street, under the Alaskan Way viaduct. Pioneer Square was not a fashionable club-and-restaurant area in 1957, but a dreary, down-and-out mission district, so Pete's was something of a bold gamble. The Poop Deck was opened in the fall of 1957 by a clever twenty-year-old jazz fan named Pete Barbas. His establishment was the first self-consciously styled modern jazz club in Seattle, mingling a "beatnik pad" decor of apple crates, wooden benches, and peanut shells on the floor with a seagoing motif of fishnets and blown-glass floats. Local painters hung their oils on the walls; a mannequin sculpted into a mermaid hung from the ceiling. Poets came to recite their work, artists sketched in the corner, and the bearded Barbas himself worked behind the bar. Every once in a while, during a set, a train would go by under the viaduct and disrupt a quiet ballad, but that, too, was part of the ambience. The place could only hold 140 customers or so, but during its five and a half years on the scene, Pete's Poop Deck was rarely empty.

"People used to sit out in the rain with newspapers over their head and have to wait till the set was over so they could probably get in and sit on a soapbox," recalls saxophonist Jabo Ward, who put in some of his finest work at Pete's. "Pete didn't care what you played as long as it was jazz. And everybody that came there—that's what they wanted to hear, was jazz. And the place stayed packed."

Barbas was a masterful publicist, securing items in the dailies on a regular basis. (The club even found its way into a Sidney Sheldon potboiler, *Rage of Angels*.) Pete's hosted the finest jazz musicians in town—as well as presenting out-of-towners such as Cal Tjader, Chris Connor, Barney Kessel, and Mongo Santamaria—establishing a standard for jazz clubs that would follow. Pops Buford led the club's first local group; the band that succeeded Pops' was fronted by a saxophone/flute double-threat of Jabo Ward and Bob Winn (a white newcomer from Detroit), with Jerry Gray (piano), Milt Garred (bass), and Bill Richardson (drums), also from the Motor City.

Pete's was the staging ground for the high point of Jabo Ward's career. Since leaving Al Pierre after his disastrous Alaska tour in 1951, Ward had led his own groups at the Far East Veterans Club, with Dee Dee Hackett doing vocal chores (1951–1953), and at the New Chinatown (1954–1956). In the Poop Deck era, Ward was smitten by the innovations of tenor saxophonist John Coltrane, who had pushed jazz harmony and improvising

Pete's Poop Deck, 1958–1961. Left to right: Jerry Gray, Bob Winn, Milt Garred, Jabo Ward, Bill Richardson. Courtesy of Pete Barbas

intensity to a new level. Attempting at first to decipher on his own the complicated ins and outs of Coltrane's approach, Ward sent for a mail-order course from the Berklee School of Music in Boston, Quincy Jones' alma mater. In 1955, Ward also began playing flute, studying with Victor Case of the Seattle Symphony and Joe Lazire, a local flute repairman. Jabo took his newly won chops into Pete's in 1958 and for the next three years knocked over audiences there. He says: "Everything came together there—people, place, owner, the music—it was terrific. Pete let us play anything we wanted, and we wanted bebop. Working for Pete for two years, like I did, there was never anything said about what I played or when I played. Nothing."

Ward's style is ferocious on tenor, mixing Coltrane, Lucky Thompson, and the note-happy aggression of Sonny Stitt into one big-toned, expressive, well-executed style, solidly in the tradition. For the Poop Deck gig, Jabo played flute and alto and tenor saxophones. His flute duets with Bob Winn at Pete's on "My

Funny Valentine" and "Little Girl Blue" are still fondly remembered.

After Pete's, Ward gave up being a leader and started to cut back on his jazz work. He had taken a day job in the 1950s, driving, delivering, and repairing golf carts. In 1966, he went to work for Texaco Oil. In 1964 he started giving private lessons and worked private parties and occasional special events. During the eighties, he was part of a popular cooperative, the Inner City Jazz Quartet, with Ernie Hatfield, white drummer Pete Madsen, and bassist Terry Morgan, which played festivals and opened for national acts, such as Freddie Hubbard. Though his appearances fell off in the late eighties, the Jackson Street veteran still is raised to the heights of enthusiasm about music:

> *What you do through your horn is project your own feelings. Whether it's slow, fast, or medium, I'm still projecting feelings, see. And soul is one of the greatest things to have in music. SOUL . . . SOUL. Project your inner self through the bell of that instrument . . .*

At some point, Jabo was replaced in the Poop Deck band by Gerald Brashear. Brashear had been gigging around the area since the Cecil Young Quartet days, although, as with his pal Milt Garred, drugs and alcohol had made his career erratic. At the Poop Deck, Brashear was famous for a melodic solo he played on congas with his elbow, as well as for his remarkable tenor and vocal chops. Brashear worked in Seattle throughout the sixties, at one point backing up Zenobia, the shake dancer, at Earl Mack's club. By then, he too had picked up Coltrane influences, adding a Trane-ish cry and modal scales to his woody tone. Brashear plays on a laid-back Wyatt Ruther album, *Easy Living with the Wyatt Ruther IV*, recorded in Vancouver, British Columbia, around 1970. By then, he sounded somewhat tired. He died soon afterwards.

The bass player in the Poop Deck band was already well-known to Seattleites through his work with Ray Charles. Since the McSon Trio days, Milt Garred had, like Pony Poindexter, spent time in prison because of his drug addiction. Garred was in and out of jail throughout the 1950s and 1960s, drinking heavily when he was trying to get off heroin, notoriously as unreliable as he was brilliant—but, along with Chuck Metcalf, he continued to be the bass player of choice for anyone in town really serious about jazz. A 1972 private recording made at Seattle Center shows Garred to have kept intact his big, boomy sound and elastic attack, while becoming even more adept at weaving a line through the harmony. Garred died in 1978.

Working with Milt and Bill Richardson in the rhythm section at the Poop Deck was pianist Jerry Gray, who had gotten started at the Lake City Tavern. Gray is an enigma. Reputed by musicians to be the best pianist who ever played in Seattle, today he is a reclusive teacher who has not performed in public for over twenty years.

When Gray was a child, his right hand had been burned in an accident, and the fingers were webbed together. To compensate, he developed his left hand to phenomenal proportions, deciding he was going to be the next Art

JABO WARD QUINTETTE

MILT GARRED bass
BILL RICHARDSON drums
BOB WINN flute - alto
Jazz
JABO WARD tenor - flute
GERRY GRAY piano

Wed • Thurs • Fri • Sat

**Jabo Ward, 1959.**
**Photo by Egill Gustafson**

Jerry Gray, 1962. Courtesy of Chuck Mahaffay

"Originals at the Piano"
Gerry Gray
Every Monday and Tuesday Evening
PETE'S POOP DECK

Tatum. He became an even more powerful player when he had his right hand operated on, around 1960.

A 1964 recording reveals Gray as a supremely logical, swinging player with crisp execution and drive, who means everything he plays and plays everything he means. In 1965, Gray arranged and played on a lovely album of standards for Joni Metcalf, *Joni Sings Porter and Ellington with the Jerome Gray Trio*, with Chuck Metcalf on bass and George Griffin on drums. The last gig anyone seems to remember him playing was around 1966. "He quit drinking, smoking, and playing music in public all in the same day," recalls Metcalf. "It was like he walked through a door into a different life."

Gray's sudden exit from the jazz life was apparently an expression of his dissatisfaction with his own progress. "I came to the wrong town," Gray told Maggie Hawthorn. "Very few people here thought of themselves as going anywhere or doing anything particularly consequential. There was a kind of 'We're just folks' attitude here. It was disastrous for me."

Gray retreated to his studio, where he wrote and published a series of method books. A slight, intense man with a cherubic face, he continues to wield a tremendous influence locally through his teaching, which is as much about method as it is a sort of counseling practice about focusing one's goals and life in the music business. Musicians from Diane Schuur to Wayne Horvitz have taken a lesson or two from this virtuoso pianist and theorist. In the nineties, Gray could be found about town, listening to the progress of his students in various clubs or catching the great piano players like Tommy Flanagan or Hank Jones when they came to town.

All the activity in the late fifties and early sixties prompted bassist Chuck Metcalf to revive his career. Metcalf had been fairly quiet throughout the 1950s, raising a family and practicing architecture. In 1960, he joined white pianist Dick Palumbi and Richardson in a house trio at the Penthouse, a posh new club at First and Cherry. When the owner began to book name players such as Dexter Gordon, Harold Land, and Carmel Jones, the Palumbi trio backed them up. In 1962, vocalist Anita O'Day hired the trio off the bandstand for a tour, which took Metcalf to Los Angeles, where he performed on television with Lou Rawls and played with Buddy Greco. Greco hired Palumbi as his accompanist, and Metcalf returned to Seattle, working jazz and commercial gigs throughout the sixties. In 1966, Metcalf and Lowell Richards started the Seattle Jazz Society, and in 1969, Metcalf toured Vietnam with pianist Overton Berry. A long commercial gig in the summer of 1972 convinced Metcalf he needed to get away from Seattle if he wanted to pursue jazz seriously, so he moved to San Francisco, where he became a first-call sideman, playing with Eddie Henderson, Sonny Simmons, Woody Shaw, Charlie Byrd, and others, and recording with vocalist Mark Murphy, avant-garde drummer Doug Hammond, and a cooperative group called San Francisco Ltd.

In 1979, Metcalf moved to New York City. The next year he was hired by Dexter Gordon for a five-month tour of Europe and the States, after which he returned to San Francisco. In 1982, Metcalf resumed his career in Seattle. With the exception of a two-year break in 1984–1985, when he lived in Wales and Holland (and recorded with pianist Albert Sarko), Metcalf has been a stalwart of the Seattle scene ever since. In 1991 he recorded *Live at the Zoo* with saxophonist Bert Wilson and released a CD of his own tunes, *Elsie Street*, in the hard-bop tradition he had learned as a young man; in 1992, he released *Help Is Coming*.

Metcalf is a solidly grounded, blues-based player whose style, knowledge, and dues-paying experiences on the road made him an elder statesman to whom local players turned for mentoring in the jazz life. His grasp of harmony and structure, particularly—perhaps a reflection of his architecture background—are a constant source of pleasure. In 1985, he was cited as one of the "bassists who have contributed to jazz music over the past 65 years" in Todd Coolman's book *The Bass Tradition*.

In 1962, Pete Barbas sold the Poop Deck. His nightclub had been part of a literal renaissance on the Seattle jazz scene as tourists and businesses rolled in with the World's Fair. The Penthouse, across First Avenue from where Al Pierre had held forth in the 1940s at the Union Club, began to bring in national acts every week. John Coltrane would eventually release an album that was recorded there, *Live in Seattle*. The Noplace, at Occidental and Washington Street, operated from 1960 to 1962, featuring Gerald Brashear, Al Larkins, and Dave Coleman, among others. The Door, an espresso coffeehouse on Sixth Avenue, also became a destination for jazz fans, where Bill Ramsay, Chuck Metcalf, Bud Schultz, Elmer Gill, Floyd Standifer, and others performed. The Townhouse, at Denny and Stewart, served for a year or so as a favorite jamming spot, as well. Between 1957 and 1963, nine Seattle clubs were presenting modern jazz—the Ebony, Flame, Mardi Gras, Dave's Fifth Avenue, Lake City Tavern, Pete's Poop Deck, the Noplace, the Door, and the Penthouse. (Another curious spot called Gabe's featured recorded jazz that fans could listen to through earphones.) Several clubs also opened to feature Dixieland, including Ronnie Pierce's establishment in Pioneer Square, the Roaring 20s club at the fairgrounds itself, and the New Washington Hotel, where Wingy Manone played. Bob Summerise, the disc jockey who had broadcast from the Flame, noted in a weekly column, "The town may seem dead, but Seattle is one of the most active jazz cities on the West Coast."

Even with the bustling jazz activity of the 1960s, some national musicians continued to think of Seattle as a remote spot in the woods where they could recuperate from the trials and tribulations of the jazz life. So it was for the pioneering violinist Joe Venuti, who visited a friend in Seattle in 1957 and moved there permanently in 1963 to "dry out." In the bargain, Venuti treated local audiences—who often had no idea who he was—to a steady diet of amazing swing violin and shenanigans until his death, in 1978.

Other musicians played important roles in the burgeoning scene of the early 1960s, as well. One was the white bassist Freddy Schreiber, a brilliant musician who grew up in Seattle and later toured and recorded with Cal Tjader. Schreiber's discovery early in life that he had a terminal liver disease seems to have given him a dark, upside-down humor that spilled into everything he did. After a *down beat* reviewer praised his playing at the expense of other players on Tjader's album *Saturday Night, Sunday Night at the Black Hawk,* Schreiber penned a retort, satirizing the inflated language of jazz critics: "I think [the reviewer] was very fair in putting down Cal and the other guys in the group," wrote the bassist, "but I really think he should have listened to me more carefully. Evidently he did not listen closely to my angular, probing lines and I am sure that not once did he take note of my relentless throbbing beat."

"Freddy was so funny," recalls Elmer Gill, who worked with the bassist at Ivar's, after Jerry Gray left the gig. "Right up until he died, he never lost his sense of humor. He was in a wheelchair and I called him up and he said, 'Man, I sure hope you're not calling me up for a gig.' This was about a week before he died." Schreiber died in 1965.

Another important musician on the early-sixties scene was Don Lanphere's old friend from Wenatchee, white pianist Jack Brownlow, about whom Paul Desmond, Dave Brubeck's saxophonist, was once reported to have said, "If I could play the piano, I'd want to sound like Jack Brownlow."

There was also Dick Palumbi's vocalist, Teddy Ross, who hit town with ten cents in his pocket and wound up on Broadway, playing

in the hit production *The Wiz*, then in the film *Arthur* (as the chauffeur). There was white comedian Pete Barbutti, a fine pianist in his own right, who cut his teeth on the Seattle scene during the World's Fair, then went on to Las Vegas and the "Tonight Show" as a comedian. Larry Rockwell, a bassist who worked with Sarah Vaughan, was also on the scene in the late 1950s. And of course, the bluesy Overton Berry, who as early as 1958 was playing with his trio at the Calypso, and would serve as Diane Schuur's accompanist during her years of struggle in the seventies and eighties before becoming one of Seattle's favorite lounge pianists.

Pete Barbas had been prescient in seeing that the Skid Road area around Pioneer Square could eventually become a lively nightclub district. It was long after he "pioneered" the area that the city followed his lead. But Barbas benefited from another development, a shift in local attitude related to the coming of the World's Fair itself. Prior to the 1950s, Seattle was a town on the margins, and apparently quite happy about it. Old Seattleites—in fact, northwesterners in general—took pride in their isolation and were almost pleased that no one knew much about them. There was a hidden quality to the place, and the natives liked to think of it as a secret. Beat writer Jack Kerouac captured this sense when he visited briefly on his way to work as a fire lookout in the Cascades, describing Seattle as the "City in the Shroud"—furtive, hidden by clouds—a little spooky, but quiet, meditative, and somewhat spiritual. It was precisely this hidden-away quality that allowed the pioneer-era bootlegging scene to flourish. Likewise, musicians who took part in these goings-on, as Jerry Gray has suggested, never imagined that what they were doing had any importance. Isolated in the northwest corner of the country, hidden by clouds, working in a market far from the pulse of things—New York, Los Angeles—they could carry on their work without anyone really paying any mind.

Sometime in the 1950s all of this changed. Seattle decided it wanted to be noticed. One of the first things it had to do to accomplish this was to shed the image of the pioneer, loggers-and-Indians town on the marshes of Elliott Bay it had been stuck with for almost a century and replace it with a more sanitized, forward-looking one. In 1951, the city started this process by replacing its traditional Potlatch Festival, during which Native Americans had gathered to trade and celebrate at various points around Lake Washington, with a Scandinavian festival based on a pirate theme. In keeping with the technology worship that had evolved around the Boeing Company and the Cold War, the festival planners plunked a hydroplane race in the middle of the event. Thus was born Seafair, which continues to this day as a source of great pleasure for children and an annual embarrassment for sophisticates, who are perhaps still not as welcome in Seattle as those city organizers would have wished.

Not long after Seafair was established, the city fathers also decided they wanted to have another fair, a big shindig that would show off their progressive and futuristic city. After many years of planning, Century-21, usually called the Seattle World's Fair, was mounted at the site of the old Civic Auditorium and Armory, both of which were converted and made part of a new civic garden christened Seattle Center. As a monument to technological futurism, the city built the Space Needle. It also invited the rest of the world in to look. Seattle's shroud was pierced.

This was a major psychological change for the city, a mood swing it hadn't known since the days of the AYP Exposition in 1909, and it closed the door forever on the innocent days of the after-hours scene on Jackson Street. Many old-timers resented the change, feeling that Seattle had been a better, less pretentious town when it was a private, unaffected affair. The curmudgeonly newspaper columnist Emmett Watson even founded a mock organization, Lesser Seattle, to commemorate his distaste for Seattle's newfound boosterism. Though Watson kept his tongue firmly in cheek, Lesser Seattle had (and has) about it a hint of Northwest truth in its parochialism and xenophobia. But the Northwest also has a genuine affection and nostalgia for such personal and human-scale activities as the scene that once flourished along Jackson Street, a scene that from the 1960s forward would become increasingly invisible and forgotten, until finally it was buried, like the Potlatch Festival itself, except in the memories of those who had once been there.

# 11 JACKSON STREET a lost legacy?

Even if Seattle had been of a mind to keep its shadow side exposed after the World's Fair, there were forces at work that would have prevented after-hours jazz from becoming a part of the program. In the mid-sixties, when rock music rose to dominate popular music, mainstream jazz nearly died out, not only in Seattle but all over the country. For almost a decade, there wasn't any room for jazz in record stores, on the radio, or in nightclubs. In Seattle, Dave's Fifth Avenue had split its bookings from the start between rock and jazz; soon it went all rock. The Mardi Gras and Poop Deck closed in the early years of the decade, and the Penthouse folded in 1968. The other clubs that had risen around the ballyhoo of the beatnik era and the World's Fair, such as the Door and the Downbeat, also went dark.

Players who couldn't adapt to the new situation often retreated from the scene in despair or died of one form of frustration or another. Ernestine Anderson stopped performing. So did Buddy Catlett. Floyd Standifer and Jabo Ward became less active. Leon Vaughn stopped playing altogether. Bob Winn, opting for commercial music and steady work, moved to Honolulu. Traff Hubert hung it up. So did Major Pigford and Roscoe Weathers. Billy Tolles and Tommy Adams turned to rock, and Tommy died young. Cecil Young and Jimmie Rodgers had both died. Bill Richardson, Vernon Brown, Gerald Brashear, Winfield King, Milt Garred, and Al Larkins followed them to the grave at the end of that difficult era. For a decade, the jazz musicians who survived were pushed aside, or forced to play more commercial music.

Just as the rock avalanche fell, the reform-minded city hall dealt the coup de grace to the last vestiges of the "tolerance policy" and the culture of corruption that went with it. In 1967, a downtown-Seattle tavern owner complained to the FBI that the cops on the beat were trying to extort protection money from him. Over the next three years, a series of investigations and a book, *On the Take*, led to an exposé of the nasty system of police payoffs and graft that had supported Seattle's gambling, prostitution, and bootlegging for more than half a century.

It was not a pretty story. It was revealed that the tolerance policy, while in itself a victimless crime that had allowed people to have a good time, also supported a system in which police officers—much like organized criminals—demanded protection money even from owners who had nothing to hide. Those who didn't "pay to stay," as the policy came to be called, were simply hounded out of business. (It was shown, for example, that the vice squad harassed gay bars, driving customers away, then demanded payments in exchange for allowing owners to reopen.) The exposé resulted in a departmental bloodbath. The police chief resigned in 1969 and the assistant police chief was indicted and convicted of perjury. Fourteen other officers resigned or took early retirement, including two assistant chiefs, two majors, one captain, three lieutenants, three sergeants, a detective, and two officers. A federal grand jury also indicted Frank Colacurcio, the reputed mobster who owned several clubs. The chief of the City Council, Charles M. Carroll, the man who had shut down the Washington Social Club as a public nuisance, admitted to taking $6,750 in bribes.

When the tolerance policy officially collapsed, it was directly supporting only two after-hours clubs, the 605 and the New Chinatown (both closed after the investigation), so the consequences for working jazz musicians were negligible. However, its timing, coinciding as it did with the rise of rock, contributed to a curious disjunction in local jazz history. For almost a decade, there was so little local jazz played in Seattle that when the music finally did make a comeback, around 1976, the fans—and even many local musicians—had no idea Jackson Street had ever existed.

Seattle musicians in the 1980s were not even aware that Quincy Jones, Ray Charles, or Patti Bown had worked in the same town they were scuffling in. Even fewer knew who Al Pierre or Bumps Blackwell were. It was as if the musical past, like the corruption that had supported it, had been expunged from the town's official history, as if it were an unpleasant memory. The result was a jazz scene sadly cut off from its own past. Older black musicians, in particular, who had participated in the lively Jackson Street era felt passed over when the jazz scene revived, somehow robbed of what should have been their own legacy.

But what is that legacy? With the Jackson Street era in full view, can it be said with any assurance that there is a relationship between the old scene and the present one? In short, does Seattle have a jazz "tradition"?

Yes. Standifer, Catlett, Anderson, and Metcalf—among others—are living testimony to the continuity of such a tradition. Their careers bridge the Jackson Street era and the present. Further, the flow from the bottle club culture to the modern jazz bistros of the contemporary scene, though less obvious, is precisely what gives Seattle jazz its authenticity and depth today.

But "tradition" is a tricky word. In the simplest sense of historical continuity, one can accurately speak of the city as having had a long, if previously unrecognized, tradition of jazz performance and players, with profound connections to the story of the music at large. Many of the musicians who still perform in Seattle trace their roots to Jackson Street; families such as the Holdens, Barnetts, and Hendrixes boast specific local lineages; and Seattle players such as Kenny G and Diane Schuur continue to make it in the mainstream. However, in the sense that "tradition" means a cultural infrastructure of elders that assigns values and creates standards, Seattle has not had a bonafide tradition, the way the East Coast does. Since the demise of Jackson Street, musical values tend to be passed on in schools, not on the street, and no one standard or style seems able to assert itself with authority.

Significant regional styles usually come about when a particular player's approach is so compelling that others imitate it. Though there were strong, individual stylists in Seattle—Dick Wilson, Fred Greenwell, and Gerald Wiggins come to mind—their approaches did not dominate other players, perhaps because these potentially influential musicians didn't stay in town long enough.

As a result, there is no significant Seattle style. However, stylistic connections between Jackson Street's bluesy bebop and the current scene persist. The legacy is rather faint, but there are threads. Most obvious is the music still being made by the survivors themselves.

In Floyd Standifer's straight-ahead bop with a modal twist, one can hear echoes of Jackson Street shuffles and blues. In Buddy Catlett, one hears the same solid time, big sound, and soulful values the bassist had when he was playing with Count Basie and Quincy Jones. In a more nostalgic vein, Catlett's Sunday-night jam sessions at Lofurno's Restaurant in the late eighties and early nineties, according to people like Sonny Booker, were the last living vestige of the feeling that existed on Jackson Street so many years ago, when instrumentalists and vocalists came by to jam and sing, and the feeling was easy and convivial. Jabo Ward's swing-to-bebop fire fit right into the Lofurno's scene. And Chuck Metcalf, though his roots lie more in the fifties, still has that link to basic swing and blues feeling that can only have come from many nights at the Elks Club. In 1990, Ward, Standifer, Catlett, Elmer Gill, and a younger drummer named Patti Padden formed the 493 Reunion Band, commemorating the after-hours scene on Jackson Street.

But if it's true that there are connections between past and present, that the Jackson Street tradition lives on in some contemporary voices, what is the quality of that tradition? Chuck Metcalf, with a gentle skepticism, is loath to exaggerate the musical standards that obtained on Jackson Street. In his reckoning, for example, it would have been hard to put together two good bebop bands in Seattle in 1950, largely because of a scarcity of "hot" drummers. There was also the problem that excellent players tended to move away:

> *All of the real heavyweights, the people that really felt themselves to be talented and really had ambitions for themselves in the music business, man, they were out of here! Quincy Jones! Out of high school,*

blam! *Patti Bown, the same way. Bill Crow went right to New York and became a success. [Bassist] Larry Rockwell went to New York. [Bassist] Freddy Schreiber went down to California and almost instantaneously was working with Cal Tjader. The really talented ones, except for Floyd and Jerry Gray and a few others, didn't stay.*

But Metcalf himself was one of the "really talented ones," and he stayed, at least until 1970. And while there is some justification to his criticisms, in voicing them he slights himself. Jackson Street didn't produce musicians to rival Dizzy Gillespie and Charlie Parker, true. But Jackson Street had so much when most people—even those who lived nearby—thought it had nothing at all, that the point would seem to be its very existence and authenticity, not its competitiveness with the national scene. Besides, Jackson Street did nurture musicians such as Quincy Jones, Patti Bown, and Freddie Greenwell, whether they stayed in town or not. And time and time again, it connected with the national scene in a way that was productive both for locals and musicians on the larger stage.

A good illustration of this kind of interchange was the contribution of alto saxophonist Joe Brazil, who arrived from Detroit in 1962. Brazil was a better mover and shaker than he was a musician, but after working at the Mardi Gras with another Detroit emigrant who arrived the same year, vocalist Woody Woodhouse, and at the Poop Deck and the Penthouse, he established the Black Academy of Music (later renamed the Brazil Academy of Music) with the notion of passing on African-American traditions to youngsters in the neighborhood. Milt Garred, Jabo Ward, Floyd Standifer, and others played and taught at the academy, and Brazil also collared name artists who came through town—including Dizzy Gillespie, Joe Henderson, and Stanley Turrentine—to come talk to the kids. It's amazing how many black musicians of a certain age mention the Black Academy of Music (BAM) as their first and only source of real jazz inspiration and education. Sam Chambliss, Ed Lee, George Hurst, Omar Brown, and the young bassist Doug Barnett, Jr. (the grandson of Powell Barnett) had some of their first chances at sight-reading big-band charts, arranging, improvising, and theory at the BAM. Brazil later recorded with John Coltrane in a marathon twelve-hour session, in Lynnwood, Washington, after Coltrane's live album was finished at the Penthouse. The tapes were issued on the LP *Om*.

Two young musicians who worked with Joe Brazil went on to prominent national careers. Bassist Rufus Reid lived in Seattle from 1966 to 1969, studying at Olympic College in Bremerton and working in Seattle at Rosellini's Four-10 and at the Checkmate, a club opened in 1966 by Sonny Booker. As a kid, Carlos Ward played with vocalist Ron Holden, keyboard man Dave Lewis, and bandleader Terry Cruise, then came to international attention in the eighties as the lead alto player with Abdullah Ibrahim's band, Ekaya. Ward, whose interests turned toward the avant-garde, often jammed at a coffeehouse called the Llahngaelhyn, just south of the University Bridge, run by an eccentric white pianist/bassist named Jerry Heldman.

A variety of very important young musicians, including Ward, Larry Coryell, Ralph Towner, Walter Zuber Armstrong, David Friesen, and Ron Soderstrom learned to improvise free jazz there. Heldman admired Scott La Faro and Gary Peacock, both bassists with a rhythmically sprung, guitar-like approach to the instrument, moving it away from timekeeping to an expressive, supple counterweave against the rhythmic line. (Peacock moved to Seattle in 1966, but was not fully active as a player until a decade later, when he joined the Cornish faculty; his influence on Heldman was through records.)

"The Llahngaelhyn had a very great influence on the music in this place," says white bassist David Friesen, who remembers jam sessions that went on all night at the club.

The Llahngaelhyn scene is a kind of missing link in Seattle jazz history. For while it was a hotbed of avant-gardism and free jazz, the music played there also remained grounded in blues, bebop, and swing tradition. Part of the reason for this was that Heldman himself had spent time on the old after-hours scene, where he had developed a firm respect for tradition. Another reason may have been the earthy, no-nonsense nature of the Northwest itself. Unlike California, Washington never seems to have abandoned a fundamental sense of swing and blues, no matter how "cosmic" its music became. This respect for fundamentals carried over in the music of the Llahngaelhyn's heirs.

Probably the most obvious example can be found in white bassist Michael Bisio, whose quintet CD, *In Seattle*, made several critical Top Ten lists in 1990. Bisio is a modern player with a Charlie Haden–like sound and a feeling for composition very much like Charles Mingus'. His music has an "inside/outside" feel, with a kind of moody space around a blues feeling in the line. White trumpeter Ron Soderstrom, who spent his formative years at the Llahngaelhyn coffeehouse learning to play free jazz, works with Bisio. There is a direct line between what's happening in Bisio's music and the aesthetics that evolved at Heldman's cafe. (Dave Friesen, who heard *In Seattle* "blindfolded," agrees: "That record we just heard, with Ron Soderstrom? That's like a very reserved, very tame [version] of [the] playing that came out of the Llahngaelhyn.")

The more Northwest music one hears, the better this seemingly tenuous bridge starts to hold up. No matter how "far out" musicians in the region seem to go, there is always a strain of healthy conservatism about line, blues, and traditional jazz feeling that anchors them, a graceful balance of heaven and earth. This certainly applies to the area's most amazing contemporary musician, saxophonist Denney Goodhew, who has recorded with white trumpet player and composer Jim Knapp on the ECM label. But it also feels accurate for Knapp himself, for the band of former Cornish students called Timebone (Briggan Krause, Arnold Hammerschlag, and Aaron Alexander), the gentle, run-on compositions of the fine pianist Dave Peck, the steady time and linear inventiveness of pianist Marc Seales, the Bill Frisell–inspired sounds of guitarist Brad Schoeppach, the open, Paul Motian–like drumming of Mike Sarin, and the world fusion creations of the Big Daddy of all Northwest groups, Oregon.

Perhaps the continuity between contemporary Seattle jazz and the Llahngaelhyn free-jazz sessions is only one of temperament, rather than an actual passing of traditions across the decades. But one has to ask why this particular blend of utopianism and common sense, of cosmic searching and earthy humility, has evolved in this corner of the world. Linking it to Seattle's background in basic blue does not seem half so far-fetched as saying it is just a matter of coincidence.

A more easily defended legacy of Jackson Street is the direct, firsthand influence the house-rocking music of Billy Tolles and Tommy Adams had on the "Northwest sound" of rockers such as the Wailers, the Kingsmen, and the Sonics. In the late 1950s and early 1960s, white kids in the Northwest seized upon black R & B with a manic, almost awkward ferociousness, epitomized by the Kingsmen's anthem, "Louie Louie," the Frantics' "Werewolf," and, later, the Sonics' "Psycho" and "The Witch." Some of this music had a jazz flavor. The Dynamics (with Larry Coryell), for example, with its horn section and keyboard, showed the cool, loping influence of "chitlins jazz." The Frantics were influenced more by the twang guitar sound of Duane Eddy, but their records were straight blues structures. White musicians such as Larry Coryell, who grew up in eastern Washington, emphasize that the cultural thrust of their music came from their admiration of black style, as personified in local musicians. "The black people were cool," says Coryell. "They had a unified culture. There was so much more emphasis on feeling, and very fundamental respect for rhythmic principles."

Black rock musicians such as Dave Lewis were influenced by the older jazz players, too. Lewis' tune "J.A.J.," also covered by the Kingsmen, was a real instrumental oddity, a series of descending seventh chords followed by a "circle of fifths" bridge. Lewis threw all manner of jazz riffs into his playing. Members of the Wailers frequented the Flame, where Floyd Standifer was playing his version of a tune the rock band would later record, "Mau Mau." Mike Burke, drummer for the Wailers, cites Mardi Gras drummer George Griffin as a major influence. Dave Holden, who had worked with Billy Tolles in the 1950s, teamed up with Gerald Frank at the Downbeat in 1961, playing jazz/rock piano. None of this early rock could have been made in this way in the Northwest if the players hadn't been getting firsthand exposure to jazz and R & B.

One of the most important new musical elements rock music brought to the front was the electric guitar and its various electronic effects. It is curious that two of rock guitar's most influential exponents—Larry Coryell and Jimi Hendrix—arose in Seattle, drew early ammu-

nition from Jackson Street, and have significant ties to jazz.

Hendrix, whose experiments with distortion and feedback on his albums *Are You Experienced?*, *Axis, Bold as Love*, and *Electric Ladyland* permanently altered the sonic landscape of both jazz and rock, was a third-generation Seattle artist. His grandparents, Nora and Ross Hendrix, had been stranded in town in 1911 while working in a vaudeville show. His father, Al (who still lives in Seattle), was an amateur tap dancer who, with Jimi's mother, became famous in the black community as a competition jitterbugger. Jimi Hendrix, who started playing guitar in 1957, was influenced as a youngster by a local white rhythm-and-blues guitarist named Joe Johansen, who was also helpful to Larry Coryell: "The thing that connected me and Jimi Hendrix was Joe Johansen. Joe was responsible for teaching me R & B tunes. Very simple." Hendrix left Seattle in 1961 and toured as a yeoman rhythm guitarist with several black bands, including the Isley Brothers and Little Richard and the Upsetters. In New York, he was exposed to the downtown bohemia coalescing around folk-rock and Bob Dylan and began to experiment with his sound.

Apocryphal stories to the contrary, Hendrix had not developed even the germ of his distortion effects in Seattle. What Hendrix did derive from his local background was simple blues discipline and form, for which there were lots of able role models on Jackson Street. The audience at Birdland had been listening to good dance music since Billy Tolles and the Savoy Boys opened there in 1941. Ultimately, that simple foundation was as important for Hendrix's development as the experimental sounds he later heard in New York and London.

**The Rocking Kings, with Jimi Hendrix, guitar, Washington Hall, 1960.**

**Courtesy of Al Hendrix**

It may also be that the easy interchange in Seattle between jazz, R & B, rock, and blues—and the relaxed mixing of the races—had some subliminal influence on Hendrix's open-mindedness toward other experimental forms. Though Hendrix never showed any interest in straight-ahead bebop, his experiments with sound and time later had a huge influence on such jazz artists as Gil Evans, Miles Davis, and the group Weather Report in the jazz/rock fusion movement. It's interesting to note that Larry Coryell, who arrived in Seattle four months after Hendrix left, was one of the prime movers in this fusion.

Coryell played with both jazz and rock musicians in Seattle, including Jimmy Hanna and the Dynamics, Overton Berry, Jerry Gray, and Chuck Mahaffay. One night in 1965, at the Black and Tan, Gene Harris, the pianist with the Three Sounds, encouraged Coryell to go to New York. Coryell drove cross-country in a Volkswagen Bug and didn't stop until he got to Manhattan. A year later, he recorded an album that brilliantly combined avant-garde improvisation with rock 'n' roll rhythms, called *Free Spirit*, with drummer Bob Moses and Portland saxophonist Jim Pepper—arguably the first jazz/rock fusion record ever made.

Coryell brought not only a solid blues, rock, and jazz foundation from Seattle, but a sense of cosmic yearning, which he attributes to the city's geographic kinship with the Far East. Is it possible Hendrix absorbed the same feeling? Looking out across Elliott Bay, with Mount Rainier looming behind, Coryell remarked that he felt a sense of possibility when he lived in Seattle, engendered by the town's isolation and the Pacific Ocean. "Seattle is not the real America," he said. "America starts on the other side of that mountain."

Floyd Standifer echoes this sentiment in a similar assessment of Seattle's place in the big picture:

> *Seattle serves a unique purpose. It's one of the loveliest incubators you'll ever run into. Seattle always was a place to get it together, or come off the road and reassess yourself. But you can't stay here, if you're going to make it big. You don't have the numbers, first of all. You don't have the market value.*
>
> *But this town will hook you. You'll always end up coming back. And the reason you come back is, the first thing you ever were was a human being. And it's the last thing you're ever going to be. This town allows you to do that. All that other stuff in between is just stuff that you learn to do.*

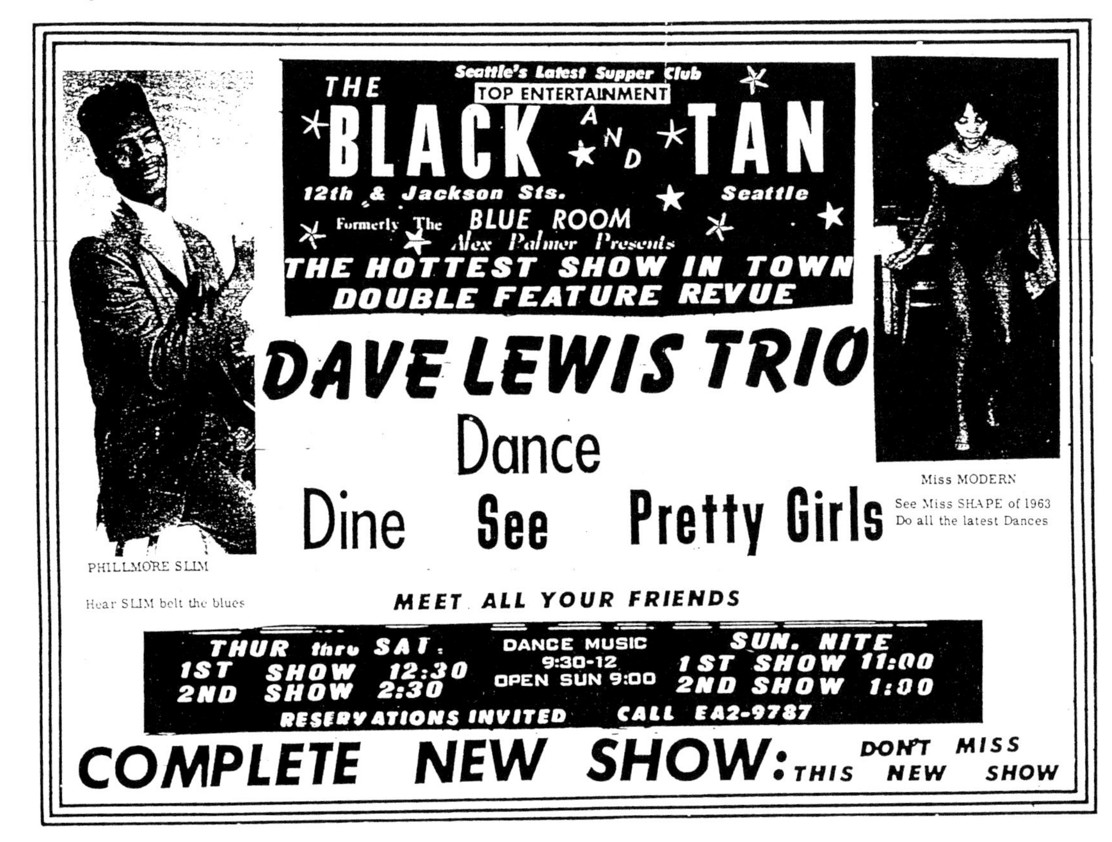

*You're looking for someplace where life can mean something, you come here.*

Coryell and Standifer are right about Seattle's human scale, natural beauty, and isolation, but the city's music also has had an impact around the world, the most far-reaching influence being that of Ray Charles, Bumps Blackwell, and Quincy Jones. The entire Motown movement was based on Charles' breakthroughs. Later, he would leap more artificial boundaries, by recording the first country-music album by a black artist. Later still, he broke out of the straitjacket of the "black artist" realm altogether, becoming a nationally loved, mainstream artist.

Bumps Blackwell's contribution to this process—referred to as "crossing over" to the white market—is less well known, but important. When Blackwell left Seattle in 1951, he went to Los Angeles, where he was hired as an A & R man by Specialty Records. Four years later, Specialty sent him to New Orleans to produce a record by an unknown artist named Richard Penniman. In "Little Richard," Blackwell finally found the target for his creative energy that he had been looking for. As the lyricist, songwriter, A & R man, or producer, Blackwell midwifed nearly all of Little Richard's important early records, which makes him one of the fathers of rock 'n' roll. He was a pioneer in a more important sense, too, in that he helped define the role of the rock producer, which has more to do with marketing and manipulating raw talent than it does with music per se. This is precisely what Blackwell did when he virtually created Richard's first hit, "Tutti Frutti," in New Orleans, by rewriting the lyrics and cajoling Richard into a relaxed mood that captured his freewheeling spirit on record. Blackwell also produced the first crossover gospel hit, Sam Cooke's "You Send Me," which helped to establish the soul-music trend.

Is it a coincidence that yet a third figure from Jackson Street, Quincy Jones, also wound up as a prime mover in "crossing over" black music? Probably not. Duke Ellington, who hated such marketplace terms as "rock," "jazz," and "funk," once told Quincy Jones that he would be the one to "decategorize American music." In his work with Michael Jackson, movie scores (*Roots*), and his 1991 CD *Back on the Block*, which proposes a unified musical lineage of jazz, R & B, funk, and rap, Jones seems to have taken on Ellington's compliment as something of a life assignment.

The "crossover" work of these three men—Bumps Blackwell, Ray Charles, and Quincy Jones—has a clear legacy in such Seattle performers as vocalist Diane Schuur and saxophonist Kenny G. Schuur's expressive and fluid style owes as much in spirit to Ray Charles as it does in fact to Dinah Washington. Kenny G's fusion of jazz technique with an R & B dance sensibility is as old as Quincy Jones.

Seattle's crossover tradition is directly related to its racially positive atmosphere in the 1940s. There was not only an unusual level of tolerance and mixing between the races, but a sense of excitement and possibility, a feeling that the old hierarchies—call it "tradition," if you like—did not apply in this little corner of the world, that a person could live up to his or her potential without worrying about the world cutting it down. Time after time, players make a point of mentioning this mellow atmosphere.

Ray Charles notes in his autobiography that "Seattle . . . was very different, because when you went to the clubs, you saw everybody —white, black—it didn't make any difference, people were just there! In Florida . . . if you worked in a white club, it was a white club, and that was that. It was new to me to go someplace and everybody was just loose and free."

Where Detroit had riots, Seattle was a town where a racial "incident" was news. Men like Quincy Jones and Billy Tolles grew up thinking that they could conquer the world. Likewise, Bumps Blackwell assumed that success was his for the taking, that he could take his "Junior Band" to an exclusive white district like Broadmoor, or to the Trianon Ballroom.

In 1983, Charles, Jones, and Blackwell celebrated their mutual background in a fiftieth birthday party for Quincy Jones, held at the Paramount Theater. One of the highlights was a tongue-in-cheek performance of the old Jackson Street war-horse "Big Fat Butterfly." When Quincy and Ray and Bumps started in on those silly lyrics—"The chick was high, / As a butterfly . . ." they cracked up laughing, and all their old friends and compatriots in the audience laughed along with them. For a brief moment, the old Jackson Street scene was alive in the room.

And then it was gone.

# selected discography

by Ken Wiley and Paul de Barros

*Dates in parentheses, where listed, are recording dates, not release dates. Releases cited are not necessarily in print.*

**Anderson, Ernestine**

*Hot Cargo* (1958). Mercury MG 20354.

*Moanin' Moanin' Moanin'* (1960). Mercury MG 20582.

*Hello like Before* (1977). Concord Jazz 31.

*Big City* (1983). Concord Jazz 214.

*When the Sun Goes Down* (1984). Concord Jazz CCD 4263.

*Be Mine Tonight* (1986). Concord Jazz CCD 4319.

**Bailey, Mildred**

*Harlem Lullaby* (1933). Academy Sound and Vision CD AFA 5065.

*Squeeze Me* (1935). Affinity CD AFS 1013.

Benny Goodman and His Orchestra. *Roll 'Em,* Vol. 1 (1939). CBS 460062-2.

*Her Greatest Performances 1929–1956,* Vols. 1–3 CBS JC 3L 22.

**Bisio, Michael**

*In Seattle* (1987). Silkheart SHLP-107.

**Blackwell, Bumps**

Little Richard. *18 Greatest Hits* (1955–57). Rhino Records RNCD 75899 (Blackwell, producer).

**Bown, Patti**

*Patti Bown Plays Big Piano* (1958). Columbia CL 1379.

Gene Ammons Quartet. *The Gene Ammons Story: Gentle Jug* (1962). Prestige P 24079.

Bill Coleman. *The Great Parisian Session.* Polydor 837235-2.

*See* Quincy Jones, *Live at the Alhambra '60* and *The Birth of a Band.*

**Bradley, Oscar**

Benny Carter and His Orchestra. *Coleman Hawkins / Benny Carter* (1943). Forlane UCD 19011.

**Brashear, Gerald**

*See* Wyatt Ruther, *Easy Living with the Wyatt Ruther IV.*

*See* Cecil Young, *Concert of Cool Jazz* and *Jazz on the Rocks.*

**Brazil, Joe**

John Coltrane. *Om,* Pts. 1 & 2 (1965). Impulse AS9140.

James Moody. *The Teachers* (1970). Perception PLP6.

Roy Ayers. *Mystic Voyage* (1975). Polydor PD6057.

**Burke, Ceele**

Louis Armstrong and His Sebastian New Cotton Club Orchestra. *Louis Armstrong: St. Louis Blues* (1930). CBS 467919-2.

**Catlett, Buddy**

Frank Foster. *Basie Is Our Boss* (1963). Argo/Cadet LP717.

Louis Armstrong and his All-Stars. Mercury 6499355.

Count Basie Orchestra. *The Count Basie Years.* Roulette RE 102.

Count Basie Orchestra. *On My Way & Shoutin' Again.* Verve MV 2647 IMS.

Bill Coleman. *The Great Parisian Session.* Polydor 837235-2.

*See* Quincy Jones, *Live at the Alhambra '60, The Birth of a Band,* and *I Dig Dancers.*

**Charles, Ray**

Maxin Trio et al. *Early Years* (1947–51). Jazz Archives No. 7, CD ZET 707.

*Spotlight on Ray Charles* (1950–?). Design Spotlight Series DLP-145.

*The Genius of Ray Charles* (1959). Atlantic SD 1312.

*Genius plus Soul Equals Jazz* (1961). Impulse.

*The Greatest Ray Charles.* Atlantic SD 8054.

**Coleman, Dave**

Freddie Slack. *Riffette* (1942). Capitol.

T-Bone Walker. "I Got a Break Baby" and "Mean Old World." *The Complete Recordings* (1942). Mosaic MD6-130.

Willie Smith. *September in the Rain* (1945). Keynote.

Billie Holiday. *Billie Holiday and Her All Stars* (1946). Verve 841434-2.

**Corcoran, Corky**

. . . and His Orchestra. *Jazz Club: Piano* (1945). Verve 840032-2.

Lionel Hampton All-Stars. *Stardust* ("Just Jazz" sessions) (1947). MCA Records MCA-198.

Harry James and His Orchestra. *The Best of the Big Bands* (1959). LRC Records CDC 8518.

**Coryell, Larry**
Free Spirits. *Out of Sight and Sound* (with Jim Pepper) (1967). ABC 593.
. . . Emily Remler Duo. *Together* (1985). Concord CCD 4289.
Shlomo Bat-Ain Group. *Distant Echoes* (1986). VeraBra Records CDVBR 2018-2.
*Don Lanphere Larry Coryell* (1990). Hep CD 2048.
Jimmy Hanna and the Dynamics. *Memory Bank.* Bolo BSLP-8003.
*See* Chuck Mahaffay, *Seattle Beat* and *The Girl from Ipanema.*

**Crow, Bill**
Stan Getz. *Plays* (1952–54). Verve 833 535-2.
Gerry Mulligan. *Live in Boston at Storyville* (1956). Pacific Jazz PJ-1228.
Gerry Mulligan. *Newport Jazz Festival* (1958). CBS 88605.
Milt Jackson with the Quincy Jones Orchestra. *The Ballad Artistry of Milt Jackson* (1959). Atlantic 7567-82269-2.
Gerry Mulligan and the Concert Jazz Band. *Live at the Village Vanguard* (1960). Verve V-8396.
Gerry Mulligan. *Night Lights* (1963). Phillips PHM 200-108.

**Cruse, Juanita**
*Juanita!* (1960). Gene Norman Presents GNP51.

**Darensbourg, Joe**
Kid Ory's Creole Jazz Band (1945). Exner 3 and 4.
Kid Ory's Creole Jazz Band (1945). Decca 25133 and 25134.
Redd Foxx & His Ding Dong Daddies, original cast. (1945).
Kid Ory's Creole Jazz Band (1950). Columbia 38955, 38956, 38957, and 38958.
Teddy Buckner and his Dixieland Five (1955). Gene Norman Presents GNP-11.
*See* John Wittwer [Trio].

**Dolphy, Eric**
*At the Five Spot,* Vols. 1–2 (1960). Prestige 7826.

**Ellington, Duke**
*Seattle Concert* (1952). Victor LJM-1002.

**Friel, Neil**
Si Zentner (1965). RCA LPM/LSP3484.
Woody Herman. *Concerto for Herd* (1967). Verve V6-8764.

**Friesen, David**
Mike Nock Quintet. *Climbing* (1979). Tomato 2696502.
Mal Waldron–David Friesen Duo. *Dedication* (1985). Soul Note SN 1178.
. . . , Jerry Heldman, and David Coleman, Jr. *Color Pool.* Muse MR 5109.

**G, Kenny**
Jeff Lorber. *Wizard Island* (1979). Arista AL9516.
*Kenny G* (1982). Arista AL9608.

**Garred, Milt**
Maxin Trio et al. *Early Years* (1947–51). Jazz Archives No. 7, CD ZET 707.

**Gill, Elmer**
*Elmer Gill Trio* (1968). Aragon ASL201.
*A Few of My Favorite Things* (1976). Rada RST 1119.
*I Can't Hear for Listening* (1981). Intermodal 1PLJ8200.

**Goodhew, Denney**
First Avenue. *First Avenue* (1980). ECM 1194(2301194).
Rich Halley. *Multnomah Rhythms* (1981). Avocet P-100-1.

**Gray, Jerry**
*See* Joni Metcalf, *Joni Sings Porter and Ellington with the Jerome Gray Trio.*

**Grimes, Herman**
Duke Ellington. *Duke Ellington* (1947). Columbia CL2522.

**Hayes, Cathi**
*It's All Right with Me* (1960). HiFi R416.
*See* The Signatures, *The Signatures Sign In* and *Prepare to Flip.*

**Heldman, Jerry**
*See* David Friesen, Jerry Heldman, and David Coleman, Jr., *Color Pool.*

**Hendrix, Jimi**
*Are You Experienced* (1967). Reprise RS6261.

**Hodges, Dean**
*See* Joni Metcalf, *Ringaround.*

**Hogan, Granville "G.T."**
Ahmad Khatab Salim and His Orchestra. *Blues Suite* (1958). Savoy SV 0142(MG121132).
Cal Massey Sextet. *The Jazz Life* (1961). Candid CCD 79019.

**Hubert, Traff**
*See* Cecil Young, *Concert of Cool Jazz* and *Jazz on the Rocks.*

**Johnson, Billy**
*See* Roscoe Weathers, *Rosco* [sic] *Weathers and His Sterling Flute & Piccolo.*

**Jones, Quincy**
Art Farmer Septet. *Plays the Arrangements and Compositions of Gigi Gryce and Quincy Jones* (1953–54). Original Jazz Classics OJC-054(P7031).
Dizzy Gillespie and His Orchestra. *Jazz Club: Big Band* (1956). Verve 840030-2.
*The Birth of a Band* (1959). Emarcy Jazz Series 818 177-1.
*Live at the Alhambra '60* (1960). JMY 1004-2.
*I Dig Dancers* (1961). Mercury 20612.

**Kelly, Red**
Dick Collins. *Horn of Plenty* (1954). Victor LJM1019.
The Modest Jazz Trio (with Jim Hall). *Good Friday Blues* (1960). Pacific Jazz PJ(ST)10.

**Knapp, Jim**
First Avenue. *First Avenue* (1980). ECM 1194(2301194).

**Lanphere, Don**
*First Sessions* (1949). Prestige PCD 24114-2.
Gene Roland. *The Band that Never Was* (1950). Spotlite SPJ141.
*Out of Nowhere* (1982). Hep Records 2019.
*Stop* (1983). Hep Records 2034.
*Don Lanphere Larry Coryell* (1990). Hep CD 2048.

**Levitt, Rod**
Dizzy Gillespie and His Orchestra. *Jazz Club: Big Band / Jazz Club: Trumpet* (1956–57). Verve 840030-2/840038-2.
*The Dynamic Sound Patterns of the Rod Levitt Orchestra* (1963). Riverside 9471.
*Insight* (1965). RCA Victor LPM-3372.

**Lewis, Dave**
"David's Mood" and "Little Green Thing." *The History of Northwest Rock,* Vols. 1 and 2, respectively (1976, 1980). The Great Northwest Music Company GNW 4003 and 4008.

**Mahaffay, Chuck**
. . . and the Individuals. *Seattle Beat* (1962). Capitol Custom SLP 1002.
. . . and the Individuals. *The Girl from Ipanema* (1964). 21 Records L2101.

**Mancuso, Gus**
*Introducing Gus Mancuso* (1956). Fantasy LP 3233.
*Music from New Faces* (1957). Fantasy LP 3282.

**McKee, Garcia**
Maxin Trio et al. *Early Years* (1947–51). Jazz Archives No. 7, CD ZET 707.

**Metcalf, Chuck**
Doug Hammond. *Reflections in the Sea of Nurnen* (1972). Tribe.
Mark Murphy. *Stolen Moments* (1978). Muse MCD 5102.
. . . Featuring George Cables. *Elsie Street* (1990). BopWare BW101.
Bert Wilson. *Live at the Zoo* (1991). 9 Winds NWCD 0138.
. . . Octet. *Help Is Coming* (1992). BopWare BW 102.
*See* Joni Metcalf, *Joni Sings Porter and Ellington with the Jerome Gray Trio.*

**Metcalf, Joni**
*Joni Sings Porter and Ellington with the Jerome Gray Trio* (1965). Camelot.
*Ringaround* (1982). Ringaround 2330.

**Meyers, Vic**
. . . and His Orchestra (1923–24). Folkways RBF17.

**Montgomery, Monk**
The Mastersounds. *The King and I* (1957). World Pacific Records PJM-405.
The Mastersounds. *A Date with the Mastersounds* (1960). Fantasy 3316.

**Moore, Phil**
Don Elliott. *Don Elliott Accompanied by Phil Moore and His Orchestra* (1957). ABC-Paramount ABC 190.

**Morton, Jelly Roll**
"Seattle Hunch." *Giants of Jazz: Jelly Roll Morton* (1929). Time-Life Records 19STL-J07.

**Oregon**
*Oregon* (1983). ECM 1258(811711-1).
*45th Parallel* (1989). Portrait OR 44465.

**Payne, Stan**
Billie Holiday. *Billie Holiday with Frankie Newton and His Orchestra* (1939). Storyville SLP 4002.

**Peacock, Gary**
Allen Youngblood. *Selah* (1984). Griot 7771.
Jay Clayton. *Live at Jazz Alley* (1987). ITM Records ITMP 970065.
Quartett. *No Secrets* (1988). New Albion Records NA 017 CD.
*Paul Bley–Gary Peacock Duet* (1989). Owl Records 058 CD.

**Peck, Dave**
*See* Bud Shank, *Tales of the Pilot.*

**Perciful, Jack**
Harry James and His Orchestra. *Jazz Club: Big Band* (1968). Verve 840030-2.

**Poindexter, Pony**
Jon Hendricks. *A Good Git-Together* (1959). World Pacific Jazz 1283.
Wes Montgomery. *Montgomeryland* (1959). Pacific Jazz Records PJ-5.
Lambert, Hendricks and Bavan. *Basin Street East* (1963). RCA LSP-2635.
Alto Summit. *Alto Summit* (1968). MPS 15192ST.

**Raglin, Alvin "Junior"**
Duke Ellington. "Black Brown & Beige." *At His Very Best* (1944). RCA Victor LPM-1715.
Al Casey. *Al Casey–Sid Catlett Quartet* (1945). Saga 6925AG.
Duke Ellington and His Orchestra. *Liberian Suite* (1947). CBS 66607.

**Rainy City Jazz Band**
*Rainy City Jazz Band* (1947). Exner 5, 6, and 7.

**Ramsay, Bill**
Frank Wess Orchestra. *Entre Nous* (1991). Concord Jazz CCD-4450.

**Reid, Rufus**
*See* Jimmy Rowles, *I Remember Bebop.*

**Reilly, Dean**
Vince Guaraldi. *Vince Guaraldi Trio* (1956). Fantasy LP3225.
Earl Hines. *Fatha Plays Fats.* Fantasy.

**Rowles, Jimmy**
Stan Getz. *Plays* (1952–54). Verve 833 535-2.
Billie Holiday. *Billie Holiday: Stormy Blues* (1955). Verve VE2-2515.
Gerry Mulligan. *Gerry Mulligan Meets Ben Webster* (1959). Verve MGV-8343.
*I Remember Bebop* (1977). Columbia C2-35381-2.
*The Peacocks* (1977). Columbia PC34873.
*Music's the Only Thing that's on My Mind* (1981). Progressive 7009.
. . . *Plays Duke Ellington and Billy Strayhorn* (1981). Columbia FC37639.

**Ruther, Wyatt**
Chico Hamilton. *Quintet* (1959). Warner Bros WB(S)1344.
*Easy Living with the Wyatt Ruther IV* (1967). Van-Los Music VLM-3605.
Fraser McPherson. *Live at the Planetarium* (1975). Concord CJ-92.
Louise Rose. *Live at the Belfry* (1978). Iona IRS78-026.

**Schreiber, Freddie**
Cal Tjader. *Saturday Night, Sunday Night at the Black Hawk* (1962). Verve 8459.

**Schuur, Diane**
*Deedles* (1984). GRP 1010.
*Timeless* (1986). Gramavision GRP-D-9540.

**Seales, Marc**
*See* Don Lanphere, *Out of Nowhere.*

**Shank, Bud**
. . . and Michel Legrand. *The Windmills of Your Mind* (1969). World Pacific ST20157.
. . . and Shorty Rogers. *California Concert* (1985). Contemporary C14012.
*Tales of the Pilot* (1990). Capri 74025-2.

**(The) Signatures**
*The Signatures Sign In.* Warner Bros.
*Prepare to Flip.* Warner Bros.

**Souders, Jackie**
. . . and His Orchestra (1926–27). Columbia 837-D, 905-D.

**Standifer, Floyd**
Northwest Jazz Sextet. *Journey Without Maps* (1979). Stan Keen Productions 7902100-S.
*See* Quincy Jones, *Live at the Alhambra '60* and *The Birth of a Band.*

**Stentz, Chuck**
Ray Borden. *Boston Bust Out* (1947–48). Hep 13.r
Nat Pierce and His Orchestra (1948). Zim 1005.

**Stentz, Jan**
*Profile* (1984). Bam J1002.

**Thurlow, Janet**
Charles Mingus. *The Complete Debut Recordings* (1953). Debut 12-DCD-4402-2.

**Turnham, Floyd**
Maxine Sullivan (1939). Victor 26237, 26260.
T-Bone Walker. "T-Bone Blues" (1940). *The Complete Recordings.* Mosaic MD6-130.
Les Hite. "Jersey Bounce" (1942). Hit 7001.
Gerald Wilson and His Orchestra (1945). Excelsior 122, 123, 127.

**Venuti, Joe**
Eddie Lang and Joe Venuti. *Stringing the Blues* (1927–32). Columbia C2L 24.
Joe Albany. *Joe Albany + Joe Venuti* (1974). Horo HDP 42.

**Ward, Carlos**
Don Cherry. *Relativity Suite* (1973). JCOA Records JCOA 1006.
Rashied Ali Quartet. *New Directions in Modern Music* (1973). Survival SR104.
Abdullah Ibrahim. *Water from an Ancient Well* (1986). Black-Hawk BKH 50207-1 D.

**Weathers, Roscoe**
Bob Keene and His Orchestra. *Stringin' Along* (1957). Andex LP3001.
*Rosco* [sic] *Weathers and His Sterling Flute & Piccolo.* Bezel Records RWS 101/102.

**Wiedoeft, Herb**
Jesse Stafford and His Orchestra (1928). The Old Masters 19.

**Wiggins, Gerald**
Les Hite. "Jersey Bounce" (1942). Hit 7001.
Chris Woods. *Quartet* (1976). Black & Blue 33100.
Major Holley. *Featuring Gerry Wiggins* (1977). Black & Blue BLA CD 233074.
*Live at Maybeck Recital Hall, Vol. 8* (1991). Concord Jazz CCD-4450.
*See* Gus Mancuso, *Introducing Gus Mancuso.*

**Wilson, Bert**
. . . and Rebirth. *Kaleidoscopic Visions* (1982). AuRoar AU-003.

**Wilson, Dick**
Andy Kirk and His Clouds of Joy. *Walkin' & Swingin'* (1936–41). Affinity AFS 1011.

**Winn, Bob**
. . . and Paul Madison. *Honolulu Sax Players* (1989). First Break Records FB 7005.

**Wittwer, John**
. . . Trio (1944). Exner 1 & 2.
Redd Foxx & His Ding Dong Daddies, original cast (1945).
*Rags Stomps and Blues* (1947). Jazz Man 18, 19, 20.

**Young, Cecil**
*Jazz on the Rocks* (1951–52). Audio Lab 1516.
. . . Quartet. *Concert of Cool Jazz* (1951–52). King LP 295-1.
. . . Quartet. Gene Norman Presents EP 102.

# notes

*Sources cited below are either the names of interview subjects (as listed in "Sources," under "Oral Histories and Interviews" and "Additional Interviews") or the authors of books or other printed matter (listed by category in "Sources"). In the case of an author with multiple bibliographic entries, the publication date of the relevant work is given in parentheses.*

**KEY**

*NW Ent = Northwest Enterprise*
*P-I = Seattle Post-Intelligencer*
*S. Times = Seattle Times*

**Chapter I**

**Jelly Roll Morton** probably played Seattle more than once. He was reported to be "on his way to the Entertainer's Club, Seattle," on 31 July 1920 and was remembered to have been in Seattle in June 1920 by Don Pasquall (Gushee). Merle I. Smith says her brother saw Morton play at the Black and Tan in the "late 1920s." Joe Darensbourg, the great Creole clarinetist who moved to Seattle in 1929, asserts that he worked with Morton there, as well. The reference to Holden is from Lomax. ■ **Background on Seattle's skid road (including *McClure's* quote):** Mumford (1980) and Morgan. ■ **Lopes, Noodles Smith, and early black settlement:** Mumford (1980). ■ **Black population statistics:** Quintard Taylor. ■ **Noodles' nickname and background:** Rowell, Williamson, Darensbourg, Gayton. ■ **The Alhambra:** Mumford (1980) dates the founding at 1922; McCarthy has the club open as early as 1920; Seattle Polk Directories begin listing the Alhambra in 1922. ■ **"Black and tan":** William Howland Kenney, *Chicago Jazz,* New York: Oxford University Press, 1993. ■ **Reb Spikes date:** McCarthy. ■ **12th and Jackson neighborhood description:** Rowell. ■ **Characterization of Noodles Smith:** *S. Times,* 15 Apr 1952. ■ **Zelma, El Bee, and Noodles quote:** Williamson. ■ **Madison neighborhood:** Mumford (1980); **LeEtta King quote:** Mumford (1986). ■ **Waldron:** Merle I. Smith. ■ **Personnel of the Odean Jazz Orchestra:** Charles Adams, trumpet; Archie Jackson, piano; Francis King, violin; Ralph Gibbs, drums and vibes; and (later) Ralph Stephens, drums. ■ **Pierce quote on Waldron:** Pierce, 3 May 1991. ■ **Barnett background:** Mumford (1980) and Doug Barnett. ■ **AYP Exposition:** Powell Barnett. The Seattle Symphony Orchestra played a symphonized rag at the Alaska-Yukon-Pacific Exposition. By this time, according to Merle Smith, several local composers, all white, had published rags, including Bernard Brin, Frederick Irwin, and Warren Camp. ■ **Anti-black union violence:** After black workers came to Franklin to work in the mines, Mumford (1980) reports that a mysterious fire killed 37 men, half of them black. ■ **Lacy's Dixieland Band:** Droker (1981). ■ **Nora and Ross Hendrix date:** Henderson. ■ **Keppard:** *S. Times,* 25 Oct 1914. ■ **Use of word "jazz" and early dissemination of jazz:** Stoddard, who writes, "I have long held the notion that black people in America and black music, such as jazz, were so widely scattered that it makes little sense to try to pin-point the music's geographical origin, much less, as some researchers have done, to try to identify a particular person like Buddy Bolden or Jelly Roll Morton as the source of the music. Rather, it is more likely the music was as widespread as blacks were and that the development of jazz took place over many years, in different places, and involved many people." ■ **The Bobby Hayes group** featured Howard Patrick (piano), who wrote "Sweet Daddy," Rhinehart (banjo), Zimmermacher (cornet)—also said to be "renowned in California"—and O'Brien (trombone). ■ **Lillian Smith performances:** *Cayton's Weekly,* 8 June 1918.

**Chapter II**

**Anti-saloon movement and liquor legal history:** Clark (1965). ■ **"The illegal stuff . . . ":** Stockley, *S. Times,* 29 Mar 1970. ■ **Forbes:** *S. Times,* 23 Mar 1931. ■ **Mud wrestlers and other nightclub details:** Foy. ■ **Reddin:** *S. Times,* 22 Mar 1970. ■ **Arrests:** *S. Times,* 2 Jan 1924. ■ **"Doorbelly":** Darensbourg. ■ **Olmsted:** *S. Times,* 3 July 1973. ■ **Oscar Holden:** Morton comments, Lomax; biographical information, Holden family. ■ **Doc Hamilton and the Barbecue Pit:** Broderick, Rochester; security system, *S. Times,* 7 Jan 1929; raid, *S. Times,* 28 July 1924; Terry Pettus comment, Emmett Watson, *S. Times,* 24 Jan 1984; "chickens" quote and Sheriff Harry Lewis story, *S. Times,* 25 May 1931; "I ask you," *S. Times,* 29 Jan 1932. ■ **Spokane music professor:** *S. Times,* 5 Feb 1925. ■ **Gill elections:** Morgan. ■ **Madge Cayton:** *Cayton's Weekly,* 1 Sep 1917. ■ **Sid Hall Orchestra:** *S. Times,* 12 May 1925. ■ **Buffano quote:** *S. Times,* 1 Mar 1928. ■ **Vaudeville-cum-jazz:** One such act that got started in Seattle was the white banjo player Eddie Peabody, who went on to considerable fame in the swing era. In 1926, Peabody put together an act at the Fifth Avenue Theatre that remained popular there throughout his career. ■ **Clayton on Harper and Fain:** Clayton. ■ **Maryland Tavern raid:** *S. Times,* 2 Jan 1928. ■ **Roadhouses:** Reddin, *S. Times,* 29 Mar 1970 and 9 Oct 1927. ■ **Varsity Vagabonds:** Foy. ■ **Darensbourg particulars:** Darensbourg. ■ **Genessee Street Shufflers:** Foy. ■ **Gerald Wells:** origins, Stoddard, Bobrow; in general, Stoddard, McCarthy. ■ **Garfield Ramblers particulars:** Emma Gayton and Leonard Gayton. ■ **Jimmy Adams performances:** *NW Ent,* 6 Apr 1931 and 18 Aug 1932; suicide, Palmer Johnson. ■ **Creon Thomas:** Henson. ■ **Leonard Gayton career:** Leonard

Gayton. ▪ **"Hub of jazz world":** Charles Taylor. ▪ **Edythe Turnham:** Placksin, Dahl, Turnham. ▪ **Location of Copper Kettle:** Emma Gayton. ▪ **Frances Turnham:** In the 1920s, the beautiful Turnham married dancer Earl Robinson and formed a successful vaudeville team, Earl and Frances, which performed at New York's Apollo Theater. ▪ **Location of Bungalow:** Rowell. ▪ **Joe Bailey:** Turnham. ▪ **1928 personnel:** business card. ▪ **Ellington quote:** Turnham. ▪ **Vido Musso incident:** Turnham scrapbook, undated article. ▪ **Woodman collaboration:** *Los Angeles Sentinel,* 1 Mar 1951. ▪ **Turnham replacing Hodges:** On 1 Mar 1951, the *Los Angeles Sentinel* reported the story, describing Turnham as a "tall, talented, young gent with a pleasing personality. . . . He is a perfect replacement for Hodges, having a style all his own and often called the greatest young altoist in local swing circles." ▪ **Mildred Bailey:** Placksin, Dahl, McCarthy, Zwisohn, liner note by Don DeMichael, *Red Norvo Giants of Jazz,* and liner note, *Mildred Bailey, Her Greatest Performances 1929– 1946*; jobs in Seattle, *S. Times,* 13 Dec 1951 and 14 Dec 1954; radio show, *down beat,* 1 Sep 1944 and 1 Feb 1945; *Time,* 20 Mar 1944. ▪ **Princess Belle:** Darensbourg, Henson. ▪ **Bungalow burns down:** *S. Times,* 5 Mar 1929. ▪ **Steamships:** *S. Times,* 12 Jan 1925. ▪ **Goode:** *NW Ent,* 28 Sep 1933. ▪ **Zelma Winslow:** arrest, *NW Ent,* 14 Sep 1993. ▪ **Chinese Gardens:** Williamson; "like nobody's business," Rowell. ▪ **Rucker with Black and Tan Orchestra:** McCarthy. ▪ **Borders:** Black Birds of Paradise, McCarthy; Elite Social Club, *NW Ent,* 6 Aug 1931; Black and Tan, *NW Ent,* 13 Apr 1933; 1938 is the last gig noted by *NW Ent;* Detroit and Fulmighter details, Palmer Johnson; Chinese Gardens arrest, Williamson. ▪ **Hong Kong Chinese Society Club:** *S. Times,* 14 Feb 1931. ▪ **Phil Moore:** Darensbourg says he worked with Moore in 1931, which is highly unlikely, since Moore would have been a mere 13 years old; "first blacks," Feather. ▪ **Barranco in Oakland:** *down beat,* 16 Dec 1949. ▪ **Souders:** "in the college style," *S. Times,* 8 Feb 1925. ▪ **Del Monte Blue Dogs:** 1928, 1929, and 1930 *Musicland* yearbooks and *S. Times,* 25 July 1929. ▪ **Goodrich Silvertown Cord Orchestra:** *S. Times,* 23 Feb 1925. ▪ **J & V Syncopators:** *S. Times,* 17 Mar 1925. ▪ **Shorty Clough personnel and gig:** 1929 *Musicland* yearbook. ▪ **Paul Clifford:** Foy. ▪ **Virgil Ireland:** Darensbourg. ▪ **Clarence Barney biography and details and date of Parker's Pavilion:** letter to author by Harold Finch, Feb 1991. ▪ **Jules Buffano:** "Mikado," *S. Times,* 28 Mar 1928; biographical details, *S. Times,* 29 Sep 1939. ▪ **Butler Hotel:** description and history, *S. Times,* Nov 1927, 20 June 1962, and 30 Oct 1983; raids, *S. Times,* 10 Aug 1924 and following. ▪ **Vic Meyers:** early life, *S. Times,* 19 Aug 1938; *Musicland* VI, no. 21, 1926; other biographical detail, Jones, Morgan; Winchell show, *S. Times,* 26 Mar 1937; raids on Alhambra and Butler, *S. Times,* 16 May 1922; interracial marriage, Morgan. ▪ **Landes Ordinance:** *S. Times,* 20 Feb, 20 Nov, and 1 Apr 1923. ▪ **"Moral menace":** *S. Times,* 31 Oct 1929. ▪ **"How Dry I Am":** *S. Times,* Nov 1927. ▪ **Card game story:** Ramage. ▪ **"Jazz and whoopee":** *S. Times,* 20 Apr 1931. ▪ **Whiteman:** *Musicland,* 25 Apr 1930, and *S. Times,* 20 Mar, 6, 8, 9, and 13 Apr 1930.

#### Chapter III

**Depression in Seattle:** Sale. ▪ **Blue Rose:** Henson. ▪ **Henson's style:** Rowles. ▪ **Princess Belle:** origins, Darensbourg; "like a schoolteacher," Henson. ▪ **Japanese businesses:** Booker, Reddick. ▪ **Tokiwa Hotel:** Henson. ▪ **Darensbourg hard-luck story:** Darensbourg. ▪ **Tootie Boyd:** Ewing, Johnson. ▪ **Whaley:** at Broadway Hall, *NW Ent,* 29 Sep 1932; to China, Johnson. ▪ **Gene Coy:** "first harbinger" conclusion based on *NW Ent* listings, Turay, Johnson; background before reaching Seattle, McCarthy. ▪ **Dick Wilson:** joins Coy, McCarthy, Johnson; biography, Chilton, Darensbourg; return to Seattle, flyer from Gay Jones archive; death, McCarthy says tuberculosis. ▪ **Raglin:** at the Congo Club, Johnson; at Ubangi, Johnson; two-necked guitar, Henson; biography after Seattle, Dance (1970), Ulanov; Three Deuces engagement, *down beat,* 3 June 1946; Seattle engagement, M.A.A. *S. Times,* 16 Dec 1941. ▪ **Wells at the Hi-Hatters:** *NW Ent,* 21 May 1931. ▪ **Black migration:** Reddick. ▪ **411 Club:** Johnson, Turay, Rowles. ▪ **Ubangi:** description and entertainers, Rowell; closure, *NW Ent,* 25 Feb 1938; Marshal Royal says Coreen Gibson, whose style was popularized by the white singer Ella Logan, developed a family act at the Ubangi that also included an older brother who started the dance craze "Peckin'," a big hit for Benny Goodman and Harry James. ▪ **Congo Club description:** Reddin, *S. Times,* 10 Mar 1963, and Johnson. ▪ **Herman Grimes:** early life, Darensbourg; Green Dot and Dutchman Tavern, Johnson, Bobrow; Ellington tenure and recordings, *Duke Ellington's Story on Records,* Luciano Mascagli, Liborio Pusciteri and Giovanni Volonte, Vol. 1946–50, Musica Jazz, Milan 1972. ▪ **Chinese Gardens:** Williamson. ▪ **State Theatre, Cocoanut Grove, Lyons' Music Hall, and Virginian:** Foy. ▪ **Shanghai jazz scene:** in general, Johnson, Clayton; Whaley's imprisonment, etc., Driggs letter to author, 22 Mar 1991. ▪ **Wayne Adams and Johnson's career after Shanghai:** Johnson.

#### Chapter IV

**Gaylord Jones' early career:** Jones. ▪ **Husky Hot Club formation:** *The Daily,* 2 Mar 1939 and following. ▪ **Bobrow conversation with President:** Bobrow. ▪ **Trianon opening and description:** *S. Times,* 19 and 21 May 1927; Young, *P-I,* 26 Oct 1975; and Marshal, *P-I,* 27 Apr 1955. ▪ **Card game anecdote:** Ramage. ▪ **Black revues:** *S. Times,* 13 Aug 1933, 20 Feb 1935, and 25 Aug 1937. ▪ **Hite:** *NW Ent,* 15 Nov 1934. ▪ **First Ellington appearance:** *S. Times,* 13 May 1934. ▪ **Hampton:** *S. Times,* 15 Aug 1935. ▪ **Gray:** *S. Times,* 3 Aug 1937. ▪ **Dorsey:** Young. ▪ **Herman quote:** Herman. ▪ **Charlie Blackwell:** Hunziker. ▪ **"Fraught with significance,"** *The Daily* article from Gay Jones archive. ▪ **First Swing Concert:** Gil Brown, *Seattle Star,* 5 Feb 1940. ▪ **Hampton concert:** M.A.A., *S. Times,* 2 Dec 1940. ▪ **Fats Waller story:** Wells, Bobrow, and *S. Times,* 11 July 1941. ▪ **Corcoran:** " . . . mother" and baseball story, Radke; fights and bus story, Kelly. ▪ **Trianon segregation:** Young writes, "For years, a Seattle city ordinance and the mind-set of John Savage kept black customers out of the Trianon." He then quotes Harris: "It was just the plain truth that if black people and white people were together at a dance there would be fights." "Spook nights" and Hampton incident, Bown and *NW Ent,* 29 Nov 1940. An attorney's search of Seattle's law library turned up no "mixed dancing" ordinance, which would have been contrary to state law, in any case. ▪ **Black Laws and Public Accommodations Act:** Mumford (1980). During the 1940s, the black population of the state increased dramatically from 7,424 to 30,691. ■ **Red-lining:** Clark (1976). ■ **"Peanut heaven":** Mumford (1986). ■ **Black population:** Reddick. ■ **Boeing hiring policy:** Clark (1976). ■ **"Separate but equal":** Droker (1976) and *NW Ent,* 19 May 1943. ■ **"White only":** *NW Ent,* 23 June 1943. ■ **Bremerton housing:** Clark (1976). ■ **Navy Commander:** *NW Ent,* 4 Apr 1943. ■ **Grill Cafe:** *NW Ent,* 9 Dec 1942. ■ **Admiral Theatre:** Clark (1976). ■ **Foundry:** *NW Ent,* 19 May 1943. ■ **Fort Lawton riot:** Mumford (1986). See Clark, Droker, and Reddick on race relations. ■ **Armstrong:** *P-I,* 5 Mar 1950. ■ **Local 493:** Siegl. ■ **Wells details:** Emmett Lewis. ■ **Pierre early life:** Spearman, Stoddard, Darensbourg. ■ **Turner quote:** Stoddard. ■ **Valhalla Hall:** *NW Ent,* 18 Aug 1932. ■ **Al's Lucky Hour:** Spearman. ■ **Union Club description:** Wanda Brown. ■ **Pierre repertoire:** Ward, Vaughn. ■ **Vernon Brown origins, early bands:** *P-I,* 1 Oct 1966. ■ **Connection to Al Pierre:** Wanda Brown. ■ **Clayton anecdote:** Clayton. ■ **Cruise birthdate and place:** 493 roster and Jabo Ward. ■ **Dee Dee Hackett and Russell Jones:** Johnson, Russell, McCarthy. ■ ***S. Times* review of Russell:** 13 Oct 1943. ■ **Eighth Avenue ordinance:** *S. Times,* 15 July 1934. ■ **Petition for black dance hall:** *S. Times,* 8 Nov 1939. ■ **"An unwritten but rigid policy** of the City Council forbidding cabarets east of Eighth Avenue in the Central portion of the city was relaxed yesterday to give Seattle's Negro community a dine-and-dance establishment at the Savoy Ballroom," *S. Times,* 19 Feb 1946.

#### Chapter V

**Description of the Jackson Street area:** composite from Greenwell, Wanda Brown, Vaughn, Wiggins. ■ **"Tolerance policy":** Chambliss, Pigford, Hilbert. ■ **Russian John:** *S. Times,* 15 Dec 1961, Graf and Foy. ■ **410B:** *S. Times,* 4 and 5 Aug 1941. ■ **Interracial marriage:** Booker, Brown, Vaughn. ■ **Early Anderson:** Anderson. ■ **Basin Street:** lottery, description of club, hours, Hilbert; Curry, Vaughn; Sammy Davis, Emmett Lewis, and Lillian Buford. ■ **Boatley:** McCarthy. ■ **Central Avenue:** Gordon. ■ **First bebop records:** Hubert. ■ **Thurlow:** first press, undated Chuck Mahaffay item in *down beat,* c. 1950; band personnel, Cleveland; performance with Quincy Jones, *S. Times,* 31 Aug 1951. ■ **JATP:** origins, *down beat,* 1 Jan 1945; first Seattle shows, *S. Times,* 29 Apr 1946. ■ **Description of Weathers:** Standifer. Weathers' departure from McShann is noted in *Northwest Herald,* 4 Dec 1945. McShann himself has confirmed in a conversation with the author that Weathers played in his band. However, Weathers insisted that he had played with McShann when Bird was in the band, and Wyatt Ruther says Weathers once showed him a photograph of McShann's band with Weathers in the saxophone section. No discographies, personnel listings, records, or photographs bear this out. ■ **Tolles update:** Tolles. ■ **Dorham on Battle of Bands:** Tolles. ■ **Early Poindexter:** Poindexter, Buford, Lewis. ■ **Wiggins:** Wiggins. ■ **Cruse:** liner notes, *Juanita!* (1958). ■ **Wanda Brown:** Wanda Brown. ■ **Description of New Orleans Club:** Friel. ■ **Evening with Billie Holiday:** Ernestine Anderson places this at the China Pheasant. ■ **Ruther:** Ruther. ■ **Ramey quote:** Dance (1970). ■ **Narcolepsy:** Boas, Wiggins. ■ **Description of Washington Social Club:** Bown, Anderson, Brown; Groves, Tolles and *S. Times,* 1 Sep 1951. ■ **Membership cards:** *S. Times,* 10 Feb 1965. ■ **Floor show:** Perkins. ■ **Hickey early life,** Hickey ■ **Jive Bombers personnel:** Moton. ■ **Lester Young:** v. Jive Bombers, *S. Times,* 5 Feb 1948; at Washington Social Club, Buchmann-Moller.

#### Chapter VI

**Chino Pozo:** The reference is correct. Chano Pozo, the original Cuban drummer in Gillespie's band, was killed 2 Dec 1948, and the little-known Chino took his place. ■ **Blackwell:** early life, Penn, Nite, White; assessment of musical ability, Catlett, Gill; Emmett Lewis remarks, "He didn't know one note big as that stove." ■ "Ceremony in Swing," *NW Ent,* 1 Dec 1939. ■ **Holiday:** *S. Times,* 9 Feb 1979. ■ **Cole:** *NW Ent,* 2 July 1947. ■ **Jordan:** *NW Ent,* 12 Jan 1949. ■ **R & B groups:** all *NW Ent.* ■ **National Guard Band:** Blackwell and *S. Times,* 1 Oct 1947. ■ **Without contract:** Charles. ■ **Mankertz:** Jones, Standifer, Hawthorn, *Seattle Spectator,* 4 Nov 1949, 2 Dec 1949, and 27 Apr 1950. ■ *Four Winds Suite*: *Seattle Spectator,* 19 Oct 1950. ■ **Jones/Hampton story:** composite from Quincy Jones, Hickey, and Thurlow. Hampton's recollections, in *Hamp,* particularly Jones telling him he wanted to be a millionaire, are erroneous. ■ **Jones recorded with Hampton** on a New York session in May 1951 that included "Hannah, Hannah," "Shalom, Shalom," "Eli, Eli (Part 1)," and "Eli, Eli (Part 2)." A live concert recording in August 1951 in Malibu features "Flying Home," "Autumn in New York," "How High the Moon," "Out of Breath," and "Hamp's Boogie Woogie." ■ **"Musical Prodigy":** *Seattle Spectator,* 19 Oct 1950. ■ **Skinner:** Jones. ■ **Jones/Thurlow at Trianon:** Thurlow. ■ **Resentment in the Hampton band:** Thurlow. ■ **Jones' family situation:** Bown. ■ **"Stone out of the ghetto":** *S. Times,* 6 Mar 1983. ■ **"Hailed as a prodigy":** *S. Times,* 25 Aug 1949, and *Seattle Spectator,* 1 June 1950. ■ **Balliett:** *New Yorker,* 16 July 1979. ■ **Francois:** *Pacific Leader,* 19 Nov 1954. ■ **Free and Easy background:** Jablonski. ■ **Music as shapes:** *Life,* Dec 1984.

#### Chapter VII

Manning, Pierce, and Kimball all assert that Pierce's was the **first "modern" big band in Seattle.** ■ **Personnel of "dream band":** Pierce band photo. ■ **Woody Isbell,** mentioned briefly in Ross Russell's biography of Charlie Parker, also performed at the Players Club, according to Manning. ■ **Bridgeford's Getz gig:** "Norm Bobrow Jazz Letter #1." ■ **Harpa's El Rancho gig:** Stetler. ■ **Greenwell with Jimmy Zito:** *down beat,* 14 Jan 1948. ■ **OWL Party:** According to Rick Anderson, in an undated *P-I* article, OWL Party nominees received a quarter of a million votes, three percent of the total vote. ■ **Reddin on the China Pheasant:** *S. Times,* 10 Sep 1945. ■ **Joni Metcalf liner quote:** *Joni!* (1969).

#### Chapter VIII

**Big Lewis:** Ernestine Anderson. ■ **Bob Braxton:** *Billboard,* 17 Dec 1949. ■ **Ray Charles' arrival in Seattle:** Jones' account jibes with McKee's but differs considerably from Charles' own story in *Brother Ray,* in which McKee plays no role in Charles' first night in town. ■ **"I didn't know anyone" and "The entertainment business":** Charles and Ritz. ■ **Delridge Housing Project:** Taylor (dissertation). ■ **LeEtta King:** Mumford (1980). ■ **Barnett:** Powell Barnett. ■ **Early recording history:** Charles and Ritz. ■ **"French and Be-Bop":** *NW Ent,* 15 June 1949. ■ **Drugs:** Charles and Ritz. ■ **Ray Charles' blindness:** According to records of the St. Augustine State School for the Blind, Charles was "totally blind" by the time he was six years old (Charles says seven). However, the expression "totally blind" is a technical term meaning the inability to read the printed word under any circumstances, even with visual aids. "Most blind people have *some* vision," according to Mary Jane Dillon, Public Information Officer for the Florida school.

#### Chapter IX

**Young at Yale:** *down beat,* 15 June 1951. ▪ **Breakfast show:** Others place these shows at the Basin Street. ▪ **The Ralph Gleason quote about Gerald Brashear** is reported by Norm Bobrow. ▪ **Rodgers' demise:** Friel. ▪ **Jackson Street Community Council:** *S. Times,* 21 July 1946. ▪ **Raids:** Yukon Club, *S. Times,* 20 July 1947; Clover Club, *S. Times,* 3 Oct 1947; Rocking Chair, *S. Times,* 27 Dec 1947; Basin Street, *S. Times,* 12 Jan 1948; "out of bounds," *S. Times,* 17 May 1948; 166 arrested, *S. Times,* 8 Oct 1948. ▪ **Gambling profits:** Chambliss. ▪ **Washington Social Club:** *NW Ent,* 16 and 17 Sep 1950. ▪ **Carroll:** Chambliss. ▪ **Dorsey:** Skreen (1975). ▪ **"The one thing which bothered me . . . ":** Charles and Ritz. ▪ **Second Herd:** Herman reports in *Woodchopper's Ball* that he was inspired to form the Second Herd after hearing ex-Seattleite Phil Moore in a Hollywood club. ▪ **Neves and Hawkins:** Catlett. ▪ **Getz arrest:** *S. Times,* 15 Feb 1954. ▪ **The Parker story:** Norm Bobrow. Bobrow drove Bird from the Evergreen Ballroom, outside Olympia (where Bird performed on the same bill with Chet Baker and Dave Brubeck), to Seattle, then billeted him in his Seattle apartment. The Seattle show was 31 Oct 1953, at the Metropolitan Theatre. Parker seemed destined never to give a solid performance in Seattle. His first confirmed appearance, on a 16 Nov 1948 Jazz at the Philharmonic session at the Moore Theatre, suffered from an inappropriate rhythm section, according to pianist Ken Boas. Saxophonist Don Lanphere recalls a later concert with Errol Garner, when Bird played well, but the date is not clear. Bird may also have played Seattle as early as 1946, on a Norman Granz show at the Moore Theatre billed as an "All-Star Jazz Concert." Though Parker's name does not appear in the ad for the show, Lester Young's does, and several Seattle musicians recall seeing Parker at the Moore Theatre at some point with Young. Ron Pierce, in particular, remembers Bird at the Moore. Parker could conceivably have been on this show, since the date, 29 Apr 1946, coincides with Bird's first, 15-month stay on the West Coast. ▪ **Dolphy service dates:** Simosko and Tepperman. ▪ **"Rock 'n' Roll Party":** Tolles. ▪ **Tommy Adams:** Not all rock drummers agree with Holden's assessment. Mike Burke, drummer with the legendary Tacoma band the Wailers, says he did not know of Tommy Adams in the 1950s. ▪ **Union merger:** Siegl. ▪ **Wittwer's reference to "steal a march" on San Francisco** stems from a 1956 refusal by Local 6 in SF to merge black and white locals, *Musicland,* 7 Dec 1956. ▪ **Count of black locals:** Ernie Lewis. ▪ **AFM count of mergers nationally:** Siegl. ▪ **Mayor Clinton:** *S. Times,* 24 July 1956, reports closing of club. Standifer tells the story of the photo with axe. ▪ **The Blue Note closed** in 1958 when the unions amalgamated, according to Chuck Metcalf, but the *S. Times* of 19 Jan 1959 notes that the club was raided as late as this date.

#### Chapter X

**Henderson:** Schuller notes that Henderson recorded the Wingy Manone riff that later became Glenn Miller's smash hit "In the Mood" as early as 1931, on "Hot and Anxious." ▪ **Basie recording** by Joe Boles. ▪ **Hampton on the Potomac:** For a somewhat different account of this famous incident, see Crow. ▪ **Voorhees article:** *P-I,* 28 Sep 1953. ▪ **Wilson:** *New York Times,* 24 Aug 1958. ▪ **Tynan:** *down beat,* 18 Sep 1958. ▪ **"Secret indictment":** Poindexter was reading about the famous Kefauver hearings in San Francisco. ▪ **Arrest and parole information:** Seattle Police Department. ▪ **Skating rink:** The building is the same as the Savoy Ballroom. ▪ **Jay McNeely** made a tape at Birdland in 1957 that was released as an LP; McNeely also recorded his only hit, "There Is Something on Your Mind," in West Seattle. ▪ **First rock 'n' roll record:** according to Pete Blecha, Seattle rock historian.

#### Chapter XI

**FBI, "bloodbath," and Carroll:** Chambliss. ▪ **Frank Colacurcio** was sentenced in 1978 to 36 years for income tax evasion. ▪ **Lofurno's restaurant closed in July 1993.** ▪ **Bisio:** National Public Radio Jazz Critics Top 10. ▪ **Friesen:** Friesen. ▪ **Influence on Northwest rock:** Seattle rocker "Little Bill" Engelhart, who had the 1959 hit "I Love an Angel," acknowledged in an interview with the author (26 July 1993) that black R & B players such as Tommy Adams had a "tremendous influence" on the early rock scene. ▪ **Blackwell and Little Richard, including "Tutti Frutti" story:** White.

# sources


**Oral Histories and Interviews**

*Transcriptions and / or tape recordings of the following oral histories and interviews are housed at Suzzallo Library, Manuscript Collection, University of Washington, Seattle, Washington. Interviews were with author unless otherwise noted.*

Alcivar, Bob. 17 June 1989. Transcript.

Anderson, Ernestine. Interview with Sandra Burlingame, 22 October 1988; with author, 10 October and 15 November 1989. Transcripts.

Barbas, Pete. Interview with Ken Maffit, 9 July 1989. Tape recording.

Barrington, Pete. 20 May 1990. Tape recording.

Boas, Ken. 18 November 1989. Transcript.

Bobrow, Norm. 5 July, August, and 15 September 1989. Transcripts.

Booker, Quentin "Sonny." Interviews with Sandra Burlingame, 31 October 1988 and 23 May 1989. Transcripts.

Bown, Patti. 18 October 1987 and 5 April 1989. Transcripts.

Brazil, Joe. 3 October 1989. Transcript.

Brown, Wanda. Interviews with Ted Dzielak, 21 February and 22 August 1989. Transcripts.

Brownlow, Jack. Interview with Adam Woog, 26 September 1989. Transcript.

Buford, Vernon "Pops." 2 June 1989. Tape recording.

Carruthers, Arnie. Interview with Joseph Murphy, 21 April 1989. Transcript.

Catlett, George "Buddy." 9 November and 23 November 1988. Transcripts.

Charles, Ray. 11 April 1991. Transcript.

Cleveland, Jimmy. 30 November 1989. Tape recording.

Coleman, Dave. Interview with Sandra Burlingame, 1 November 1988. Transcript.

Coryell, Larry. 29 August 1989. Transcript.

Crow, Bill. 11 November 1989. Transcript.

Davis, Ralph. 22 March 1989. Tape recording.

Foy, Jack. 2 December 1989. Transcript.

Friel, Neil. 2 June 1989. Transcript.

Friesen, David. 20 September 1989. Transcript.

Gatewood, Donald. 5 September 1989. Tape recording.

Gill, Elmer. 23 October 1988. Transcript.

Gilles, Jim. Interview with Lynn Darroch, 22 October 1989.

Greenwell, Fred. Interview with Jim Wilke, 31 January 1988. Transcript.

____________. 24 April 1990. Tape recording.

Hatfield, Ernie. 18 May 1987. Tape recording.

Hayes, Cathi. 20 April 1990. Tape recording.

Heldman, Jerry. 21 December 1989. Tape recording.

Henson, Julian. 20 January 1991. Tape recording.

Hickey, Al. Interview with Lynn Darroch, 24 June 1992. Tape recording.

Hilbert, Al. 16 August 1989. Tape recording.

Hill, Alphonse. Interview with Ted Dzielak, 5 September 1989. Transcript.

Holden, Dave. 12 April 1991. Tape recording.

Holden, Grace and Bob, Jimmy and Leala. Interview with author and Ted Dzielak, 4 June 1989. Transcript.

Hubert, Traff. Interview with Jim Wilke, 21 March 1989. Transcript.

Johnson, Palmer. Interviews with author and Jim Wilke, 20 November 1988; 16 October, 23 October, 4 November, 26 November, and 17 December 1989. Transcripts.

Jones, Gaylord. 24 March and 24 April 1989. Transcripts.

Jones, Melody. Interviews with Susan Golden, 10 January 1988 and 8 November 1989. Transcripts.

Jones, Quincy. 5 December 1989. Transcript.

____________. 17 August 1990. Tape recording.

Keen, Stan. Interview with Mark Solomon, 29 August 1988. Transcript.

Kelly, Red. 23 May and 5 June 1989. Transcripts.

Kimball, Kenny. Interviews with Ken Maffit, 19 February and March 1989. Transcripts.

Lanphere, Don. Interviews with Joe Murphy, 14 September and 28 September 1988. Transcripts.

Lewis, Emmett. Interview with Ted Dzielak and Marianne Jones, 7 October 1989. Transcript.

Lewis, Ernie. 15 December 1990. Tape recording.

Mahaffay, Chuck. Interviews with Mark Solomon, 2 October and 8 November 1989. Transcripts.

Mancuso, Gus. 2 December 1989. Transcript.

Manning, Don. Interview with Lynn Darroch, 30 September 1989. Transcript.

McKee, Garcia. 17 March 1991. Tape recording.

Metcalf, Chuck. Interviews with Mark Solomon, September 1988. Transcripts.

Montgomery, Buddy. 1 June 1990. Tape recording.

Morehouse, Rollie. Interview with Ken Maffit, 26 September 1989. Transcript.

Ostransky, Leroy. 7 July 1989. Tape recording.

Perciful, Jack. Interviews with Keith Raether, 11 September, 15 September, and 19 September 1989. Transcripts.

Perkins, Zenobia. 16 June 1989. Tape recording.

Pierce, Ron. Interviews with Ken Maffit, 14 May and 16 May 1989. Transcripts.

Pigford, Major. Interview with Ted Dzielak, 24 January 1989. Transcript.

Ramage, Chet. 9 May 1990. Tape recording.

Ramsay, Bill. Interviews with Joe Murphy, 9 March and 18 April 1989. Transcripts.

Reid, Rufus. 3 September 1988. Transcript.

Reilly, Dean. 20 May 1990. Tape recording.

Rowell, Bruce. 28 August 1990. Tape recording.

Rowles, Jimmy. 1 December 1989. Transcript.

Russell, Bob. Interviews with Ted Dzielak, 7 March and 6 April 1989. Transcripts.

Ruther, Wyatt. 18 May 1990. Transcript.

Standifer, Floyd. 27 September and 18 October 1988. Transcripts.

Steele, Gary. Interview with Rick Leppanen, 23 September 1989. Transcript.

Stentz, Chuck. Interview with Joe Murphy, 6 September 1989. Transcript.

Stetler, Dave. Interview with Joe Murphy, 13 December 1989. Tape recording.

Taylor, Charles. Interviews with Ted Dzielak, 29 December 1988 and 10 February 1989. Transcript.

Thurlow, Janet. 30 November 1989. Transcript.

Tolles, Billy. 30–31 January 1990. Tape recording.

Turay, Al. Interview with Ted Dzielak, 8 February 1989. Transcript.

Turnham, Floyd. 3 December 1989. Transcript.

Vaughn, Leon. 21 September and 27 September 1989. Transcripts.

Ward, Jabo. Interview with Joe Murphy, 27 January 1989. Transcript.

Wiggins, Gerald. 4 December 1989. Transcript.

Williamson, Evelyn, and Marshal Royal. 11 April 1991. Tape recording.

Winn, Bob. Interview with Adam Woog, May 1989. Transcript.

Wittwer, John. Interviews with Pete Leinonen, 27 November 1989 and 28 June 1990. Transcripts.

### Additional Interviews

*Interviews with author unless otherwise noted.*

Anderson, Don. 1992.

Barnett, Doug II. 19 January 1988.

Barnett, Doug III. 18 January 1988.

Barnett, Powell. University of Washington Northwest Collection. Transcript.

Blackwell, Robert A. "Bumps." Interview with Roberta Penn, 5 December 1983. Tape recording.

Brown, Wanda. 16 September 1989.

Eckstine, Ed. 24 January 1990.

Ewing, Vivian. Interview with Ted Dzielak, 18 August 1989.

Gayton, Emma. Interview with Ted Dzielak, 2 March 1989.

Gayton, Leonard. Interview coordinated by Esther Mumford. King County Black Oral History Project. Oral History Collection, Washington State Archives, Olympia. Transcript.

Gillespie, John Birks "Dizzy." 4 September 1989.

Graf, Bob. 9 November 1989.

________. February 1991.

Gray, Jerry. Interview with Maggie Hawthorn. Maggie Hawthorn Archive, Music and Art Division, Seattle Public Library. Transcript.

Hilbert, George. 26 April 1991.

Hunziker, Bill. 15 July 1991.

Johnson, Palmer. 10 January 1990.

Kelly, Bev. 26 April 1991.

Lewis, Charles. Interview coordinated by Esther Mumford. King County Black Oral History Project. Oral History Collection, Washington State Archives, Olympia. Transcript.

Montgomery, Monk. Interview with Maggie Hawthorn. Smithsonian Collection.

Moton, John. Interview with Ted Dzielak, 9 October 1990.

Pierce, Ron. 3 May 1991.

Pierre, Neva. 1 May 1991.

Radke, Fred. 4 May 1991.

Standifer, Floyd. 28 August 1992.

Stentz, Jan. 11 July 1991.

### Books

Allen, Linda. *Washington Songs and Lore.* Spokane: Melior, 1988.

Anderson, Martha. *Black Pioneers of the Northwest.* Seattle: By the author, 1980.

Avery, Mary W. *Washington: A History of the Evergreen State.* Seattle: University of Washington Press, 1965.

Barney, Bigard. *With Louis and the Duke.* New York: Oxford University Press, 1986.

Barto, Harold, and Catherine Bullard. *History of the State of Washington.* Boston: D.C. Heath and Co., 1947.

Broderick, Henry. *Early Seattle Profiles.* Seattle: Dogwood Press, 1959.

Bruyninckx, Walter. *60 Years of Recorded Jazz, 1917–1977.* Mechelen, Belgium: By the author, 1978–1983.

Cayton, Horace R. *Long Old Road.* Seattle: University of Washington Press, 1970.

Chambliss, William. *On the Take.* Bloomington, Ind.: Indiana University Press, 1978.

Charles, Ray, and David Ritz. *Brother Ray.* New York: Dial Press, 1978; New York: Warner, 1979.

Charters, Samuel B., and Leonard Kunstadt. *Jazz: A History of the New York Scene.* New York: Doubleday, 1962; New York: Da Capo Press, 1984.

Chilton, John. *Who's Who of Jazz.* New York: Time-Life Records, 1978.

Clark, Norman H. *The Dry Years: Prohibition and Social Change in Washington.* Seattle: University of Washington Press, 1965.

________. *Washington: A Bicentennial History.* New York: Norton, 1976.

Clayton, Buck, assisted by Nancy Miller Elliott. *Buck Clayton's Jazz World.* New York: Oxford University Press, 1987.

Collier, James Lincoln. *Benny Goodman and the Swing Era.* New York: Oxford University Press, 1989.

Crow, Bill. *Jazz Anecdotes.* New York: Oxford University Press, 1990.

Crowther, Bruce. *Gene Krupa: His Life and Times.* New York: Universe Books, 1987.

Dahl, Linda. *Stormy Weather: The Music and Lives of a Century of Jazz Women.* New York: Pantheon Books, 1984.

Dance, Helen. *Stormy Monday: The T-Bone Walker Story.* Baton Rouge: Louisiana State University Press, 1987.

Dance, Stanley. *The World of Count Basie.* New York: Scribner, 1980.

____________. *The World of Duke Ellington.* New York: Scribner, 1970; New York: Da Capo Press, 1980.

____________. *The World of Swing.* New York: Da Capo Press, 1974.

Darensbourg, Joe, as told to Peter Vacher. *Jazz Odyssey.* Baton Rouge: Louisiana State University Press, 1987.

Driggs, Frank, and Lewine Harris. *Black Beauty, White Heat: A Pictorial History of Classic Jazz 1920–1950.* New York: Morrow, 1982.

____________. "Andy Kirk's Story," in *Jazz Panorama*, edited by Martin Williams. New York: Collier, 1964.

Dryden, Cecil. *Dryden's History of Washington.* Portland, Ore.: Binfords and Mort, 1968.

Eckland, K.O. *Jazz West.* Carmel-by-the-Sea, Calif.: Cypress, 1986.

Moritz, Charles, ed. "Jones, Quincy Delight." *Current Biography.* 1977.

Elliott, Eugene Clinton. *A History of Variety-Vaudeville in Seattle,* University of Washington Publications in Drama, edited by Glenn Hughes. Seattle: University of Washington Press, 1944.

Feather, Leonard, and Ira Gitler. *Encyclopedia of Jazz in the Seventies.* New York: Horizon Press, 1976.

Feather, Leonard. *Encyclopedia of Jazz in the Sixties.* New York: Bonanza Books, 1961.

____________. *Encyclopedia of Jazz.* New York: Bonanza Books, 1962.

Ficken, Robert E., and Charles P. LeWarne. *Washington: A Centennial History.* Seattle: University of Washington Press, 1988.

Giddins, Gary. *Celebrating Bird.* New York: Beach Tree Books (Morrow), 1987.

Gordon, Robert. *Jazz West Coast.* London: Quartet Books, 1986.

Hampton, Lionel, with James Haskins. *Hamp.* New York: Warner Books, 1989.

Handy, D. Antoinette. *Black Women in American Bands and Orchestras.* Metuchen, N.J.: Scarecrow Press, 1981.

____________. *The International Sweethearts of Rhythm.* Metuchen, N.J.: Scarecrow Press, 1983.

Hawes, Hampton, and Don Asher. *Raise Up Off Me.* Coward McCann, 1974; New York: Da Capo Press, 1979.

Henderson, David. *'Scuse Me While I Kiss the Sky: The Life of Jimi Hendrix.* New York: Doubleday, 1978; Bantam Books, 1981.

Herman, Woody, and Stuart Troup. *The Woodchopper's Ball.* New York: Dutton, 1990.

Horricks, Raymond. *Quincy Jones.* New York: Hippocrene Books, 1985.

Jablonski, Edward. *Harold Arlen: Happy with the Blues.* New York: Doubleday, 1961.

Jones, Nard. *Seattle.* New York: Doubleday, 1972.

Kernfeld, Barry, and Stanley Sadie, eds. *The New Grove Dictionary of Jazz.* New York: Grove's Dictionaries of Music, 1988.

Klinkowitz, Jerome. *Listen: Gerry Mulligan.* New York: Schirmer Books, 1991.

Korall, Burt. *Drummin' Men.* New York: Macmillan, 1990.

Lomax, Alan. *Mr. Jellyroll.* Berkeley: University of California Press, 1973 (first edition, 1950).

Lyons, Len. *The Great Jazz Pianists: Speaking of Their Lives and Music.* New York: Quill, 1983.

McCarthy, Albert. *Big Band Jazz.* New York: Putnam, 1974.

Morgan, Murray. *Skid Road.* New York: Viking Press, 1951.

Mumford, Esther. *Seven Stars and Orion.* Seattle: Ananse Press, 1986.

____________. *Seattle's Black Victorians 1852–1901.* Seattle: Ananse Press, 1980.

Newell, Gorden, and Joe Williamson. *Pacific Coast Liners.* Seattle: Superior, 1959.

Ostransky, Leroy. *Jazz City.* N.J.: Prentice-Hall, 1978.

Placksin, Sally. *American Women in Jazz.* Wideview, 1982.

Poindexter, Pony. *The Pony Express: Memoirs of a Jazz Musician.* West Germany: j.a.s. publikationen, 1985.

Ramsey, Doug. *Jazz Matters.* Fayetteville: University of Arkansas Press, 1989.

Reisner, Robert George. *Bird: The Legend of Charlie Parker.* New York: Citadel Press, 1962.

Russell, Ross. *Bird Lives!* 1972. Reprint. London: Quartet Books, 1988.

____________. *Jazz Style in Kansas City and the Southwest.* 1971. Reprint. Berkeley: University of California Press, 1973.

Sale, Roger. *Seattle Past to Present.* 1976. Reprint. Seattle: University of Washington Press, 1978.

Schuller, Gunther. *The Swing Era.* New York: Oxford University Press, 1989.

____________. *Early Jazz.* New York: Oxford University Press, 1968.

Shapiro, Harry, and Caesar Glebbeek. *Jimi Hendrix: Electric Gypsy.* New York: St. Martin's Press, 1990.

Shapiro, Nat, and Nat Hentoff, eds. *Hear Me Talkin' To Ya.* New York: Rinehart and Co., 1955; New York: Dover, 1966.

Simon, George. *The Big Bands.* New York: Schirmer Books, 1981.

Simosko, Vladimir, and Barry Tepperman. *Eric Dolphy.* New York: Da Capo Press, 1979.

Smith, Merle Irene. *Seattle Had a Tin Pan Alley, Too!* Seattle: By the author, 1989.

Southern, Eileen. *The Music of Black Americans.* New York: Norton, 1971.

Spiedel, Bill. *Doc Maynard.* Seattle: Nettle Creek, 1978.

Stearns, Marshall. *The Story of Jazz.* New York: Oxford University Press, 1956.

Stoddard, Tom. *Jazz on the Barbary Coast.* Chigwell, Essex: Storyville, 1982.

Ulanov, Barry. *Duke Ellington.* New York: Creative Age Press, 1946.

Unterbrink, Mary. *Jazz Women at the Keyboard.* Jefferson, N.C., and London: McFarland, 1983.

Waldron, Frank. *Syncopated Classic.* Seattle: By the author, 1924.

White, Charles. *The Life and Times of Little Richard.* New York: Harmony Books, 1984.

Williams, Martin, ed. *Jazz Panorama.* New York: Collier, 1964.

__________________. *Jelly Roll Morton.* New York: A.S. Barnes, 1962.

Woodfin, Henry. "Ray Charles," in *Jazz Panorama,* edited by Martin Williams. New York: Collier, 1964.

#### Daily Newspapers

(Multiple References)

*The Daily* [University of Washington]. 1 March 1939; 2 June 1939; 21 April 1954; 22 January 1959.

*New York Times.* 18 November 1980; 13 January 1985; 22 September 1989.

*Seattle Post-Intelligencer.* 15 November 1896–11 March 1983.

*Seattle Times.* 23 November 1901–14 May 1989.

*Tacoma News Tribune.* 11 February 1955; 2 September 1962; 14 February 1968; 8 June, 19 June 1969; 11 September 1971; 11 March 1973; 12 February 1975; 8 February 1987.

#### Daily Newspapers

(Single Reference)

"Tacoma Orchestra Plays 'Round the World." [Tacoma] *Ledger*, 26 December 1926.

[Seattle] *Pacific Leader.* 19 November 1954.

Clark, Doug. "Jazz Musician Spent Life Concealing Fantastic Secret." [Spokane] *Spokesman-Review,* 31 January 1989.

Gelman, Mitch. "Idolmaker to Many, but Not Himself." *Los Angeles Herald Examiner,* 20 August 1981.

Hilburn, Robert. "So Long, 'Tutti-Frutti,' Hello, God." *Los Angeles Times,* 16 August 1981.

March, John. "On the Black and White Keys." *Idaho Statesman,* 14 March 1971.

Newell, Berniece E. "Originator of 'Jazz' in 347th Orchestra." *Trench and Camp,* 25 November 1917.

Winslow, Valerie. "Palmer Johnson Is 'Cooking' in Bellevue." *Bellevue* [Washington] *Journal-American,* 28 January 1977.

#### Periodicals and Magazines

*Cayton's Weekly* [Seattle]. 1 September 1917–21 February 1920.

*down beat.* 1 January 1942–21 April 1954.

*Earshot Jazz* [Seattle]. 1984–1992.

*The Enterprise* [Seattle]. 18 September 1925; 30 April 1926.

*The Facts* [Seattle]. 3 August 1962.

*Musicland* [Journal of Seattle Musicians' Union Local 76]. 1926–1957.

*Northwest Enterprise* [Seattle]. 1 January 1931–28 December 1950.

*Northwest Herald* [Seattle]. 5 January 1944–18 December 1945.

*Puget Sound Observer* [Seattle]. 27 March 1957–23 April 1958.

*Puget Sound Trail* [College of the Puget Sound, Tacoma] 6 February, 1 May 1947; 7 May 1948; 6, 13 May 1949.

*Seattle Republican.* August 1909–August 1920.

*The Spectator* [Seattle University]. 4 November, 2 December 1949; 30 March, 27 April, 1 June, 19 October 1950; 13 January 1955.

#### Periodical and Magazine Articles

"An Addiction to Music." *Crescendo International,* January 1987.

"Bass Fiddler Junior Raglin." *Life,* 25 September 1944.

"Floyd Turnham and Britt Woodman with Duke Band." *Los Angeles Sentinel,* 1 March 1951.

"Out of Nowhere." *Jazz Journal,* February 1987.

"Spinning Wheel Cabaret, Seattle." *Billboard,* 17 December 1949.

"Turnham Band Clicks." *California Eagle,* 12 August 1948.

Burnett, Stan. "Seattle JAZZ Scene." *Columns,* April 1957.

de Barros, Paul. "Back on the Block." *Alaska Airlines Magazine*, May 1990.

______________. "Black Jazz." *Washington,* September/October 1989.

______________. "The Comeback of Ms. Metcalf." *Seattle Weekly,* 25 February 1981.

Douglas, Patrick. "The Gaytons." *Seattle,* January 1969.

Droker, Howard. "On the Pay Streak at the Alaska-Yukon-Pacific Exposition." *Portage,* Summer 1981.

______________. "Seattle Race Relations During the Second World War." *Pacific Northwest Quarterly,* October 1976.

Evans, Gary. "Don Lanphere." *Saxophone Journal,* November/December 1988.

Frykman, George. "The Alaska-Yukon-Pacific Exposition." *Pacific Northwest Quarterly,* July 1962.

George, Nelson, and others. "The Many Worlds of Quincy Jones: 40th Anniversary." *Billboard,* 9 December 1989.

George, Nelson. "Quincy Jones." *Musician,* May 1983.

Giddins, Gary. "Joe Venuti: A Penchant for Mayhem." *Village Voice,* 28 August 1978.

Gushee, Lawrence. "A Preliminary Chronology of the Early Career of Ferd 'Jelly Roll' Morton." *American Music,* Winter 1985.

______________. "How the Creole Band Came to Be." *Black Music Research Journal* 8, no. 1, 1988.

______________. "New Orleans–Area Musicians on the West Coast, 1908–1925." *Black Music Research Journal* 9, no. 1, 1989.

Hawthorn, Maggie. "Fifty Years of Quincy Jones." *Seattle Weekly,* 9 March 1983.

King, Terry. "Big Bands in Seattle." *Seattle Weekly,* 6 June 1984.

Lees, Gene. "Fiddler Joe." *Jazzletter,* September 1988.

Leo, Melody. "The Music Business—Tough but Worth It." *Art Circle,* July 1975

Lunn, Chris. "Jack Perciful." *Victory Music,* April 1989.

Penn, Roberta. "Robert 'Bumps' Blackwell." *The Rocket,* April 1985.

Reddick, L.D. "The New Race Relations Frontier." *Journal of Education Sociology,* November 1945.

Robinson, Louis. "Quincy Jones." *Ebony,* June 1972.

Rochester, Junius. "Doc Hamilton; King of Seattle's Speakeasy Living." *Seattle Weekly,* 2 February 1983.

Stimson, William. "Bing We Hardly Knew Ye." *Pacific Northwest,* December 1987.

Sutherland, Sam. "Music-Biz Veteran Bumps Blackwell Has Been Running His Own Academy." *Record World,* no date.

Umphrey, Wallace. "New Orleans in Seattle." *The Jazz Record,* December 1944.

Wittwer, John. "A Tribute to Joe Darensbourg." *The Jazz Record,* no date.

**Pamphlets, Liner Notes, Programs, Private Publications, Ephemera, and Unpublished and Miscellaneous Material**

Broderick, Henry. Pamphlet. "Prohibition." Seattle: Dogwood Press, 1968. Seattle Public Library Northwest Collection.

DeMichael, Don. Liner note. *Red Norvo* (Giants of Jazz Series) (1980). Time-Life STLJ14.

Exner, Frederick B. Liner note. *Kid Ory, b/w Johnny Wittwer* (1945). Exner 1 and 2.

Gleason, Ralph. Liner note. *Introducing Gus Mancuso* (1956). Fantasy LP 3233.

Gray, Jerry. Letter to author. 20 February 1988.

Holden, Ron. Letter to author. 27 September 1983.

Ingram, Adrian. Pamphlet. "Wes Montgomery." Ashley Mark, 1985.

Kimball, Kenny. Letter to author. 11 February 1991.

Zwisohn, Laurence J. . Pamphlet. "Bing Crosby: A Lifetime of Music." Los Angeles: Palm Tree Library.

Siegl, Eleanor. "The Amalgamation of the Colored and White Musicians' Unions in Seattle." Term paper (University of Washington), 1966. American Federation of Musicians Local 76 Archive.

Smith, Merle. Letter to author. 15 April 1990.

Taylor, Quintard. "History of Blacks in the Pacific Northwest." Ph.D. diss., University of Minnesota, 1978.

Charter document, Northwest Jazz Workshop. 1 June 1956.

Chronology of engagements, Floyd Turnham.

Chronology of engagements, Jabo Ward.

Curriculum vitae, Kenny Kimball.

Discography, Don Lanphere, compiled by Lanphere.

Discography, Cecil Young, compiled by Traff Hubert. 1992.

Flyer, Kenneth Patchen Poetry and Jazz Reading. Maggie Hawthorn Archive, Seattle Public Library.

Index card file, Seattle theaters. *Seattle Times* Library.

Index card file, theater performances 1940–1964. *Seattle Times* Library.

Membership brochure, Seattle Jazz Society. 1966.

Newsletter. Seattle Jazz Society. June, December 1966; November, December 1976.

Newsletter, "Trianon Saturday Night." 15 February 1941.

Photograph caption, Ron Pierce band.

Press biography, Robert A. "Bumps" Blackwell.

Press biography, George "Buddy" Catlett.

Press biography, David Friesen. Creative Service.

Press biography, David Friesen. Palo Alto Jazz.

Press biography, Elmer Gill.

Press biography, Quincy Jones. A & M Records.

Press biography, Quincy Jones. Quincy Jones Productions.

Press biography, Floyd Standifer.

Press biography, Floyd Turnham.

Press biography, Bob Winn.

Press package, Blackwell's Academy of the Performing Arts.

Press package, David Friesen.

Program, Lake City Tavern, Seattle. 18 August 1955.

Program, "Quincy Jones: A Seattle Celebration" 50th Birthday Party, Seattle. 11 March 1983.

Program, Relatives of Old-Timers of Washington State (ROOTS) Tenth Anniversary Reunion Reception. September 1982.

Program, SeaFair Jazz Festival. 5 August 1956.

Résumé, Patti Bown.

Résumé, Wyatt Ruther.

Union roster, [Seattle] Local 493. American Federation of Musicians Local No. 76 Archive. 14 January 1958.

# acknowledgments

In 1987, when Kjris Lund, then Executive Director of the King County Arts Commission, heard I was interested in researching jazz in Seattle, she suggested I contact Charles Payton at the Cultural Resources Historic Preservation Program to see about funding for oral history interviews. That was the beginning of *Jackson Street After Hours*. I want to thank Kjris for encouraging me at that time and, later, for guiding me through the political maze of Washington State Centennial funding. Without her help, it's doubtful this project would have gotten off the ground. I also owe many thanks to Charles for his contacts and moral support, and to Charlotte Jacobs at the King County Centennial Commission for sticking by the project.

To Quincy Jones, for giving this project his time and credibility and for convincing R. C. that it was worth his time, I offer thanks, as well. I also thank the Black Heritage Society — Ralph Hayes, Joe Warner, Jim Yarbrough, and particularly historian Esther Mumford, who generously shared information, leads, and her meticulous sense of scholarship. To Al Smith, who not only offered his collection of vintage photographs but arranged several important interviews, many thanks, as well.

I could not have found a more dedicated, thorough, and enthusiastic research assistant than Ted Dzielak. I thank him now for the many hours he spent in libraries, making lists, photocopying, and compiling information; for the grant proposals he wrote to support the project; and for the stimulating conversations we had over two years as the concept for the book took shape. I also thank research aides Paul Titialii and Mike Galligan, and Jane Lambert at the Cornish College of the Arts for providing those aides through a credit program.

My grateful appreciation also goes out to Bill Crow, who not only endured an entire oral history interview by telephone but donated valuable research from the Institute for Jazz Study, in Rutgers. Thanks also to Kevin Whitehead for assistance in several research matters and his critical reading of the manuscript, and to Floyd Standifer for his guidance in the early stages of the project, access to rare tapes, and a critical reading. My deepest appreciation goes to Audrey Houck of the *Seattle Times* library, for her patient assistance; to Julia Braun and Chet Ramage of the American Federation of Musicians Local 76, for theirs; and to the Tacoma, Portland, Los Angeles, and San Francisco union locals for various other information. Thanks also, for help in various other ways, to Merle I. Smith, Norm Bobrow, Linda Allen, Traff Hubert, Frank Driggs, Jerry Gray, Judy de Barros, Lawrence Gushee, Lola Pedrini, Ken Wiley, John McDonough, Jan Stentz, Roberta Penn, Al Hendrix, Don Duncan, and Mark Troxel.

Oral history is an art form in itself, and I would have been poorer for not having consulted at length with Dan Morgenstern of the Institute for Jazz Study and Bob Rusch of *Cadence*. Thanks to both of them and to oral historians Peter Heffelfinger of Anacortes and Sharon Boswell of the Washington State Oral History Society. The oral histories themselves were conducted by a patient cadre of inquiring souls, to whom I am grateful: Ted Dzielak, Kate Smith, Ken Maffit, Joe Murphy, Adam Woog, Sandy Burlingame, Mark Solomon, Jim Wilke, Lynn Darroch, Susan Golden, Marianne Jones, Keith Raether, Rick Leppanen, and Pete Leinonen.

And to the transcribers who patiently took each word off the tapes, thank you, as well: Jeff Kahrs, Karen Rahl, Sandra Burlingame, Beatriz Pascual, Nancy Slote, Mark Troxel, Susan Golden, Aleta Ashlock, Carmen Jones, Julie Johnson, Carolyn Mandile, Linda Grotefendt, Evelyn Roehl, Marcia Haines, Sarah Wilson, Jerry Alexander, Gwen Gottberg, Lara Morrison, Mary Scott, Marlene Stone, Hap Hanchett, Delva Earl and Rick Huey. Thanks also to Ron Hall for coordinating volunteer transcribers; Phyllis Hatfield for the loan of a transcribing machine; Nola Freeman for guidance in working with seniors; Jim Wilke for his special help on the Palmer Johnson interview; the Refugee Women's Alliance for the loan of tape recorders; Caren Adams, Earshot Jazz, KPLU-FM, and United Way for helping provide volunteer transcribers; and Joe Canale of Acoustic Imports for his technical assistance.

Gracious thanks to those who offered support and help in other areas: Julie Niebuhr Eulenberg, *Alaska Airlines Magazine,* and Peter Davenport, for sticking by the project in its difficult "horse latitudes."

Thanks to Nick Allison, for his judicious and sensitive editing and for taking on this project when he had so many other things to do; likewise, to designer Art Chantry, whose love of Northwest music shines through on every page. Thanks to the folks at Earshot Jazz, who supported this project after I left the organization, not only with operational funds but with moral support, volunteer help, and a spur-of-the-moment subsidy for plane tickets to interview Ray Charles.

Thanks to all the generous funders and friends who have supported *Jackson Street* through grants to Earshot as an organization and to Eduardo Calderón and myself as individual artists: Seattle Arts Commission, King County Arts Commission, Tacoma Arts Commission, Washington State Arts Commission, Washington Commission for the Humanities, Artist Trust, Allied Arts, King County Centennial Commission, King County Cultural Resources Historic Preservation Program, Court Productions, the Alpac Corporation, Washington Mutual Savings Bank, Paul Fishburg, Barbara Erwine, and Whit Symmes.

Thanks to my family, for enduring the long hours, days, weeks, months, and years this project demanded. And, finally, to all the musicians and others who took the time out to be interviewed and share their scrapbooks and memorabilia for this project — thank you.

# index

## C

## D



## E

## F



## G

## N

## O



## P–Q



## R

## S

## T

## U–V



## W

## X–Z

Benham Studio Gallery

©1993 Eduardo Calderón

Paul de Barros is an author and music critic, and a contributing writer for *The Seattle Times*. His reviews have appeared in numerous publications, including *The Washington Post, The San Francisco Chronicle, Modern Drummer,* and *Musician,* and he has served as a juror for national jazz competitions. Mr. de Barros founded Seattle's Earshot Jazz, a nonprofit arts organization, and he is program director for Northwest Folklife.

Eduardo Calderón is an award-winning photographer who has exhibited in Seattle, Los Angeles, and Lima, Peru. He received an Artist Fellowship from the National Endowment for the Arts in 1992. His work is included in many Northwest collections.